RELIGION AND THE MEDIEVAL AND EARLY MODERN GLOBAL MARKETPLACE

Religion and the Medieval and Early Modern Global Marketplace brings together scholars from a variety of disciplines to examine the intersection, conflict, and confluence of religion and the market before 1700.

Each chapter analyzes the unique interplay of faith and economy in a different locale: Syria, Ethiopia, France, Iceland, India, Peru, and beyond. In ten case studies, specialists of archaeology, art history, social and economic history, religious studies, and critical theory address issues of secularization, tolerance, colonialism, and race with a fresh focus. They chart the tensions between religious and economic thought in specific locales or texts, the complex ways that religion and economy interacted with one another, and the way in which matters of faith, economy, and race converge in religious images of the pre- and early modern periods. Considering the intersection of faith and economy, the volume questions the legacy of early modern economic and spiritual exceptionalism, and the ways in which prosperity still entangles itself with righteousness.

The interdisciplinary nature means that this volume is the perfect resource for advanced undergraduates, postgraduates, and scholars working across multiple areas including history, literature, politics, art history, global studies, philosophy, and gender studies in the medieval and early modern periods.

Scott Oldenburg specializes in early modern literature and culture at Tulane University. He is the author of *Alien Albion: Literature and Immigration in Early Modern England* and *A Weaver-Poet and the Plague: Labor, Poverty, and the Household in Shakespeare's London* as well as articles on various early modern topics.

Kristin M. S. Bezio is an Associate Professor at the University of Richmond. Publications include *Staging Power in Tudor and Stuart English History Plays*; "Munday I Sweare Shalbee a Hollidaye" in *Études Anglaises*; and *William Shakespeare & 21st Century Culture, Politics, and Leadership* with Anthony Russell.

RELIGION AND THE MEDIEVAL AND EARLY MODERN GLOBAL MARKETPLACE

Edited by Scott Oldenburg and Kristin M. S. Bezio

Routledge
Taylor & Francis Group
LONDON AND NEW YORK

First published 2022
by Routledge
2 Park Square, Milton Park, Abingdon, Oxon OX14 4RN

and by Routledge
605 Third Avenue, New York, NY 10158

Routledge is an imprint of the Taylor & Francis Group, an informa business

British Library Cataloguing-in-Publication Data
A catalogue record for this book is available from the British Library

Library of Congress Cataloging-in-Publication Data
Names: Oldenburg, Scott K., 1969- editor. | Bezio, Kristin M. S., editor.
Title: Religion and the medieval and early modern global marketplace / edited by Scott Oldenburg and Kristin M. S. Bezio.
Description: Abingdon, Oxon ; New York, NY : Routledge, 2022. | Includes bibliographical references and index.
Identifiers: LCCN 2021020281 | ISBN 9780367536749 (hbk) | ISBN 9780367536756 (pbk) | ISBN 9781003082842 (ebk)
Subjects: LCSH: Economics--Religious aspects--History. |
Religion--Economic
aspects--History. | Commerce--Religious aspects--History.
Classification: LCC HB72 .R45132 2022 | DDC 330--dc23
LC record available at https://lccn.loc.gov/2021020281

ISBN: 978-0-367-53674-9 (hbk)
ISBN: 978-0-367-53675-6 (pbk)
ISBN: 978-1-003-08284-2 (ebk)

DOI: 10.4324/9781003082842

Typeset in Bembo
by KnowledgeWorks Global Ltd.

CONTENTS

FIGURES

CONTRIBUTORS

Sara Aponte-Olivieri completed a Ph.D. in French literature from the Université Grenoble Alpes and has an upcoming book titled *La Prudence d'après Michel de Montaigne et Baltasar Gracián*. She currently teaches Spanish at Adelphi University.

David Beeler earned his Ph.D. in history from the University of South Florida in 2019. He is currently an adjunct instructor of Humanities at the University of South Florida and an adjunct instructor of history at St. Petersburg College.

Kristin M. S. Bezio is an Associate Professor at the University of Richmond. Publications include *Staging Power in Tudor and Stuart English History Plays*; "Munday I Sweare Shalbee a Hollidaye" in *Études Anglaises*; and *William Shakespeare & 21st Century Culture, Politics, and Leadership* with Anthony Russell.

Sara González Castrejón is a Researcher at the Faculty of Communication Sciences, Tourism, and Psychology at Universidad de San Martín de Porres (Lima, Peru). She specializes in Andean rural religious heritage. Her publications include: *Templos virreinales de la sierra de Oyón y Huaura: estudio artístico e iconográfico* (Lima: USMP & Obispado de Huacho, 2019), 'Las iglesias virreinales de los valles de los ríos Huaura y Checras: patrimonio religioso y turismo en la sierra de Lima' (*Turismo y Patrimonio* 12, 2018), "Las efigies de los Incas en el Ms. 1551 de la Biblioteca Angelica (Roma) y los 'cuadernos de mano' de Francisco Fernández de Córdova," in A. Vázquez Varela, F. Eissa-Barroso and S. Espelt-Bombin, *Élites, representación y redes atlánticas en la Hispanoamérica moderna* (Michoacan, Mexico: El Colegio de Michoacán, A.C., 2017), and "Making Pre-Hispanic History in Viceregal Peru: Colonial 'Portraits' and Painted Dynasties of the Inca Kings," *History of Humanities*, Volume 1, Number 2, Fall 2016.

Cecilio M. Cooper holds a Ph.D. (with distinction) in African American studies and a graduate certificate in critical theory from Northwestern University. Currently, Dr. Cooper serves as a Forsyth Postdoctoral Research Fellow in the History of Art at the University of Michigan-Ann Arbor. Over 2021–22, they will also be an American Antiquarian Society-National Endowment for the Humanities Fellow.

Lorenz A. Hindrichsen trained in medieval and early modern literature at Zurich and Aberdeen, writing his M.A thesis on social codes in Chaucer's *Canterbury Tales*, and his Ph.D. on representations of ethnicity in Shakespeare and Renaissance art. His main research interests include race and gender from the Middle Ages to the Romantic period, ecocriticism, trauma theory, and graphic novel. Lorenz teaches English at Copenhagen International School.

Maya Mathur is a Professor of English at the University of Mary Washington. Her scholarship on early modern drama has been published in *A Cultural History of Comedy*, the *Journal for Medieval and Early Modern Studies*, and *Early Theater*, among other venues. Her current research examines representations of race, caste, and gender in Indian film adaptations of Shakespeare.

Scott Oldenburg specializes in early modern literature and culture at Tulane University. He is the author of *Alien Albion: Literature and Immigration in Early Modern England* and *A Weaver-Poet and the Plague: Labor, Poverty, and the Household in Shakespeare's London* as well as articles on various early modern topics.

Manuel J. Ortuño is a Professor Emeritus of Spanish at Baylor University where he served for a decade and a half as Chair of the Department of Modern Languages and Cultures. His areas of scholarly research are Spain's late medieval and early modern works of literature, particularly those that develop religious themes, and the ongoing influence that they have had on Hispanic America. Among his published articles are "Religious Ritual in the Poetry of Francisco de Quevedo," *Revista de Estudios Hispánicos* (1981), "Revisions and Their Significance in Quevedo's 'Poema heroico a Cristo Resusitado,'" *Hispanófila* (1984), and "The Spanish Franciscans of Twentieth-Century Texas and the Role of Mediterranean Culture in Their Ministry," *Catholic Southwest: A Journal of History and Culture* (2001).

Luis Josué Salés is an Assistant Professor and chair of religious studies at Scripps College. He specializes in postcolonial, queer, and feminist approaches to premodern Christianities at the intersection of Africa, Asia, and Eastern Europe. Luis is especially interested in long-neglected African Christian voices from Egypt, Nubia, and Ethiopia, gender and sexuality in late ancient and medieval Christian martyrologies and hagiographies, and the role of Aristotelian philosophy in facilitating early Christian-Muslim discourse in the Umayyad and Abbasid Caliphates.

Ian R. Simpson is an Assistant Professor at the Faculty of Archaeology at Leiden University. His research investigates relationships between religion, market exchange, the environment, and materiality, with a focus on early Islamic and medieval history. He has conducted archaeological investigations at Jarash in Jordan, examining evidence of commerce, household, and industry with the aim of understanding interaction between early Muslim communities and other groups. His work also examines heritage in society from critical and anthropological perspectives, including the demands and expectations of mobilizing heritage in environmental, community, and memory projects, and how to improve collaborative and participatory methods in heritage projects.

Anne L. Williams is an Assistant Professor of Art History at the University of Hong Kong. She is the author of *Satire, Veneration, and St. Joseph in Art, c. 1300–1550* (Amsterdam: Amsterdam University Press, 2019). She has published articles on sanctity, humor, rhetoric, and devotional and ecclesiastical art from c. 1300–1600.

ACKNOWLEDGMENTS

The generosity of time and effort across borders made this volume possible. In addition to the conscientious work of the contributors writing from various corners of the globe, we thank Cassie Price (University of Richmond) for her meticulous attention to and feedback on the chapters. We also thank the Routledge editorial staff, especially Izzy Voice and Laura Pilsworth. A good deal of the research herein stems from archival work. We thank the Church of San Miguel Arcángel de Cayma for permitting the use of the photographs in chapter six; the Ministry of Cultural Heritage and Tourism, Museale della Toscana, Pinacoteca Nazionale di Siena, Nationalmuseet, Copenhagen, Musée de la Chartreuse, Douai, LWL-Museum für Kunst und Kultur, Münster, the Metropolitan Museum of Art, New York, and Stuart Whatling for permission to reproduce the images in Chapter 7; Þingeyrar Church and photographer Katharina Kley for permission to reproduce photographs in Chapter 9; and Church of Santa María, Terrasa and Museo del Prado-Pinture, Madrid, Spain (both via Alamy) for permission to use images for Chapter 10. Finally, Scott Oldenburg wishes to thank Michelle Kohler for her patience and support throughout this project.

INTRODUCTION

Scott Oldenburg

When English East India Company man Richard Cocks arrived in Japan in 1613 with the goal of establishing a trading post there, he found that Spanish, Portuguese, and Dutch merchants had already made significant inroads and that Chinese merchants, too, had a stake in the island nation. Although neither the Spanish nor the Portuguese had established permanent trading posts in Japan, the missionaries who traveled with them had managed to convert significant numbers of Japanese to Catholicism. While the motivation for evangelizing in Japan may have been the care of souls, the merchants were not unaware of the trade benefits of spreading their religion. As Cocks traveled through Japan he observed, "Yt seemeth there is many papistes in these partes, which would doe us a mischeefe yf they could."[1] After traveling through Omura (for Cocks, "Umbra"), he writes, "Their hatred against us (I meane them of Umbra) is per meanes of the padrese or pristes, who stered them up against us to make us odious to the Japons, for they are all, or the most part, papisticall Christians in Umbra."[2] Cocks attempted to apprise locals of what for him were crucial differences among the dominant Western European religions. Although Japanese rulers found it difficult to distinguish between the theology of Catholics and Protestants, the distinction nonetheless enabled the Spanish and Portuguese merchants to stoke distrust of their Protestant competitors.

Although Cocks expresses surprise and dismay at his encounters with local Japanese Catholics, he may well have been sent to Japan precisely to destabilize the Catholic hold on trade there.[3] For roughly a decade Cocks had served as a spy in France where he reported to the Earl of Salisbury, and he continued to send reports to Salisbury from Japan. Cocks actively lobbied to have the Catholics exiled—how effective he was is unclear, but the Japanese did eventually banish Christians as well as Buddhists, thus diminishing the hold Spanish, Portuguese,

DOI: 10.4324/9781003082842-1

Dutch, and Chinese merchants had on Japan, but this was also the prequel to the closing of Japan's ports to foreign merchants altogether.

The influx of foreign goods and the religions that came along with them appeared to pose a threat of outside influence to the recently established Tokugawa regime. Masterless samurai, dubbed *kabukimono* (loosely translated as "eccentrics"), found in their access to a new global marketplace an expression of their social and political discontent, donning flamboyant silks from abroad and smoking tobacco brought to Japan from the Americas by way of European merchants.[4] Hyper-masculine in their self-presentation, the *kabukimono* formed the basis for the stock protagonist of the earliest of Japan's kabuki theater (named for its depiction of the samurai). Tellingly, Izumo no Okuni, the woman credited with inaugurating the dramatic form, performed her masterless samurai with rosary beads and a cross hanging from the neck, signs that he consumed not only foreign goods but also foreign religion. Okuni's standard skit involved her *kabukimono* character attempting a tryst with a courtesan.[5] There is considerable debate about how the popular performance was received, but it seems not much of a stretch to see the prominent place of the symbols of Catholicism as rendering the samurai at least somewhat hypocritical, engaged in an empty embrace of the foreign religion as casually as he might embrace his courtesan.[6]

In this instance, religion emerges not as the sincere belief Cocks hoped he might leverage at the marketplace, but rather as just another commodity trafficked by foreign merchants. The point is furthered in the Japanese "Tale of the Christian" (1639) which describes a Jesuit missionary arriving with European merchants as a grotesque "phanstasm more terrible than the most ferocious monster," and rather like "a long-necked demon of the sort that disguise themselves as Buddhist lay-priests in order to trick people."[7] Here the Europeans themselves are rendered monstrous others, and the trickery of the inhuman friar overlays with the empty signs of faith in the kabuki theater or deception at the marketplace.

In this brief overview of religion and the market of early modern Japan—and its encounters with the religions and markets of other nations—one may glean some of the key themes of this volume of essays, developed more intricately in the chapters that follow. Objects of religious veneration might circulate as marketable commodities; they might serve as signs of political or economic identities; matters of faith might frame (or be framed) by the experience of the marketplace; religion traveled with merchants and might be used to gain leverage at the marketplace; and, recognizing this latter point, states might attempt to enforce or banish religion from the market altogether. Political power and individual identity meet at the crossroads of religion and the marketplace.

It is no surprise, of course, that religion and economy comprise significantly overlapping spheres in pre- and early modern life. Indeed, the notion of an autonomous economic and religious sphere might well be deemed anachronistic to the early modern period.[8] Whether attending a mosque, synagogue, church, or temple, early modern subjects heard about the evils of avarice and the importance of redistributing one's wealth. They read about injunctions against interest, or about prophets objecting to enslavement. Still, this was a period of major investment in trade with the expectation of returns, the establishment of joint companies, and the horrors of the transatlantic slave trade. And these economic activities gave rise to encounters with non-Western religious outlooks and thus perceived opportunities for evangelism, which would, in turn, as Cocks and those like him understood it, result in preferred access to the marketplace. It should further be noted that religion was not merely gilding of filthy lucre. The conversion of enslaved peoples to Christianity may have aimed at greater control over the enslaved, but the enslaved also often developed their own vital, theologically informed critique of enslavement.[9] Similarly, in his *Nueva Corónica y Buen Gobierno* (1615), the Inca Felipe Guaman Poma de Ayala petitions Spain for better governors and priests, at one point presenting the image of an Inca and a Spaniard conversing; the Inca asks the Spaniard what he eats, and the Spaniard replies, "Este oro comemos" (we eat this gold). Not unlike the interpretation of Okuni's *kabukimono* above, the *Corónica* thus held the Spanish colonial project up to the religious standards they had imposed on the Inca.[10]

This volume might usefully be compared to the *Religion and Trade: Cross-Cultural Exchanges in World History, 1000–1900*, edited by Francesca Trivellato, Leor Halevi, and Caátia Antunes.[11] Building on the tradition of Fernand Braudel and Philip D. Curtin, the essays that make up *Religion and Trade* focus primarily on trade with a sense that religious concerns were ultimately dwarfed by the lure of commodities and profit. While we do not necessarily contest this framing, the present volume is interested in the manifold ways matters of faith interacted with marketplace phenomena—anxieties about the intermixing of secular markets and the sacred objects, the trade in altar pieces and religious imagery, and the economics of such images, as well as the ways in which religion helped or hindered market activities and, conversely, how market activity facilitated or complicated the spread of specific religions. By the same token, while several of the following chapters delve into cross-cultural encounters, others explore specific regional intersections of religion and the market, inviting readers to draw their own comparativist conclusions. Finally, the exceptionalism that came along with faith (not to mention national mercantile projects) frequently led to racialization and attempts to legitimate conquest and enslaving of peoples.

The dual focus on religion and marketplace, the chapters that make up this volume do not easily fall into what Sanjay Subrahmanyam calls "ersatz Weberianism," a de facto Eurocentrism that sees Christianity as the preeminent force behind modern economic development.[12] Several chapters delve into exclusively Western European, Christian material, but others investigate the intersection of religion and the marketplace in Syria, Ethiopia, and Peru without giving precedence to European perspectives. Moreover, this volume does not attempt to present a comprehensive history of the interrelations of religion and the global marketplace, nor could it given the diverse religions, cultures, and economic practices across continents and centuries that comprise its scope. Even the very best of largescale scholarly examinations of religion and economy, like Joost Hengstmengel's *Divine Providence in Early Modern Economic Thought* or Silvia Federici's remarkable *Caliban and the Witch* have their blindspots–nuances within their scope and whole continents outside of it. Such largescale narratives of economic and religious change have their place, but this volume sets out to examine particularities, episodes, and phenomena that might support or undermine or offer alternatives to distant readings of religion and the marketplace. This volume provides a series of case histories, which, it is hoped, will lead to further investigations into the complex interplay of religion and the marketplace in different regions and moments, particularly those that transcend or challenge the historical tendency of centering European Christianity.

Despite the diverse approaches and regional focuses of the chapters that make up *Religion in the Medieval and Early Modern Global Marketplace*, these ten chapters can be usefully grouped into three distinct categories. The first four chapters chart the tensions between religious and economic thought in specific locales or texts. The next three chapters look at the complex ways religion and economy interacted with one another as markets became increasingly global, particularly in colonial or proto-colonial settings. The last three chapters look at the way matters of faith, economy, and race converge in religious images of the pre- and early modern periods.

In alluding to Matthew 22:21 ("Render unto Caesar that which is Caesar's") in chapter one's title, David Beeler reminds us that scripture long involved itself in political economy. Beeler charts the way the economic decision-making of the Dutch province Groningen was informed by Calvinist leaders in a province with a significant Catholic population throughout the seventeenth century. Through analysis of Groningen's domestic as well as international trade, Beeler shows a gradual yet fraught process of secularization of the early modern marketplace in the Netherlands. In chapter two Ian R. Simpson reveals the ways that, despite the centrality of mosques, markets in medieval Syria-Palestine facilitated not only trade, but also interreligious contact. The various kinds of contact at the market made for fluid identities irreducible to particular religious affiliation. Here the confluence of various religions at the marketplace ruptures traditional identities. Similarly, in chapter three, Manuel Ortuño examines King Enrique's 1474 letter establishing an annual trade fair in Paradas, Spain. Although the letter infused political and religious authority, the trade fair was ordained to be a space where Christians, Muslims, and Jews could freely trade without interference. This is all the more surprising given that the *Reconquista* of the southern region of Spain was still incomplete at the time. It would seem that economic pressure to keep the marketplace open overrode preoccupation with xenophobia until Granada fell to Catholic Spanish powers. Still, that Enrique ordered local magistrates to protect the religious diversity at the market suggests at least some antipathies about matters of faith as they became entangled with trade. Sara Aponte-Olivieri's reading of Michel Montaigne's *Essais* in chapter four pursues such anxieties. Committed to his aristocratic identity, Montaigne, argues Aponte-Olivieri, regards with disdain the intermingling of the sacred and the prophane from the domestic space of the middling sort's shop in France to attempts at conversion in the New World.

If allowing merchant adventures to go forward with missionary adjuncts produced anxiety in aristocrats in Europe, the meaning of "heathen" goods imported to Europe introduced another kind of anxiety. In chapter five Maya Mathur examines the writings of East India Company men Sir Thomas Roe and Edward Terry who try to allay such fears by framing their mercantile project as fulfilling God's purpose, a holy war by other means, which would break up the stronghold the Ottoman Empire had on trade routes. We have then dual anxieties—for Montaigne a worry about mingling religion and the market, for Terry and Roe a fear of the consequences for not doing so. Chapter six picks up where these anxieties leave off. Here Sara González Castrejón traces the history of unique Catholic icons in Peru from the sixteenth through the nineteenth centuries. In what she cautiously compares to market pressures, what began as evangelical efforts to convert and subdue indigenous peoples of Peru gave way to subtle negotiations whereby saints' images were imbued with local meaning and indigenous aesthetics. It is perhaps this autonomy once religion enters the market, that so worried early modern subjects like Montaigne, in some ways the corollary to efforts by the likes of Cocks to use religious affiliation as a way of opening up markets.

As one may detect in the examples of Peru and India, efforts at conversion that went with commerce were not always purely aimed at the saving of souls or merely facilitating exchange but rather at attempts at domination. In Chapter 7, Luis Salés shows that intense Jesuit attempts at converting Abyssinians to Catholicism were imagined as a prelude to broader colonial efforts in Ethiopia and its surroundings. Salés documents the successful resistance to this incursion led in part by Wälättä Pęṭros, memorialized by the seventeenth-century Ethiopian hagiography about her, the *Gädlä Wälättä Pęṭros.*

Despite attempts at promoting tolerance at the marketplace (observed in the first three chapters of this volume), inter-religious encounters might also create animosity. Salés points out that the Jesuit missionary Pedro Paéz looked with disdain on (among other things) the Abyssinian practice of teaching girls to read scripture, while Gälawdewos, the author of the *Gädlä Wälättä Pęṭros,* frequently refers to "the filthy faith of the Europeans."[13] Righteousness coupled with competition for resources might thus lead to claims of racial or cultural superiority. In chapter eight, Anne Williams explores such instances in depictions of Joseph of Nazareth, associated as he was with the material well-being of the household. As market capitalism developed alongside increased contact among disparate peoples in the Mediterranean, notes Williams, depictions of Joseph as the household's saintly treasurer at times gave way to, among other things, anti-Semitic satire. A similar dynamic appears in chapter nine where Lorenz Hindrichsen examines the commodification of race in an altarpiece and a baptismal font found in a parish church in Northern Iceland. The baptismal font features an irenic scene of Ethiopian conversion while the altarpiece frames two Black Africans as Christ's sadistic torturers. As Hindrichsen shows, the images participated in broad patterns of European fantasies about racial difference and domination but also retained local meanings for the congregants of the remote Parish Church.

Finally, from the market for racialized religious images, chapter ten by Cecilio M. Cooper examines antiblack racism in depictions of the Miracle of the Black Leg. The pre-modern vision of a (non-racialized) leg being amputated from one person and surgically attached to another was, as cross-cultural encounters, colonial enterprises, and the transatlantic slave trade increased in the early modern period, racialized into the image of an Ethiopian's leg amputated and grafted onto a white European body. Cooper's careful exegesis exposes the ways religions, markets, and medical discourses combined to mystify antiblack racism as the miraculous triumph of Christianity and science.

This volume ends with an epilogue by co-editor Kristin M. S. Bezio reflecting on the connections between these chapters on religion in the medieval and early modern market and our present moment. What is the legacy of early modern economic and spiritual exceptionalism? In what ways does prosperity still entangle itself with righteousness? Bezio offers some insights on these questions. None of these chapters should be seen as end points, however. On the contrary, it is hoped that these ten case studies covering disparate locales and centuries might provide useful starting points for considering the intersection of faith and economy in a wide variety of disciplines.

Given the brutal record of colonization that followed so many joint incursions of merchants and missionaries, it was perhaps not unwise, then, for the early modern Japan encountered by Richard Cocks to be suspicious of and ultimately close its markets to foreign merchants. Okuni's satirical presentation of the masterless samurai, after all, pointed to anxieties about the influence of foreign goods on the social and political stability of the island (similar, perhaps, to Montaigne's own anxieties about change manifested in the mingling of the sacred and the profane). Spanish, Portuguese, Dutch, English, and Chinese merchants all converged on Japan, as they had done elsewhere, conflating the conversion of resources to profit with the conversion of souls. The demand for exotic goods went along with a desire to efface differences of belief. Like Ethiopia, Japan resisted such attempts. While we may see the economic and cultural exchanges of the global marketplace as abundantly progressive, when it came to the respect of diverse cultures, absolute faith in the market risked being at the same time recklessly regressive.

Notes

1 Richard Cocks, *Diary of Richard Cocks, Cape-Merchant in the English Factory in Japan, 1615–22*, Vol. 1, Ed. Edward Maunde Thompson (London: Printed for the Hakluyt Society, 1883), 171.
2 Ibid, 139.
3 Timon Screech, "The English and the Control of Christianity in the Early Edo Period," *Japan Review* 24 (2012): 3–40 and 13–15.

4 Harry Harootunian, *Uneven Moments: Reflections on Japan's Modern History* (New York: Columbia University Press, 2019), 79–80.
5 Yoko Takakuwa, "Performing Marginality: The Place of the Player and of 'Woman' in Early Japanese Culture," *New Literary History* 27.2 (1996): 213–25 and 213–15; and Galia Todorova Gabrovska, "Onna Mono: The 'Female Presence' on the Stage of the All-Male Traditional Theatre," *Asian Theatre Journal* 32.2 (2015): 387–415 and 389–92.
6 On debates on how subversive or conservative early kabuki theater was, see Takakuwa, 215–8; Gabrovska, 389.
7 Alexander Curvelo, "The Disruptive Presence of the Namban-jin in early Modern Japan," *Journal of the Economic and Social History of the Orient*, 55.2/3 (2012): 581–602 and 592.
8 Recent work suggests that even today religion and economy might not be as separate as we would like to think. See Daromir Rudnyckyj and Filippo Osella (eds.), *Religion and the Morality of the Market* (Cambridge: Cambridge University Press, 2017).
9 See, for example, Kristen Block, *Ordinary Lives in the Early Caribbean: Religion, Colonial Competition, and the Politics of Profit* (Athens: University of Georgia Press, 2012), 51–64; Jon F. Sensbach, *Rebecca's Revival: Creating Black Christianity in the Atlantic World* (Cambridge: Harvard University Press, 2006).
10 Felipe Guamán Poma de Ayala, *El Primer Nueva Corónica y Buen Gobierno*, Vol. 2 (Mexico: Fundacion Biblioteca Ayacuch, 1980), 371. On this reading of the text, see Francisco Ramírez Santacruz and Héctor Costilla Martínez, "Diego Muñoz Camargo y Felipe Guaman Poma de Ayala," *Revista de Crítica Literaria* Latinoamericana 43.86 (2017): 151–70 and 162–5; and Rocío Quispe-Agnoli, "'Yo y el Otro': Identidad y Alternidad en la 'Nueva Corónica y Buen Gobierno," *MLN* 119.2 (2004): 226–51.
11 Francesca Trivellato, Leor Halevi, and Caátia Antunes, *Religion and Trade: Cross-Cultural Exchanges in World History, 1000–1900* (Oxford University Press, 2015).
12 Sanjay Subrahmanyam, "Introduction," *Merchant Networks in the Early Modern World, 1450–1800* (London: Routledge, 2016), xii.
13 Gälawdewos, *The Life and Struggles of Our Mother Walatta Petros: A Seventeenth-Century African Biography of an Ethiopian Woman,* Trans. Wendy Belcher and Michel Kleiner (Princeton: Princeton University Press, 2015), 152, 154, 155, 180, and 228.

Bibliography

Block, Kristen. *Ordinary Lives in the Early Caribbean: Religion, Colonial Competition, and the Politics of Profit.* Athens: University of Georgia Press, 2012.

Cocks, Richard. *Diary of Richard Cocks, Cape-Merchant in the English Factory in Japan, 1615–1622*, Vol. 1, ed. Edward Maunde Thompson. London: Printed for the Hakluyt Society, 1883.

Curvelo, Alexander. "The Disruptive Presence of the Namban-jin in Early Modern Japan." *Journal of the Economic and Social History of the Orient*, 55.2/3 (2012): 581–602.

de Ayala, Felipe Guamán Poma. *El Primer Nueva Corónica y Buen Gobierno*, Vol. 2. Mexico: Fundacion Biblioteca Ayacuch, 1980.

Gabrovska, Galia Todorova. "Onna Mono: The 'Female Presence' on the Stage of the All-Male Traditional Theatre." *Asian Theatre Journal*, 32.2 (2015): 387–415.

Gälawdewos. *The Life and Struggles of Our Mother Walatta Petros: A Seventeenth-Century African Biography of an Ethiopian Woman*, Trans. Wendy Belcher and Michel Kleiner. Princeton: Princeton University Press, 2015.

Harootunian, Harry. *Uneven Moments: Reflections on Japan's Modern History*. New York: Columbia University Press, 2019.

Quispe-Agnoli, Rocío. "'Yo y el Otro': Identidad y Alternidad en la 'Nueva Corónica y Buen Gobierno." *MLN*, 119.2 (2004): 226–51.

Rudnyckyj, Daromir and Filippo Osella, eds. *Religion and the Morality of the Market*. Cambridge: Cambridge University Press, 2017.

Santacruz, Francisco Ramírez and Héctor Costilla Martínez."Diego Muñoz y Felipe Guaman Poma de Ayalan." *Revista de Crítica Literaria Latinoamericana*, 43.86 (2017): 151–70.

Screech, Timon. "The English and the Control of Christianity in the Early Edo Period." *Japan Review*, 24 (2012): 3–40.

Sensbach, Jon F. *Rebecca's Revival: Creating Black Christianity in the Atlantic World*. Cambridge: Harvard University Press, 2006.

Subrahmanyam, Sanjay. "Introduction." *Merchant Networks in the Early Modern World, 1450–1800*. London: Routledge, 2016.

Takakuwa, Yoko. "Performing Marginality: The Place of the Player and of 'Woman' in Early Japanese Culture." *New literary History*, 27.2 (1996): 213–25.

Trivellato, Francesca, Leor Halevi, and Caátia Antunes. *Religion and Trade: Cross-Cultural Exchanges in World History, 1000–1900*. Oxford: Oxford University Press, 2015.

1

RENDER UNTO CAESAR

Religious thought, trade, and secular authority in Groningen during the Dutch Golden Age

David Beeler

The Dutch province of Groningen and its capital city, also named Groningen, have long been a bit of an oddity within the broader Dutch Republic. Located nearly 200 km northeast of Amsterdam and The Hague (i.e., the entrepôt of the Dutch economy and the center of Dutch political life, respectively), Groningen was, as Jan van den Broek argued, set apart from the rest of the Dutch Republic, both physically and mentally.[1] Although the city of Groningen was an important hub for trade with Northern Germany, it never achieved the sort of economic successes that were experienced in Holland's more prosperous maritime centers.[2] Groningen was also plagued by incessant political feuding, which, on occasions, led to violent protests and riots. In the historiography, these moments of social disorder are typically described as having been driven by economic or political grievances, whereas religious riots were said to have been rare, limited to the first quarter of the century, and largely inconsequential.[3]

Thus, it is tempting to interpret the economic and political history of seventeenth century Groningen in strictly secular terms. Such an approach aligns with the typical trajectory of early modern studies which, broadly speaking, interprets the rise of capitalism and nation-states as part and parcel of the decline of religious convictions. Of course, religious, economic, and political concerns were inexorably linked in the early modern period, and there are inevitable pitfalls associated with isolating these themes into separate spheres of study.[4] Furthermore, the extent to which religious convictions intermingled with secular concerns in the Dutch Republic varied from province to province, and even from town to town. Sir William Temple may have stood in awe of the religious diversity that he witnessed in Holland, writing that, "Of all other Religions, every man enjoys the free exercise in his own Chamber, or his own House, unquestioned and unespied," but could that same degree of toleration be found throughout the

DOI: 10.4324/9781003082842-2

country?[5] Had Temple observed Groningen as closely as Holland, he may have found a bit more nuance in his conclusions.

Dutch religious toleration in the seventeenth century was first and foremost related to economic pragmatism, social order, localism, and political expediency.[6] And while some Dutch cities, especially those with large mercantile industries, such as Amsterdam, adopted models of relative toleration, Groningen was far less accommodating.[7] With these things in mind, this chapter explores the intersection of religious thought, economic decision-making, and secular authority in Groningen during the Dutch Golden Age (c. 1600–1700). Groningen is a unique case study in this regard, in part because it has been an understudied region of the Dutch Republic, but also because of its unusual reputation for political instability and civic disobedience. Furthermore, the seventeenth century was a period in which Groningen was very much coming of age. As a united province, Groningen was, for all intents and purposes, annexed into the Dutch Republic in 1594, and although its publicly recognized Reformed Church enjoyed the backing of the new government, large swaths of the population remained Catholic. It is perhaps no coincidence then, that during the course of the seventeenth century, some of Groningen's most significant economic and political rivals were also religious dissenters, namely Catholics and their sympathizers.

This chapter examines three main religious undercurrents that both influenced and justified economic decision-making in Groningen during the Dutch Golden Age. First, the longstanding, and sometimes contentious, relationship that existed between Groningen's Reformed government and its Catholic population. Second, Groningen's remarkable contrast to the other Dutch provinces regarding the war effort against Portugal; territorial claims in Brazil; and support of the Dutch West-India Company (WIC), even after suffering horrendous financial losses. These decisions were informed not only by a desire for higher returns on their investments but also by their brand of militant Calvinism, which fostered plenty of anti-Catholic sentiment. Finally, this chapter analyzes the role of religious thought and secular authority in economic decision-making in Groningen's domestic marketplace. Driven by a shared desire for prosperity and social order, Groningen's economic decision-making followed an Erastian trajectory that subordinated not only dissenting religious groups but also its own Reformed Church, often, and somewhat paradoxically, in the name of divine providence.

A "Very Bitter Bile": pluralism in Groningen's marketplace

At the turn of the seventeenth century, Groningen witnessed the beginnings of what would be a gradual secularization process, even if the inhabitants may not have immediately recognized it as such. The first step in this process was the removal of Catholics, and later even Remonstrant Calvinists, from positions of authority. One of the early milestones toward this end was an event known as Rennenberg's *verraad* (betrayal). In the spring of 1580, the Count of Rennenberg

Georges de Lalaing (1550–1581), who was also the Stadholder of Groningen and a staunch Catholic, broke his promise to support the Dutch rebels in their Revolt against Spain and shifted his allegiance to the Spanish King Philip II. As a result of Rennenberg's betrayal, the capital city of Groningen remained in Catholic-minded hands for the next 14 years, while the surrounding countryside (also known as the Ommelanden) continued to support the Dutch rebels. The situation fueled resentment and distrust between Protestants and Catholics, as well as between the city and countryside, for decades to come.

Of course, there were additional reasons for Dutch Protestants to fear Catholics and their sympathizers, including the Spanish Council of Troubles (1567–1576), the debilitating effects of siege warfare in Haarlem and Leiden in the 1570s, the fall of Antwerp in 1585, as well as a handful of Catholic martyrs willing to kill, and be killed, for the cause.[8] As Scott Oldenburg has shown in his work on early modern immigration, these events not only promoted a transnational Protestant identity, but also prompted thousands of Dutch Calvinists to flee the Netherlands and seek shelter among other likeminded Protestant communities in England.[9] After the turn of the seventeenth century, there was a sharp decline in Catholic martyrdom and Dutch refugees, but Calvinist anxieties related to the potential for Catholic violence persisted in the Republic for decades to come.[10] The Dutch Reformed Church received the backing of the government in the second decade of the century, but much of the Dutch population remained Catholic, and outside of the Maritime Provinces, Catholics tended to make up the majority of the population.[11] This was especially true in Groningen, where, even after the Dutch Army captured the capital city from its Catholic leaders in 1594—and for all intents and purposes, forced it into the Dutch Republic—membership to the Reformed Church remained a minority.

Groningen's Reformed Church and government displayed mixed feeling regarding their Catholic neighbors, but legal and economic pragmatism often compelled coexistence and relative toleration. Both the Union of Utrecht (1579) (the treaty between the Dutch provinces, often considered to be the Republic's constitution), and Groningen's *Tractaat van Reductie* (1594) (the official agreement that joined the capital city of Groningen with the Ommelanden into a single province, also named Groningen), emphasized the importance of "freedom of conscience," stipulating that "no one should be inquired, investigated, or disputed regarding his conscience."[12] What concerned Dutch authorities, even those who were devout Calvinists, was not necessarily individual beliefs, but rather public displays of dissent.[13] As Benjamin Kaplan explains:

> Dutch law defined any worship that involved a gathering of different families as a public event, a "conventicle," and proscribed it. But within the confines of their home, it permitted individuals and single families to do as they pleased ... Thus, "freedom of conscience" really meant freedom of private, domestic worship.[14]

Freedom of conscience also entailed a shared desire for economic prosperity and social order. Public acts of dissent that disrupted trade, commerce, or posed some other threat to the community—through verbal, intellectual, and physical confrontations—had to be checked immediately. As was the case throughout early modern Europe, social order was paramount.

Pluralism and "freedom of conscience" may have been begrudgingly tolerated in the Dutch Republic, but in their drafting of the Reductie, Groningen's new government declared that throughout the province "no other religion except the Reformed religion shall be practiced."[15] This, of course, was easier said than done, and practically speaking would never be accomplished. Catholic beliefs and traditions were simply too embedded in Groningen's culture to be uprooted by the stroke of a quill. In addition, Groningen's Reformed government struggled to accurately identify those who were truly Reformed. There was no law requiring Groningers to attend Reformed Church services, much less one that required Groningers to become official members of the Reformed Church.[16] Of those who considered themselves Protestants, many were known simply as "sympathizers," meaning that although they regularly attended Reformed services, they did not necessarily embrace *all* of the teachings and rituals of the Reformed Church.[17] This diversity, which could to some extent be found throughout Protestant Europe, contributed to a distinction between an invisible church of personal beliefs, and a visible church that was, in the words of Kevin Chovanec, "mixed with hypocrites."[18]

Identifying one's true religious convictions was equally difficult for those living outside of the city. Jonathan Israel, for example, has shown that most of the population along the Dutch-German border "constituted a non-confessionalized, or barely confessionalized, bloc, undecided and unformed, attracting fierce disapproval of committed men on both sides."[19] One of those who sought to change this was the Jesuit priest and missionary Franciscus Mijleman (1610–1667). In his *Ommelands Eer* (Ommeland's Honor) (1664), Mijleman described how he held secret Catholic meetings at night in the Groningen countryside, and circumvented the Reformed authorities by disguising himself as a cattle trader.[20] For nearly 30 years, Mijleman traveled from village to village, staying in each one for about five or six weeks, before moving on to the next.[21] During that time, he estimated that he had corrected the religious *errores* (errors) of hundreds of non-Catholics, thus bringing them back into the fold of the true *Moederkerk* (Mother Church).[22]

Mijleman also described how many of the Catholic priests in the countryside lived and worked among the peasantry according to the Cistercian Order. They spent their days performing manual labor, cultivating the earth, feeding cattle, digging peat, building roads and bridges, embanking land to divert water, and trading goods in the marketplace.[23] In this way, they blended in with their rural communities, forging bonds of friendship, patronage, and clientage with other farmers and villagers. This pattern is consistent with the "putting-out system," in which merchants remedied labor shortages by hiring a wide range of laborers from the countryside, many of whom were presumably from different confessions.[24]

The diversity of religious groups in Groningen's countryside may have also acted as a counterweight to the increasing secular authority in the city. At the turn of the seventeenth century, when Groningen's new Reformed government ordered their soldiers to commence a *zuivering* (cleansing) of the monasteries, they did so in a relatively orderly and peaceful manner.[25] Catholic altars were indeed demolished, statues of saints were cleared away, and interior walls were painted over; however, most of these acts were carried out behind closed doors and under the supervision of the government.[26] In the years that followed, Groningen's Reformed government continued to confiscate monastic goods, which they then "secularized," meaning that they sold them and used the proceeds to fund public construction projects.[27] Of utmost importance was the construction of the University of Groningen in 1614, as well as the maintenance of the mighty *Martinitoren* (St. Martin's Church Tower), which seventeenth-century Groningers boasted was the tallest in the world, rivaled only by the Biblical Tower of Babel.[28] Because it was the secular government, and not a religious mob, that had carried out this cleansing, the implications went well beyond religious purification, ultimately subordinating the Reformed Church—and indeed all churches—to the Dutch state.

After the secular government had stripped the monasteries of their religious objects, it was that same government that filled the religious power vacuum that it had created. In short, the cleansing in Groningen followed a certain Erastian trajectory, whereby the secular government became the de facto "new sacred community."[29] To varying degrees, this pattern occurred throughout the Republic as Dutch secular leaders increasingly defined their cities and provinces in accordance with Calvinist ideals, while paradoxically excluding the Reformed Church from actual governance.[30] Gradually, Dutch secular authorities extended their control over what they referred to as the "Public Church" by supervising church meetings and paying the salaries of its ministers.[31] Even the final rules governing religious toleration in each city were not decided by the Reformed Church's consistory, or an ecclesiastical panel, but, rather, by the municipal governments, which "appointed 'political commissioners' to control the consistories from within."[32]

Groningen's municipal government, or magistracy, was a group of 4 mayors and 12 city councilmen, who collectively referred to themselves as the *senatus sanctus* (Holy senate) and likened themselves as a God-fearing and God-serving oligarchical body.[33] The minimum formal requirements for becoming a member of the city council was that one had to be at least 25 years old, considered a good patriot, have assets with a value of at least 3,000 thalers (daalders, the equivalent of 4,500 Caroliguilders), and a member of the Reformed Church.[34] This last requirement—membership to the Reformed Church—was often more so in name than in practice, but Groningen's city council nevertheless attempted to tighten restrictions on other religious groups—especially Catholics—whenever possible. In September 1601, for example, the government hung a legal placard reminding the citizenry that it was forbidden to practice any other religions except the Reformed.[35] The placard went on to warn the populace that those who were baptized outside of the Reformed Church could face imprisonment, those who attended baptisms outside of the Reformed Church would be fined, and children from marriages outside of the Reformed Church would be deemed illegitimate and prohibited from receiving inheritance.[36]

By the second half of the century, Catholics still made up approximately 30%–50% of the Dutch population, although their standing in Groningen did not improve all that much.[37] In August 1665, for example, as the Bishop of Münster, Christoph Bernhard von Galen (1606–1678), prepared to invade the Eastern Netherlands, Groningen's city council dismissed a number of guildmembers under the simple charge of *niet zijnde gereformerd* (not being Reformed).[38] And, in October 1665, the magistracy ordered all of the Catholic inhabitants to register with the authorities and surrender any weapons "that might be used to the detriment of the city."[39] Catholics throughout Groningen were placed under house arrest, their homes were subject to be searched, and they were ordered to keep a lantern at their front door that was to remain lit all night.[40] Any Catholics who violated these measures were subject to having their property confiscated.[41]

The degree to which dissenting religious groups obeyed all of these requirements, and the extent to which the city's threats were actually carried out, are difficult to determine. Andrew Pettegree and Arthur der Weduwen, for example, have shown that placards often became "a target for mockery, anger and dissent."[42] Kees Boterbloem writes that, "the Dutch … paid mere lip-service to the idea of being a messianic nation, uniquely chosen to rescue true Christianity with fire and sword from the corrupt Catholic Church."[43] Willem Frijhoff, too, has argued that in most cases, enforcing such laws amounted simply to an act of *oogluiking* (turning a blind eye).[44] This apparent ambivalence could also be transactional, as many dissenting religious groups paid authorities bribes known as *compositie* (recognition money), "in effect," as Hank van Nierop writes, "buying religious freedom for themselves."[45]

Groningen's legal officials could hardly identify everyone who was Catholic, much less compel them to pay. Instead, more often than not, the municipal and provincial authorities simply settled for an oath of loyalty and a promise that the individual in question would not harm the Reformed Church.[46] These oaths seem to have been sufficient for the government, who's primary concern was social order, but they offered little reassurance to the militant Calvinists who lived among them. One Calvinist school director in Middelstum, for example, complained that the presence of so many Catholics in the village was like a *zeer bittere galle* (very bitter bile) lodged in the bowels of the community.[47] The expression likely stemmed from Acts 8:23, which describes greed and worldly ambitions as a sinful entrapment and a corruption of the true faith, and thus, should be expelled from the village, city, state, etc. Dutch Calvinists wrestled with these sentiments. On the one hand, there was the perceived duplicity of their Catholic neighbors, as evidenced by their long history of victimization at the hands of Spanish Catholics during the Eighty Years' War (1568–1648)—as well as the potential repercussions from God for even allowing pluralism in the first place.[48] On the other hand, there was the practical and pragmatic matter of trade, which not only required, but rewarded, those who were willing to interact with strangers.

Militant Calvinism and the Dutch West-India Company

The market, in all of its forms, was not a religiously neutral space; rather, it was, in the words of Dave Postles, "socially inhabited," a place of "social negotiation as well as a place of conflict."[49] Early modern markets contained both sacred and profane qualities, and served as an arena for religious identity and civic pride. Groningen's marketplace was no different. Of course, in most cases, those who bought and sold goods in the marketplace, including those from dissenting religious faiths, did so not as radical reformers hell bent on conflict and disorder, but as fellow citizens and residents carrying out mundane responsibilities necessary for daily life. On rare occasions, heretics, atheists, and other extremists could also be found in in the marketplace. In Groningen's countryside, one might encounter the infamous Marie *'t wikwief van Kolham* (the fortune teller of Kolham), who was said to have maintained a steady book of business, as did Albert Johan, nicknamed *Smeerhans* (Greasy/Dirty Hans), who earned a living as a healer.[50] Smeerhans became so popular that even a local reverend paid him four *Rijksdaalders* and some green cheese in exchange for healing his horses.[51] There was also Rembt Backer, who was arrested in 1629 for meddling with supernatural forces, although it is unclear what became of him.[52] These characters existed in a precarious social space, where their *duivelkunsten* (devil arts) always placed them at risk of the authorities shutting them down, or worse.[53]

Another example appears in 1626, when one Bartholomaeus Barckman was banished after debating with an innkeeper regarding whether or not magicians existed.[54] Certain that they were real, the innkeeper cited Exodus 7 and 8, which speaks of Egyptian wizards, before asking Barckman, somewhat rhetorically, "Was the Bible not the word of God?"[55] It must have been an absolute shock when Barckman replied "No … What is God? Who has seen God? They are fables."[56] This statement alone thrust Barckman to the margins of Dutch society. In the seventeenth century, it was rare to meet someone who openly denied the existence of magic, much less God. Those who did were linked to the devil and ostracized from the community. Timothy 5:22 warns that one should not partake in "other men's sins: keep thyself pure," and on this it seems that all of the major confessions agreed.[57] Even in the tolerant Dutch Republic, those who were deemed to be dangerous pariahs had to be removed for the good of the community. For his part, Barckman was banished for heresy, and like so many others who questioned the status quo, he has disappeared into obscurity. Despite attempts to exclude people of other faiths from their respective communities, the marketplace—and the need to buy and sell goods from one another—compelled people of different faiths to interact.

For early modern Protestants, this interaction was not by chance, but was more likely part of God's great design. In 1673, the Groningen Reformed Minister Gregorius Mees declared that, "Upon creation, God gave mankind the ability to draw upon his natural thriftiness, and to trade with all earthly creatures."[58] As Joost Hengstmengel has articulated, this "universal economy," or the understanding that God had intentionally distributed resources and raw materials around the world, was necessary in order to bring people into contact with one another:[59]

> The observation that not all necessary and useful things are found everywhere was almost universally related to divine providence. God himself introduced this form of economic inequality when creating the world. His material gifts were not distributed evenly, but literally scattered over the surface of the earth ... The Creator's higher aim was to make the nations of the world mutually dependent. The lack of certain necessary products in one country after all forced it to obtain them elsewhere, preferably through the peaceful means of trade.[60]

Along these lines, Willem Frijhoff, too, has shown that Europeans' interests in the East and West were derived from their respective "orientation in the world."[61] In an early modern European mindset, the East represented the beginning of the world (i.e., the sun rising in the East), whereas the West represented the future, and the end (i.e., the sun setting in the West).[62] Thus, there is a sort of manifest destiny at work here and the potential to fulfill that perceived mission—as evidence of God's elect—inspired many Dutch Calvinists to throw their support behind the West India Company. As Frijhoff summarizes, the WIC "evoked so much more passion than the [Dutch] East India Company," because Dutch Calvinists "saw more of a future for Christianity in Brazil than in the Indonesian archipelago."[63] But, as the WIC's profits lagged around mid-century, the religious motivations for trans-Atlantic trade were tested, and many Dutch provinces ultimately fled from the WIC venture. Groningen, however, did not.

In the summer of 1661, after decades of fighting for control of Brazil, the Dutch Republic and Portugal entered into a peace treaty. Weary from war, and with little profit to show for it, most of the Dutch regents were eager to end the hostilities, but these negotiations would come at a heavy price. The Portuguese agreed to compensate the Dutch Republic for some of its financial losses, but in exchange, the WIC was required to abandon all of their commercial, colonial, and territorial interests in Brazil. For most WIC investors, especially those in Holland, the "loss" of Brazil could not come soon enough. The WIC had been hemorrhaging money for years, and, after the loss of Recife in 1654, it was clear that Brazil was a lost cause, and that the company itself was in serious financial trouble.[64] On the Amsterdam exchange, WIC share prices declined steadily for almost two decades, from approximately *f*134 (1640), to *f*46 (1645), to *f*14 (1650), to *f*10 (1655), and practically worthless throughout the remainder of the 1650s.[65] By the early 1660s, most of the Dutch provinces wanted to liquidate both the Brazil venture and the WIC in their entireties. Here again, Groningen refused.

Groningen's provincial leaders, investors, and directors remained steadfastly committed to the war effort against Portugal, and to the belief that the WIC could turnaround their financial misfortunes.[66] They contended that the decline in the WIC's share price was the result of Portuguese and Catholic duplicity.[67] The roots of this argument stemmed from distrust of Spanish and Portuguese Catholics during the Eighty Years War and gained momentum during the Twelve Years' Truce (1609–1621), especially following the religious debates between the more liberal Remonstrants and the militant Counter-Remonstrants during the National Synod of Dordt (1618/1619).

Groningen's Reformed government played important roles in all of these pivotal events. They tipped the scales of the Synod in favor of militant orthodoxy by sending six delegates, all of whom were staunch Counter-Remonstrants.[68] Groningen's government also required that the Theology Department at the University of Groningen be staffed with Counter-Remonstrants, beginning with Franciscus Gomarus (1563–1641), the leader of the Counter-Remonstrant movement, who served as professor of theology from 1618 until his death in 1641, followed by his protege, the French minister Samuel Maresius (1599–1673), from 1643 to 1673.[69] The Counter-Remonstrants witnessed further gains following the *Grote Vergadering* (Great Assembly) (1651), which made "Calvinist orthodoxy as defined by the Synod … the exclusive creed authorized in public life."[70] Decades later, the results of the Great Assembly and Synod of Dordt were still celebrated in Groningen. In 1673, the Groningen Reformed minister Gregorius Mees declared that "the [old] division in the church was like Satan's gunpowder, which he used to burn the divine service, but he can burn us no more, because it [the division] is now outside the bosom of the church of our fatherland."[71] Thus, there was little question as to where Groningen's Reformed government and Reformed Church stood in matters of religious preference.

Groningen's support for the Counter-Remonstrant movement carried over to the aforementioned WIC venture. Gomarus, for example, argued that the company had received "God's blessing," because it was inflicting harm on the papal religion.[72] Indeed since its inception—just 2 years after the Synod of Dordt—the WIC was recognized as a "Counter-Remonstrant enterprise," so much so that Catholic and Remonstrant investors boycotted purchasing shares in the company.[73] This is somewhat striking since the Counter-Remonstrants, who, despite having the backing of the government, were still a minority among the Dutch population, and the WIC surely would have stood a better chance had it not alienated so many potential investors. As Kees Boterbloem has shown in his lucid study on early modern capitalism: "Offending religious sensibilities was not very wise if one wanted to capitalize on trading opportunities."[74]

In addition to its commercial undertakings, the Counter-Remonstrants were also attracted to the WIC's military, colonizing, and Christianizing objectives.[75] This unique blend of secular and spiritual missions was praised by Counter-Remonstrants, many of whom associated orthodox Calvinism with assertiveness, profit-seeking, patriotism, heroism, and even violence, when necessary.[76] The Flemish merchant Willem Usselincx (1567–1647), for example, was a leading advocate for the WIC, and one who "dreamed of a God-fearing empire, of flourishing commercial and agricultural colonies where God's word would be preached in the true Calvinist manner."[77] For Usselinx, the company's aims were not solely profit, but also colonization, because of its potential to spread the true faith.[78] If and when profit followed, it was further evidence of God's providence.

Other Counter-Remonstrant preachers agreed. In his sermons and publications, the Zeeland minister, Godfried Udemans (1581/2–1649), combined didactic lessons on morality, ethics, faith, and divine providence with more temporal concerns such as trade and seafaring. On the title page of his most famous work, *'t Geestelyck roer van 't coopmaans schip* (The spiritual helm of the merchant's vessel) (1638), Udemans included the verse: "Behold also the ships, which though they be so great, and are driven of fierce winds, yet are they turned about with a very small helm, whithersoever the governor listeth" (James 3:4). The divine power of wind—which could be created and controlled only by God—powered these massive ships across unfathomable seas, and it was only with God's grace that the captains could successfully maneuver such vessels.

Of course, there were also secular interests, such as political leaders who expected the WIC to secure military advantages against their rivals, and investors who demanded competitive dividends and capital gains. In these pursuits, the WIC's track record was not exceptional, but on rare occasion it managed to please most of its stakeholders. On September 8, 1628, for example, the WIC Admiral Pieter Heyn (1577–1629) captured the Spanish silver fleet off the coast of Cuba, a colossal prize netting the WIC an estimated 11 million guilders worth of gold and silver.[79] In Groningen, this unprecedented event encouraged a new generation of young men, including numerous orphans to forgo their apprenticeships and try their luck as sailors. They hoped to follow in the footsteps of Piet Heyn—who began as a simple sailor and rose to the rank of Lieutenant-Admiral of Holland—and they risked everything, including a modest, yet stable economic existence on land, in the pursuit of the old cliché: gold, glory, and God.[80]

Adventurers were not the only ones to take on additional risks. Investors, too, many of whom had benefited from the growth of the Dutch economy in the early seventeenth century, wagered their newfound wealth in various investments, including overseas ventures and domestic trade. In Groningen, much of this new wealth flowed through the *Collecthuis* ([Tax] Collection House)—later renamed the *Goudkantoor* (Gold Office)—a government office responsible for the maintenance of various financial accounts. The building itself was constructed in 1635 in the Grote Markt (the large market square in the center of the city), where it still stands today. On the façade above the entrance, one can still read the words, *Date Caesari quae sunt Caesaris* (Render unto Caesar that which is Caesar's). Neither the location, nor the messaging, were coincidental, and here again, the Erastian implications are obvious. The passage was of course taken from Matthew 22:21 and was meant to be a reminder to the citizenry that although Groningen's political leaders were secular figures, they were nevertheless ordained by God, and therefore should be obeyed.

If the Collecthuis, which held some of the city's largest investment accounts, represented one end of the economic spectrum, then the other end of the spectrum could be found, both literally and figuratively, on the opposite side of the marketplace. There, along the southern side of the *Martinikerk*, stood the *Boter en Broodhuisje* (Butter and Bread House), a small building where the poor received food and other forms of charity throughout the seventeenth century. Above the entrance was a sign that read: *bedenck de armen in u testamenten want ghij hebt geen beter renten* (remember the poor in your testaments [wills] because you have no better interest). The word "interest" is a bit of a double entendre, meaning both financial interest and spiritual interest. In other words, charitable gifts to the church, and by extension to the poor, were the best investments one could make (i.e., they had a high return on investment—the highest in fact), because they helped secure one's place in heaven.[81] This position is somewhat counterintuitive to orthodox Calvinism which emphasized that salvation was predetermined by God, not by charitable works. As Anne McCants explains, this phenomenon is sometimes referred to as "bourgeois secularism," and implies that many Dutch elites paid little attention to the finer points of predestination, which ultimately allowed "civic concerns" to take "precedence over ecclesiastical ones."[82]

Domestic trade and the monopolization of secular power

Although Groningen's Reformed government was relatively weak at the turn of the seventeenth century, it nevertheless benefitted from its proximity to the Grote Markt and to other hegemonic institutions in the city. This positional superiority was both bolstered and challenged vis-à-vis the city's management of the marketplace. This was especially the case regarding a controversial law known as the *stapelrecht* (staple rights), which required all goods not intended for personal consumption to be sold at specific markets set forth by the city before they could be offered in secondary markets. In addition, all merchants were required to register with the city's *hoofdmannenkamer* (the chief judicial chamber in Groningen), which, incidentally was the same institution responsible for enforcing the *stapelrecht*.[83] In short, the *stapelrecht* provided the city with a de facto monopoly over the flow of commodities that were in high demand. The situation was made more complicated by Groningen's regents, who politicized the law by paying off certain farmers and villages, as well as by erecting bureaucratic institutions along the canals through which these goods were shipped.[84] Thus, for many farmers in the Ommelanden, the *stapelrecht* was at once an economic hindrance, a symbol of political oppression, and a source of bitterness throughout the century.

The Ommelanders were also plagued by a lack of political and religious cohesion, which prevented them from unifying in any meaningful way against the city's oligarchs. Still, the farmers and villagers in the countryside made use of rhetorical devices, such as the motto *liever Turksch dan Groningsch* (rather Turks than Groningers [city dwellers]), which appeared in print and in popular culture.[85] This was a play on the slogan, *liever Turks dan Paaps* (rather Turks than papists), which was commonly used throughout the Dutch Republic during the Revolt against Catholic Spain.[86] For contemporaries, the message was clear: the Turks, who, for the Dutch had long been a generic symbol of Muslim barbarism, cruelty, and evil, would nevertheless be preferable overlords in comparison to those who were currently in charge (i.e., the Spanish Catholics in the case of the Dutch Revolt; the Reformed municipal government in the case of Groningen).[87] The saying was a bit tongue and cheek, of course, as neither would have been content with Turkish overlords. The exaggeration, however, emphasized the point.

Despite the animosity, some, such as the Groningen syndic, Bernard Alting (c. 1600– a. 1655), implored the city and countryside to set aside their differences, not only for commercial interests but also for their spiritual wellbeing. In the vein of Christian neighborliness—as Jesus had commanded "Love thy neighbor as thyself" (Matthew 22:39)—Alting argued that a town's honor was deeply linked to the reputation of its marketplace, and that the disputes between these "neighbors" were harmful to each other.[88] Alting's critique earned him numerous enemies among the city council members, who forced him to resign from his post in 1643, and then revoked his citizenship in 1644, effectively severing him from the community.[89] Nevertheless, in 1648, he published what would become his most famous work, *De Pilaren ende Peerlen van Groningen* (The Pillars and Pearls of Groningen). In his treatise, Alting described the "pillars" (i.e., the province's institutions) as necessary for Groningen's prosperity, the most important of which was the "general pillar" (i.e., the union between the city and the countryside).[90]

Alting was a conservative Calvinist and his commentary was deeply informed by his faith. The very reference to pearls—which were understood as a symbol of perfection, virtue, honor, and chastity—would have invoked further Biblical references, such as those found in Matthew 13:45-46.[91] The content of Alting's work was also couched in a Calvinist worldview that was preoccupied with uncovering evidence of God's providence, specifically as it related to the prosperity of Groningen. To this end, Alting's writing reminded his readers of Emperors Julian and Hadrian, both of whom had attempted to rebuild the city of Jerusalem, but because their attempts were in bad faith, God thwarted their efforts: "God continued to show his wrath against that city [Jerusalem]," and that "the entire work was thrown into disarray, leaving many of the Jews shaking under the ruins."[92] Alting held up Rome as another infamous example, writing that God had turned this "once great and powerful city, into a city for sale, lost by hatred, discord, self-serving benefits, a stiff-headed council, greedy wars, and cruel tyrants ... only then did it fall to the barbarians."[93] The implications for Groningen were the same: corrupt leaders and self-serving policies tempted God's wrath, which could potentially be visited on the entire community.

Alting also used Holland, and the city of Amsterdam in particular, as ideal examples of the spiritual and temporal potential for Groningen:

> people will read of Holland's prosperity ... and we must say that the Lord has done it; it is a miracle in our eyes. But the Almighty has placed a column on which all of Holland's prosperity rests: its waterways and the sea, through which commerce travels. Without them, the cities of Holland would not have become what they are now. In Holland, and especially in the cities, there is an abundance of everything that can be obtained from any region of the world.[94]

He explained further that with Amsterdam, which was known in the past for having poor air, land, and waterways, one could nevertheless "see what the Lord has done with this city ... stocking an infinite amount of merchants' goods and riches ... [and] all of this is grounded on a single foundation ... trade."[95] Thus, in Amsterdam, God had given mankind a shining example of what He desired: peaceful trade. Alting hoped that this model would be applied to Groningen, and he drove the point home in no uncertain terms, brazenly declaring that "whoever disputes this is either ignorant in the affairs of Groningen, a fool, or both."[96]

Alting's critique also called into question the theological issue of whether or not Christians had the right to criticize their secular leaders. On this point, Calvin was clear that they should not. Calvin generally held a low opinion of humanity, was fearful of anarchy, and therefore promoted the idea that secular leaders should be obeyed. He emphasized that magistrates were not only secular leaders, but also ministers, or servants, of God, and that even leaders who seemed evil should be obeyed, because their authority was derived from God.[97] Romans 13:1-2, for example, instructed Christians to obey their secular rulers, because "the powers that be are ordained of God. Whoever therefore resisteth the power, resisteth the ordinance of God, and they that resist shall receive to themselves damnation."[98] By 1650, even Alting capitulated to this line of reasoning, writing that "what can still be expected is known only to God, who appoints bad administrators when he torments the people with misfortune and disaster."[99] Alting's change in attitude contributed to the restoration of his citizenship in 1650, and his return to employment with the municipal authorities in 1653.[100] As was often the case, Groningen's political elites fostered an environment of deference, loyalty and subordination, while attempting to avoid physical conflict, social disorder, and civic disobedience.

Alting's concession was part of a broader trend of submission among Groningen's citizenry to the secular government. Perhaps the most striking examples of this came in the aftermath of the Groningen guild riots (1657 and 1662). These riots grew from grievances among the guild members (many of whom were Catholic) over municipal leaders' repeated attempts to undercut guild profits by raising taxes and tariffs, as well as by preventing the guilds from officially participating in the political process.[101] The riot of 1657 was exceptionally violent. The mayor Johan Tjassens barely escaped with his life, taking refuge in the *Martinikerk*, while rioters destroyed his house.[102] Rioters also vandalized the home of the councilor Gerhard Buningh, emptying out his stores of wine and beer while he went into hiding in the city.[103] The entire event was not only dangerous, but also embarrassing for the city council. So, when the guilds rioted again in 1662, the city took extraordinary measures to crush the uprising. The stadholder's soldiers were called in, not only from Groningen, but also from the surrounding provinces of Friesland and Drenthe, to assist in the arrests of the belligerent guild members and to restore social order in the city. When the smoke cleared, numerous guild members were arrested, at least four ringleaders were banished, and one was beheaded in the Grote Markt. Those guild members who were allowed to remain in the city were forced to sign an agreement, albeit under duress, that they would never again engage in any clandestine meetings or political interference.[104]

Over the course of next few years, the municipal government continued to chip away at their economic, political, and religious rivals in the guilds. In their consolidation of power, the mayors and city councilors prohibited the reading and circulation of pamphlets that critiqued the government and even ordered some of these to be burned publicly by the city's executioner.[105] They also completely abolished the role of the guild *bouwmeester* (literally meaning architect, because of their love of public buildings, but in reality was a representative for the guilds to express grievances to the city council), and, following the ringing of the bells in the Grote Markt, the town crier read a new set of regulations meant to limit the power of the guilds.[106] Some of these new regulations appeared in a subsequent publication meant to "secure the government against any future seditions and riots."[107]

What is most striking, however, is that the authorities laid the blame for the riots not necessarily on economically or politically oppressed citizens (i.e., guild members), but on dissenting religious groups (mainly Catholics), as well as foreigners. They declared that, in order to prevent future uproars, "from now on, no persons coming in from outside to become citizens of this city will be accepted unless they are of the Reformed religion, and they will be required to bring a certificate with them explaining where they have lived or have stayed in recent times."[108] For the secular authorities, foreigners were a double-edged sword, necessary to bolster the population and local economy, but also bringing with them unwelcomed cultural baggage (i.e., foreign languages, dissenting religions, and unfamiliar behaviors or patterns of practice). Of these, dissenting religious groups were the most concerning because of their potential to disrupt the social order. As the new regulations stipulated: "from now on, no one will be chosen as a lieutenant or any other leading position in the burgher company unless he is committed to the Reformed religion and is likewise required to make an oath of fidelity."[109] Both the disputes over the *stapelrecht* and the guild riots have long been described as economic and political grievances, but they were also clearly informed by religious convictions.

Conclusion

In 1665, and again in 1672, the Catholic Bishop of Münster Christoph Bernhard von Galen, whom the Dutch mockingly nicknamed *Bommen Berend* because of his fondness for artillery tactics, launched two failed military invasions against Groningen. By this point, Groningen's regents had been compelled to raise dramatic sums of money to bolster the city's military defenses. To accomplish this, they increased taxes, issued high-interest bonds, and borrowed heavily from the Holland debt market.[110] These decisions had devastating effects on the Groningen economy, but they nevertheless helped save the city from being overrun by a Catholic tyrant. For the Groningers, it seemed that God, too, had played a vital role in the outcome as rains, floods, and diseases did more to wipe out the enemy's siege camps than any pitched battle. In the Dutch collective memory, these victories also reflected a broader "Batavian historical mythology" that celebrated Dutch (i.e., Calvinist) superiority over their Roman (i.e., Catholic) barbarism.[111]

Seventeenth-century Groningers took pride in their city, even as many others in the Republic—especially the elites in Holland—saw it as little more than a distant buffer zone meant to protect their "Dutch garden" (i.e., the entrepôt of the Dutch economy) from foreign aggression.[112] As orthodox-leaning Calvinists, Groningen's Reformed government saw its political autonomy as instrumental to the province's success and survival. Their economic decisions followed this line of reasoning and were based not only on the potential for profit and loss, but also on their spiritual wellbeing. The history of early modern Groningen is, like many early modern histories, told as a story of secularization, in which political conflict and intolerance paved the way for a more modern and more worldly future. Driven by a shared desire for prosperity and social order, Groningen's economic decision-making may have followed an Erastian trajectory, but Groningen's secularization story is nuanced by the deep interchange of religious thought that nevertheless influenced those decisions. As a site of economic, political, and cultural exchange, the interactions in Groningen's marketplace were dictated not only by shrewd businessmen and political elites, but also by diverse religious convictions.

Notes

1 Jan van den Broek, *Groningen, een stad apart: over het verleden van een eigenzinnige stad (1000–1600),* (Groningen: Uitgeverij Van Gorcum, 2007), this is the overall thesis of Van den Broek's research; see also Jonathan I. Israel, *The Dutch Republic: Its Rise, Greatness, and Fall, 1477–1806* (Oxford: Oxford University Press, 1998), 589–90.

2 Israel, *The Dutch Republic*, 331, Israel describes the Republic as "a land with two economies, that of the west expanding, dynamic, and prosperous, and that of the inland provinces largely stagnant and much poorer." Although Groningen had a port on the North Sea, Delfzijl, the province's economy was generally more in line with the inland provinces.

3 Albert Buursma, *"Dese bekommerlijke tijden": Armenzorg, armen en armoede in de stad Groningen 1594–1795* (Assen: Koninklijke Van Gorcum, 2009), 337; Rudolf M. Dekker, *Holland in beroering: oproeren in de 17de en 18de eeuw* (Baarn: Ambo, 1982), 23–37; see also Rudolf M. Dekker, "Women in Revolt: Popular Protest and Its Social Basis in Holland in the Seventeenth and Eighteenth Centuries," *Theory and Society* 16, no. 3 (1987): 337–39.

4 For example, see Benjamin J. Kaplan, *Divided by Faith: Religious Conflict and the Practice of Toleration in Early Modern Europe* (Cambridge, MA: Harvard University Press, 2007), 177–79; and Joost Hengstmengel, *Divine Providence in Early Modern Economic Thought* (London: Routledge, 2019), 56–7 and 64–5.

5 Sir William Temple, *Observations Upon the United Provinces of the Netherlands* (London: A. Maxwell, 1673), 178.

6 For example, see Israel, *The Dutch Republic*, 675–6; and Peter van Rooden, "Jews and Religious Toleration in the Dutch Republic," in R. Po-Chia Hsia and Henk van Nierop, eds., *Calvinism and Religious Toleration in the Dutch Golden Age* (Cambridge: Cambridge University Press, 2002), 132.

7 Benjamin J. Kaplan, "'Dutch' Religious Tolerance: Celebration and Revision," in R. Po-Chia Hsia and Henk van Nierop, eds., *Calvinism and Religious Toleration in the Dutch Golden Age* (Cambridge: Cambridge University Press, 2002), 16.

8 Israel, *The Dutch Republic*, 157–61.

9 Scott Oldenburg, *Alien Albion: Literature and Immigration in Early Modern England* (Toronto: University of Toronto Press, 2014), 8.

10 Kees Boterbloem, *The Dirty Secret of Early Modern Capitalism: The Global Reach of the Dutch Arms Trade, Warfare and Mercenaries in the Seventeenth Century* (New York: Routledge, 2019), 84. These were some of the last Catholic martyrs in the Dutch Republic as there were virtually none in the seventeenth century; see also Pieter Christiaensz Bor, *Oorsprongk, begin, en vervolgh der Nederlandsche oorlogen*, vol. 1–4 (Amsterdam, 1679–1684), vol. III, 815, and vol. IV, 528, In 1584, for example, a Spanish Catholic named Balthasar Gérard assassinated Willem "the Silent" van Oranje; in 1594, a Catholic priest named Michiel Renichon attempted to assassinate Maurits and his brother, Frederick Henry; and in 1599, a Catholic zealot named Henrik van Achterveld stabbed the Reformed minister Francsicus Schorinckmannus (Schurichman) to death following a sermon in front of everyone in the church.

11 Henk van Nierop, "Sewing the Bailiff in a Blanket: Catholics and the Law in Holland," in R. Po-Chia Hsia and Henk van Nierop, eds., *Calvinism and Religious Toleration in the Dutch Golden Age* (Cambridge: Cambridge University Press, 2002), 108.

12 Reductie van de stad Groningen, July 23, 1594, https://dutchrevolt.leiden.edu/dutch/bronnen/Pages/1594%2007%2023%20ned.aspx, accessed June 1, 2020.

13 Kaplan, *Divided by Faith*, 108–09.

14 Kaplan, *Divided by Faith*, 178–9.

15 Reductie van de stad Groningen, July 23, 1594, https://dutchrevolt.leiden.edu/dutch/bronnen/Pages/1594%2007%2023%20ned.aspx, accessed June 1, 2020.

16 Kaplan, *Divided by Faith*, 241–2.

17 Kaplan, *Divided by Faith*, 241–2. There were no legal consequences for being a "sympathizer," although there were social consequences such as exclusion from Communion.

18 Kevin Chovanec, *Pan-Protestant Heroism in Early Modern Europe* (Cham, Switzerland: Palgrave Macmillan, 2020), 17.

19 Israel, *The Dutch Republic*, 366.

20 Geert Aeilco Wumkes, *De Gereformeerde Kerk in de Ommelanden tusschen Eems en Lauwers (1595–1796)* (Groningen: P. Noordhoff, 1904), 22.

21 Wumkes, *De Gereformeerde Kerk in de Ommelanden*, 22.

22 Joep van Gennip, *Controversen in context: Een comparatief onderzoek naar de Nederlandstalige controversepublicaties van de jezuïeten in de zeventiende-eeuwse Republiek* (Hilversum: Uitgeverij Verloren, 2014), 541.
23 Johan Adriaan Feith, *Wandelingen door het Oude Groningen: de straten en hare namen, uithangtekens van herbergen, muren en torens, poorten en wallen, bestaande en verdwenen oude gebouwen, en andere onderwerpen oorspronkelijk verschenen in de Groningsche Volksalmanakken van 1891 tot 1908* (Groningen: B.V. Foresta, 1974), 6–7.
24 Jan de Vries, *The Economy of Europe in an Age of Crisis, 1600–1750* (Cambridge: Cambridge University Press, 1976), 96.
25 W. J. Formsma, ed., *Historie van Groningen: Stad en Land* (Groningen: Wolters-Noordhoff, 1981), 361.
26 Formsma, *Historie van Groningen,* 361. A number of relics, including the alleged arm of John the Baptist, disappeared without a trace.
27 Feith, *Wandelingen door het Oude Groningen,* 28. The secularization of monastic property continued throughout the seventeenth century and was used to fund the construction of the University of Groningen in 1614, as well as the maintenance of guesthouses, hospitals, and the *Martinikerk*. Also, in 1664, the city purchased the Jesuit House, which they then converted into a prison, known as "Het Pontje," and then later into a hospital, and finally into a school.
28 Arie Theodorus van Deursen, *De hartslag van het leven: studies over de Republiek der Verenigde Nederlanden* (Amsterdam: Bert Bakker, 1996), 160.
29 Willem Frijhoff, "Religious Toleration in the United Provinces: from 'Case' to 'Model'," in R. Po-Chia Hsia and Henk van Nierop, eds., *Calvinism and Religious Toleration in the Dutch Golden Age* (Cambridge: Cambridge University Press, 2002), 31.
30 Willem Frijhoff, "Was the Dutch Republic a Calvinist Community? The State, the Confessions, and Culture in the Early Modern Netherlands," in A. Holenstein, T. Maissen, and M. Prak, eds., *The Republican Alternative: The Netherlands and Switzerland Compared* (Amsterdam: Amsterdam University Press, 2008), 110.
31 Kaplan, *Divided by Faith,* 176–7.
32 Frijhoff, "Was the Dutch Republic a Calvinist Community," 112.
33 Guido de Bruin, *Geheimhouding en Verraad,* 194–5.
34 Hidde Feenstra, *Spinnen in het web: Groningse regenten in relatie tot het omringende platteland tijdens de Republiek* (Assen: Uitgeverij Van Gorcum, 2007), 33.
35 Formsma, *Historie van Groningen,* 367.
36 Formsma, *Historie van Groningen,* 367.
37 Frijhoff, "Was the Dutch Republic a Calvinist Community," 106.
38 A. J. Smith, "De eerste Bisschoppelijke Invasie," in *Groningsche volksalmanak voor het jaar 1903* (Groningen: E.B. van der Kamp, 1902), 156.
39 Groninger Archieven, Toegang 2041, Inv. 2086, "Resolutie van burgemeesteren en raad van Groningen dat in de burger vaandels het geweer van de pausgezinden zal worden afgenomen en dat in huizen, kelders en kamers zal worden onderzocht naar geweer en andere zaken die tot nadeel van de stad zouden kunnen worden gebezigd," 9 October 1665.
40 Groninger Archieven, Toegang 2041, Inv. 2086, October 9, 1665.
41 Groninger Archievan, Toegang 2041, Inv. 2086, October 9, 1665.
42 Andrew Pettegree and Arthur der Weduwen, *The Bookshop of the World: Making and Trading Books in the Dutch Golden Age* (New Haven, CT: Yale University Press, 2019), 207.
43 Boterbloem, *The Dirty Secret of Early Modern Capitalism,* 84.
44 Frijhoff, "Religious Toleration in the United Provinces," 28.
45 Van Nierop, "Sewing the Bailiff in a Blanket," 109.
46 Wumkes, *De Gereformeerde Kerk in de Ommelanden,* 17.
47 Wumkes, *De Gereformeerde Kerk in de Ommelanden,* 17.
48 Kaplan, *Divided by Faith,* 69.

49 Dave Postles, "The Market Place as Space in Early Modern England," Social History 29, no. 1 (February 2004): 41, 55.
50 Van Deursen, *De hartslag van het leven*, 157; Formsma, *Historie van Groningen*, 393.
51 Formsma, *Historie van Groningen*, 393; Kornelis ter Laan, *Groninger Encyclopedie* (Groningen, 1954/55).
52 Formsma, *Historie van Groningen*, 393.
53 I.A. Nijhoff, *Bijdragen voor vaderlandsche geschiedenis en oudheidkunde* (Arnhem: I.A. Nijhoff en Zoon, 1859), 66–67.
54 Formsma, *Historie van Groningen*, 393.
55 Formsma, *Historie van Groningen*, 393.
56 Van Deursen, *De hartslag van het leven*, 157; Wiebe Bergsma, *Tussen Gideonsbende en publieke kerk: een studie over het gereformeerd protestantisme in Friesland, 1580–1650* (Hilversum: Uitgeverij Verloren, 1999), 351.
57 1 Tim. 5:22 King James Version; see also Kaplan, *Divided by Faith*, 69 and75–6.
58 Gregorius Mees, *Hagars Dienst onder de Vrye Sara* (Groningen, 1673), 25.
59 Joost Hengstmengel, *Divine Providence in Early Modern Economic Thought* (London: Routledge, 2019), 56–7 and 64–5.
60 Hengstmengel, *Divine Providence in Early Modern Economic Thought*, 56–7.
61 Willem Frijhoff, *Fulfilling God's Mission: The Two Worlds of Dominie Everardus Bogardus, 1607–1647*, translated by Myra Heerspink Scholz (Leiden: BRILL, 2007), 299.
62 Frijhoff, *Fulfilling God's Mission*, 299.
63 Frijhoff, *Fulfilling God's Mission*, 299.
64 Pieter Jan van Winter, *De Westindische Compagnie ter kamer Stad en Lande* "s-Gravenhage: Martinus Nijhoff, 1978), 155; see also Pepijn Brandon, *War, Capital, and the Dutch State (1588–1795)* (Leiden: BRILL, 2015), 107.
65 Jonathan I. Israel, *Dutch Primacy in World Trade, 1585–1740* (Oxford: Clarendon, 1989), 163–8, "Under the first and last 'governor-general' of Dutch Brazil, Count Johan Maurits of Nassau-Siegen, in the years 1637–1644, the fortunes of the WIC in Brazil reached their zenith," but by the mid-1640s, "directors and investors alike were filled with apprehension about the future."
66 The provinces of Utrecht, Groningen, Gelderland and Zeeland also initially refused to negotiate a cease-fire with Portugal, but after talks with Holland, these provinces reversed course and supported the peace treaty.
67 Cornelis van de Haar, *De Diplomatieke Betrekkingen Tussen de Republiek en Portugal, 1640–1661* (Groningen: J. B. Wolters, 1961), 173.
68 Feith, *Wandelingen door het Oude Groningen*, 28.
69 Formsma, *Historie van Groningen*, 372, Gomarus rejected the more liberal teachings of the Remonstrant forefather, Jacobus Arminius (1560–1609).
70 Frijhoff, "Was the Dutch Republic a Calvinist Community," 104.
71 Mees, *Hagars Dienst onder de Vrye Sara*, 154.
72 Van Winter, *De Westindische Compagnie*, 13–4.
73 Frijhoff, *Fulfilling God's Mission*, 287–90.
74 Boterbloem, *The Dirty Secret of Early Modern Capitalism*, 84, Many thanks to Professor Boterbloem for reminding me of how shrewd, clever, and resourceful early modern merchants were in their pursuits for profit.
75 Frijhoff, *Fulfilling God's Mission*, 287–90.
76 Joris van Eijnatten, "War, Piracy and Religion: Godfried Udemans' Spiritual Helm (1638)," *Grotiana* 26, no.1 (November 2007), 194.
77 Frijhoff, *Fulfilling God's Mission*, 287.
78 Van Winter, *De Westindische Compagnie*, 43–4.
79 Israel, *Dutch Primacy in World Trade,* 162–3.
80 Arie Theodorus Van Deursen, *Plain Lives in a Golden Age: Popular Culture, Religion, and Society in Seventeenth-Century Holland*, trans. Maarten Ultee (New York: Cambridge University Press, 1991).

81 George Frans Hooijer, "'Geen beter renten'": Een studie naar de functie van het begrip hemelrente in opschriften in de Republiek der Zeven Verenigde Nederlanden tussen 1600 en 1800" (Ph.D. dissertation, Vrije Universiteit Amsterdam, 2019), https://research.vu.nl/en/publications/geen-beter-renten-een-studie-naar-de-functie-van-het-begrip-hemel.
82 Anne E. C. McCants, *Civic Charity in a Golden Age: Orphan Care in Early Modern Amsterdam* (Chicago: University of Illinois Press, 1997), 189–90.
83 Formsma, *Historie van Groningen*, 236–7.
84 Formsma, *Historie van Groningen*, 310–1.
85 Formsma, *Historie van Groningen*, 237.
86 Formsma, *Historie van Groningen*, 237, Additional examples of this can be seen in a number of sixteenth-century sources, most notably on the *Geuzenpenning* (Sea Beggars' medallion) (1574), which reads "*liver Turcx dan Paus*" (rather Turks than the Pope), and in the pamphlet *Den Spaenschen ende Arragoenschen spiegel* (The Spanish and Aragonese Mirror) (1599), both found in the Rijksmuseum.
87 Kees Boterbloem, *The Fiction and Reality of Jan Struys, A Seventeenth-Century Dutch Globetrotter* (New York: Palgrave Macmillan, 2008), 134–5.
88 J. A. Feith, *Groningsche Volksalmanak voor het jaar 1905* (Groningen: Erven B. van der Kamp, 1904), 94–5.
89 Feith, *Groningsche Volksalmanak*, 94–5.
90 Bernard Alting, *De Pilaren ende Peerlen van Groningen: Tractaet, betoonende waer op de Welvaert van in die Stadt is staende, ende waer door zy meest is geciert*, Vol. 1 (Groningen: Johannes van Velsen, 1710).
91 David Kunzle, *From Criminal to Courtier: The Soldier in Netherlandish Art, 1550–1672* (Leiden: BRILL, 2002), 380–3, "The kingdom of heaven is likened to the pearl …" and "Jesus was the pearl brought forth by the Virgin."
92 Alting, *De Pilaren ende Peerlen*, 14.
93 Alting, *De Pilaren ende Peerlen*, 16.
94 Alting, *De Pilaren ende Peerlen*, 20–1.
95 Alting, *De Pilaren ende Peerlen*, 23–4.
96 Alting, *De Pilaren ende Peerlen*, 30.
97 Jean Bethke Elshtain, *Sovereignty: God, State, and Self* (New York: Basic, 2008), 87.
98 Rom. 13:1–2 King James Version.
99 Groningen Archieven, Toegang 835, Inv. 293, Nr. 1, "Bernhard Alting, "Oud en nieuw Groningen," 1648; See also, Van den Broek, Groningen, een stad apart, 158.
100 P. Brood, A.H. Huussen Jr., and J. van der Kooi, eds., *Nieuwe Groninger Encyclopedie* (Groningen: REGIO-Projekt Uitgevers, 1999), 42.
101 Maarten Prak, *Citizens without Nations: Urban Citizenship in Europe and the World c. 1000–1789* (Cambridge, UK: Cambridge University Press, 2018), 72–3.
102 Formsma, *Historie van Groningen*, 251.
103 Groninger Archives, Hendrikus Oktavius Feith, Register van het Archief van Groningen (Groningen: A.L. Scholtens, 1856), 127; see also Lieuwe van Aitzema, Historie of Verhael Saken van staet en oorlogh … Vierde deel ('s Gravenhaghe: Johan Veely, 1669), 131–2; and Formsma, *Historie van Groningen*, 251.
104 Jan de Groot, G. Warnars, S. Luchtmans, J. Luchtmans, A. Blusse, P. Blusse, and V. van der Plaats, *Tegenwoordige staat der Vereenigde Nederlanden; een en twintigste deel; Vervattende het vervolg der Beschryving van Stad en Lande* (Netherlands: Shouten, 1794), 160; Formsma, *Historie van Groningen*, 255.
105 Groninger Archieven, "Catalogue of pamphlets," nr. 185–203, De Bruijn bij nr. 671 (August 29, 1663); see also P.J. Blok and P.C. Molhuysen *Nieuw Nederlandsch biografisch woordenboek, Deel 5* (Leiden: A.W. Sijthoff, 1921), 707; N. Tonckens "Het proces-Schulenborgh (1662) in het licht van de stadhouderlijke politiek in Stad en Lande," in *Groningse Volksalmanak* (Groningen, 1963), 65–98; Groninger Archieven, Toegang 2041, Inv. 1200, "Plakkaat van burgemeesteren en raad van Groningen woorbij het boekje getiteld

"Prodromus Schulenburgicae defensionis" wordt verklaard te zijn een "calumnieus, injurieus en seditieus" geschrift, hetwelk door de scherprechter in het openbaar zal worden verbrand," August 29, 1663.

106 Groninger Archieven and Hendrik Octavius Feith Jr., *Regeringsboek der provincie Groningen* (Groningen: Oomkens, 1850), 21–2.

107 Groninger Archieven, Toegang 740, Inv. 148, Publicatie van borgemeesteren ende raedt betreffende de pointen dienen tot redress van de voorgevallene desordres inde regeringe ende securiteyt voor 't toecomende tegens alle sedition ende oproer. Gedrukt, March 23, 1663.

108 Groninger Archieven, Toegang 740, Inv. 148.

109 Groninger Archieven, Toegang 740, Inv. 148.

110 Alberto Feenstra, "Hiding in a Twilight Zone: Credible Commitment in the Dutch Republic and Groningen's 1680s Default," *Historie & Mesure* XXX, no. 2: 79–116.

111 Simon Schama, *The Embarrassment of Riches: An Interpretation of Dutch Culture in the Golden Age* (London: Vintage Books, 1997), 75–7.

112 Brandon, *War, Capital, and the Dutch State*, 75.

Bibliography

Primary Sources, Manuscripts

"Catalogue of Pamphlets." nr. 185–203. De Bruijn bij nr. 671. 29 August 1663.

Feith, Hendrikus Oktavius. *Register van het Archief van Groningen*. Groningen: A. L. Scholtens, 1856.

Feith, J. A. "Introduction." Inventory of the Judicial Archives. Groninger Archieven (Groningen Archives)

Toegang 835, Inv. 293, Nr. 1. Bernhard Alting, "Oud en nieuw Groningen." 1648.

Toegang 740, Inv. 148. "Publicatie van borgemeesteren ende raedt betreffende de pointen dienen tot redress van de voorgevallene desordres inde regeringe ende securiteyt voor 't toecomende tegens alle sedition ende oproer. Gedrukt." 23 March 1663.

Toegang 2041, Inv. 1200. "Plakkaat van burgemeesteren en raad van Groningen woorbij het boekje getiteld 'Prodromus Schulenburgicae defensionis' wordt verklaard te zijn een 'calumnieus, injurieus en seditieus' geschrift, hetwelk door de scherprechter in het openbaar zal worden verbrand." 29 August 1663.

Toegang 2041, Inv. 2086. "Resolutie van burgemeesteren en raad van Groningen dat in de burger vaandels het geweer van de pausgezinden zal worden afgenomen en dat in huizen, kelders en kamers zal worden onderzocht naar geweer en andere zaken die tot nadeel van de stad zouden kunnen worden gebezigd." 9 October 1665.

Primary Sources, Print

Alting, Bernhard. *De Pilaren Ende Peerlen van Groningen: Tractaet, betoonende waer op de Welvaert van in die Stadt is staende, ende waer door zy meest is geciert*. Groningen: Samuel Pieman, 1710.

Bor, Pieter Christiaensz. *Oorsprongk, begin, en vervolgh der Nederlandsche oorlogen*, 4 vols. Amsterdam: de wed. van Joannes van Someren, Abraham Wolfgangh, Hendrick en Dirck Boom, 1679–1684.

Mees, Gregorius. *Hagars Dienst onder de Vrye Sara*. Groningen: Dominicus Lens, 1673.

Reductie van de stad Groningen, 23 July 1594, https://dutchrevolt.leiden.edu/dutch/bronnen/Pages/1594%2007%2023%20ned.aspx, accessed 1 June 2020.

Temple, Sir William. *Observations upon the United Provinces of the Netherlands*. London: A. Maxwell, 1673.

Van Aitzema, Lieuwe. *Historie of Verhael van Saken van staet en oorlogh, in ende omtrent de Vereenigde Nederlanden: Beginnende met het jaer 1657, ende eyndigende met het jaer 1663. Vierde deel.* 's-Gravenhaghe: Johan Veely, 1669.

Secondary Sources

Bergsma, Wiebe. *Tussen Gideonsbende en publieke kerk: Een studie over het gereformeerd protestantisme in Friesland, 1580–1650*. Hilversum: Uitgeverij Verloren, 1999.

Boterbloem, Kees. *The Fiction and Reality of Jan Struys: A Seventeenth-Century Dutch Globetrotter*. New York: Palgrave Macmillan, 2008.

Boterbloem, Kees. *The Dirty Secret of Early Modern Capitalism: The Global Reach of the Dutch Arms Trade, Warfare and Mercenaries in the Seventeenth Century*. New York: Routledge, 2019.

Brandon, Pepijn. *War, Capital, and the Dutch State (1588–1795)*. Leiden: Brill, 2015.

Buursma, Albert. *"Dese bekommerlijke tijden": Armenzorg, armen en armoede in de stad Groningen 1594–1795*. Assen: Koninklijke Van Gorcum, 2009.

Chovanec, Kevin. *Pan-Protestant Heroism in Early Modern Europe*. Cham: Palgrave Macmillan, 2020.

De Bruin, Guido. *Geheimhouding en Verraad: De geheimhouding van staatszaken ten tijde van de Republiek (1600–1750)*. 's-Gravenhage: SDU Uitgeverij, 1991.

De Groot, Jan, G. Warnars, S. Luchtmans, J. Luchtmans, A. Blusse, P. Blusse, and V. van der Plaats. *Tegenwoordige staat der Vereenigde Nederlanden; een en twintigste deel; Vervattende het vervolg der Beschryving van Stad en Lande*. Netherlands: Shouten, 1794.

Dekker, Rudolf M. *Holland in beroering: Oproeren in de 17de en 18de eeuw*. Baarn: Ambo, 1982.

Dekker, Rudolf M. "Women in Revolt: Popular Protest and Its Social Basis in Holland in the Seventeenth and Eighteenth Centuries." *Theory and Society*, 16.3 (1987): 337–62.

De Vries, Jan. *The Economy of Europe in an Age of Crisis, 1600–1750*. Cambridge: Cambridge University Press, 1976.

Elshtain, Jean Bethke. *Sovereignty: God, State, and Self*. New York: Basic, 2008.

Feenstra, Albert. "Hiding in a Twilight Zone: Credible Commitment in the Dutch Republic and Groningen's 1680s Default." *Historie & Mesure* XXX.2 (2015): 79–116.

Feenstra, Hidde. *Spinnen in het web: Groningse regenten in relatie tot het omringende platteland tijdens de Republiek*. Assen: Uitgeverij Van Gorcum, 2007.

Feith, Hendrik Octavius Jr. *Regeringsboek der provincie Groningen*. Groningen: Oomkens, 1850.

Feith, Johan Adriaan. *Groningsche Volksalmanak voor het jaar 1905*. Groningen: Erven B. van der Kamp, 1904.

Feith, Johan Adriaan. *Wandelingen door het Oude Groningen: De straten en hare namen, uithangteekens van herbergen, muren en torens, poorten en wallen, bestaande en verdwenen oude gebouwen, en andere onderwerpen oorspronkelijk verschenen in de Groningsche Volksalmanakken van 1891 tot 1908*. Groningen: B.V. Foresta, 1974.

Formsma, W.J., ed. *Historie van Groningen. Stad en Land*. Groningen: Wolters-Noordhoff, 1981.

Frijhoff, Willem. "Religious Toleration in the United Provinces: From 'Case' to 'Model.'" In *Calvinism and Religious Toleration in the Dutch Golden Age*, eds. R. Po-Chia Hsia and Henk van Nierop, 27–52. Cambridge: Cambridge University Press, 2002.

Frijhoff, Willem. *Fulfilling God's Mission: The Two Worlds of Dominie Everardus Bogardus, 1607–1647*. Trans. Myra Heerspink Scholz. Leiden: Brill, 2007.

Frijhoff, Willem. "Was the Dutch Republic a Calvinist Community? The State, the Confessions, and Culture in the Early Modern Netherlands." In *The Republican Alternative: The Netherlands and Switzerland Compared*, eds. A. Holenstein, T. Maissen, M. Prak, 99–122. Amsterdam: Amsterdam University Press, 2008.

Hengstmengel, Joost. *Divine Providence in Early Modern Economic Thought*. London: Routledge, 2019.

Hooijer, George Frans. "'Geen beter renten': Een studie naar de functie van het begrip hemelrente in opschriften in de Republiek der Zeven Verenigde Nederlanden tussen 1600 en 1800." Ph.D. dissertation, Vrije Universiteit Amsterdam, 2019. https://research.vu.nl/en/publications/geen-beter-renten-een-studie-naar-de-functie-van-het-begrip-hemel.

Hsia, R. Po-Chia, and Henk van Nierop, eds. *Calvinism and Religious Toleration in the Dutch Golden Age*. Cambridge: Cambridge University Press, 1993.

Israel, Jonathan I. *Dutch Primacy in World Trade, 1585–1740*. Oxford: Clarendon Press, 1989.

Israel, Jonathan I. *The Dutch Republic: Its Rise, Greatness, and Fall, 1477–1806*. Oxford: Oxford University Press, 1998.

Kaplan, Benjamin J. "'Dutch' Religious Tolerance: Celebration and Revision." In *Calvinism and Religious Toleration in the Dutch Golden Age*, eds. R. Po-Chia Hsia and Henk van Nierop, 8–26. Cambridge: Cambridge University Press, 2002.

Kaplan, Benjamin J. *Divided by Faith: Religious Conflict and the Practice of Toleration in Early Modern Europe*. Cambridge: Harvard University Press, 2007.

Kunzle, David. *From Criminal to Courtier: The Soldier in Netherlandish Art, 1550–1672*. Leiden: Brill, 2002.

McCants, Anne E. C. *Civic Charity in a Golden Age: Orphan Care in Early Modern Amsterdam*. Chicago: University of Illinois Press, 1997.

Molhuysen, P. C., and P. J. Blok, eds. *Nieuw Nederlandsch Biografisch Woordenboek Deel 5*. Leiden: A. W. Sijthoff, 1921.

Nijhoff, I. A. *Bijdragen voor vaderlandsche geschiedenis en oudheidkunde*. Arnhem: I. A. Nijhoff en Zoon, 1859.

Oldenburg, Scott. *Alien Albion: Literature and Immigration in Early Modern England*. Toronto: University of Toronto Press, 2014.

Pettegree, Andrew and Arthur der Weduwen. *The Bookshop of the World: Making and Trading Books in the Dutch Golden Age*. New Haven: Yale University Press, 2019.

Postles, Dave. "The Market Place as Space in Early Modern England." *Social History*, 29.1 (2004): 41–58.

Prak, Maarten. *Citizens without Nations: Urban Citizenship in Europe and the World c.1000–1789*. Cambridge: Cambridge University Press, 2018.

Schama, Simon. *The Embarrassment of Riches: An Interpretation of Dutch Culture in the Golden Age*. London: Vintage Books, 1997.

Smith, A. J. "De eerste Bisschoppelijke Invasie." In *Groningsche volksalmanak voor het jaar 1903*. 116–78. Groningen: E. B. van der Kamp, 1902.

Ter Laan, Kornelis. *Groninger Encyclopedie 2 Delen*. Groningen: 1954–1955.

Tonckens, N. "Het proces-Schulenborgh (1662) in het licht van de stadhouderlijke politiek in Stad en Lande." In *Groningse Volksalmanak*. Groningen: 1963.

Van de Haar, Cornelis. *De Diplomatieke Betrekkingen Tussen de Republiek en Portugal, 1640–1661*. Groningen: J. B. Wolters, 1961.

Van den Broek, Jan. *Groningen, een stad apart: Over het verleden van een eigenzinnige stad (1000–1600)*. Groningen: Uitgeverij Van Gorcum, 2007.

Van Deursen, Arie Theodorus. *Plain Lives in a Golden Age: Popular Culture, Religion, and Society in Seventeenth-Century Holland*. Trans. Maarten Ultee. New York: Cambridge University Press, 1991.

Van Deursen, Arie Theodorus. *De hartslag van het leven: Studies over de Republiek der Verenigde Nederlanden*. Amsterdam: Bert Bakker, 1996.

Van Eijnatten, J. "War, Piracy and Religion: Godfried Udemans' Spiritual Helm (1638)." *Grotiana*, 26.1 (2007): 192–214.

Van Gennip, Joep. *Controversen in context: Een comparatief onderzoek naar de Nederlandstalige controversepublicaties van de jezuïeten in de zeventiende-eeuwse Republiek*. Hilversum: Uitgeverij Verloren, 2014.

van Nierop, Henk. "Sewing the Bailiff in a Blanket: Catholics and the Law in Holland." In *Calvinism and Religious Toleration in the Dutch Golden Age*, eds. R. Po-Chia Hsia and Henk van Nierop, 102–11. Cambridge: Cambridge University Press, 2002.

Van Rooden, Peter. "Jews and Religious Toleration in the Dutch Republic." In *Calvinism and Religious Toleration in the Dutch Golden Age*, eds. R. Po-Chia Hsia and Henk van Nierop, 132–47. Cambridge: Cambridge University Press, 2002.

Van Winter, Pieter Jan. *De Westindische Compagnie ter kamer Stad en Lande*. 's-Gravenhage: Martinus Nijhoff, 1978.

Wumkes, Geert Aeilco. *De Gereformeerde Kerk in de ommelanden tusschen Eems en Lauwers (1595–1796)*. Groningen: P. Noordhoff, 1904.

2

THE MARKET THAT BINDS US

Religious exchange in medieval Syria-Palestine

Ian R. Simpson

The emergence of a new social and religious movement that took over the political administration of Syria-Palestine in the seventh century CE, only much later to be known as Islam, comprises a compelling example of religion in its wider articulation in society. According to tradition, the Prophet Muhammad was a member of the Quraysh tribe, a powerful merchant group in Mecca and the caravan trade of the Hijaz region located in the northwest of the Arabian Peninsula. Merchants and long-distance trade would come to play a central role in the market exchange economy of the Middle East. Early medieval trade and commerce built on pre-existing mercantile activity in the region and were revitalized by the formation of the early Islamic empires. Long-distance trade was helped by the new Muslim political administration of large territories known as the *dar al-Islam* (but not to the exclusion of other social groups) and interconnected vast regions, resulting in the development of specialized occupations and new technologies in medieval cities. As highly valued and economically important professions, trade and commerce were focused on marketplaces, evidenced by different types of markets in medieval Syria-Palestine,[1] including urban marketplaces, festival markets, and trading ports. The thriving market activity of early medieval times in the region was also enabled through a highly monetized economy, as shown by ample amounts of coinage found frequently in marketplace sites and other urban contexts, and by the number and activity of mints attested by numismatic evidence.[2] Principles of law and duties in social and economic life were laid out in diverse writings collectively known as *fiqh* (Islamic jurisprudence), which included conduct in commercial business and investment.[3] Various works discussed the ethics of trading practices, such as al-Ghazali's (1058–1111) practical handbooks in his work *Ihya' 'Ulum al-Din* (The Revival of the Religious Sciences),[4] and technical treatises set out the supervision of trade and commerce entrusted to the *muhtasib*—the market inspector.[5] Notably, this was a commercial culture open to cooperation and

DOI: 10.4324/9781003082842-3

partnerships between different social groups, including non-Muslim merchants of diverse affiliation who were able to practice commercial agency in the marketplace, albeit they were, in principle, subject to paying higher rates than Muslims.

Addressing the social co-constitution of markets and religion with a focus on medieval Syria-Palestine in the period 700–1500 CE, I argue that market exchange had a crosscutting effect on religious affiliation and that medieval marketplaces facilitated interreligious relations of difference *and* commonality in which people were enmeshed in urban centers of medieval Syria-Palestine and in networks of exchange over long distance. I will discuss these effects by considering three different aspects of the market in turn: the participation of religious communities and merchants in commerce and trade, marketplaces in cities, and the materiality of exchange goods. At the start of this period, urban marketplaces expanded, and congregational mosques were founded as a new type of building and sanctuary in cities. The mosque and expanding marketplaces were sometimes closely associated, and a changing commercial culture featuring mostly everyday, but also new, religious attributes, ostensibly Muslim (such as Quranic inscriptions), emerged gradually in the cityscape and in the exchanges between people of diverse backgrounds and cultural connections. The relationship between religion and the market in medieval Syria-Palestine can be illustrated by drawing on archaeological and historical studies of merchants and trade, urban marketplaces and associated material culture, raising questions concerning religious change and how social interaction in the market contributes to producing new religious forms and might play a role in the long-term, gradual pattern of a shift to predominantly Muslim populations in medieval times.

In studying social interaction in practice, any account that employs categories of Muslim and non-Muslim does not necessarily imply individuals or communities sharply defined along religious boundaries or distinctions alone, and it is with this in mind that I discuss the relations between religion and the market.[6] A frequently discussed domain of religious interaction is historical evidence for intellectual exchange, particularly interreligious polemics and Christians involved in theological and philosophical discussions in the ninth to twelfth centuries in Baghdad and translating written works into Arabic.[7] Intellectual exchange took place in the other direction as well, with early Islam and translations of the Bible into Arabic having an influence on Christian and Jewish identities and traditions.[8] However, although interfaith exchange in intellectual dialogue is perhaps the most discussed form of interreligious exchange, it may not have been as significant in wider society as other fields of interaction between social and religious groups, such as in the social dimension of the market. Religion and the market, when examined cross-culturally and in their historical variation, can be seen as actively shaping the social dimensions of each other. For instance, the history of usury in medieval Europe shows that the Church influenced the economy, but attitudes of the Church also responded in relation to economic changes.[9] The market can therefore be considered as a site of social interaction and negotiation, and as an interface with religion. Yet in treatments of predominantly Muslim societies, there has been a tendency to assume that Islam is an overarching force that solely determined the structure and politics of medieval and Islamic societies.[10] This normative view of Islam as highly-deterministic oversimplifies the ways in which religion is related to and can be shaped by other spheres of social life. Tracing the relations between religion and the social constitution of historical markets addresses this shortcoming and is part of wider, ongoing engagement with the general problem of understanding religion and economy in tandem raised by Max Weber.[11]

Markets and commerce in the medieval Middle East

Studies of market exchange in early medieval *Bilad al-Sham* (the Arabic historical term for the region of Greater Syria, referred to here as Syria-Palestine) cover road networks and transport,[12] production in the urban economy,[13] markets associated with Hajj routes,[14] the nature of market exchange,[15] coinage,[16] ceramic products traded in these networks,[17] and trade between Byzantium and the Islamic state.[18] Alongside this evidence of production, goods, trade routes, and marketplace activities we have legal texts on commerce and financial investment dating from the early Islamic period, which form part of the wider body of Islamic jurisprudence,[19] as well as limited amounts of documentary forms (mainly from Egypt) attesting to how business was organized, such as contracts, letters of agreement, and accounts lists,[20] while a broader array of sources is available from the eleventh century onwards that can be studied.[21]

Trade in the late antique and early medieval East Mediterranean has been discussed mainly in terms of economic activity and growth,[22] and while this research offers a rich picture of the provenance, distribution and types of goods, market sites, trade routes, infrastructure, prices and market behavior, and scales of exchange in the transition to medieval times, these accounts tend not to explore how trade may play a role in enabling, effectuating, or constraining religion in market practices and marketplaces. Yet the archaeological and historical data do indicate a significant relationship between trade and social agency, such as a rise in the social mobility of commercial manufacturers and merchants in urban settings in the sixth to tenth centuries, or the reshaping of the local, agrarian economic basis as more people became merchants and benefitted from interconnected trade networks and the growth in commerce.[23] I suggest that such findings result from trade and exchange as an observable set of practices that drive or enable social interaction and change among Muslims, Jews, Christians, and others.

Individual cities in medieval Syria-Palestine with well-preserved archaeological remains, complemented by historical sources, are fruitful settings in which to investigate the interaction between different religious communities because they hosted existing cultural-religious traditions and Islamic social formations set against an industrializing and commercializing market exchange economy. In the early medieval cities of Syria-Palestine and the wider region, urban centers, which already included markets, churches, synagogues, and temples, began incorporating mosques and extending or modifying marketplaces. At the same time, new religious features and text emerged in a changing commercial culture with early Muslim attributes. These sources can broaden our historical understanding of religion's varying role in commercialization and its market interactions, and allow us to explore the significance of matters such as individuals participating in trade, the social and commercial location of mosques, and the expression and ambiguity of religious identity in material culture.

The formation of Islam, as a new social and religious movement in the seventh century, implies the emergence of new religious identities and practices. In the early medieval Middle East, as Islamic culture and society developed in diverse ways against a backdrop of Muslim political rule, I argue that business practices, social intermingling in marketplaces and the production, exchange, and consumerism of goods played a role in constituting and maintaining social relations of difference *and* similarity that bound urban society together, and this is essential to understanding the interaction of religious groups and their relations of difference and similarity.

Under the initial expansion of Islam, the shift to Islamic state administration is evidenced in distinctive and widespread forms and changes representing the new Muslim authorities and leaders, such as Islamic coinage, weights and measures, and changes in administrative organization of territories. Ruling authorities can wield their power in ways that cultivate a given religious practice or impose religious ideology, including in economic life. The productive tensions between state authority and other agents vying for economic influence,[24] and the way markets enable ideological distribution,[25] constitute forms of power such as restrictions, licensing, taxation, and regulations on ownership which are central to statecraft. Following Foucault's thinking,[26] expressions of religiosity in commercial culture and everyday products can enable ways of articulating religion in technological authorship and disciplinary practices. However, religion in wider society is not shaped solely by the rulers. While there was a largely Muslim political administration and a body of Islamic principles, and while the medieval centuries saw a large-scale shift to a predominantly Muslim population, marketplaces and their associated domains of craft production, exchange, and consumerism can be considered as everyday sites where individuals of different religious (and other types of) affiliation could negotiate their commonalities and differences. In this sense, the view here shares some of the analytical lens of Block,[27] whose study of the large-scale shift from religion to race in the seventeenth century Caribbean also explores religion through everyday social relationships and interactions. In the much earlier periods encompassing the expansion of Islam, the notable shift was, by contrast, the commercializing and industrializing trend in early medieval cities of the Middle East. Although there are considerable differences between the early medieval Middle East and early modern period of the Americas and Europe, comparative studies of marketplaces across medieval times and geographies can enrich our understanding of religion in society by tracing the social articulation of religion in everyday life afforded by the market and marketplaces. Religious identity can be gauged historically by observing cultural contradictions and discontinuities at the level of practice, some of which may reflect the authority and ideology of the Church, Muslim political administration or legal doctrine, but which also reflect the actual practicalities of social interaction and social arrangements of doing commercial business.

The continued spread of Islam as a cultural, social, political, and religious movement in the early medieval periods can be attributed to a range of driving factors. Large numbers of converts to Islam is not one of the reasons in the first centuries of Islam, and the early conversion that did take place has mistakenly been seen by some as involuntary and the result of Islamic "military conquest."[28] Most major cities and towns in the regions surrounding Damascus and Jerusalem conceded peacefully to Muslim armies at the time of the Islamic expansion into Syria-Palestine (635–640 CE). Conversion to Islam was mostly far from involuntary or forced as a result of these initial military and political takeovers, and conversion was limited at first in Syria-Palestine and Egypt, with personal and religious rights of non-Muslims guaranteed by treaty in many cities in Syria-Palestine.[29] Explaining the growing appeal of a Muslim orientation through the medieval periods requires addressing processes other than discrete and swift acts of conversion, for under the early Islamic expansion, entering into treaties with Muslim leaders ensured religious rights and community roles and institutions of the existing diverse populations, while protective *dhimmi* status was granted to non-Muslim religious groups living within the Islamic state, according to the *ahl al-dhimma* (people of the covenant). This meant that Jews and Christians continued to hold high-level positions in government across the early and medieval Islamic dynasties, and it gave people the protection and freedom to practice religion and commerce and to own property, while also obligating non-Muslims to pay a poll tax known as the *jizya* to the Islamic state.

Hence, addressing the relationship between religion and the market as a domain of interreligious interaction can contribute to understanding these interreligious contours of life and the pattern of gradual increase in affiliation with Islam during the medieval periods. Religious conversion is socially and historically multifaceted,[30] and explanation is in general underdeveloped regarding the social role of market in broadening the appeal of religious groups and extending their power relations. It is by taking the view that marketplaces are sites of social negotiation and interreligious interaction that I reflect broadly on some lines of evidence of markets and commerce in the Middle East in the eighth to fifteenth centuries. Focusing on spatially situated and contextualized examples of social interaction, occupations, and exchange goods can illuminate the intersection of religion and market, and the ways in which expressions of faith are embodied or enabled in the built environment, such as mosques within marketplaces, and in the practices of craft specialists, merchants, and market supervisors. These lines of evidence about markets and exchange form an important domain of underlying historical circumstances that I argue enabled not only everyday expressions of spiritual and religious lives in marketplaces, but also facilitated the structural interreligious relations of commonality and difference in which people were enmeshed in urban centers of medieval Syria-Palestine.

Participation in the market

People of different religious affiliation mixed closely and interacted in the everyday course of life in the medieval Middle East. For instance, the Cairo Geniza—a documentary trove preserved in a synagogue which relates to medieval commerce, everyday life, and interreligious relations in the region—shows that Jews, Christians, and Muslims in Fustat (the capital of Egypt in the 7–12th centuries) often lived next door to each other, rented housing from each other, owned property in partnership with each other, and were all active in the multitude of different markets in the city.[31] This pattern is found more widely too, with urban populations of the Syria-Palestine region in the early and medieval Islamic states consisting of Muslims and non-Muslims living side-by-side or interacting within towns, while cities with separate quarters or neighborhoods for different religious identities were less common. Historical sources do attest to the stationing of Arab troops in garrison towns, known as *amsar* (singular *misr*), built under Muslim caliphs in the seventh century, which appear to be more significant in Iraq, although archaeology has also uncovered examples of early Islamic garrisons in the East Mediterranean in the form of permanent settlements that had been developed from what were probably military encampments, such as at Hadir Qinnasrin and Aylah, as well as revealing other settlement types that were newly established in the early Islamic period, such as the town of Anjar in Lebanon and rural castle-estates.[32] At any rate, it is the urban pattern of assorted communities in interaction that seems to strengthen after the initial change to Muslim rule as cities developed and served as focal points for surrounding rural areas. However, the relations among religiously and linguistically diverse populations living in cities such as Baghdad and Cairo, and Jews, Christians, and Muslims living under the same governing state in this period, cannot be squarely understood in terms of modern notions of cosmopolitanism or multiculturalism. While protected status was granted to *dhimmis*, there were also attitudes and injunctions that implied the exclusion of others outside one's own faith group and created tangible, yet often flexible, boundaries and hierarchies in society, such as a degree of social inferiority among *dhimmis*.

Rather, the gradual shift to a Muslim majority in medieval Syria-Palestine and the wider region was likely related to many processes, including the growth of market exchange facilitating greater social intermingling and interreligious exchange locally and over distance, as well as widespread linguistic Arabization and other factors. There is a need to address how market-related aspects of life afforded social interaction between Muslim and non-Muslim merchants. This market interaction took place not only at the level of demand and consumption, but also in the bureaucratic and supply side of industry, commerce, and trade. While many studies are concerned with communities of one particular religion, they tend to overlook the processes of exchange between different religious groups, and there is a need to address this historical pattern and the prevalence of cities with multiple religious communities interacting with each other. An inquiry is needed that addresses how different social groups act and influence each other in ways that market exchange encourages, such as by reinterpreting or amending their existing principles or traditions to legitimate business practices. On this problem, relations between religious groups have often been reduced to opposing religious traditions and institutions, following a conception of religions as distinct and bounded systems of symbols.[33] Instead, I am interested in examining how the interaction between different religious groups in the market produces and reshapes social categories of identity.

Commercial partnerships between Jews, Christians, and Muslims were commonplace, as attested by examples of *commenda*—business agreements allowing one partner to supply the capital and another to carry out the trade.[34] In particular, the Cairo Geniza demonstrates the crucial role of Jewish merchants, and other non-Muslims, in long-distance trade, especially with South Asia. Commercial transactions involved mutual trust and cooperation between different religious affiliations, and if cooperation in business life cut across religious boundaries as the norm, one might interpret religious identity as playing no role in business relations, but it did, and it needs to be understood as a layer of complexity that played a role within commerce and market life. For instance, non-Muslims were subject to paying special customs duties for importing goods, and in one business letter that Goitein[35] highlighted, we learn of someone writing from Alexandria (in Egypt) to his brother, who was an India trader, to dispatch his goods with Muslim agents in order to avoid import duties for non-Muslims. In other words, the Cairo Geniza documents show that the way business agreements and partnerships were arranged in practice were crosscutting of religious orientation, even while the survival of this evidence in a medieval synagogue repository reflects a Jewish institutional practice.

Egypt, Syria-Palestine, Iraq, and the Arabian Peninsula traded eastwards and westwards, across the Indian Ocean and the Mediterranean respectively. While Jews, Christians, Muslims, Armenians, Persians, and others were all involved in trade, the activity or inclusion of different groups in economic life varied depending on historical context and place (although the variation we see is also a result of the nature and availability of historical sources).[36] For instance, by the thirteenth century the Indian Ocean trade, especially the lucrative market for spices, came into the hands of mainly Muslim-Karimi traders and consignments financed by Muslim capital, to the loss of Jewish merchants working in the sector.[37] The Karami were centered on Egypt, formed of tightly knit, intermarried groups living under Mamluk rule (1250–1517), a period that was marked by a shift from previous cooperation to increasing anti-Christian polemics due to external factors. Types of trust and cooperation between merchants[38] were a factor and could play a role when it came to merchants' identities and restrictive dominance over commerce and trade. Yet there was to be expected great variation between places and over time in the access and competition of non-Muslims as well as diverse Muslim sects, and in negotiating how values and principles were actually applied in commerce and trade.

Religious identity was also enmeshed in the social contours and control of markets in the medieval Mediterranean. By the twelfth century onwards the Western Mediterranean had been able to substitute imports from Syria-Palestine and Egypt with production from its own workshops, for example in dyes and silks, and in some cases exported goods eastwards that were manufactured partly using supplies from Syria-Palestine and Egypt. The historian Ashtor[39] saw this development through a lens of decline of the medieval Middle East, but these relationships have more recently been recognized in terms of the interdependence of markets, despite territorial confrontation across the Mediterranean.[40] Merchants from Alexandria, Cairo, Damascus, Genoa, and Venice wanted to maintain their foothold for trading with each other rather than lose it due to political-territorial differences, and market exchange acted as a driver of ongoing interreligious interaction.

The mutual interaction between eastern and western networks of merchants was a concern of Latin Christian authorities, who attempted to impose embargoes to prohibit trade with Syria-Palestine. At the same time, merchants depended on the connective nature of the market and actively resisted such restrictions. The history of slavery trade in the Mediterranean provides an example of this overwhelming binding effect of market exchange between diverse groups of merchants. In principle, Christians, Jews, and Muslims were not permitted to enslave individuals of the same faith, respectively, but, in practice, ethnicity, race, and language were also taken as categories of difference, meaning that, for instance, Italian Christians enslaved Orthodox Christians and Muslim Arabs enslaved Circassians or Muslim Turks.[41] This underlying religious difference was all the more significant due to the competitive and confrontational relations that arose from the twelfth and thirteenth century onwards between the Latin Christian crusader powers and the Mamluk state in Egypt and Syria-Palestine. Enslaved individuals were expected to change affiliation to that of their master, hence enslaved people from the Black Sea region, whom Mamluk merchants traded by land and sea, were crucial to maintaining the Muslim Mamluk military. Italian merchants were also heavily involved in the Black Sea slavery trade, with Genoa and Venice effectively gaining control over it during the reign of the Mamluks. Against this background of competing states, Barker[42] describes how Christian crusade strategists proposed banning trade in enslaved people in their embargo against the Mamluks, and yet in reality Genoa and Venice continued to supply slaves to the Mamluks because they depended on Mamluk control over the spice market and India trade.

Marketplace sites and urban mosques

In the first centuries of Islam, urban marketplaces were expanded, indicating a high level of economic activity that is also reflected in the development of financial systems and commercial products.[43] Urban marketplaces appear to be characteristic of medieval Islamic cities. The physical marketplace, known as the *suq* in Arabic, could also be found at sites associated with specific festivals and rural fairs, trading ports, and slavery. Studies of commerce and trade in Late Antiquity show that monetized markets and specialized production were already pivotal to the urban economy, and archaeological studies have found that shortly before and after the arrival of Muslim governance, trade between towns in Syria-Palestine was facilitated by a renewal of urban facilities and urban marketplaces were further developed.[44] At Baysan (in Palestine/Israel) a building inscription attributes the construction of a *suq* to the patronage of the Umayyad caliph Walid II, while at Tadmur (Roman Palmyra in Syria) there are remains of extensive rows of shops dating from the early Islamic period that were built over former streets—to name two examples excavated in cities that are unpopulated ruins today. Some of the old *suq* areas in populations centers today, such as Khan el-Khalili in Cairo and others in Jerusalem, Damascus, and Aleppo, and the well-preserved Khan Mirjan, a fourteenth century medieval market hall in Baghdad—although renewed and rebuilt over centuries—are examples of significant urban marketplaces that were first developed in medieval times.

Central urban marketplaces were often associated with congregational mosques, a pattern that seems typical of medieval Islamic cities, if not early Islamic cities, too. Congregational mosques and town or district mints that issued coinage were both features common to many urban centers under Muslim administration in medieval Syria-Palestine. Some argue that the pattern of mosques embedded within city markets demonstrates a more pronounced link between religion and commerce in medieval Islamic societies compared to the Byzantine East Mediterranean that preceded. Urban markets could be used to subsidize the mosque and building of other infrastructure,[45] at least as far as later medieval centuries are concerned, if not already in earlier periods, and urban markets were spatially organized partly according to types of product and occupation,[46] with more valuable goods sold closer to the center, where the principal mosque was emplaced, which is reason to associate certain goods and occupations with the mosque. However, it was only recently that a clearer picture of mosque building in the eighth century and onwards has been established due to renewed archaeological attention.

For example, in the central area of Jarash city (Classical Gerasa) in Northern Jordan, which was transformed in several phases of redevelopment from Roman times to the early medieval period, a substantial congregational mosque was constructed in the early eighth century—the first major mosque in this city—at a central intersection of streets.[47] Recent excavations and records of unpublished excavations conducted during the British Mandate in Jordan show that the early mosque at Jarash was embedded in a planned *suq*/marketplace made up of shop-lined streets and related marketplace infrastructure, built with substantial limestone masonry. These buildings dominated the central streets in the sixth to ninth or tenth centuries,[48] making the streets a more important place for social interaction, and marked a change from the former porticoed streets, open plazas, forums, and theaters, which had by then been converted for other purposes. This early medieval cityscape had been shaped by a long historical process that began in Late Antiquity.[49] At Jarash, the early congregational mosque was inserted in the city at the crossroads of the Cardo main street and the South Decumanus street—Roman thoroughfares that continued to serve as main paths of movement in the early medieval period, but now transformed from wide, porticoed affairs into bustling market streets lined with extended shops or entirely new shops. The market streets connected the mosque in a way that made it both central and relatively easy to reach from different districts of the city, and the mosque's emplacement at a central street intersection underlines its centrality in the city. When considering the early mosque of Jarash in terms of the building's prominence, its nodal position in the city, and its contextual relationship to surrounding spaces, it is clear that a distinction was created by streets becoming increasingly commercial and intersecting in the mosque-market area, and that this area was subject to the movement of a high number of people from different parts of the city, which increased the likelihood of interreligious social transaction taking place in the mosque-marketplace node.

In the case of Jarash, the mosque's emplacement contrasts with many sanctuaries built previously in the city—churches, a synagogue, and temples—both in terms of location and accessibility or boundedness. Many churches are nestled within districts toward the edge of the city, such as the Church of Saints Peter and Paul and the Church of Procopius, while other churches, for example, the monumental churches in the main ecclesiastical complex, are not located at crossroads. The monumental church buildings, and earlier temples too, also display far more circumscribed or hierarchical access than the early mosque. In the case of the mosque, a transitional space in the form of an open outer platform inserted between the mosque and the street conferred a degree of openness to the building within the mosque-shops conjunction, rather than a highly-bounded site of assembly that was socially exclusive, and the mosque also opened on three sides directly onto streets in the market area. These points suggest there was a degree of circulation and gathering of people through the mosque's internal courtyard space. So overall, the early Islamic market street intersection was predominantly experienced in terms of shops, the mosque, and interconnecting paths and spaces of movement and interaction, and it was therefore likely that the mosque-marketplace zone facilitated intermingling between people from different parts of the city.[50]

By building a mosque at the intersection of busy market streets lined with shops in the city center, a formal and close link between shops and the mosque as a sanctuary and transactional social space was established. Although the roles that early mosques played are not clear, they were likely social spaces of debate and learning, as well as sanctuaries. The spatial relationship between shops and mosques made the link between practicing prayer, prostration, and buying and consuming things. There was a ritualization of both practices in tandem. In addition, this was happening in a setting of social gathering, interaction, and transaction between non-Muslims and early followers of the Muslim movement. I suggest that this context created liminal possibilities between the social and material spaces of exchange in the shop streets and the mosque as a site of various types of gathering, rather than an exclusively bounded site of assembly. The early mosque-marketplace relationship linked together prayer, prostration, and negotiating over and consuming things, and suggests a potential ritualization of these practices in tandem in a setting of social gathering, interaction, and transaction between non-Muslims and early followers of the Muslim movement. The relationship would have facilitated a degree of intermingling and "passage-potential" social transactions with economic implications or outcomes.

The open courtyard of congregational mosques and the context of many central urban mosques can be understood as places in which existing Christian and Jewish communities came to interact with early Muslim followers. This was facilitated by the open courtyard spaces of mosques constructed next to bustling market streets with lots of social and material transactions taking place. The likelihood afforded by this situation of non-Muslims participating in "ritualized" practices and festivals associated with the mosque, and of Muslims participating in Christian, Jewish, or pagan culture—through talismans, oracles, and so on—during the early Islamic period should be taken seriously.[51] Meeting in mosque spaces might have resulted in ritualizing the social transactions between Christians, Jews, and early Muslims. This is a different view from the functionalist understanding of mosque courtyard design and size as reflecting the size of the local Muslim community alone. The functionalist approach to mosques, which focuses only on assumed, pre-existing needs of Muslims and assumes social boundedness, cannot account for the ways that early Islamic urban mosques may have been significant in the lives of non-Muslims, and cannot account for social fluidity and change over time relating to the marketplace context of exchange, intermingling, and interreligious interaction. With the idea that marketplaces can be conceived as culturally and socially transformative sites,[52] the view I take here avoids the idea of one-way Islamization of the town or definitively Muslim symbols and instead highlights the potentiality of fluidity and interaction in the religion-marketplace relationship among non-Muslims and early followers of the Muslim movement.

Early medieval mosques were located in commercially-oriented zones within cities where a significant amount of exchange occurred, and a notion of transactional building space and place is appropriate to understand this relationship between religion and marketplace. In the early medieval period, at least, especially from the eighth to ninth centuries, the first wave of urban mosque-marketplaces cannot be understood only as a new building for Muslims to pray, but as an interreligious relationship that shaped the commonality and difference of different identities in medieval Syria-Palestine. The mosque-marketplace site is mimetically and discursively different to the urban context of churches in the preceding Byzantine East Mediterranean that functioned as "neighborhood" churches, but by the Middle Islamic period, the relationship may have changed again in cities as mosques came to be built in individual neighborhoods, increasingly reflecting the much older patterns.

While it makes sense that early mosques in cities across the Middle East were planned as part of enacting a new political and religious ideology on a regional scale, and may be considered a symbolic expression of this, there is more to mosques when the contingent aspects of their emplacement and context within city marketplaces are taken into consideration. The above discussion of the mosque and the marketplace shows there is a gap in our understanding between, on the one hand, political-religious ideology and the notion of mosques as a symbol of a political-religious culture, and, on the other, the contexts of individual mosques. Reductive and functionalist views of medieval mosques as symbolic expressions of religious ideology have limitations because they cannot account adequately for the situated outcomes of individual mosques, or for the local aspects of their initial emplacement.

Religiosity in exchange goods

While merchants and marketplace infrastructure are significant aspects of the relationship between markets and religion to consider in early medieval Syria-Palestine, trade goods and consumer items are also important to consider because they constitute a material basis or vehicle for cultural and religious meaning, for instance when embellished with Muslim, Christian or Jewish visual motifs and writing. Exchange items in the marketplace were manufactured locally or in production centers and their circulation and consumption were facilitated by urban and regional markets. The most apparent way that expressly Muslim religious ideas circulated in material culture was through the entextualization of Islam in the form of calligraphy, epigraphy, and inscriptions. This began with the shift to Arabic as the language of state administration but also in other areas as writing became a major part of decoration and design, especially from the eighth century onwards: epigraphy in state coinage, which, after a period of transitional Byzantine-Islamic issues, became fully-Arabized linguistically; inscriptions in Arabic were often part of architectural and building programs under the patronage of Muslim rulers; the twinned production of Qurans and the development of Arabic calligraphy became a discipline in itself; and mobile objects were in some cases embellished with pious expressions, such as the opening phrase in Quranic verses, the *bismillah* (in the name of God, the Merciful, the Compassionate), although this is not an exclusively Muslim phrase.

The circulation of goods due to market exchange is important because it enables material things to acquire cultural, social and religious meaning and appeal in society. The market exchange and circulation of goods implies there are social actors who craft, trade, and consume the material items in a marketplace. While the cultural dimension of consumer goods is often studied through consumption and consumerism,[53] this focus tends to divorce demand from supply and production. Such an approach risks overlooking the interplay between manufacturers, merchants, and consumers of different religious identities, and hence, there is a greater need to trace the links between manufacturers, merchants, and consumers. In the medieval Middle East, the influence of Muslim, Christian, Jewish, and other cultural features varies across contexts of production, marketplace, and consumption, suggesting that we should consider how producers, traders, and consumers influence or negotiate with each other from their different positions in the market.

Ceramic, glass, and metal products, for instance, were important items in exchange relations in the marketplace in early medieval societies in Syria-Palestine.[54] As ritual or religious objects circulated with the help of a city's marketplace, which can be conceived as a culturally and socially transformative site,[55] such objects imbued the lives of different groups brought together by the marketplace with social and religious meaning outside strictly institutional contexts. For instance, there was a type of glass vessel intended for pilgrims to use as a ritual flask that was produced in Jerusalem in the seventh and eighth centuries "expressly for a Muslim market,"[56] which emerged alongside others attributed to production for Christian or Jewish clientele. As with lamps that were decorated with spiritual symbolic designs, the "pilgrim" flasks express an everyday religiosity that circulated beyond written doctrine and designs that vary in terms of the images they carry while sharing a common form and ritual use. Exchange relations fostered the integrating of knowledge and practices over time between religious traditions, such as between Christians and Muslims, which can be seen in the case of the trading of decorated ostrich eggs, which have symbolic meaning and material value passed on in both early Christian and Muslim usage.[57] Market exchange carried such objects beyond the city, too, facilitated by the *suq*, trade, and regional markets in early medieval societies. Archaeologists have for example found mass-produced inscribed lamps made in Jarash at other sites in Northern Jordan in varying distances from Jarash (Kafr Batna at 142 km, Qasr al-Hallabat at 46 km, and Rujm al-Kursi at 34 km), suggesting that their spiritual and symbolic content circulated and was known across a regional network of towns and settlements.

In some cases, this accretion of knowledge and practices resulted in forms that appear ambiguous from a perspective of Islam or Christianity as a bounded, normative tradition. In this regard, theoretical reflection on the productive outcomes of in-between, liminal situations,[58] and the ambiguity of meaning in material culture, which is multiply coded and multidimensional,[59] can be helpful to make sense of the transformation of the discourses of symbols during the early medieval period by viewing the materiality and circulation of goods facilitated by the market as a field of liminality and ambiguity around which recognition of new forms and social structure occurs. Among the inscribed lamps of the eighth century produced at Jarash in large quantities using mold-made manufacturing and large industrial kilns, there are several examples of such ambiguity. Interestingly, these examples employ textual content that is not attributable exclusively to Christian or Muslim tradition, but to both at the same time, and such forms are facilitated by market exchange kindling processes of religious accretion and pluralism in society.[60] In this sense the medieval marketplace, in general, can be conceived as a field of ambiguity, liminality, and accretion, out of which recognition of structure emerged that, on the one hand, may have broadened the appeal of Islam and extended its authority as a political or moral form, while on the other also facilitated non-Muslim groups in locally recasting and negotiating their identity in the cityscape beyond the spaces of mosque, church, or synagogue.

A later example of religious identity in material culture and the market can be seen in a series of inlaid metal objects manufactured in Syria and Egypt in the first half of the thirteenth century bearing figurative motifs and Arabic epigraphy that seem to consist of a mixture of Christian themes and Muslim influence.[61] Although the exact manufacturers and intended audience are not known, the craftwork has been described as constituting a multi-layered Christian-Islamic encounter in which Christian motifs "were carefully chosen to include only those episodes acceptable to Muslims, specifically from the infancy and life of Jesus, omitting episodes dealing with his death and divinity. The inclusion of Christian subjects within a wider repertoire of Islamic figural representations on these metalwork pieces elucidates an expanded overriding iconographic system of a shared visual culture, with indigenous Christians and Muslims as participants and inhabitants of the same visual universe."[62] These metalwork objects appear to reflect the way Christians had been shaped by Islamic culture and society, and they were produced for the market and an audience possibly of Muslims or Christians alike, whether they belonged to local Christian groups or to Crusaders. The market acted as a driver or facilitator of these interreligious products, and their circulation and consumption imply an audience for whom a combination of Christian and Muslim content made sense or that they could identify with. Manufacturers may have recognized that there was a market for such work, and in this way the market has the effect of drawing together different religions. It is through, at least in part, the above cultural exchanges in market products that identities were co-shaped across religious affiliation and beyond institutional constraints.

Conclusion

The contours of market relations are more complex than any singular model might assume, as seen in the evidence for the multiple ways that market exchange in the medieval Middle East brought different religious communities into interaction and negotiation. The question of religion's varying part in commercialization and trade in the medieval Middle East can be productively illuminated in terms of the ways different religious communities are able to participate in commercial business as merchants, are encouraged to interact in physical marketplaces, and have agency in crafting, trading, and consuming goods with a religious identity or material religiosity.

Rather than Jews, Christians, and Muslims interacting through the marketplace as strictly defined groups, a dimension of commonality between these social and religious categories was enabled by interaction in marketplaces and by the materiality of objects. Although the present argument tends toward emphasizing the fluidity between social and religious categories, I have as a starting point considered Muslims and non-Muslims with the result of overlooking other distinctions such as Muslim communities divided more by school of thought, family, tribe, and so on.

The commonality and shared dimension of market exchange that cross-cut religious categories were enabled by the market gathering together diverse individuals and groups and creating their interaction. In other words, the shared aspects and commonality of medieval markets were engendered through relations of religious difference, rather than in spite of them; having a religious affiliation, different sets of values and traditions being brought together and negotiated, and accommodating or shifting religious affiliation were part and parcel of the social life of marketplaces. Although market exchange and the livelihoods that relied on it could be subject to territorial confrontation and competition along religious-political lines, the history of commerce and trade in the medieval Middle East shows there was an interdependence of markets and merchants between regions and this had a dependency effect that eclipsed religious-political efforts to restrict trade and kept diverse groups in interaction. The medieval marketplace, as discussed in this chapter in terms of interconnected merchant networks, business agreements and partnerships, social intermingling in marketplaces, and market goods, forms an interreligious field of social interaction and enables room for negotiation, differentiation, and the crosscutting of identity within the common setting of market exchange.

Notes

1 André Binggeli, Foires et pèlerinages sur la route du Hajj: à propos de quelques sanctuaires chrétiens et musulmans dans le sud du Bilād al-Šām d'après le *Kitāb al-azmina* d'Ibn Māsawayh (9e s.) *ARAM* 19 (2007); Patricia Crone, *Meccan Trade and the Rise of Islam* (Princeton: Princeton University Press, 1987); Rebecca M. Foote, "Commerce, Industrial Expansion, and Orthogonal Planning: Mutually Compatible Terms in Settlements of Bilad Al-Sham During the Umayyad Period," *Meditarch* 13 (2000); Clive Foss, "Syria in Transition, A.D. 550–750: An Archaeological Approach," *Dumbarton Oaks Papers* 51 (1997); Alan Walmsley, "Production, Exchange and Regional Trade in the Islamic East Mediterranean: Old Structures, New Systems?," in *The Long Eighth Century: Production, Distribution and Demand*, ed. Inge Lyse Hansen and Chris Wickham (Leiden: Brill, 2000).

2 "Coinage and the Economy of Syria-Palestine in the Seventh and Eighth Centuries CE," in *Money, Power, and Politics in Early Islamic Syria: A Review of Current Debates*, ed. John F. Haldon (Farnham: Ashgate, 2010).

3 For a brief introduction to Islamic legal sources relating to commercial practice in the medieval Mediterranean, see R. Stephen Humphreys, *Islamic History: A Framework for Inquiry*, Rev. ed. (London: I.B. Tauris & Co, 1991).

4 S. M. Ghazanfar and A. Azim Islahi, "Economic Thought of an Arab Scholastic: Abu Hamid Al-Ghazali (A.H. 450–505/A.D. 1058–1111)," *History of Political Economy* 22, no. 2 (1990); Abraham L. Udovitch, *Partnership and Profit in Medieval Islam* (Princeton, NJ: Princeton University Press, 1970).

5 C. Cahen, M. R. M. Talbi, et al., R. Mantran, A. K. S. Lambton, and A. S. Bazmee Ansari, "Ḥisba," in *Encyclopaedia of Islam*, eds. P. Bearman, T. Bianquis, C. E. Bosworth CE, et al. (Leiden: Brill, 2012).

6 Recent discussions of historical evidence argue strongly against assumptions of communities differentiated along religious or legal terms in any narrow sense in early Islamic societies. See for instance Sidney Harrison Griffith, *The Church in the Shadow of the Mosque: Christians and Muslims in the World of Islam* (Princeton, NJ: Princeton University

Press, 2008); Robert G. Hoyland, ed. *Muslims and Others in Early Islamic Society* (Aldershot: Ashgate, 2004); Milka Levy-Rubin, *Non-Muslims in the Early Islamic Empire: From Surrender to Coexistence* (Cambridge: Cambridge University Press, 2011); Arietta Papaconstantinou, "Between *Umma* and *Dhimma*: The Christians of the Middle East under the Umayyads," *Annales islamologiques* 42 (2008).

7 For example Damien Janos, ed. *Ideas in Motion in Baghdad and Beyond: Philosophical and Theological Exchanges between Christians and Muslims in the Third/Ninth and Fourth/Tenth Centuries* (Leiden: Brill, 2015).

8 For example J. J. van Ginkel, H. L. Murre-van den Berg, and Theo Maarten van Lint, eds., *Redefining Christian Identity: Cultural Interaction in the Middle East since the Rise of Islam* (Leuven: Uitgeverij Peeters, 2005); David M. Freidenreich and Miriam B. Goldstein, *Beyond Religious Borders: Interaction and Intellectual Exchange in the Medieval Islamic World* (Philadelphia: University of Pennsylvania Press, 2012).

9 J. Gilchrist, *The Church and Economic Activity in the Middle Ages* (New York: St. Martin's, 1969); Giacomo Todeschini, *Il Prezzo Della Salvezza: Lessici Medievali Del Pensiero Economico* (Rome: La Nuova Italia Scientifica, 1994).

10 Neil Asher Silberman, "Thundering Hordes: The Image of the Persian and Muslim Conquests in Palestinian Archaeology," in *Studies in the Archaeology of Israel and Neighboring Lands in Memory of Douglas L. Esse*, ed. S. R. Wolff (Chicago: Oriental Institute of the University of Chicago, 2001); Aini Linjakumpu, *Political Islam in the Global World*, 1st ed. (Reading: Ithaca Press, 2008).

11 Weber, in *The Protestant Ethic and the Spirit of Capitalism with Other Writings on the Rise of the West* (Oxford: Oxford University Press, 2009 [1930]), examined the influence of religion in economic life under modern industrialization, proposing that the tradition of Puritan asceticism and rational thinking led to the emergence of capitalism in Europe. Weber contrasted this view with a characterization of the ethics of Eastern religions, most notably Islam, as part of a patrimonial and feudal society that resulted in an irrational economy. The Protestant ethic has, at least by some interpreters, been posited as a strong or causal theory about Calvinism precipitating modern capitalism (see discussion in Bryan S. Turner, *Weber and Islam: A Critical Study* [London: Routledge, 1998]).

12 Such as studies in Alyssa A. Bandow, "The Late Antique Economy: Infrastructures of Transport and Retail," in *Local Economies?: Production and Exchange of Inland Regions in Late Antiquities*, ed. Luke Lavan (Boston: Brill, 2015).

13 Fanny Bessard, "The Urban Economy in Southern Inland Greater Syria from the Seventh Century to the End of the Umayyads," *Late Antique Archaeology* 10, no. 1 (2013).

14 Binggeli, "Foire Et Pèlerinages Sur La Route Du Hajj: À Propos De Quelques Sanctuaires Chrétiens Et Musulmans Dans Le Sud Du Bilad Al-Šam D'après Le Kitab Al-Azmina D'ibn Masawayh (9e S.)."

15 Jean-Michel Carrié, "Were Late Roman and Byzantine Economies Market Economies? A Comparative Look at Historiography," in *Trade and Markets in Byzantium*, ed. Cécile Morrisson (Washington, DC: Dumbarton Oaks Research Library and Collection, 2012).

16 Walmsley, "Coinage and the Economy of Syria-Palestine in the Seventh and Eighth Centuries CE."

17 Such as studies listed in Stefano Costa, "Late Antique Economy: Ceramics and Trade," in *Local Economies?: Production and Exchange of Inland Regions in Late Antiquities*, ed. Luke Lavan (Boston: Brill, 2015).

18 Marlia Mundell Mango, *Byzantine Trade, 4th–12th Centuries: The Archaeology of Local, Regional and International Exchange: Papers of the Thirty-Eighth Spring Symposium of Byzantine Studies, St John's College, University of Oxford, March 2004*, Society for the Promotion of Byzantine Studies Publications 14 (Farnham, England: Ashgate, 2009).

19 Udovitch, *Partnership and Profit in Medieval Islam.*

20 Gladys Frantz-Murphy, "A New Interpretation of the Economic History of Medieval Egypt: The Role of the Textile Industry 254–567/868–1171," *Journal of the Economic and Social History of the Orient* 24, no. 3 (1981); Shelomo Dov Goitein and Mordechai Akiva Friedman, *India Traders of the Middle Ages: Documents from the Cairo Geniza: India Book, Part One*, Études sur le judaïsme médiéval (Leiden: Brill, 2008).

21 For example Jessica Goldberg, *Trade and Institutions in the Medieval Mediterranean: The Geniza Merchants and Their Business World*, (Cambridge: Cambridge University Press, 2012).

22 Michael Decker and Sean A. Kingsley, *Economy and Exchange in the East Mediterranean During Late Antiquity* (Oxford: Oxbow, 2001); Sean Kingsley, "Late Antique Trade: Research Methodologies and Field Practices," in *Theory and Practice in Late Antique Archaeology*, ed. Luke Lavan and William Bowden (Leiden: Brill, 2003); Mango, *Byzantine Trade, 4th–12th Centuries: The Archaeology of Local, Regional and International Exchange: Papers of the Thirty-Eighth Spring Symposium of Byzantine Studies, St John's College, University of Oxford, March 2004*; Cécile Morrisson, *Trade and Markets in Byzantium*, Dumbarton Oaks Byzantine Symposia and Colloquia (Washington, DC: Dumbarton Oaks Research Library and Collection, 2012).

23 Mark R. Cohen, *Maimonides and the Merchants: Jewish Law and Society in the Medieval Islamic World*, 1st edition. ed., (Philadelphia: University of Pennsylvania Press, 2017); Alan Walmsley, *Early Islamic Syria: An Archaeological Assessment* (London: Duckworth, 2007), 119.

24 Gracia Clark, *Traders Versus the State: Anthropological Approaches to Unofficial Economies*, Westview Special Studies in Applied Anthropology (Boulder: Westview Press, 1988).

25 Ellen Hertz, *The Trading Crowd: An Ethnography of the Shanghai Stock Market*, (Cambridge: Cambridge University Press, 1998).

26 Michel Foucault, *The Order of Things: An Archaeology of the Human Sciences* (London: Tavistock, 1966); *The Archaeology of Knowledge* (London: Tavistock, 1969).

27 Kristen Block, *Ordinary Lives in the Early Caribbean: Religion, Colonial Competition, and the Politics of Profit*, Early American Places (Athens: University of Georgia Press, 2012).

28 For example in Jean Ensminger, "Transaction Costs and Islam: Explaining Conversion in Africa," *Journal of Institutional and Theoretical Economics* 153, no. 1 (1997).

29 John F. Haldon, ed. *Money, Power and Politics in Early Islamic Syria: A Review of Current Debates* (Farnham: Ashgate, 2010).

30 Andrew Buckser and Stephen D. Glazier, eds., *The Anthropology of Religious Conversion* (Lanham: Rowman & Littlefield, 2003); Tijana Krstic, *Contested Conversions to Islam: Narratives of Religious Change in the Early Modern Ottoman Empire* (Stanford: Stanford University Press, 2011).

31 Shelomo Dov Goitein, *A Mediterranean Society: The Jewish Communities of the Arab World as Portrayed in the Documents of the Cairo Geniza, Vol. 2, The Community* (Berkeley: University of California Press, 1967), 290–92.

32 Walmsley, *Early Islamic.*

33 Clifford Geertz, "Religion as a Cultural System," in *Anthropological Approaches to the Study of Religion*, ed. Michael Banton (New York: F.A. Praeger, 1966).

34 Goitein, *A Mediterranean Society* 294–95.

35 Ibid., 295.

36 Maya Shatzmiller, C. E. Bosworth, and W. Heffening, "Tid̲jāra," in *Encyclopaedia of Islam*, ed. P. Bearman, et al. (Brill Online, 2008).

37 Janet L. Abu-Lughod, *Before European Hegemony: The World System A.D. 1250–1350* (Oxford, UK: Oxford University Press, 1989).

38 See for example Sebouh Aslanian, "Social Capital, 'Trust' and the Role of Networks in Julfan Trade: Informal and Semi-Formal Institutions at Work," *Journal of Global History* 1, no. 3 (2006).

39 Eliyahu Ashtor *The Medieval Near East: Social and Economic History* (London: Variorum Reprints, 1978).

40 David Abulafia, "The Impact of the Orient: Economic Interactions between East and West in the Medieval Mediterranean," in *Across the Mediterranean Frontiers: Trade, Politics and Religion, 650–1450: Selected Proceedings of the International Medieval Congress, University of Leeds, July 10–13, 1995, July 8–11, 1996*, ed. Dionisius A. Agius and Ian Richard Netton (Turnhout: Brepols, 1997); Ian R. Simpson, "Framings of Capitalism and the Archaeology of Sugar in the Islamic Mediterranean," *Historical Archaeology* 53, no. 3 (2019).

41 Hannah Barker, *That Most Precious Merchandise: The Mediterranean Trade in Black Sea Slaves, 1260–1500,* The Middle Ages Series (Philadelphia: University of Pennsylvania Press, 2019).
42 Ibid.
43 Rebecca M. Foote, "Umayyad Markets and Manufacturing: Evidence for a Commercialized and Industrializing Economy in Early Bilad Al-Sham" (Doctoral dissertation, Harvard University, 1999).
44 K. As'ad and F. M. Stepniowski, "The Umayyad Suq from Palmyra," *Damaszener Mitteilungen* 4 (1989); Elias Khamis, "Two Wall Mosaic Inscriptions from the Umayyad Market Place in Bet Shean/Baysān," *Bulletin of the School of Oriental and African Studies* 64, no. 2 (2001); Israel Roll and Etan Ayalon, "The Market Street at Apollonia-Arsuf," *Bulletin of the American Schools of Oriental Research* 267 (1987); Ian Simpson, "Market Buildings at Jarash: Commercial Transformation at the Tetrakionion in the 6th to 9th Centuries CE," *Orient-Archäologie* 24 (2008).
45 Randi Deguilhem, "The Waqf in the City," in *The City in the Islamic World*, ed. Salma Khadra Jayyusi, et al. (Leiden: Brill, 2008).
46 Ernst J. Grube and George Michell, *Architecture of the Islamic World: Its History and Social Meaning* (New York, NY: Thames and Hudson, 1984); Andre Raymond, "Islamic City, Arab City: Orientalist Myths and Recent Views," *British Journal of Middle Eastern Studies* 21, no. 1 (1994).
47 Alan Walmsley, "The Friday Mosque of Early Islamic Jarash in Jordan," *Journal of the David Collection* 1 (2003).
48 Simpson, "Market Buildings at Jarash."
49 Luke Lavan, *Local Economies?: Production and Exchange of Inland Regions in Late Antiquities* (Boston: Brill, 2015); Morrisson, *Trade and Markets in Byzantium.*
50 Ian R. Simpson, "Religious Redirection: Muslim-Christian Market Interaction in Early Islamic Syria-Palestine" (Doctoral dissertation, Stanford University, 2016).
51 Aziz Al-Azmeh, *The Emergence of Islam in Late Antiquity: Allah and His People* (Cambridge: Cambridge University Press, 2014), 95.
52 Kalman Applebaum, "The Anthropology of Markets," in *A Handbook of Economic Anthropology*, ed. James G. Carrier (Cheltenham: Edward Elgar, 2005); Virgil Henry Storr, "The Social Construction of the Market," *Society* 47, no. 3 (2010).
53 Michel de Certeau, *The Practice of Everyday Life* (Berkeley: University of California Press, 1984); Daniel Miller, *A Theory of Shopping* (Cambridge: Polity, 1998).
54 For example, see studies listed in Costa, "Late Antique Economy: Ceramics and Trade."
55 Applebaum, "The Anthropology of Markets." Storr, "The Social Construction of the Market."
56 Julian Raby, "In Vitro Veritas. Glass Pilgrim Vessels from 7thCentury Jerusalem," in *Bayt Al-Maqdis: 'Abd Al-Malik's Jerusalem*, ed. Julian Raby and Jeremy Johns (Oxford: Oxford University Press, 1992), 113.
57 Nile Green, "Ostrich Eggs and Peacock Feathers: Sacred Objects as Cultural Exchange between Christianity and Islam," *Al-Masaq: Islam and the Medieval Mediterranean* 18, no. 1 (2006).
58 Victor Turner, *The Ritual Process: Structure and Anti-Structure* (London: Cornell University Press, 1977 (1969)).
59 Robert W. Preucel and Ian Hodder, "Material Symbols," in *Contemporary Archaeology in Theory*, ed. Robert W. Preucel and Ian Hodder (Oxford: Blackwell, 1996).
60 Krisztina Kehl-Bodrogi, Barbara Kellner-Heinkele, and Anke Otter-Beaujean, eds., *Syncretistic Religious Communities in the Near East* (Leiden: E.J. Brill, 1997); Anita Maria Leopold, "Syncretism and the Interaction of Modes of Religiosity: A Formative Perspective on Gnostic-Christian Movements in Late Antiquity," in *Theorizing Religions Past: Archaeology, History, and Cognition*, ed. Harvey Whitehouse and Luther H. Martin (Walnut Creek: AltaMira Press, 2004); Janet McIntosh, *The Edge of Islam: Power, Personhood, and Ethnoreligious Boundaries on the Kenya Coast* (Durham: Duke University Press, 2009); Yetkin Yildirim, "The Medina Charter: A Historical Case of Conflict Resolution," *Islam & Christian-Muslim Relations* 20, no. 4 (2009).

61 Robert Hillenbrand, *Islamic Art and Architecture* (London: Thames and Hudson, 1999); Eva R. Hoffman, "Christian-Islamic Encounters on Thirteenth-Century Ayyubid Metalwork: Local Culture, Authenticity, and Memory," *Gesta* 43, no. 2 (2004).

62 Hoffman, "Christian-Islamic Encounters" 132.

Bibliography

Abulafia, David. "The Impact of the Orient: Economic Interactions between East and West in the Medieval Mediterranean." In *Across the Mediterranean Frontiers: Trade, Politics and Religion, 650–1450: Selected Proceedings of the International Medieval Congress, University of Leeds, 10–13 July 1995, 8–11 July 1996*, eds. Dionisius A. Agius and Ian Richard Netton, 1–40. Turnhout: Brepols, 1997.

Abu-Lughod, Janet L. *Before European Hegemony: The World System A.D. 1250–1350*. Oxford: Oxford University Press, 1989.

Al-Azmeh, Aziz. *The Emergence of Islam in Late Antiquity: Allah and His People*. Cambridge: Cambridge University Press, 2014.

Applebaum, Kalman. "The Anthropology of Markets." In *A Handbook of Economic Anthropology*, ed. James G. Carrier, 275–89. Cheltenham: Edward Elgar, 2005.

As'ad, K., and F. M. Stepniowski. "The Umayyad Suq from Palmyra." *Damaszener Mitteilungen*, 4 (1989): 205–23.

Ashtor, Eliyahu. *The Medieval Near East: Social and Economic History*. London: Variorum Reprints, 1978.

Aslanian, Sebouh. "Social Capital, 'Trust' and the Role of Networks in Julfan Trade: Informal and Semi-Formal Institutions at Work." *Journal of Global History*, 1.3 (2006): 383–402.

Bandow, Alyssa A. "The Late Antique Economy: Infrastructures of Transport and Retail." In *Local Economies?: Production and Exchange of Inland Regions in Late Antiquities*, ed. Luke Lavan, 83–9. Boston: Brill, 2015.

Barker, Hannah. *That Most Precious Merchandise: The Mediterranean Trade in Black Sea Slaves, 1260–1500*. The Middle Ages Series. Philadelphia: University of Pennsylvania Press, 2019.

Bessard, Fanny. "The Urban Economy in Southern Inland Greater Syria from the Seventh Century to the End of the Umayyads." *Late Antique Archaeology*, 10.1 (2013): 377–421.

Binggeli, André. "Foire Et Pèlerinages Sur La Route Du Hajj: À Propos De Quelques Sanctuaires Chrétiens Et Musulmans Dans Le Sud Du Bilad Al-Šam D'après Le Kitab Al-Azmina D'ibn Masawayh (9e S.)." *ARAM*, 19 (2007): 559–82.

Block, Kristen. *Ordinary Lives in the Early Caribbean: Religion, Colonial Competition, and the Politics of Profit*. Athens: University of Georgia Press, 2012.

Buckser, Andrew, and Stephen D. Glazier, eds. *The Anthropology of Religious Conversion*. Lanham: Rowman & Littlefield, 2003.

Cahen, C., Talbi, M. R. M., Mantran, R., Lambton, A. K. S., and Bazmee Ansari, A. S. "Ḥisba," in *Encyclopaedia of Islam, Second Edition*, edited by Bearman, P., Th. Bianquis, Th., Bosworth, C. E., van Donzel, E. and Heinrichs, W. P. Brill Reference Online, 2012. Accessed August 28, 2020. http://dx.doi.org/10.1163/1573-3912_islam_COM_0293

Carrié, Jean-Michel. "Were Late Roman and Byzantine Economies Market Economies? A Comparative Look at Historiography." In *Trade and Markets in Byzantium*, ed. Cécile Morrisson, 13–26. Washington, DC: Dumbarton Oaks Research Library and Collection, 2012.

Clark, Gracia. *Traders versus the State: Anthropological Approaches to Unofficial Economies*. Boulder: Westview Press, 1988.

Cohen, Mark R. *Maimonides and the Merchants: Jewish Law and Society in the Medieval Islamic World*. 1st ed. Philadelphia: University of Pennsylvania Press, 2017.

Costa, Stefano. "Late Antique Economy: Ceramics and Trade." In *Local Economies?: Production and Exchange of Inland Regions in Late Antiquities*, ed. Luke Lavan, 91–130. Boston: Brill, 2015.

Crone, Patricia. *Meccan Trade and the Rise of Islam*. Princeton: Princeton University Press, 1987.

de Certeau, Michel. *The Practice of Everyday Life*. Berkeley: University of California Press, 1984.

Decker, Michael, and Sean A. Kingsley. *Economy and Exchange in the East Mediterranean During Late Antiquity*. Oxford: Oxbow, 2001.

Deguilhem, Randi. "The Waqf in the City." In *The City in the Islamic World*, eds. Salma Khadra Jayyusi, Renata Holod, Attilio Petruccioli and André Raymond, 923–50. Leiden: Brill, 2008.

Ensminger, Jean. "Transaction Costs and Islam: Explaining Conversion in Africa." *Journal of Institutional and Theoretical Economics*, 153.1 (1997): 4–29.

Foote, Rebecca M. "Commerce, Industrial Expansion, and Orthogonal Planning: Mutually Compatible Terms in Settlements of Bilad Al-Sham During the Umayyad Period." *Meditarch*, 13 (2000): 25–38.

———. "Umayyad Markets and Manufacturing: Evidence for a Commercialized and Industrializing Economy in Early Bilad Al-Sham." Doctoral dissertation, Harvard University, 1999.

Foss, Clive. "Syria in Transition, A.D. 550–750: An Archaeological Approach." *Dumbarton Oaks Papers*, 51 (1997): 189–269.

Foucault, Michel. *The Archaeology of Knowledge*. London: Tavistock, 1969.

———. *The Order of Things: An Archaeology of the Human Sciences*. London: Tavistock, 1966.

Frantz-Murphy, Gladys. "A New Interpretation of the Economic History of Medieval Egypt: The Role of the Textile Industry 254–567/868–1171." *Journal of the Economic and Social History of the Orient*, 24.3 (1981): 274–97.

Freidenreich, David M., and Miriam B. Goldstein. *Beyond Religious Borders: Interaction and Intellectual Exchange in the Medieval Islamic World*. Philadelphia: University of Pennsylvania Press, 2012.

Geertz, Clifford. "Religion as a Cultural System." In *Anthropological Approaches to the Study of Religion*, ed. Michael Banton, 1–46. New York: F.A. Praeger, 1966.

Ghazanfar, S. Shaik M., and A. Azim Islahi. "Economic Thought of an Arab Scholastic: Abu Hamid Al-Ghazali (A.H. 450–505/A.D. 1058–1111)." *History of Political Economy*, 22.2 (1990): 381–403.

Gilchrist, J. *The Church and Economic Activity in the Middle Ages*. New York: St. Martin's Press, 1969.

van Ginkel, J. J., H. L. Murre-van den Berg, and Theo Maarten van Lint, eds. *Redefining Christian Identity: Cultural Interaction in the Middle East since the Rise of Islam*. Leuven: Uitgeverij Peeters, 2005.

Goitein, Shelomo Dov. *A Mediterranean Society: The Jewish Communities of the Arab World as Portrayed in the Documents of the Cairo Geniza, Vol. 2, the Community*. Berkeley: University of California Press, 1967.

Goitein, Shelomo Dov and Mordechai Akiva Friedman. *India Traders of the Middle Ages: Documents from the Cairo Geniza: India Book, Part One*. Études sur le judaïsme médiéval. Leiden: Brill, 2008.

Goldberg, Jessica. *Trade and Institutions in the Medieval Mediterranean: The Geniza Merchants and Their Business World*. Cambridge: Cambridge University Press, 2012.

Green, Nile. "Ostrich Eggs and Peacock Feathers: Sacred Objects as Cultural Exchange between Christianity and Islam." *Al-Masaq: Islam and the Medieval Mediterranean*, 18.1 (2006): 27–66.

Griffith, Sidney Harrison. *The Church in the Shadow of the Mosque: Christians and Muslims in the World of Islam*. Princeton: Princeton University Press, 2008.
Grube, Ernst J., and George Michell. *Architecture of the Islamic World: Its History and Social Meaning*. New York: Thames and Hudson, 1984.
Haldon, John F., ed. *Money, Power and Politics in Early Islamic Syria: A Review of Current Debates*. Farnham: Ashgate, 2010.
Hertz, Ellen. *The Trading Crowd: An Ethnography of the Shanghai Stock Market*. Cambridge: Cambridge University Press, 1998.
Hoyland, Robert G., ed. *Muslims and Others in Early Islamic Society*. Aldershot: Ashgate, 2004.
Humphreys, R. Stephen. *Islamic History: A Framework for Inquiry*. Rev. ed. London: I.B. Tauris & Co., 1991.
Janos, Damien, ed. *Ideas in Motion in Baghdad and Beyond: Philosophical and Theological Exchanges between Christians and Muslims in the Third/Ninth and Fourth/Tenth Centuries*. Leiden: Brill, 2015.
Kehl-Bodrogi, Krisztina, Barbara Kellner-Heinkele, and Anke Otter-Beaujean, eds. *Syncretistic Religious Communities in the Near East*. Leiden: E.J. Brill, 1997.
Khamis, Elias. "Two Wall Mosaic Inscriptions from the Umayyad Market Place in Bet Shean/ Baysān." *Bulletin of the School of Oriental and African Studies*, 64.2 (2001): 159–76.
Kingsley, Sean. "Late Antique Trade: Research Methodologies and Field Practices." In *Theory and Practice in Late Antique Archaeology*, eds. Luke Lavan and William Bowden. 113–38. Leiden: Brill, 2003.
Krstic, Tijana. *Contested Conversions to Islam: Narratives of Religious Change in the Early Modern Ottoman Empire*. Stanford: Stanford University Press, 2011.
Lavan, Luke. *Local Economies?: Production and Exchange of Inland Regions in Late Antiquities*. Boston: Brill, 2015.
Leopold, Anita Maria. "Syncretism and the Interaction of Modes of Religiosity: A Formative Perspective on Gnostic-Christian Movements in Late Antiquity." In *Theorizing Religions Past: Archaeology, History, and Cognition*, eds. Harvey Whitehouse and Luther H. Martin, 105–23. Walnut Creek: AltaMira Press, 2004.
Levy-Rubin, Milka. *Non-Muslims in the Early Islamic Empire: From Surrender to Coexistence*. Cambridge: Cambridge University Press, 2011.
Linjakumpu, Aini. *Political Islam in the Global World*. 1st ed. Reading: Ithaca Press, 2008.
Mango, Marlia Mundell. *Byzantine Trade, 4th–12th Centuries: The Archaeology of Local, Regional and International Exchange: Papers of the Thirty-Eighth Spring Symposium of Byzantine Studies, St John's College, University of Oxford, March 2004*. Society for the Promotion of Byzantine Studies Publications 14. Farnham: Ashgate, 2009.
McIntosh, Janet. *The Edge of Islam: Power, Personhood, and Ethnoreligious Boundaries on the Kenya Coast*. Durham: Duke University Press, 2009.
Miller, Daniel. *A Theory of Shopping*. Cambridge: Polity Press, 1998.
Morrisson, Cécile. *Trade and Markets in Byzantium*. Dumbarton Oaks Byzantine Symposia and Colloquia. Washington, DC: Dumbarton Oaks Research Library and Collection, 2012.
Papaconstantinou, Arietta. "Between *Umma* and *Dhimma*: The Christians of the Middle East under the Umayyads." [In Spanish]. *Annales Islamologiques*, 42 (2008): 127–56.
Preucel, Robert W., and Ian Hodder. "Material Symbols." In *Contemporary Archaeology in Theory*, eds. Robert W. Preucel and Ian Hodder, 299–314. Oxford: Blackwell, 1996.
Raby, Julian. "In Vitro Veritas. Glass Pilgrim Vessels from 7th-Century Jerusalem." In *Bayt Al-Maqdis: 'Abd Al-Malik's Jerusalem*, eds. Julian Raby and Jeremy Johns, 113–83. Oxford: Oxford University Press, 1992.

Raymond, Andre. "Islamic City, Arab City: Orientalist Myths and Recent Views." *British Journal of Middle Eastern Studies*, 21.1 (1994): 3–18.

Roll, Israel, and Etan Ayalon. "The Market Street at Apollonia-Arsuf." *Bulletin of the American Schools of Oriental Research*, 267 (1987): 61–7.

Shatzmiller, M., Bosworth, C. E., and W. Heffening, "Tidjāra," in *Encyclopaedia of Islam, Second Edition*, edited by P. Bearman, Th. Bianquis, C. E. Bosworth, E. van Donzel, and W. P. Heinrichs. Amsterdam: Brill Reference Online, 2012. Accessed August 28, 2020. www.http://dx.doi.org/10.1163/1573-3912_islam_COM_1218.

Silberman, Neil Asher. "Thundering Hordes: The Image of the Persian and Muslim Conquests in Palestinian Archaeology." In *Studies in the Archaeology of Israel and Neighboring Lands in Memory of Douglas L. Esse*, ed. S. R. Wolff, 611–23. Chicago: Oriental Institute of the University of Chicago, 2001.

Simpson, Ian. "Market Buildings at Jarash: Commercial Transformation at the Tetrakionion in the 6th to 9th Centuries C.E." *Orient-Archäologie*, 24 (2008): 115–24.

———. "Market Buildings at Jarash: Commercial Transformation at the Tetrakionion in the 6th to 9th Centuries C.E." In *Residences, Castles, Settlements. Transformation Processes from Late Antiquity to Early Islam in Bilad Al-Sham (Proceedings of a Colloquium on Late Antique and Early Islamic Archaeology in Bilâd Al-Shâm. Deutsches Archäologisches Institut, Orient-Abteilung, Damascus, 5–9 November 2006)*, eds. Karin Bartl and Abd al-Razzaq Moaz, 115–24. Rahden: Verlag Marie Leidorf, 2008.

Simpson, I. R. "Framings of Capitalism and the Archaeology of Sugar in the Islamic Mediterranean." *Historical Archaeology*, 53.3 (2019): 591–610.

———. "Religious Redirection: Muslim-Christian Market Interaction in Early Islamic Syria-Palestine." Doctoral dissertation, Stanford University, 2016.

Storr, Virgil Henry. "The Social Construction of the Market." *Society*, 47.3 (2010): 200–6.

Todeschini, Giacomo. *Il Prezzo Della Salvezza: Lessici Medievali Del Pensiero Economico*. Rome: La Nuova Italia Scientifica, 1994.

Turner, Bryan S. *Weber and Islam: A Critical Study*. London: Routledge, 1998.

Turner, Victor. *The Ritual Process: Structure and Anti-Structure*. London: Cornell University Press, 1977 (1969).

Udovitch, Abraham L. *Partnership and Profit in Medieval Islam*. Princeton: Princeton University Press, 1970.

Walmsley, Alan. "Coinage and the Economy of Syria-Palestine in the Seventh and Eighth Centuries CE." In *Money, Power and Politics in Early Islamic Syria: A Review of Current Debates*, ed. John F. Haldon, 21–44. Farnham: Ashgate, 2010.

———. *Early Islamic Syria: An Archaeological Assessment*. London: Duckworth, 2007.

———. "The Friday Mosque of Early Islamic Jarash in Jordan." *Journal of the David Collection*, 1 (2003): 110–31.

———. "Production, Exchange and Regional Trade in the Islamic East Mediterranean: Old Structures, New Systems?." In *The Long Eighth Century: Production, Distribution and Demand*, eds. Inge Lyse Hansen and Chris Wickham, 265–343. Leiden: Brill, 2000.

Yildirim, Yetkin. "The Medina Charter: A Historical Case of Conflict Resolution." *Islam & Christian-Muslim Relations*, 20.4 (2009): 439–50.

3

KING ENRIQUE IV OF CASTILLA AND THE CHRISTIAN UNDERPINNINGS OF HIS LETTER ON TRADE FAIRS

Manuel J. Ortuño

In 1474, the last year of Enrique IV's two-decade reign, he and a member of his advisory council, Rodrigo Ponce de León, Marquis of Cádiz, and Count of Arcos, became closely associated with one another when the king assumed the task of extricating the marquis from an increasingly violent feud with the Duke of Medina Sidonia. Once royal emissaries assured the duke that he and the marquis would benefit equally and in a similar manner from the final negotiated settlement, the two adversaries quickly agreed to a cessation of hostilities.[1] Soon afterward, Don Rodrigo asked the king to approve the establishment of an annual trade fair in the town of Paradas, a part of his feudal holdings near the city of Sevilla. In a four-page letter to the Paradas town council and residents, the king granted the marquis's wish and described the way in which the fair would be conducted.[2] When this heretofore unpublished document is examined in light of the king's 1459 letter describing the first trade fairs he founded, the progress that was made in royal policy during the intervening years becomes apparent immediately.[3] The newly devised business plan for large-scale, long-distance trade is at once inspirational, and eminently practical.

The joint effort of King Enrique and the Marquis of Cádiz to promote commerce was not a rare undertaking. From the early Middle Ages onward monarchs often cooperated with landed nobility and Church organizations in the establishment of regional trade fairs. The first recorded initiation of such a business venture was by Dagobert I of France (629–39), who noted the increased commercial activity that occurred in the town of Saint-Denis on the outskirts of Paris when locals and pilgrims participated in the week-long celebration of their patron's annual feast day. Wishing to impart a measure of structure and control to this beneficial but free-wielding commerce, King Dagobert granted the Abbey of St. Denis the privilege of serving as host of the event, and he ceded to the abbot and friars the royal tolls and revenues paid by traders and other attendees. At

DOI: 10.4324/9781003082842-4

first, the buying, selling and exchanging of agricultural produce, honey, and wine occurred among residents of Northern France, but in the following centuries the goods traded became more varied, and the fair began to attract merchants from the Netherlands, Germany, and England.[4] Another concurrent development was the founding of similar trade fairs in neighboring kingdoms, the exceptions being those of the Iberian Peninsula owing to the Muslim invasion in 711, which resulted in the rapid occupation of all but its northernmost reaches. For half a millennium this corner of Southwestern Europe remained part of the Islamic world.[5]

In the mid-twelfth century, however, the three small Iberian kingdoms in the north, Aragón, Castilla, and Portugal, through coordinated warfare and shrewd bargaining, began to regain one after another the lands occupied long ago by the Muslim invaders from North Africa. The military success of the Christians continued into the third quarter of the thirteenth century, at which time the only remaining kingdom still ruled by the invaders' descendants was Granada. Along the frontier separating Christian and Muslim territory, the newcomers engaged in periodic military operations ranging from skirmishes to full-fledged offensives, but the defenders were able to prevent significant advances because of Granada's mountainous terrain and its fortified Mediterranean seaports to which African coreligionists delivered supplies and additional manpower. The lulls in fighting and the maintenance of a territorial status quo, both of which lasted until the fourth quarter of the fifteenth century, facilitated Castilla's use of the central grasslands of the peninsula for sheep raising as well as for the development of very lucrative wool trade with Italy and Northwestern Europe.

The increase in wealth generated by international commerce accelerated urbanization throughout the continent, which in turn led to unprecedented social problems.[6] Church leaders and statesmen in widely disseminated written works addressed the human suffering and conflict that occurred in cities, and soon a preferred remedy emerged. Pope Innocent III in two of his sermons and Thomas Aquinas in a number of his collected theological treatises agreed that the virtue of charity had to be practiced conscientiously and more extensively by all, whatever one's place of residence, social class, or religion might be. A similar theme appeared in two of *Las siete partidas*, a comprehensive legal code assembled by King Alfonso X of Castilla: part one dealt with cannon law and part five with contracts, many of which were related to commerce.[7] As one might expect, the New Testament served as the ultimate source of the Christian teachings and practices that would be applied to ailing municipalities. All of these works seem to have had an impact on the formulation of King Enrique's trade policy, and specifically on the composition of his 1474 letter to the people of Paradas. The letter's most pertinent source with a broad circulation, however, was the *Ars dictaminis*, the equivalent of modern-day handbooks on composing business letters.[8] With regard to the letter's form, King Enrique scrupulously adhered to the rules of the *Ars dictaminis*, and I argue that within those contours he worked creatively to impart a decidedly Christian tone and message to his letter. He included explicit references to God and Jesus Christ in the salutation and valediction, respectively, and in the body of the letter, he insisted that the readers and listeners comply fully with a set of trade fair regulations consisting of interdependent religious and marketplace practices. Documentary evidence from the 1480s indicates that the king's masterful intermingling of Roman Catholic ethos and sound trade policy was financially very successful, and, as this chapter will go on to show, his regulations for the Paradas fair, in particular their Christian underpinnings, would prove to be equally relevant and effective on the other side of the Atlantic in New Spain—a colonial realm wholly unforeseen at the time of the letter's composition.

Analysis and interpretation of the text

From the very first line of the Paradas letter, as opportunities to convey its Christian message became apparent to the king, he cleverly exploited them. According to the *Ars dictaminis*, a required formal aspect of business letters is that they reflect the existing socio-political hierarchy.[9] The king therefore opened, not with a greeting addressed to the recipients, but rather by identifying himself and listing his many royal titles. He began by stating his given name preceded by a widely used and rather modest title of respect. The immediate insertion of a parenthetical expression continued to tone down the pride of place by humbly observing that he, like every other human being, received undeserved favors dispensed by their generous and loving deity: "Don Enrique, by the grace of God, King of Castilla, of León, of Toledo, ... "[10] Once the rest of his kingdoms and principalities were named, he turned to the inhabitants of Paradas and addressed them in hierarchical order beginning with government officials, followed by groups of high socio-economic standing, next came workers with specialized training, and in closing, the many were singled out who contributed to the community's wellbeing simply by pursuing their positive thoughts and activities: "[this concerns] you, the Council, [namely] the Governor, Magistrates, Constable, and all Councilors, [the town's] gentlemen and squires, its skilled laborers, and finally everyone of good will in Paradas.... " (1, 3–4)

The body of the letter, if it is to conform to *dictaminis* rules, must begin with a brief narrative that apprises readers and listeners of the basic substance of the communication.[11] The king, therefore, conveyed the following information:

> ... because Don Rodrigo Ponce de León, Marquis of Cádiz, ... asked it of me as a favor, ... and moreover because [the town of Paradas] ... is likely to grow in population and size, and being located, as it is, very close to [the Kingdom of Granada] border, ... I find [it economically] advantageous, as well as supportive of my wish to favor you now and forever, that there be in said town a trade fair every year.... (1, 5–10)

Given the point that the king made in the salutation regarding his own relationship with God, here at the beginning of the body of the letter he endeavored to lead the marquis's vassals and peasants, as well as the duke and his people, to the realization that the establishment of the Paradas regional fair would be understood best as an instance of the bestowal of divine grace.[12] No matter how unworthy the two groups had become because of their hatred of each other and the violence in which they engaged, their loving heavenly Father decided to intervene and to prompt Don Rodrigo's request for a fair and King Enrique's willingness to grant it.

The letter continues with an outline of a series of hard and fast regulations that will prevail during the 20-day-long fair. The first three rules are fundamentally important in that each illustrates the king's plan to adhere to certain Christian beliefs while employing related business practices which tend to be profitable. Although it is a somewhat convoluted restatement of Luke 3:11, the king announced first that he would share his wealth with those less fortunate than he. The instrument employed in accomplishing this would be an exemption from the royal tax on transactions: "… [the fair will] be free of the *alcabala* [tax] and … [the event will] last for 20 days beginning on the 20th day of March and ending on the 10th day of April" (1, 11–12).[13] Worthy of note is that early in the thirteenth century Pope Innocent III issued a pronouncement on the need for more charity toward individuals and groups residing in municipalities. St. Thomas Aquinas included similar ideas in one of his treatises. He clarified that "… some have defined alms as being a deed whereby something is given to the needy, out of compassion and for God's sake …," and then he warned, "We should not lavish our wealth on others all at once, we should dole it out by degrees." Furthermore, "… we are warned to be careful in giving alms, and to give, not to one only, but to many, that we may profit many."[14] From the perspective of doing business effectively, this tax relief measure, by leaving in the merchants' hands money and/or goods that otherwise would have gone to the king, had the potential for making the fair especially profitable in that it would allow more numerous and larger volume sales, purchases, and exchanges to take place. Whoever the merchants might be, they would benefit financially, as would non-business people who acquired products for personal use. The total absence of taxation contrasted sharply with the selective approach that King Enrique took in a letter describing the fairs he had founded in the first few years of his reign. Those earlier trade events were announced as essentially tax-free, but with a handful of specific exceptions; the *alcabala*-bearing items were meat, fish, wine, flour, bread, woolen cloth, and linens.[15] For the relatively small upper and middle classes, their spending capability was at a level that made taxed staple nourishment and durable cloth easily affordable while still enabling them to purchase such tax-free luxuries as condiments and embroidered silk. The very large lower class, however, was so impoverished that its members struggled to buy necessities, and seldom if ever could they afford an item that was not taxed. This inequity became patently clear to King Enrique, and he decided to do away with it.

More directly expressed was the Christian admonition found in Luke 10:30–37 that the whole of humankind, in its great diversity and varying needs, is to be treated as if all were good neighbors.[16] The welcome extended by King Enrique was quite detailed, and it attempted to include everyone in the known world:

> And I wish and command that each and every person, of whatever station, economic level, or dignity, be they Christian, Jew, or Moor, ... be allowed to attend said fair and to send [others there] safely with all their merchandise, [personal] property, [etc.] ... And I wish and it is my will to grant that all people, men as well as women, from said town and its surrounding area, as well as from ... other kingdoms and dominions of mine and from elsewhere ... attend said fair .... (1, 17 and 2, 1–3)

Unfortunately, the king's inclusive, virtually universal, invitation plus his assurance of effective safety measures to protect attendees and their property began to contrast at times with the experience of the general public and soon would stand in diametric opposition to the policies advocated by future monarchs of Spain.[17] In this portion of the letter Enrique IV took his lead and even some of his wording from an illustrious predecessor of his, Alfonso X: "... we decree that all persons who resort to the fairs in our kingdoms, not only Christians but also Jews and Moors, and also those who at any other time visit our dominions ... shall be safe and secure in body, property, merchandise, and all their effects." [18] From the business perspective the very large and diverse group of fair participants and their protection from lawless elements would tend to broaden the range of goods in supply and in demand. For example, upper socio-economic exporter/importers would gravitate toward offering fine merino wool and expecting in exchange luxury textiles, while lower-class merchants would deal in coarser fibers and rough durable cloth. Likewise, male and female customers wishing to purchase fabric for a new wardrobe would expect a broad assortment of different colors and textures.[19]

The next regulation involved fair participants with previously incurred debt and their creditors who presented valid documentation and demanded payment. Generally, the king prohibited the latter from pursuing their debt collection during the fair, but once it was over and the borrowers had returned home, the lenders' efforts to settle accounts could resume. The king's directive is again to love your neighbors whoever they might be, but in this case, the focus is not on the scriptural teaching but on the actions that should follow.[20] The obvious argument against on-site debt collection is that an unexpected surrender of currency and/or goods by traders attending the fair might diminish or, in extreme cases, completely destroy their buying, selling, and exchanging plans. The king phrased his protection of debtors as follows:

> neither they nor their ... associates [will] be delayed, detained or arrested, nor their goods, beasts of burden, merchandise, or other items of theirs be seized for indebtedness, not even [for] debts they or their associates owe and have to pay in whatever form either to me ... or to other persons regardless of notes, proofs, pledges, or [threats of] reprisal. (2, 6–9)[21]

There is, however, one important exception to the ban on debt collection at a trade fair, and the reason for it is a most valid one: its procedures tend to foster large-scale, long-distance commerce. Typically, in the course of a year, merchants attended a number of regional fairs, and occasionally some individuals, after having negotiated an attractive transaction, discovered that it could not be completed because of a miscalculation of the where-with-all to do so. The usual solution to the problem was that the better-funded and supplied merchant would grant the necessary amount of credit to his/her counterpart, provided the latter indicated in writing that the debt would be paid in full at the next fair in which both intended to participate, provided the time lapse did not exceed one year.[22] In King Enrique's words, the only way that the general prohibition of debt collection at a trade fair could be circumvented is "… if such [written demands for payment] state specifically that the debt must be settled at said fair…" (2, 11–12). This special procedure for granting and paying off loans among trade-fair merchants not only made possible the original transaction, but also others at the later fair because the repaid coin and/or goods, now in the hands of the lender merchant, could be used for new purchases and exchanges.

Here, at the midpoint in the king's list of six trading regulations, he turned away from those actively engaged in commerce and directed his attention to a number of officials and staff members within the royal bureaucracy who would be instrumental in making the fair function properly. His purpose was twofold: to go on record regarding the obligations of the bureaucrats named and, at the same time, to impart to the residents of Paradas as complete an understanding as possible of how the fair would be conducted. This is an opportune moment to share with the readers of this study an overview of the form and content of the entire body of the letter. If we look backward at the three Christian modes of behavior and their associated business maneuvers, and then forward toward the three distinct portions that remain of the body of the letter, then an integrated and symmetrical structure becomes apparent. The three religious/commercial initiatives in the first half of the body of the letter are: 1) sharing wealth through tax exemption; 2) neighborly treatment of all merchants and other attendees as a way of enhancing supply and demand; and 3) Church and state sanctioned loans in order to facilitate transactions. Together they form an updated and intricately coordinated Christian business strategy that may falter. If it does, then any setbacks must be addressed before serious damage is done to the fair. The king therefore in the remaining half of the body of the letter gave appropriate orders of both a preventive and emergency nature to a triple alliance of helpers: 1) the royal bureaucracy; 2) the king's vassals and subjects taken as a whole; and 3) his newly organized criminal justice agents.

As mentioned above, all of those who were addressed in part 1 of the second half of the letter's body were members of the royal bureaucracy; more specifically, they dealt in various ways with financial matters. The first to be singled out by the king was responsible for gathering taxes, and they received notification of the special exemption from the *alcabala* that had been granted to the Paradas fair. Next in line were the king's senior accountants who were to oversee new economic policies that would result in the increase or decrease of royal funds, and they in the course of their duties might have to communicate in writing with the Paradas council and its accountants. The last subgroup of bureaucratic officials brought into the loop consisted of the royal chancellor and his support staff. Not until the beginning of the eleventh century, when the practice of letter writing became increasingly institutionalized, did popes, emperors, kings, and prelates add these highly skilled administrators to their households and entourages. It was they who kept track of all incoming and outgoing written communication.[23] King Enrique commanded that the royal chancery process meticulously the various pieces of correspondence having to do with the Paradas fair. Finally, the king's awareness that the complex machinery of government at times may work at cross-purposes led him to call upon the above bureaucrats as well as others to cooperate with one another in order to identify and remove any obstructions to optimum trading conditions that might occur at the soon-to-be established fair:

> … I command my various treasurers, tax collectors, major and minor agents, guarantors, inspectors, receivers, and others who now assess and collect … my *alcabalas* from said town, that henceforth … they not demand or take [these taxes] … from said people who have come to said fair …. And I order that my senior accountants place permanently in my Amendment Books this letter … according which the proceeds from my *alcabalas* are to be rendered from now forward in the town of Paradas …. And [furthermore] with regard to the matter [of taxation, I order] you [my senior accountants] to make available and send forward this and other letters and papers of mine as may be necessary. Because of this [latter directive] I order my chancellor, notaries, and their assistants who affix my royal seal, to review, seal, and remit … each item. I want, and it is my wish and will, that you [as a group] be careful and thorough now and forever, not to allow interference to occur [between the privileges enjoyed by Paradas] and other laws, codes, rights, ordinances, rulings, and sanctions. (2, 12–17 and 3, 2–11)

Those addressed in part 2 of the second half of the letter body included every one of Enrique IV's able-bodied and well-intentioned vassals and subjects, and they were all charged with protecting the person, and possessions of fair attendees. The language used implied that principally men were to make this effort, but because women were not specifically excluded, some might have heeded and followed the directive. The list began with those having significant authority and power: dukes, counts, and other feudal lords and ladies; masters of military orders; priors or prioresses of large religious communities; and wealthy commoners. Others were enlisted who wielded power by virtue of their membership on an advisory council, be it the king's very own or one for which the purview was a city, town, or village. Also enjoined in the security effort, despite their limited authority and means, were gentlemen, squires, and workers of all kinds:

> ... by means of this my letter ... I order dukes, counts, marquises, wealthy [entrepreneurs], masters of [military] orders, priors [of religious communities]... members of my council, judges of the royal court ... as well as all [municipal] councils, magistrates, mayors, constables, councilmen, gentlemen, squires, skilled laborers, and all men [and women] of good will who reside in ... my kingdoms and dominions who are now living and those yet to be, and [finally I turn] to each and every one of my vassals, subjects, and all native-born persons, regardless of social status or financial condition, or preeminence or dignity, and I command all of you ... to assist and defend now and always the people who participate in the fair and consent and allow them all to travel unimpeded to and from the event .... (3, 21–24 and 4, 1–8)

Because the above group was enormous and heterogeneous, they would tend to operate less effectively than those in group 1 who followed the chain of command from the king, to his top officials, and finally to their assistants. Clearly, the tax-free status of the fair would be well protected, but the security of the fair's many and diverse participants remained uncertain because it depended in large part on an individual taking the initiative in a potentially dangerous confrontation between merchants and thieves. Although there were always some proactive people at every level of society who indeed would follow through on the king's orders, a second subgroup would be reluctant to become involved because they were minimally endowed with the requisite virtues. The third and last kind of people who would react to the call were not helpers but rapacious feudal lords, recalcitrant municipal officials, swindlers, highwaymen, and assorted ne'er-do-wells who, given the opportunity, would victimize fair participants. As we shall see presently in part 3, King Enrique had in readiness a force of justice agents who would prompt many of the reluctant to perform their duty and also would ensure that the incorrigible received the punishment they deserved.

Shortly after ascending the throne in 1454, Enrique saw the need to improve the way in which local law enforcement brotherhoods functioned. Over time, he gathered them into regional associations, and in 1473 at a meeting in Villacastín, a village near Segovia, he was able to bring to fruition a plan conceived almost two decades earlier and never fully realized: namely, the presence throughout his realms of a coordinated and effective police force answerable to him.[24] Its preferred name would become the *Santa Hermandad* (Holy Brotherhood), but King Enrique's designation was *mis justicias* (my justice agents). With regard to the Paradas fair, these law officers, assisted by town criers and public scribes, were responsible for making known to the attendees of the event each of the royal regulations. The agents' most challenging duties were related to the interface of law enforcement with the actions of the accused and the accusers. The critical objective was to serve the alleged culprits with valid subpoenas to appear before the royal court:

> ... I command that the above-mentioned justice agents arrange to have everything contained in this letter proclaimed [and posted] by town criers and public scribes ... in plazas, markets and other such places that all will be informed. And once done, ... if some person or persons take action contrary to my security measures and assurances, they must stop and legal proceedings against them and their property are to be initiated and pursued to the fullest extent of the civil and criminal legal code for having disobeyed or ignored written orders of their rightful king and lord. And neither the [accused] nor the [accusers] should do anything more in any way under penalty of [loss] of my favor, privation of positions, and confiscation of goods and properties .... I order that the individual who [originally] shared my letter with the accused subpoena him/her/them to appear before me in my court within 15 days, wherever they may be when served. (4, 13–23)

As the body of the letter drew to a close, King Enrique demonstrated again how faithfully he was following the *Ars dictaminis* format. There are two approaches that members of the hierarchy may use when they inform subordinates of their obligations, and the king employed both.[25] Accordingly, the first half of the body announced the benefits to be gained by doing what is required, and the second described the punishment that the inattentive and disobedient would undergo. In each of the six subsections, the king provided substantive detail on how the most important aspects of the Paradas fair would be regulated. At the same time, he was busy molding the text into an attractively written work which in many ways was like a well-crafted short story or narrative poem. Most worthy of praise are the king's broad and fitting vocabulary, his engaging but authoritative tone, and his ingenuity in moving forward in each of the two thematically related portions of the body of the letter. The smooth transition from the multifaceted body to the valediction would be an artistic challenge because a business letter's closing lines are devoted mostly to such mundane facts as place and date of composition and the name of the secretary who put pen to paper. Surprisingly, the king was able to use some of this humdrum information to create a complex visual image that conveyed additional Christian teachings he deemed relevant to the Paradas fair.[26]

King Enrique's path to an impressive conclusion began with noting the importance of paperwork and signatures in relation to those accused of disobeying the Paradas fair regulations: "I order that the public scribe who is enlisted to prepare the subpoena document sign it so that I can confirm how [my subjects] comply with my rule, which is made known to you through this signed and sealed letter of mine, ..."(4, 25–27). The last eight words of the foregoing quotation served also to begin the valediction:

> ... this signed and sealed letter of mine [issued] in Madrid on the 15th day of September, in the year one thousand four hundred and seventy-four since the birth Our Lord Jesus Christ: I the King, (signature); I Juan de Oviedo, secretary to Our Monarch, at his command had it copied [by royal scribes]. (4, 27–29)

The current day, month, and year were expressed in terms of the lapse of time "since the birth of Our Lord Jesus Christ," and the latter part of this phrase became the first and most important stroke in the creation of a hierarchical tableau of four beings. In order to add the remaining three and thus complete the mental image, one must think in terms of titles plus names and recall that in the letter there are exactly four who are identified by using both. Even individuals with social stature and an important role to play in the fair, such as the head of the Paradas town council and the royal chancellor, were identified only by title and remained nameless. Our Lord Jesus and the second figure, King Enrique IV, had their unique personal identities, but the third and the fourth, in addition to being themselves, represented their segment of society. Figure number three, Rodrigo Ponce de Leon, Marquis of Cadiz, who was mentioned in the letter's narrative, represented the aristocracy, and number four, Secretary Juan de Oviedo, the lower classes.

Worthy of note is that the more attentive and perceptive of those who read and listened to the Paradas letter would have shared among themselves and with others their discovery of the valediction's image and its obvious meaning. In short, the trade fair was bestowed by the grace of God, and secondly, Enrique IV's business plan, with its attention to Christian teachings and practices, would be notably successful as long as he and his successors on the throne followed and enforced its six basic regulations. Of course, the aristocracy and the lower classes had to abide by the rules, but equally important for them was that they strive always to work together in harmony despite their social, economic, and religious differences.

Founding, growth, suspension, and disappearance of the Paradas trade fair

The fair's demise in spite of its growth becomes more understandable if one first considers, and then takes into account, the adverse feelings that a large number of titled noblemen and three younger members of the royal family had toward King Enrique. This elite socio-political group was notably tradition-bound and self-serving, and by the late1450s it was criticizing openly several of the king's practices and policies. One of the former was his gracious treatment of those who constituted the "other," that is, he was inclined to choose his most trusted council advisers from among "new men" in the sense of their being young in years or having been elevated recently to noble status. And it was they, not his critics, who most often benefitted from customary royal patronage and largess.[27] An especially despised policy was the king's staunch opposition to long, devastating wars. With respect to military action in and around the Kingdom of Granada, Enrique preferred a strategic use of limited warfare followed by skillful diplomacy. His adversaries, however, were committed to an all-out offensive ending in total conquest.[28] Such a large increase in territory under Christian control would call for land grants to noblemen, plus awards of the most distinguished titles of duke and marquis for exemplary feats on the battlefield.

By the spring of 1465 the king's critics were in open rebellion and had agreed upon a daring solution to their predicament: the removal of Enrique from the throne by force of arms and the replacement of him with his 12-year-old half-brother, Alfonso.[29] A war of succession dragged on for three years, mainly because the king and his supporters proved to be formidable opponents. The uprising came to a sad, unforeseen end with Alfonso's death in July of 1468 after a brief illness. The equally weary rebel and loyalist leaders arranged to meet in early September to negotiate their differences and to secure peace. The resulting compromise stated the following: Enrique will remain king until his death; Isabel, Alfonso's 17-year-old sister, will be granted the title of princess and heir to the throne of Castilla; the king, in the roll of foster-father of the princess, will originate all marriage plans.[30] This agreement brought about a fragile peace and less overt criticism of Enrique's rule. In the fall of 1469, the indomitable Isabel chose as her spouse Fernando, prince and heir to the throne of Aragón, married him in secret, and thus violated the negotiated settlement. Another year elapsed before the king felt sufficiently secure on the throne to revoke Isabel's title and to name as the future Queen of Castilla his eight-year-old daughter Juana.

During the waning months of 1474, Don Rodrigo, the Paradas town council, and the area's residents worked diligently toward making an unqualified success of the trade fair's fast-approaching inauguration. As fate would have it, they were dealt three blows in rapid succession, which together made it doubtful that the fair would ever be launched. King Enrique, while hunting in a forest near Madrid, suffered an apparently non-life-threatening fall from his horse, but died the following day, December 13, 1474. Within 36 hours Isabel and her retinue, who were ensconced in the palace of Segovia, made their way to a platform overlooking the city's main plaza where heralds, amid much fanfare, proclaimed her Queen of Castilla. Months earlier Fernando had been summoned to Aragón on an urgent matter, and upon his hurried return to Castilla, an agreement naming him joint monarch was adopted on January 15, 1475.[31]

As a result of these events, the more controversial initiatives taken by Enrique in the final year or two of his reign, which included the Paradas fair, were in danger of being countermanded by Fernando and Isabel. The enactment of such rollbacks, however, had to proceed with caution because the royal couple and their supporters among the titled nobility might differ on particular matters of state. To lose even one powerful ally because of an unpleasant disagreement could have dire consequences, especially if the forces that favored Princess Juana as queen were to call for a war of succession. Don Rodrigo understood this, and he quickly devised a scheme in which a well-chosen accomplice was able to obtain royal approval for the fair. The marquis approached Don Alonso Enríquez, Admiral of Castilla, a resident of Sevilla, and supporter of Fernando and Isabel. Don Rodrigo, in a conversation with Don Alonso, underscored the value of the fair to the city and convinced him to write a carefully contrived letter to the king and queen. In it the admiral requested a particular favor related to sea-borne commerce, which, if granted, would be tantamount to royal approval of the fair. The timing and success of these machinations are a matter of record: "1475 A.D. In this year at the request of Don Alonso Enríquez, Admiral of Castilla, the dock on the Sevilla River, at which commercial goods previously were unloaded, was moved by the City, in accordance with the command of the King and Queen, to a location adjacent to the Gold Tower where it currently remains, issued in Segovia on the 15th of February."[32] The Paradas annual fair was inaugurated on the appointed date, March 20, 1475, and the following 20 days of trading met, and perhaps even surpassed, the expectations of its organizers and participants.

By early May, however, the anticipated war of succession had reached an advanced stage of preparation and was about to commence. Though this was a reasonable cause for concern, the celebration of the fair was in no way impeded because major military actions, without exception, took place far to the north of Andalucía in the Kingdoms of León and Castilla. The remote theater of war gave Don Rodrigo, Don Alonso, and many other noblemen from the southern border region sufficient justification to remain neutral and not to support with additional combatants the queen they preferred. The tide of war eventually favored Fernando and Isabel for various reasons, one being the engaged presence of the king and queen on the battlefield, a feat that the younger princess was incapable of duplicating. The better part of 1479, February through September, was devoted to the negotiation of two treaties: one secured peace and the other decided Juana's future. She had to renounce forever her claim to the throne, which she did, and was then given the choice between an arranged marriage and the religious life; she willingly chose the latter and lived to the age of 68.[33]

The war to reconquer Granada (1482–1492), declared and carried out by Fernando and Isabel, led in a few years to the suspension of the Paradas fair. Ironically, the spark that ignited the war was struck unintentionally by the Marquis of Cádiz when he, his troops, and those of some other Andalusian nobles launched a surprise attack on the town of Alhama. The operation resulted in many Moorish casualties and the liberation of a large number of Christian captives. During the war's first three years its skirmishes and battles resembled, in their use of infantry and light cavalry, those that had been fought intermittently along the Granada border for over two centuries.[34] Eventually, such military action placed in jeopardy Paradas-fair participants and their possessions. Just prior to the 1485 celebration of the fair, Don Rodrigo issued a proclamation, which ostensibly was an assurance of the security he would provide, but could be interpreted also as advanced notice of the inevitable suspension of the fair until the return of peace. Included in this brief and troubling communication, however, are some favorable facts and associated figures that are of considerable significance:

> I, Don Rodrigo Ponce de León, Marquis of the City of Cádiz, ... by means of the present communique extend my safety net to all people from every social rank, ... and to their merchandise, goods, beasts of burden, and other things ... being brought to the fair that is customarily held in my town of Paradas ... beginning on the fifteenth day of March and ending on the fifteenth day of April, ... [issued] in my town of Marchena on the tenth day of March in the year of Our Savior Jesus Christ one thousand four hundred eighty-five.[35]

The implication of the above opening and closing dates of the Paradas fair is that after its first few celebrations the number of participants and transactions experienced so steep an increase that the trading period had to be lengthened from the original 20 days to a more accommodating 30 days. King Enrique's inspired combination of selected Christian teachings and corresponding business practices quickly proved to be a most effective way of stimulating a regional economy. The remaining seven years of the Granada war, during which the Paradas fair remained suspended, were fought with new weaponry and different tactics and strategies. For both sides, the increased use of cannons and muskets made infantry and cavalry, as well as once-reliable fortifications, more vulnerable. The Moorish dependence on supplies and reinforcements from North Africa led to a naval blockade of Málaga, which required the building of additional war ships including some outfitted with cannons. Learning how to use and effectively coordinate these recently developed elements of the military might, unfortunately, prolonged the war and added to the loss of lives and treasure.[36] Finally, on January 2, 1492, at the main entrance to the surrounded city of Granada, King Boabdil handed over its keys to King Fernando and Queen Isabel.

March 15th, the customary opening day of the Paradas fair, was barely two and a half months away, and therefore the preparations necessary for the resumption of trading after so many years of suspension could not be completed until the following spring, that of 1493. During the intervening fourteen and a half months, two very different sets of circumstances prevailed, which ultimately resulted in the decision not to reinstate the fair. Don Rodrigo, who had fought courageously throughout the Granada war, died on September 27, 1492, at the age of 48.[37] None of his heirs or associates could have championed before the king and queen the continuation of the fair as convincingly as he. The other series of developments began with the arrival of Columbus in Lisbon on March 4, 1493, after completing his first voyage to the Americas. Within days he had informed the King of Portugal in person and Fernando and Isabel in writing of the lucrative trade possibilities associated with the people and lands he had claimed for the Kingdom of Castilla.[38] When compared to the enormously broadened commercial horizons made possible by Columbus's navigational skills, the Paradas fair became a matter of so little import that it no longer merited royal attention and simply ceased to exist.

Enrique IV's transatlantic legacy

Like countless other royal documents, the Paradas letter was relegated to a Madrid archive where it probably was consulted by only a few interested readers from the late fifteenth through the early years of eighteenth centuries. During the long reign of Felipe V (1713–1746), in all likelihood Enrique IV's letter attracted much more attention because of its relevance to the current king's proposed reorganization of Spain's overseas commerce and associated royal revenues, particularly the *alcabala*.[39] The document's well-crafted text no doubt was examined by the monarch's ministers, and the benefits that could accrue from the relationships between Christian doctrine and sound business practices sparked their interest. After sharing the letter with the king they agreed that the Viceroy of New Spain, his ministers, and the leaders of the merchant community should experience the strong impact of Enrique IV's words. Royal scribes copied the text, forwarded it to Mexico City where those charged with the task of improving commercial policy found that a number of its insights had applicability to their assignment.

God's benevolence toward the inhabitants of New Spain with respect to large-scale commerce was clearly evident in its abundant silver deposits, the ingredients for the much-valued cochineal red dye, as well as a geographical location that facilitated trade in European and Asian luxury goods arriving respectively via the Cádiz-Veracruz and the Manila-Acapulco sea routes.[40] Given the diversity of the Viceroyalty's population, all of whom engaged in buying and selling regardless of race, ethnicity, religion, or gender, indeed should be treated as good neighbors. Especially notable in the Paradas letter was the overarching principle upon which commerce is based: namely, the maintenance of harmonious interaction within a hierarchically-arranged ensemble of two individuals and two social groups: Jesus Christ is the leader, followed by Spain's sovereign, then by the aristocracy, which included the viceroy, his ministers, other nobles, prelates, and wealthy commoners, and finally by the lower classes.

A remaining and most problematic item in Enrique IV's letter was the need to share the royal wealth with merchants and others by exempting them from the *alcabala*. It took several decades before a zero sales and exchanges tax was integrated into the standard operating procedures of two of Mexico's busiest commercial venues. The town of San Juan de los Lagos, in the Viceroyalty's west central region at a distance of 75 miles from the city of Guadalajara, was the location of one annual trade fair; the other took place in the northeastern frontier area in the fortified town of Saltillo, and both had the distinction of being the destination of religious pilgrimages, which later evolved into major commercial events held respectively in early December and in late September, each for 15 days.[41] Throughout most of the eighteenth century the *alcabala* tax on sales and exchanges, which ranged from two to eight percent, continued to be collected at the fairs, but in 1797 King Carlos III granted the San Juan event exemption from the royal tax. Extensive quantitative data exist for the San Juan fair during the years 1792–1808, and they indicate a sharp rise in the number and value of transactions precisely at the turn of the century. A probable scenario for this change in revenue collection and the associated growth in trade is that a number of merchants in the Guadalajara area, sometime in the second half of the eighteenth century, obtained a copy of the Paradas letter and cited its tax policy for regional fairs in a petition sent to the viceroy and ultimately to King Carlos III. Gratified by their success and wishing to see it duplicated, they contacted colleagues in Saltillo, passed on the Paradas letter, and advised that they also submit a tax-exemption petition. In 1814 King Fernando VII granted *alcabala*-free status to the Saltillo fair.[42]

Several bits of information related to the Baylor University manuscript provide factual support for the above speculations. Enrique IV's letter was copied onto paper that bears a watermark traceable to Franco Flor, a manufacturer, and exporter of paper goods located in Cataluña, Spain. A watermark of his, which consists of the depiction of a rosary and the initial F, appears on paper he produced in the early 1750s.[43] When a shipment of that paper arrived in New Spain, it was distributed first to large centers of the population like Guadalajara and eventually to nearby towns like San Juan de los Lagos. The Enrique IV letter in the Texas Collection bears the Franco Flor watermark with the initial and the rosary, and therefore, the copying was done either in the above city or town sometime in the second half of the eighteenth century. As the beginning of the nineteenth century approached, the royal letter then made its way from the Guadalajara/San Juan region to Saltillo. Additional supporting evidence of the route that the Baylor manuscript has traveled comes from the twentieth and twenty-first centuries. A long-time dealer in Old-West rare books and manuscripts located in New York City, Lindley Eberstadt, began in the 1940s to buy and sell printed and handwritten items in Spanish from various places in Latin America, including Mexico.[44] When he died in 1975, a Texas entrepreneur bought his entire inventory, transported it to Austin, and within a year or two had sold almost all of it to university libraries and archives.[45] What remained consisted of three bundles of unsorted Spanish language documents that a Baylor University benefactor purchased in 1985 and donated to the Baylor University Texas Collection.[46] These successive buyers and sellers did not examine the bundles' contents with care, and therefore Enrique IV's letter was never identified and separated from the other documents among which it lay buried. Not until early 2011, when my research interests led me to the Texas Collection in search of primary sources, did I locate the document boxes to which the items in the three bundles had been transferred. I began examining their contents, and after skimming one after another dozen of items having to do with business dealings in Northeastern Mexico during the early nineteenth century, the following marginal note on the first page of a four-page manuscript caught my attention: "Copy of the royal decree granting the fair to the town of Paradas."

The above fortuitous occurrences spanning almost three centuries and taking place in Spain, Mexico, and the United States were instrumental in bringing to light an extraordinary, late-medieval royal document on how to improve and expand large-scale, long-distance commerce. Enrique IV's letter, however, goes beyond a mere compendium of instructions on how to conduct a regional trade fair. The carefully constructed core of the plan, with its deliberately crafted rhetoric, showcases how the interface of religious practice and commercial enterprise can benefit a wide range of fair attendees from Southern Spain and beyond. The intersection of commerce with religion provides safeguards intended to mitigate selfishness on the part of attendees and to reduce predatory business practices. Through this felicitous integration of religion and commerce, fair participants are urged to work harmoniously with such governmental groups as the royal bureaucracy and law enforcement in order to achieve a common goal—the greater and more equitable distribution of the fair's goods. As those in attendance go about their tasks, they can comply at the same time with Enrique IV's loftier directives and contemplate their loving God in whom they believe, foster goodwill toward humankind in its diversity, and share in the wealth of their heavenly Father's creation.

Notes

1 Juan Luis Carriazo Rubio, *La casa de Arcos entre Sevilla y la frontera de Granada, 1374–1474* (Sevilla: Univ. de Sevilla, 2003), 376–84.

2 Copia de la Real Zédula para la feria de la villa de Paradas, Eighteenth-century copy of 15th century decree by King Enrique IV, 1474, Rowe Collection, Baylor University Texas Collection. May be accessed at https://digitalcollections-baylor.quartexcollections.com/Documents/Detail/eighteenth-century-copy-of-15th-century-decree-by-king-enrique-iv-1425-1474/841260.

3 Enrique IV, "Al concejo de Murcia notificándole la creación de dos ferias anuales en Segovia," in Juan Torres Fontes, *Estudios sobre la 'Crónica de Enrique IV' del Dr. Galíndez de Carvajal* (Murcia: Consejo Superior de Investigaciones Científicas, 1946), 477–79. See also William D. Phillips, *Enrique IV and the Crisis of Fifteenth-Century Castile* (Cambridge, MA: Medieval Acad. of America, 1978), 58–9.

4 Charles Verlinden, "Markets and Fairs," in *Economic Organization and Policies in the Middle Ages*, ed. M. Postan and E. Rich (Cambridge: Cambridge Univ. Press, 1965), 120–21; Steven A. Epstein, *An Economic and Social History of Later Medieval Europe, 1000–1500* (New York: Cambridge Univ. Press, 2009), 81–4.

5 María Rosa Menocal, *The Ornament of the World: How Muslims, Jews, and Christians Created a Culture of Tolerance in Medieval Spain* (New York: Little, Brown & Co., 2002), 24–9; Olivia R. Constable, *Trade and Traders in Muslim Spain: The Commercial Realignment of the Iberian Peninsula, 900–1500* (Cambridge: Cambridge Univ. Press, 1994), 209–13 and 227–31.

6 James F. Powers, "Towns on the Edge: Twelfth-Century Municipal War Policy in Leon-Castile and France," in *The Emergence of Leon-Castile c.1065–1500*, ed. J. Todesca (Dorchester, UK: Dorset Press, 2015), 33–36 and 44–5; Epstein, *Economic History of Europe*, 232–5.

7 James W. Brodman, *Charity & Religion in Medieval Europe* (Wash. D.C.: Catholic Univ. of Amer. Press, 2009), 14–29 and 178–82; Elizabeth L. Gerhardt, "See How They Love One Another: A Short History of Medieval and Reformation Poor Relief," in *Orthodoxy and Orthopraxis*, ed. D. R. Cullum (Eugene, OR: Pickwick Publ., 2020), 209–17.

8 Les Perelman, "The Medieval Art of Letter Writing: Rhetoric as Institutional Expression," in *Textual Dynamics of the Professions: Historical and Contemporary Studies of Writing in Professional Communities*, ed. C. Bazerman (Madison: University of Wisconsin Press, 1991), 97–119; Malcolm Richardson, "The *Ars dictaminis*, the Formulary, and Medieval Epistolary Practice," in *Letter-Writing Manuals and Instruction, from Antiquity to the Present*, ed. C. Poster and L. Mitchell (Columbia: University of South Carolina Press, 2007), 52–66.

9 Perelman, "Medieval Letter Writing," 110–11; Richardson, "Medieval Epistolary Practice," 62–4.

10 Enrique IV, "Feria de Paradas," page 1, line 1. Henceforth quotations from the Paradas letter will be followed immediately by page and line numbers in parentheses. For more on the concept of divine grace, see Bruce M. Metzger, *The New Testament: Its Background, Growth, and Content*, 3rd ed. (Nashville: U. of TN, Abingdon Press, 2003), 276–7.

11 Perelman, "Medieval Letter Writing," 107–10.

12 Metzger, *New Testament*, 278–80.

13 Adolfo Carrasco Martínez, "Alcabalas y renta señorial en Castilla: Los ingresos fiscales de la Casa del Infantado," *Cuadernos de Historia Moderna*, 12 (1991), 111–12 and 120–2; Miguel-Ángel Ladero Quesada, *Las ferias de Castilla: Siglos XII a XV* (Madrid: Imprenta Taravilla, 1994), 102–3.

14 Gerhardt, "Medieval Poor Relief," 212–4 and St. Thomas Aquinas, *Summa Theologica*, vol. 3 (Westminster, MD: Christian Classic, 1981), 1318 and 1326.

15 Enrique IV, "Dos ferias en Segovia," 477.

16 Metzger, *New Testament Content*, 186–7.

17 Thomas Devaney, *Enemies in the Plaza: Urban Spectacle and the End of Spanish Frontier Culture, 1460–1492* (Philadelphia: Univ. of PA Press, 2015), 7–8 and 74–7.

18 *Las Siete Partidas*, trans. S. P. Scott, (New York: Commerce Clearing House, 1931), 1058. See also James W. Brodman, "The *Siete partidas* and the Law of Charity in Thirteenth-Century Castile," 81–86 in *The Emergence of León-Castile c.1065–1500* edited by J. J. Todesca, 81–91.

19 Ladero Quesada, *Ferias de Castilla*, 102.

20 Metzger, *New* Testament, 191–2. Epstein, *Economic and Social History*, 233–6 and 247–8.

21 Especially noteworthy is that the king in his evenhandedness includes himself among all the others who must wait until the trade fair is over in order to collect the debts owed them.

22 Ladero Quesada, *Ferias de Castilla*, 86–91; Abelardo del Vigo Gutiérrez, *Cambistas, mercaderes y banqueros en el Siglo de Oro español* (Madrid: Biblioteca de Autores Españoles, 1997), 41–2.

23 Perelman, "Medieval Letter Writing," 98–9.

24 Phillips, *Enrique IV of Castile*, 60–2 and 117–8.

25 Perelman, "Medieval Letter Writing," 112–13; Richardson, "Epistolary Practice," 62–4.

26 Jacques Le Goff, *The Medieval Imagination*, trans. A. Golfhammer (Chicago: University of Chicago Press, 1992), 1–2.

27 James H. Burns, *Lordship, Kingship, and Empire: The Idea of Monarchy, 1400–1525* (New York: Oxford University Press, 1992), 75–8.

28 José Luis Martín, *Enrique IV de Castilla: rey de Navarra, príncipe de Cataluña* (Hondarribia: Nerea, 2003), 103–4.

29 Jocelyn N. Hillgarth, *The Spanish Kingdoms 1250–1516,* II (Oxford: Oxford Univ. Press, 1978), 333–4.

30 Phillips, *Enrique IV of Castile*, 106–8.

31 John Edwards, *Ferdinand and Isabella* (London: Pearson, 2005), 1–2 and 11–2.

32 Diego Ortiz de Zúñiga, *Anales eclesiásticos y seculares de la muy noble y muy leal Ciudad de Sevilla*, III (Madrid: Imprenta Real, 1796), 71–2.

33 Edwards, *Ferdinand and Isabella*, 12–21.
34 Joseph F. O'Callaghan, *The Last Crusade in the West: Castile and the Conquest of Granada* (Philadelphia: University of Pennsylvania, 2014), 129–32.
35 Rodrigo Ponce de León, "Cédula de seguro dada a las personas que asistieran a la feria que desde el 15 de marzo al 15 de abril que se celebraba en Paradas," Marchena, March 10, 1485. Sección Nobleza, Archivo Histórico Nacional, OSUNA, C.140, D.177.
36 O'Callaghan, *Last Crusade*, 159–67 and 184–93.
37 Juan Luis Carriazo Rubio, "Los Ponce de León y la Capitanía de Sevilla," *Historia, Instituciones, Documentos*, 31 (2004): 131–32.
38 Elizabeth M. Willingham, *The Mythical Indies and Columbus's Apocalyptic Letter: Imagining America in the Late Middle Ages* (Chicago: Sussex Academic Press, 2016), 10–12.
39 Alan Knight, *Mexico, the Colonial Era* (Cambridge: Cambridge University Press, 2002), 240–69; José Cuello, "The Economic Impact of the Bourbon Reforms and the Late Colonial Crisis of Empire at the Local Level: The Case of Saltillo," *The Americas*, 44 (1988): 303–7.
40 Joost Hengstmengel, *Divine Providence in Early Modern Economic Thought* (London and New York: Routledge, 2019), 44–51, and Elena Phipps, *Cochineal Red: The Art History of a Color* (New Haven: Yale University Press, 2010), 12–17 and 29–36.
41 María Ángeles Gálvez and Antonio Ibarra, "Comercio local y circulación regional de importaciones: la feria de San Juan de los Lagos en la Nueva España," *Historia Mexicana*, 46, no. 3 (1997): 581–3; Jesús F. Teja, "St. James at the Fair: Religious Ceremony, Civic Boosterism, and Commercial Development on the Colonial Mexican Frontier," *The Americas*, 57 (2001): 395–416.
42 Teja, "Fair on the Mexican Frontier," 409.
43 Oriol Valls i Subirá, *The History of Paper in Spain: XVII–XIX Centuries* (Madrid: Empresa Nacional de Celulosas, 1982), 145. See also the appendix, p. 230, for the watermark design.
44 Karl Brown, ed., *The Annotated Eberstadt Catalogs of Americana,* II (New York: Argosy-Antiquarian, 1965), Catalogs 131 and 132.
45 John Holmes Jenkins, *Audubon, and Other Capers: Confessions of a Texas Bookmaker* (Austin: Pemberton Press, 1976), 108 and 111–13.
46 See Baylor University Library. Texas Collection Records, John N. Rowe III, accession number 2750.

Bibliography

Alfonso X King of Castilla. *Las Siete Partidas*, Trans. S. P. Scott. New York: Commerce Clearing House, 1931.

Aquinas, St. Thomas. *Summa Theologica*, Trans. Fathers of the English Dominican Province. 4th ed., vol. 3. Westminster: Christian Classics, 1981.

Brodman, James W. *Charity & Religion in Medieval Europe*. Washington: Catholic University of America Press, 2009.

———. "The *Siete Partidas* and the Law of Charity in Thirteenth-Century Castile." In *The Emergence of León-Castile c. 1065–1500*, ed. J. J. Todesca, 81–91. Dorchester: Dorset Press, 2015.

Brown, Karl, ed. *The Annotated Eberstadt Catalogs of Americana*, vol. II, catalogs 131 and 132. New York: Argosy-Antiquarian, 1965.

Carrasco Martínez, Adolfo. "Alcabalas y renta señorial en Castilla: Los ingresos fiscales de la Casa del Infantado." *Cuadernos de Historia Moderna*, 12 (1991): 111–22.

Carriazo Rubio, Juan Luis. *La casa de Arcos entre Sevilla y la frontera de Granada, 1374–1474*. Sevilla: Universidad de Sevilla, 2003.

Constable, Olivia R. *Trade and Traders in Muslim Spain: The Commercial Realignment of the Iberian Peninsula, 900–1500.* Cambridge: Cambridge University Press, 1994, 199–209 and 227–229.

Cuello, José. "The Economic Impact of the Bourbon Reforms and the Late Colonial Crisis of Empire at the Local Level: The Case of Saltillo." *The Americas*, 44 (1988): 301–23.

del Vigo Gutiérrez, Abelardo. *Cambistas, mercaderes y banqueros en el Siglo de Oro español.* Madrid: Biblioteca de Autores Españoles, 1997.

Devaney, Thomas. *Enemies in the Plaza: Urban Spectacle and the End of Spanish Frontier Culture, 1460–1492.* Philadelphia: University of Pennsylvania Press, 2015.

Edwards, John. *Ferdinand and Isabella.* London: Pearson, 2005.

Enrique IV King of Castilla. "Copia de la Real Zédula para la feria de la villa de Paradas, Madrid, 1474." John N. Rowe III papers, accession no. 2750, box 7, folder 26, The Texas Collection, Baylor University. https://digitalcollections-baylor.quartexcollections.com/Documents/Detail/eighteenth-century-copy-of-15th-century-decree-by-king-enrique-iv-1425-1474/841260

———. "Al concejo de Murcia notificándole la creación de dos ferias anuales en Segovia." In *Estudios sobre la 'Crónica de Enrique IV' del Dr. Galíndez de Carvajal*, ed. Juan Torres Fontes, 477–79. Murcia: Consejo Superior de Investigaciones Científicas, 1946.

Epstein, Steven A. *An Economic and Social History of Later Medieval Europe, 1000–1500.* New York: Cambridge University Press, 2009.

Gálvez, María Ángeles and Antonio Ibarra. "Comercio local y circulación regional de importaciones: la feria de San Juan de los Lagos en la Nueva España." *Historia Mexicana*, 46.3 (1997): 581–616.

Gerhardt, Elizabeth L. "See How They Love One Another: A Short History of Medieval and Reformation Poor Relief." In *Orthodoxy and Orthopraxis*, ed. D. R. Cullum, 209–25. Eugene: Pickwick Publications, 2020.

Hengstmengel, Joost. *Divine Providence in Early Modern Economic Thought.* London: Routledge, 2019.

Hillgarth, Jocelyn N. *The Spanish Kingdoms 1250–1516*, vol. II. Oxford: Oxford University Press, 1978.

Holy Bible, New Catholic Edition. New York: Catholic Publishing Co., 1964.

Jenkins, John H. *Audubon, and Other Capers: Confessions of a Texas Bookmaker.* Austin: Pemberton Press, 1976.

Knight, Allan. *Mexico, the Colonial Era.* Cambridge: Cambridge University Press, 2002.

Ladero Quesada, Miguel-Ángel. *Las ferias de Castilla: Siglos XII a XV.* Madrid: Imprenta Taravilla, 1994.

Le Goff, Jacques. *The Medieval Imagination*, Trans. A. Golfhammer. Chicago: University of Chicago Press, 1992.

Martín, José Luis. *Enrique IV de Castilla: rey de Navarra, príncipe de Cataluña.* Hondarribia: Nerea, 2003.

Menocal, María Rosa. *The Ornament of the World: How Muslims, Jews, and Christians Created a Culture of Tolerance in Medieval Spain.* New York: Little, Brown & Co., 2002.

Metzger, Bruce M. *The New Testament: Its Background, Growth, and Content.* 3rd ed. Nashville: University of Tennessee, Abingdon Press, 2003.

O'Callaghan, Joseph F. *The Last Crusade in the West: Castile and the Conquest of Granada.* Philadelphia: Univ. of Pennsylvania Press, 2014.

Ortiz de Zúñiga, Diego. *Anales eclesiásticos y seculares de la muy noble y muy leal Ciudad de Sevilla*, vol. III. Madrid: Imprenta Real, 1796.

Perelman, Les. "The Medieval Art of Letter Writing: Rhetoric as Institutional Expression." In *Textual Dynamics of the Professions: Historical and Contemporary Studies of Writing in Professional Communities*, ed. C. Bazerman. Madison: University of Wisconsin Press, 1991:97-119.

Phillips, William D. *Enrique IV and the Crisis of Fifteenth-Century Castile*. Cambridge: Medieval Academy of America, 1978.

Phipps, E. *Cochineal Red: The Art History of a Color*. New Haven: Yale University Press, 2010.

Ponce de León, Rodrigo. "Cédula de seguro dada a las personas que asistieran a la feria que desde el 15 de marzo al 15 de abril que se celebraba en Paradas." Marchena, March 10, 1485. Sección Nobleza, Archivo Histórico Nacional, OSUNA, C.140, D.177.

Powers, James F. "Towns on the Edge: Twelfth-Century Municipal War Policy in Leon-Castile and France." In *The Emergence of Leon-Castile c. 1065–1500*, ed. J. J. Todesca, 33–45. Dorchester: Dorset Press, 2015.

Richardson, Malcolm. "The *Ars dictaminis,* the Formulary, and Medieval Epistolary Practice." In *Letter-Writing Manuals and Instruction, from Antiquity to the Present*, eds. C. Poster and L. Mitchell, 52–66. Columbia: University of South Carolina Press, 2007.

Teja, Jesús F. "St. James at the Fair: Religious Ceremony, Civic Boosterism, and Commercial Development on the Colonial Mexican Frontier." *The Americas*, 57 (2001): 395–416.

Valls i Subirá, Oriol. *The History of Paper in Spain: XVII–XIX Centuries*, vol. III, Trans. S. Nicholson. Madrid: Empresa Nacional de Celulosas, 1982, 145. See also the appendix, p. 230, for the watermark design.

Verlinden, Charles. "Markets and Fairs." In *Economic Organization and Policies in the Middle Ages*, eds. M. Postan and E. Rich, 120. Cambridge: Cambridge University Press, 1965.

Willingham, Elizabeth M. *The Mythical Indies and Columbus's Apocalyptic Letter: Imagining America in the Late Middle Ages*. Chicago: Sussex Academic Press, 2016.

4

MATERIAL AND PROVIDENTIAL ECONOMIES IN MONTAIGNE'S *ESSAIS*

Sara Aponte-Olivieri

Economic matters are not removed from spiritual concerns in the early modern world, in which Michel de Montaigne's (1533–1592) *Essais* emerged.[1] From the economic imagery in the Gospels to the implementation of the tithe, material wealth has had sacred usages and meanings within Christian theology and institutions. Encompassing both prevision and provision, the notion of Divine Providence, for example, was pivotal in the economic thought of the time. In the words of Joost Hengstmengel, "the finger of God was observed in international trade ..., the social division of labour ..., the formation of value and prices ..., the interplay of self-interested individuals in society," as well as "poverty and inequality."[2]

The rich semantic history of the term *economy* condenses this adjacency between the spiritual and the material.[3] In Xenophon and Aristotle, *oikonomia* initially designated the arts of managing the household—a meaning maintained in the Middle French *yconomie*—and of administering the city.[4] From indicating the governance of the *oikos* and the *polis*, the term takes on a spiritual sense in Christian theology. In Paul's *Epistles* and patristic thought, *oikonomia* becomes equated with divine incarnation and revelation, as well as, by extension, the visible fulfillment of a providential and redemptive plan for humankind. The latter, in turn, is upheld as a model of temporal administration, to be imitated and actualized by those considered to be the earthly representatives and ecclesial instruments of this divine economy. The concept of *oikonomia* will equally encompass all endeavors to conciliate temporal power and prudential agency with spiritual principles and aims. More precisely, in Marie-José Mondzain's terms, this "divine economy" becomes the "natural model of all exchanges and consumptions."[5] The concept of *dispensatio*, one of the Latin translations of *oikonomia*, expresses the divine expenditure and deployment of a plan into the visibility of human history, thus constituting the theological basis of fiscal thought around profits and losses, as Mondzain argues.[6] Under this conceptual umbrella come

DOI: 10.4324/9781003082842-5

together nature (*phusis*) and providence (*pronoia*), as well as prudence (*phronesis*) and strategy, articulated into dispositions, arrangements, and functional orders geared toward profits and benefits, either spiritual or material.[7]

Keeping in perspective this notional *continuum* and employing close readings of selected passages, the following chapter will focus on the convergence within Montaigne's writing of different forms of human economic activity with the notions of a providential *oikonomia* ordering human affairs. Our understanding of the economic in this chapter will be wide-ranging, from domestic management and mercantile activity to imperial profit. Early modern France saw the rise of a merchant class and the ensuing replacement of feudalism by emerging capitalism. These transformations leave their mark in the *Essais*, a trace that has elicited different readings.[8] Louis van Delft, for instance, saw a form of "inner capitalism" (*capitalisme intérieur*) in Montaigne's application of economic imagery to the social and the affective.[9] Somewhat more accurately, Philippe Desan has discerned in Montaigne's writing an ambivalent stance between the values of both systems, combining an explicit disdain for the emergent merchant paradigm with an exaltation of aristocratic virtue and honor expressed at times, nonetheless, through commercial metaphors.[10] Montaigne's ambivalence becomes particularly salient when some of these economic themes intersect with representations of a celestial *Providentia* overseeing the fulfillment of transcendent plans as well as the satisfaction of concrete needs.

In spite of its skepticism surrounding providential thinking (Nicola Panichi will go as far as to speak of historical anti-providentialism), Montaigne's text does contend with the question of Divine Providence, a doctrine central to both Catholic and Protestant theology in the sixteenth century.[11] The phrase *Providence divine* explicitly appears on two occasions in the *Essais*, in chapters "Of custom, and not easily changing an accepted law" (*De la coustume et de ne changer aisément une loy receüe*, I, 23) and "That our desire is increased by difficulty" (*Que nostre desir s'accroit par la malaisance*, II, 15).[12] In I, 23, Providence is manifest through its miraculous works, departures from the ordinary that are its unique prerogative and which are out of bounds for human action.[13] The Providential and the prudential operate within strictly distinct regimes, with the mystery of incarnation being the unique object of legitimate human imitation. II, 15 depicts a *Providence divine* that permits schism and disorder within the Church, employing them for its own ends.[14] The conflict, paradoxically, serves to rekindle dormant zeal among the faithful within an economic functioning of Providence, offsetting the allowed loss (*perte*) and damage (*dommage*) against a higher gain (*gain*) and advantage (*utilité*).

Both passages are infused by the Augustinian notion of a gap between opaque and puzzling providential operations on the one hand and, on the other hand, human, prudential expectations around them.[15] The three chapters containing the passages that we will analyze revolve, to a significant extent, around economic (in the wide sense of the term) questions of self-regulation, religious usage, and imperial control. Within this general thematic orientation, and within the settings of the monastery, the shop, and the galleon, the satisfaction of material needs and the pursuit of profit unfold against a providential horizon. According to Desan, the only acceptable form of material prosperity in the *Essais* is dependent on fortune as well as the "generosity of Providence" (*bon vouloir de la Providence*), a claim that will be examined in the following paragraphs.[16]

The monastery (I, 14)

The overarching theme of the ethical *mesnagement* of a subjective economy runs through the chapter titled "That the taste of good and evil depends in large part on the opinion we have of them" (*Que le goust des biens et des maux depend en bonne partie de l'opinion que nous en avons*, I, 14), a reworking of the Stoic argument that a subject's internal disposition gives ultimate form and meaning to the external circumstances it encounters. The subject is thus identified as a kind of *oikonomos*, ultimate manager of the reality processed by their judgment and perceptions. After comparing this inner appraisal with material valuation, Montaigne concludes that "we are great economizers of our expenditure" (*nous sommes grands mesnagers de nostre mise*).[17]

Within this argument, the question of wealth administration occupies an important place and is coupled with religious references in some passages. When mentioning the expulsion of the Jews in 1492 under Isabella I of Castile and Ferdinand II of Aragon, Montaigne highlights the roles played by both monetary transactions and a high level of duplicity within the royal plan of religious unification. This example, ending in tragedy in the sea, will be echoed regarding the *conquista* in "Of coaches" (*Des coches*, III, 6).[18] Penitent practices and pecuniary gain coincide in an illustration of "contempt for pain" (*mespris de la douleur*), while the asceticism of Cardinal Borromeo, born into riches and nobility, is extolled a few paragraphs later.[19]

In this chapter, Montaigne also narrates his evolving approaches to money in three stages: prodigality, avarice, and a virtuous form of *nonchalance*.[20] His first stage of fortunate and unfettered prodigality runs counter to both his own later foresight (*providence*) and most managers' (*mesnagers*) calculations.[21] In contrast to a majority of managers' *oikonomia*, this first stage also appears equally aligned with a higher and wider-scale functioning represented by both the stars (*astres*) and a majority of people. These two last elements foreshadow the reference to Divine Providence that appears a few lines later: "In our present great drought of devotion, we have thousands and thousands of congregations which spend life comfortably, expecting every day from the liberality of heaven what they need for dinner."[22] Heavenly generosity provides material sustenance and ease of existence to a multitude of religious communities, institutions characterized in this passage by constant faith. In this passage, the divine provision bestowed on these communities could be read as an example of *providentia specialissima* addressed to a particular group given the prevailing lack of devotion of the age.[23]

This theological example underpins an ethical argument for generosity in which prodigality is described with indulgence, an aspect reminiscent of the parable of the prodigal son. This indulgent view of prodigality stands in contrast to the censure applied to its opposite vice, the deadly sin of avarice, which characterizes the second stage of the narrated ethical progression, also emblematic of capital accumulation.[24] Although presented as a flaw, Montaigne's youthful prodigality, closer to the manner of the *gentilhomme* or nobleman, is integrated into an equilibrium of loans and repayments sealed by the social bond of friendship.[25] Within this functioning, the young man's prodigality is articulated with the ambiguous virtue of "a thrifty and somewhat deceptive loyalty" (*loyauté mesnagere et aucunement piperesse*) consisting of conspicuous efforts at repayment eliciting further indulgence from his benefactors.[26] The adjective *mesnagere* here suggests the establishment of a sufficiently functional exchange of benevolent gestures between both parties engendered by the recipient's signs of loyalty. We can sense a parallel between this first period, with its themes of reciprocity, loyalty, and reliance on the stars, and the faithfulness ascribed to the congregations. A similar theological parallel can also be drawn with the third and last period of this moral evolution, in which yet another providential example, the case of the "old prelate," is evoked.[27] There is once again an analogy between Montaigne's disposition toward wealth and the prelate's generosity and confidence (*fiance*), which are in turn also favored by God. The term *fiance*, spanning the meanings of trust, guarantee, certainty, good faith, and faithfulness, is key in this passage.[28]

By its inclusion within an account of evolving ways of managing material wealth, the example of divine provision toward the religious communities implicitly reinforces the more indulgent standpoint identified in the description of Montaigne's first period. The prelate's example, bearing some analogies to Borromeo's, realizes a similar function within the description of the third and final period. With miraculous undertones, a perfect arrangement of his revenue unfolds out of his sight and beyond his handling, while he maintains his focus on spiritual matters. A form of divine provision and *mesnagement* appears to order the prelate's material conditions, seemingly in response to his faith. Around the notions of regulation, balance, and pleasure, this providential illustration echoes and magnifies the harmonious arrangement of wealth and of inner disposition that Montaigne attributes to himself at the end of his progression.

In a chapter that upholds the soul's dominance over fortune, these two representations of extraordinary providential favor place the narrator's own assays in material and subjective *mesnagement* within a transcendent *oikonomia* that subsumes them—alongside all human economic and prudential striving—while also sanctioning and heightening them on a rhetorical level.[29]

The shop (I, 56)

"Of prayers" (*Des prieres*, I, 56) opens with a distinction between two orders. Montaigne introduces his musings on prayer as mere "formless and unresolved notions" (*fantaisies informes et irresolues*), to be distinguished from the judgment (*jugement*) of Church authorities.[30] Individual and idiosyncratic considerations are placed in a realm with its own codes, beneath, and apart from the order of ecclesiastical guidance. After declaring his submission to the "holy teachings of the Church Catholic, Apostolic and Roman" (*saintes prescriptions de l'église catholique, apostolique et romaine*), he tackles the chapter's stated topic, that of prayer, through a providential perspective:

> I may be mistaken but, seeing that we have been granted by special grace and favour a set form of prayer prescribed and dictated to us, word by word, by God's own mouth, it has always seemed to me that we should use it more commonly.[31]

The *Pater noster* (Lord's prayer) in particular is identified as part of divine revelation, and, as Montaigne describes further, prayer in general punctuates and structures key quotidian moments into a sacred cycle. After this representation of prayer in providential and structuring terms, Montaigne underscores the discrepancy between "our designs and enterprises" (*nos desseins et entreprises*) and divine justice, as well as the ascendancy of the latter's "dictates" (*raison*) over "our requests" (*nos demandes*).[32] Moreover, unrighteous prayers or those interspersed with habitual sin, like that of avarice, "as if by compensation and compromise" (*comme par compensation et composition*), summon divine punishment.[33] Within this mixing falls the "fruit and emolument" (*fruit et emolument*) of certain categories of mortally sinful economic activity.[34] A few paragraphs later, the practice of psalm-singing is framed, along similar thematic lines, within the same principle of ordered distinction and against the dissonance of a merchant backdrop:

> It is not without good reason, it seems to me, that the Church has forbidden the indiscriminate, thoughtless and indiscreet use of those venerable sacred songs which the Holy Ghost dictated through David. We must only bring God into our activities with reverence and attentiveness full of honor and respect. That Word is too holy to serve merely to exercise our lungs and to please our ears; it must be rendered by our hearts not by our tongues. It is unreasonable to permit some shop-boy to amuse himself playing about with it while his mind is on silly frivolous matters. Nor, certainly, is it right to see the Sacred Book of the holy mysteries of our faith dragged about through hall or kitchen.[35]

In these two counter-exemplary scenes within a shop and a kitchen, sacred practices, and objects regulated by Church authority collide with commercial and domestic economies, realms for which Montaigne repeatedly and vehemently conveys his distaste, thus reasserting his noble status.[36] In the first scene, the sacred verses of the *Psalms* are profaned by a hypothetical *garçon de boutique*'s singing, a reference to Protestant worship.[37] It seems relevant to begin by noting that this "shop-boy" ("shop apprentice," in Frame's translation) figure appears twice briefly in the *Essais,* functioning as a liminal figure between the sacred and the profane in this passage, and between virtue and vice in the chapter "Of the inconsistency of our actions" (*De l'inconstance de nos actions*, II, 1).[38]

The shop-boy's scene has a number of overlapping terms and images with the introductory paragraph regarding the Lord's prayer. These overlaps create a series of symmetrical contrasts, which highlight the overarching logic of separation and distinction structuring this rigorist chapter.[39] Firstly, corporeal imagery links both passages. The prayer's words are transmitted through God's mouth, a biblical image that also underscores the incarnational dimension of divine *oikonomia* in Christian theology. In contrast, the Psalm's verses are defiled through the *garçon*'s lungs and tongue while pleasing "our ears."

Secondly, both the prayer and the psalm verses have been providentially dictated (*dictée* appears in both passages), given—especially in the case of the former—by "special grace and favour" (in Frame's translation, "a particular favor of divine goodness"; *une faveur particuliere de la bonté divine*). As the objects of a providential revelation and of a religiously ordered *usage*, a term also figuring in both passages, they are embedded in a sacred *oikonomia.* The usages, however, of the prayer given by Jesus and of the songs inspired by the Holy Spirit to David are defined differently within this economy. While the prayer's usage is prescribed (*prescripte*) to all (*nous*) and ought to, according to Montaigne, be more ordinary (*ordinaire*), the songs were given to David, and their inappropriate usage is proscribed (*defend*) by the Church.[40]

As Alain Legros has pointed out, the *garçon de boutique*'s "indiscriminate, thoughtless and indiscreet" (in Frame's translation, "promiscuous, reckless, and indiscrete"; *promiscue, temeraire et indiscret*) usage of the Psalms disrupts, just like the decried rise of Protestantism in the same chapter, the distinctions between the ordinary and the extraordinary, as well as the sacred and the profane, drawn by this *oikonomia.*[41] The Latin *promiscuus* designates that which is mixed and indistinct, counter to any idea of a divine economy, while *temerarius* and *indiscretus* point to thoughtlessness, precipitation, and confusion, two terms with strong theological connotations.[42]

In addition to these forms of boundary-crossing, hubristic excess, and indistinction, the sung verses' simultaneous unfolding alongside "silly frivolous matters" in the shop-boy's mind (in Frame's translation, "vain and frivolous thoughts"; *vains et frivoles pensemens*) and their playful, informal usage goes, as the passage states, against *raison,* or reason, a term appearing three times in this passage and linked in the chapter with divine order, thus subverting the verses' providentially assigned role. The term *raison* opening the scene in the kitchen, belonging to the B addition (*Ny n'est certes raison…*), connects it to the preceding A text and further dramatizes the profanation of the verses by representing the material object in which they are inscribed, the Bible, being tossed through (the verb *tracasser* expresses agitated and fast movements) the domestic spaces of a hall and a kitchen.[43] The handling of scripture represented in these scenes in the context of the Wars of Religion (1562–1598) condenses Montaigne's Catholic anxieties over Protestantism and his aristocratic unease with commerce. These jarring juxtapositions of sacred elements against profane backgrounds epitomize the religious conflicts and economic shifts challenging the modes of devotion and production to which Montaigne adhered, albeit as a lesser member of the nobility with Protestant ties.[44]

The galleon (III, 6)

The chapter "Of coaches" (*Des coches,* III, 6) is notorious for its digressive style, leaping though various subjects. Theological and economic themes intertwine throughout this elliptic construction. One of its initial theological references paints a picture of divine provision dispensing circumstances proportional to the capacities to manage them.[45] Some pages later, prolonging this topic of distribution, the question of royal spending comes into focus, including the uses of largesse in maintaining political power and a laudatory reference to Pope Gregory XIII's architectural patronage.[46]

Further in the chapter, the subjects of a decaying world and the encounter with a new one emerge. The argument "Our world has just discovered another one" (*Nostre monde vient d'en trouver un autre*), encompassing the association "Old World vice and cruelty/New World virtue," occupies the center of the chapter, as noted by Edwin Duval.[47] This encounter is presented as a catastrophe. Contrary to the harmonious political *oikonomia* imagined under an idealized and hypothetical Greek or Roman colonization of the Amerindians, Spanish "commerce" (*mercadence*) and "trading" (*trafique*) perpetrated by "conquistadors" depicted "as monstrously cruel *avares*" produces *mechaniques victoires* contrary to both moral and social nobility.[48]

Taking his indictment into theological terrain, Montaigne underscores the indistinctness between Spanish evangelization and plunder, including a description of the captured and ransomed Atahualpa being baptized in the midst of his execution, a scene, like the shop-boy's in I, 56, also featuring the dissonant encounter of the sacred and the profane.[49] The following passage draws a stark contrast between the violence and voracity of the *conquista* with both the hollowness of its religious justification and its lack of providential aegis:

> If they had proposed to extend our faith, they would have reflected that faith is not spread by possession of territory but by possession of men, and they would have been more than satisfied with the murders brought about by the necessity of war, without adding to these an indiscriminate butchery, as of wild animals, as universal as fire and sword could make it, after purposely sparing only as many as they wanted to make into miserable slaves for the working and service of their mines: with the result that many of the leaders were punished with death by order of the kings of Castile, who were justly shocked by the horror of their conduct; and almost all were disesteemed and loathed. God deservedly allowed this great plunder to be swallowed up by the sea in transit, or by the intestine wars in which they devoured one another; and most of them were buried on the spot without any profit from victory.[50]

The Spanish conquest's focus on land and gold counters its declared objective of extending the faith and the identity of its agents as instruments of a divine *oikonomia*. While partially acquiescing to some degree of violence, this passage underscores a rupture between two economies: the economy of redemption outlined in Christian theology and the economic enterprise of imperial expansion. Christendom's drive toward concrete gains, construed by some as an instrument of a providential plan, is portrayed as beastly and savage, precisely the traits that were imputed to the massacred and enslaved peoples.[51] The examples that follow further undermine the interpretation of the conquest and colonization of the Americas as realizations of a sacred plan.

Much like the propagation of Christianity, royal punishment by the Spanish kings does not usher in divine favor. It is interesting to note how this motif of retribution obliquely reemerges in the reference to God opening the next sentence. An instance of providential *permissio* looms over shipwrecks and internecine feuds that thwart profit from the decried pillaging.[52] The adverb *meritoirement*, or in a praiseworthy way (translated by Frame as "deservedly"), accompanying it suggests fulfillment of justice, amplifying the previous reference to royal punishment and adding a punitive nuance to the calamities allowed by Providence.[53]

The images of submersion and devouring evoke primordial and fratricidal forms of chaos. The themes of providential *oikonomia* and human economic activity strongly intersect around those of order and chaos in this chapter. The establishment of a system of extraction and profit from the New World by Europeans disrupts the order of these societies that Montaigne sees as reflections of a cosmic, divinely-established order. And the divine order reflected in these shattered societies ultimately allows, in turn, some of the decried *grands pillages*" to end in fruitlessness and stagnation.

Both instances of disarray unfolding through divine permission—widespread spoliation and incidents of curtailed profit—overshadow an imperial project headed by the failing "thrifty and prudent prince" (*prince mesnager et prudent*) alluded to further in this passage, Philip II of Spain.[54] Like the *mesnagers* from I, 14, the quality of being *mesnager*, with its domestic connotations, appears under a disqualifying light. In spite of his supposed prudential attributes, the king known as *El Prudente* is unable to bring forth the foreseen prosperity, finding himself overwhelmed by contingency, including the original uncoined form of the found gold, used for the ornament of palaces and temples, as well as in service of visibility and royal kinship. The king's ineffectual prudence, untouched by divine favor, could be read as a warning against the excesses of human rationality and volition, as well as against analogizing the prudential to the providential.

The monumental exhibition of gold in the New World is also closer to the aristocratic codes of generosity and thus more analogous to the handling of wealth favored by Providence.[55] Furthermore, as Jonathan Patterson points out, "Inca and Aztec gold is venerated as a quasi-sacred text," a detail that connects this passage to the one in I, 56 regarding the Bible.[56] The circulation favored by the Europeans does not bode well. Under God's subtly punitive *permissio*, material gains and mastery over causality elude both the Spanish *mesnager*'s prudence and the retributive measures effected by his predecessors.

In conclusion, the management of subjective inclinations, the ordering of devotional practices as well as the administration of an empire, central topics of the chapters from Michel de Montaigne's *Essais* considered in this article, echo the ancient notion of *oikonomia*. Within this thematic framing, the reception or acquisition of material resources and wealth intersect with providential operations and dispositions in the analyzed passages. These human and divine spheres of action clash and align in ways that confirm some previous readings of Montaigne's economic and theological sensibilities, such as Desan's thesis regarding the morally and spiritually legitimate forms of material prosperity represented in the *Essais*. Disruptions of divine order in the form of avarice, profanation, and spoliation are linked to capital accumulation, mercantile activity, and imperial expansion. Under the guise of a *garçon de boutique* or a *conquistador*, both Protestantism and the ultra-Catholic Spanish Empire, through the displacement of sacred verses and ornamental gold out of their legitimate ambits, fall, in dissonant, grotesque, and catastrophic scenarios, outside of providential favor.

Inversely, generosity, trust, and faithfulness deployed among friends and within religious communities appear in alignment with, and under the favor of, a providential order. Like faith in divine provision and good faith toward fellow beings, papal patronage of architectonic works as well as the ornamental and monumental uses of gold by the original inhabitants of the New World, mirroring a cosmic and providential order, are presented under an equally approving perspective. In spite of his circumspection regarding providential explanations of events, especially those favorable to the factions emitting them, in these passages Montaigne alleges examples of divine order, reward, and punishment which uphold his ethical, political, and religious allegiances as a French Catholic aristocrat.

Notes

1 See Giacomo Todeschini, *Les Marchands et le Temple*, trans. Ida Giordano and Mathieu Arnoux (Paris: Albin Michel, 2017), which examines the sacred status of economic thought within medieval Christianity. See also Nathan Eubank, *Wages of Cross-Bearing and Debt of Sin: The Economy of Heaven in Matthew's Gospel* (Berlin/Boston: De Gruyter, 2013).

2 Joost Hengstmengel, *Divine Providence in Early Modern Economic Thought* (New York: Routledge, 2019), 200.

3 The following lines paraphrase Marie-José Mondzain's chapter "Oikonomia," in *Vocabulaire européen des philosophies*, ed. Barbara Cassin (Paris: Seuil, 2004), 872–6.

4 See Louis van Delft's synthesis of the uses of the term in "Montaigne et l'économie du moi," in *Les spectateurs de la vie: Généalogie du regard moraliste* (Québec: Presses de l'Université Laval, 2005), 93.

5 Mondzain, "Oikonomia," 874.

6 Mondzain, "Oikonomia," 874.

7 Mondzain, "Oikonomia," 875.

8 Jonathan Patterson provides a recent outline at the start of his chapter on Montaigne, "Montaigne's Avarice," in *Representing Avarice in Late Renaissance France* (Oxford University Press, 2015), 204–6.

9 Van Delft, "Montaigne et l'économie du moi," 111.
10 Philippe Desan, "Économie," in *Dictionnaire Montaigne*, ed. Philippe Desan (Paris: Classiques Garnier, 2018), 543–8.
11 Nicola Panichi, "Première partie. Anti-providentialisme historique," *Les liens à renouer*, trans. Jean-Pierre Fauquier (Paris: Honoré Champion, 2008), 41; Hengstmengel, *Divine Providence*, 22.
12 For a more detailed picture of the topic of Providence in the *Essais*, see Alain Legros, "Montaigne Between Fortune and Providence," in *Chance, Literature, and Culture in Early Modern France*, ed. John D. Lyons and Kathleen Wine (Farnham, England: Ashgate, 2009), 17–30. The *Essais* comprise three books and three textual layers (designated by the letters A, B, and C) corresponding to different stages of the text between 1580 and 1595. We will be referring to books in Roman numerals, followed by Arabic numerals indicating the chapter and the letter indicating the textual layer. We will be indicating the page number where the referred passage appears in the three quoted editions of the *Essais*: Donald Frame's translation, in *The Complete Works* (London: Everyman's Library, 2003), M. A. Screech's translation, in *The Complete Essays* (London: Penguin, 2003), and the Villey-Saulnier edition, *Essais* (Paris: Presses Universitaires de France, 2004).
13 Montaigne, *The Complete Works*, trans. Frame, 107 (*The Complete Essays*, trans. Screech, 137); Montaigne, *Essais*, Villey-Saulnier edn., 121.
14 Montaigne, *Essais*, Villey-Saulnier edn., 615; Montaigne, *The Complete Works*, trans. Frame, 566 (*The Complete Essays*, trans. Screech, 698).
15 See Elaine Limbrick, "Montaigne et saint Augustin," *Bibliothèque d'Humanisme et Renaissance* 34, no.1 (1972): 49–64.
16 Philippe Desan, *Les commerces de Montaigne: Le discours économique des Essais* (Paris: A.-G. Nizet, 1992), 80.
17 Montaigne, *The Complete Works*, trans. Frame, 51 (*The Complete Essays*, trans. Screech, 66); Montaigne, *Essais*, Villey-Saulnier edn., 62. On Montaigne's use of the vocabulary of *mesnagement*, see George Hoffmann, *Montaigne's Career* (Oxford: Clarendon Press, 1998) and Felicity Green, *Montaigne and the Life of Freedom* (Cambridge: Cambridge University Press, 2012).
18 Montaigne, *Essais*, Villey-Saulnier edn., 53; Montaigne, *The Complete Works*, trans. Frame, 42 (*The Complete Essays*, trans. Screech, 55–56). Regarding III, 6, see below in this chapter.
19 Montaigne, *The Complete Works*, trans. Frame, 49 (*The Complete Essays*, trans. Screech, 64); Montaigne, *Essais*, Villey-Saulnier edn., 61; Montaigne, *The Complete Works*, trans. Frame, 50 (*The Complete Essays*, trans. Screech, 65); Montaigne, *Essais*, Villey-Saulnier edn., 61–2.
20 On Montaigne's *nonchalance* see Corinne Noirot-Maguire, "Careful Carelessness: Montaigne's Curious Nonchalance," in *"Revelations of Character": Ethos, Rhetoric and Moral Philosophy in Montaigne*, ed. Corinne Noirot-Maguire and Valérie Dionne (Newcastle, England: Cambridge Scholars Publishing, 2007), 11–30. See also Green, *Montaigne and the Life of Freedom*, 141–84.
21 "*Je me remettois de la conduitte de mon besoing … la pluspart du monde vit ainsi.*" Montaigne, *Essais*, Villey-Saulnier edn., 63 B; for the English translation, see Montaigne, *The Complete Works*, trans. Frame, 52 (*The Complete Essays*, trans. Screech, 67).
22 Montaigne, *The Complete Works*, trans. Frame, 52 (*The Complete Essays*, trans. Screech, 67); "*En une si grande siccité de devotion … ce qu'il faut à leur disner.*" Montaigne, *Essais*, Villey-Saulnier edn., 63 B.
23 Hengstmengel, *Divine Providence*, 22. For a summary of the different theological classifications of providential action, see chapter 2.
24 In Luke 15: 11–32. Alain Legros has identified another echo of this parable in chapter I, 56, in a different passage from the one considered here. See "Justice divine et juges romains dans *Essais*, I, 56, 'Des prières'," *Bulletin de la Société des Amis de Montaigne* VIII, no. 21–22 (2001): 253. Desan, *Les commerces de Montaigne*, 88–9. See the rest of Desan's analysis of Montaigne's three periods. For an alternative analysis of the topic of avarice in the *Essais*, see Patterson, "Montaigne's Avarice."
25 Desan, *Les commerces de Montaigne*, 91.

26 Montaigne, *The Complete Works*, trans. Frame, 51 (*The Complete Essays*, trans. Screech, 66); Montaigne, *Essais*, Villey-Saulnier edn., 63.
27 "*Je vis du jour à la journée, et me contente d'avoir dequoy suffire aux besoings presens et ordinaires; aux extraordinaires toutes les provisions du monde n'y sçauroyent baster.*" Montaigne, *Essais*, Villey-Saulnier edn., 65 B. For the English translation, see Montaigne, *The Complete Works*, trans. Frame, 54 (*The Complete Essays*, trans. Screech, 70); "*Et loue grandement la fortune d'un vieil prelat … partant la favorise Dieu volontiers.*" Montaigne, *Essais*, Villey-Saulnier edn., 66 C. For the English translation, see Montaigne, *The Complete Works*, trans. Frame, 55 (*The Complete Essays*, trans. Screech, 70–1).
28 "Fiance," *Dictionnaire du Moyen Français (1330–1500)*, http://www.atilf.fr/dmf.
29 Hengstmengel, *Divine Providence*, 22–4.
30 Montaigne, *The Complete Works*, trans. Frame, 278 (*The Complete Essays*, trans. Screech, 355); Montaigne, *Essais*, Villey-Saulnier edn., 317–8 A.
31 Montaigne, *The Complete Essays*, trans. Screech, 355–6 (*The Complete Works*, trans. Frame, 278–9); Montaigne, *Essais*, Villey-Saulnier edn., 318 C; "*Je ne sçay si je me trompe … l'usage plus ordinaire que nous n'avons.*" Montaigne, *Essais*, Villey-Saulnier edn., 318 A.
32 Montaigne, *The Complete Works*, trans. Frame, 279 (*The Complete Essays*, trans. Screech, 356); Montaigne, *Essais*, Villey-Saulnier edn., 318 A.
33 Montaigne, *The Complete Works*, trans. Frame, 279 (*The Complete Essays*, trans. Screech, 357); Montaigne, *Essais*, Villey-Saulnier edn., 319 A.
34 Montaigne, *The Complete Works*, trans. Frame, 280 (*The Complete Essays*, trans. Screech, 357–8); Montaigne, *Essais*, Villey-Saulnier edn., 320 C.
35 Montaigne, *The Complete Essays*, trans. Screech, 358–9 (*The Complete Works*, trans. Frame, 281); "*Ce n'est pas sans grande raison … le Sainct livre des sacrez mysteres de nostre creance.*" Montaigne, *Essais*, Villey-Saulnier edn., 320–1 A–B.
36 Desan, "Économie," 545. See also Desan's biography of Montaigne, *Montaigne: A Life*, trans. Steven Rendall and Lisa Neal (Princeton: Princeton University Press, 2017).
37 A future editor of the *Essais*, the calvinist Simon Goulart, seemed particularly bothered by this passage, judging by his modifications and suppressions. See Alain Legros, "Ce qui gênait Simon Goulart dans le chapitre 'Des prieres' (Montaigne, *Essais*, I, 56)," *Bibliothèque d'Humanisme et Renaissance* 67, no. 1 (2005): 79–91.
38 Montaigne, *The Complete Works*, trans. Frame, 296 (*The Complete Essays*, trans. Screech, 380); Montaigne, *Essais*, Villey-Saulnier edn., 337 A. In this passage, interestingly, avarice produces virtue in the *garçon de boutique*. On this figure, see Patterson, "Montaigne's Avarice," 230–1.
39 See Vincent Carraud, "Avoir l'âme nette: Scepticisme et rigorisme dans 'Des prières'," in *Dieu à nostre commerce et société: Montaigne et la théologie*, ed. Philippe Desan (Geneva: Droz, 2008), 73–90.
40 Montaigne's distinction reflected the prevailing Catholic practice. See Louis Fitzgerald Benson, *John Calvin and the Psalmody of the Reformed Churches* (Grand Rapids, MI: Christian Classics Ethereal Library, 1907), 33–5.
41 Legros, "Ce qui gênait Simon Goulart," 90.
42 The religious warnings against *jugements téméraires*, or rash judgements, as well as against lack of *discretio* are commonplace.
43 See Alain Legros, "Bible," *Dictionnaire Montaigne*, 197–201. See also Marianne Meijer, "Montaigne et la Bible," *Bulletin de la Société des Amis de Montaigne* V, no. 20 (1976): 23–57.
44 See Desan's biography, *Montaigne: A Life*.
45 "*Dieu donne le froid selon la robe, et me donne les passions selon le moien que j'ay de les soustenir.*" Montaigne, *Essais*, Villey-Saulnier edn., 900 B. For the English translation, see Montaigne, *The Complete Works*, trans. Frame, 833 (*The Complete Essays*, trans. Screech, 1019).
46 Montaigne, *The Complete Works*, trans. Frame, 835–40 (*The Complete Essays*, trans. Screech, 1021–7); Montaigne, *Essais*, Villey-Saulnier edn., 902–7 B–C.
47 Montaigne, *The Complete Essays*, trans. Screech, 1029 (*The Complete Works*, trans. Frame, 842); Montaigne, *Essais*, Villey-Saulnier edn., 908 B; Edwin Duval, "Lessons of the New World: Design and Meaning in Montaigne's 'Des Cannibales' (I:31) and 'Des Coches' (III:6)," *Yale French Studies*, no. 64 (1983): 106.

48 The adjective "mechanique" refers to manual or artisanal labor, see *Dictionnaire du Moyen Français*, http://www.atilf.fr/dmf; Montaigne, *The Complete Works*, trans. Frame, 844 (*The Complete Essays*, trans. Screech, 1031); Montaigne, *Essais*, Villey-Saulnier, edn., 910 B; Patterson, "Montaigne's Avarice," 231. On these two terms, see Desan, "Économie," 545.
49 Montaigne, *The Complete Works*, trans. Frame, 845 (*The Complete Essays*, trans. Screech, 1032–3); Montaigne, *Essais*, Villey-Saulnier edn., 912 B.
50 Montaigne, *The Complete Works*, trans. Frame, 846 (*The Complete Essays*, trans. Screech, 1034); "*S'ils se fussent proposés d'estendre nostre foy ... sans aucun fruict de leur victoire,*" Montaigne, *Essais*, Villey-Saulnier edn., 913 B.
51 See Frank Lestringant, "Avarice et voyage," *Seizième Siècle*, 4, no. 4 (2008): 159–63.
52 Legros highlights the vocabulary of *permissio* in this passage, as well as in II, 15, 615 mentioned above ("Montaigne Between Fortune and Providence," 24–5). Daniel Ménager interprets this passage as an example of divine punishment through natural causes ("Montaigne et les jugements de Dieu," *Bulletin de la Société des Amis de Montaigne* VIII, no. 21–2 [2001]: 245).
53 *Dictionnaire du Moyen Français*, http://www.atilf.fr/dmf. Reinforcing this nuance, Juan Durán Luzio has drawn parallels, through the theme of divine punishment through shipwreck, between this passage and two passages in Bartolomé de las Casas' *Brevísima relación de la destrucción de las Indias* in his argument regarding a possible influence of the latter over the former ("Bartolomé de las Casas y Michel de Montaigne," *Revista Chilena de Literatura*, no. 37 [1991]: 18–9).
54 Montaigne, *The Complete Works*, trans. Frame, 846 (*The Complete Essays*, trans. Screech, 1034), Montaigne, *Essais*, Villey-Saulnier edn., 913.
55 Desan, *Les commerces de Montaigne*, 207–14.
56 Patterson, "Montaigne's Avarice," 231.

Bibliography

Cited editions of the Essais

de Montaigne, Michel. *The Complete Works*, Trans. Donald Frame. London: Everyman's Library, 2003.

de Montaigne, Michel. *The Complete Essays*, Trans. M. A. Screech. London: Penguin Books, 2003.

de Montaigne, Michel. *Essais*. Villey-Saulnier edition. Paris: Presses Universitaires de France, 2004.

Secondary Sources

Benson, Louis Fitzgerald. *John Calvin and the Psalmody of the Reformed Churches*. Grand Rapids: Christian Classics Ethereal Library, 1907.

Carraud, Vincent. "Avoir l'âme nette: Scepticisme et rigorisme dans 'Des prières'." In *Dieu à nostre commerce et société: Montaigne et la théologie*, ed. Philippe Desan, 73–90. Geneva: Droz, 2008.

Desan, Philippe. *Les commerces de Montaigne: Le discours économique des Essais*. Paris: A.-G. Nizet, 1992.

Desan, Philippe. *Montaigne: A Life*, Trans. Steven Rendall and Lisa Neal. Princeton: Princeton University Press, 2017.

Desan, Philippe. "Économie." In *Dictionnaire Montaigne*, ed. Philippe Desan, 543–8. Paris: Classiques Garnier, 2018. DOI: 10.15122/isbn.978-2-406-08314-6.p.0541.

Duval, Edwin M. "Lessons of the New World: Design and Meaning in Montaigne's 'Des Cannibales' (I:31) and 'Des Coches' (III:6)." *Yale French Studies*, 64 (1983): 95–112. DOI: 10.2307/2929953.

Eubank, Nathan. *Wages of Cross-Bearing and Debt of Sin: The Economy of Heaven in Matthew's Gospel*. Berlin: De Gruyter, 2013.

"Fiance." *Dictionnaire du Moyen Français (1330–1500).* http://www.atilf.fr/dmf.

Green, Felicity. *Montaigne and the Life of Freedom.* Cambridge: Cambridge University Press, 2012.

Hengstmengel, Joost. *Divine Providence in Early Modern Economic Thought.* New York: Routledge, 2019.

Hoffmann, George. *Montaigne's Career.* Oxford: Clarendon Press, 1998.

Legros, Alain. "Justice divine et juges romains dans *Essais*, I, 56, 'Des prières'." *Bulletin de la Société des Amis de Montaigne,* VIIIe série.21–22 (2001): 251–62.

Legros, Alain. "Ce qui gênait Simon Goulart dans le chapitre 'Des prieres' (Montaigne, *Essais*, I, 56)." *Bibliothèque d'Humanisme et Renaissance*, 67.1 (2005): 79–91.

Legros, Alain. "Bible." In *Dictionnaire Montaigne*, ed. Philippe Desan, 197–201. Paris: Classiques Garnier, 2018. DOI: 10.15122/isbn.978-2-406-08314-6.p.0167.

Lestringant, Frank. "Avarice et voyage." *Seizième Siècle*, 4.4 (2008): 149–70. www.jstor.org/stable/25598622.

Limbrick, Elaine. "Montaigne et saint Augustin." *Bibliothèque d'Humanisme et Renaissance*, 34.1 (1972): 49–64.

Luzio, Juan Durán. "Bartolomé de las Casas y Michel de Montaigne." *Revista Chilena de Literatura*, 37 (1991): 7–24. https://www.jstor.org/stable/40356603.

Meijer, Marianne. "Montaigne et la Bible." *Bulletin de la Société des Amis de Montaigne, Ve série.*20 (1976): 23–57.

Ménager, Daniel. "Montaigne et les jugements de Dieu." *Bulletin de la Société des Amis de Montaigne,*VIIIe série.21–22 (2001): 241–50.

Mondzain, Marie-José. "Oikonomia." In *Vocabulaire européen des philosophies*, ed. Barbara Cassin, 872–6. Paris: Seuil, 2004.

Noirot-Maguire, Corinne. "Careful Carelessness: Montaigne's Curious Nonchalance." In *"Revelations of Character": Ethos, Rhetoric and Moral Philosophy in Montaigne*, eds. Corinne Noirot-Maguire and Valérie Dionne, 11–30. Newcastle: Cambridge Scholars Publishing, 2007.

Panichi, Nicola. *Les liens à renouer: Scepticisme, possibilité, imagination politique chez Montaigne*, Trans. Jean-Pierre Fauquier. Paris: Honoré Champion, 2008.

Patterson, Jonathan. "Montaigne's Avarice." In *Representing Avarice in Late Renaissance France*, 201–42. Oxford: Oxford University Press, 2015.

Todeschini, Giacomo. *Les Marchands et le Temple: La société chrétienne et le cercle vertueux de la richesse du Moyen Âge à l'Époque moderne,* Trans. Ida Giordano and Mathieu Arnoux. Paris: Albin Michel, 2017.

Van Delft, Louis. "Montaigne et l'économie du moi." In *Les spectateurs de la vie: Généalogie du regard moraliste*, 93–112. Québec: Presses de l'Université Laval, 2005.

5

BARBAROUS CUSTOMES

Mughal Might and Anglican Virtue in the Journals of Thomas Roe and Edward Terry

Maya Mathur

On January 8, 1615, King James I gave in to repeated urging by the directors of the East India Company (EIC) and issued a Royal Commission appointing Sir Thomas Roe the first English ambassador to the court of the Mughal emperor, Jahangir (1605–1627).[1] The EIC's directors believed that an official Embassy would establish closer ties between the courts of James and Jahangir and allow them to expand their existing trading privileges in India. *The Embassy of Sir Thomas Roe* (1899), a collection of Roe's journal and letters, is accordingly a cornerstone for scholarship on early English attitudes toward the Mughal Empire. In 1616, Roe was joined by the chaplain, Edward Terry, whose *Voyage to the East Indies* (1654) combines observations on Roe's Embassy with commentary on the religious, social, and economic landscape he encountered in India.[2] Terry's and Roe's accounts reflect both their anxieties about dealing with representatives from the wealthy and powerful Mughal Empire and their faith that they were equal to the task at hand. As the citizens of a small island with limited trading rights in India, Terry and Roe emphasize their roles as representatives of a Christian nation and advocate for free trade to address the disparity in wealth and status between their hosts and themselves. Terry's *Voyage* and Roe's *Embassy* incorporate early modern discourses of providentialism and mercantilism in order to claim that the English deserved a greater share of the Indian market than their rivals, the Portuguese, and the Dutch.

Studies of Terry and Roe have drawn attention to their sense of alienation in the face of a foreign language, religion, and customs; their desire to attain the wealth and status of the Mughals; and their belief that their religious affiliation and capacity for peaceful trade would allow them to overcome their anxieties and realize their economic ambitions.[3] While existing studies examine Terry and Roe's diplomatic engagement with the Mughal court, this chapter focuses on the intersection of religious and economic discourse in their accounts. To

DOI: 10.4324/9781003082842-6

this end, I outline Terry and Roe's concern that the military aggression of the Portuguese Estadio da India and the Dutch Vereenige Oost-Indische Compagnie (VOC) would hinder their ability to make inroads in the Indian marketplace and obtain a formal trading contract with Mughals. In the *Voyage* and *Embassy*, Terry and Roe seek to allay these anxieties by presenting the religious and moral virtues of the EIC's representatives as their greatest asset. Their writing on the subject has affinities with defenses of the EIC by the early modern mercantilists, Edward Misselden, and Thomas Mun, who argued that, in addition to benefiting its shareholders, the EIC's ventures enriched the nation and signaled the triumph of Christianity over Islam. Similar religious and economic imperatives shape the *Embassy* and *Voyage*, which attribute the corporation's ability to outmaneuver its rivals to the moral virtue of its agents.

Terry's *Voyage* and Roe's *Embassy* were written centuries before the EIC established formal settlements in India. Nonetheless, like other early English travelers to wealthy Islamic empires, Terry and Roe express awe at the grandeur of the Mughal court and orientalist distaste for the sexual and economic profligacy of its emperor, Jahangir. In their studies of early modern travel writing, Richmond Barbour and Kate Teltscher held that English views of Jahangir as an Eastern tyrant stemmed from their anxieties over their lack of authority in the Mughal court.[4] Jyotsna Singh and Ania Loomba complicate this picture by treating early English descriptions of India as signs of an incipient colonial ideology that divided the world into a superior Christian self and inferior Indian "other." Singh writes that English travelers like Terry held no authority in the nations they visited, but nonetheless displayed a "colonizing moral imagination, mapping, and cataloguing the alien lands and people through the prism of a supposedly normative English Protestantism … [that] elides profitable and providential trade."[5] In her investigation of Roe, Loomba posits, "despite being conscious of his status as a supplicant for trading privileges in India, Roe's journal and letters… are thick with references to English and Christian superiority that we associate with a later period."[6] As Singh and Loomba demonstrate, Terry and Roe claimed that their position as virtuous Christians justifies their demand for greater concessions from the Mughal government.[7]

The religious framework that Terry and Roe use to separate Christians from non-Christians is accompanied by a political discourse in which they distinguish their position as subjects of a benevolent English monarch from that of their Indian counterparts who are forced to serve an Eastern tyrant. The historian Sanjay Subrahmanyam notes that Roe's account is rife with the "topoi of Oriental Despotism: absence of laws, arbitrary royal power and a penchant for blood-lust, absence of private property."[8] These tropes allow Roe in particular to portray the EIC's desire for a signed contract with favorable terms as an honest and rational goal while treating the Mughals' resistance to those terms as the manifestation of a corrupt political system. Rita Banerjee argues that Roe's negative treatment of the Mughal court is a strategic choice that he uses to flatter his elite English audience. She writes, "By consciously overlooking similarities and emphasizing the opposition between the Mughals and the English, Roe seeks to build a framework of contrasts within which he fixes India as the polar opposite of England."[9] Roe heightens the differences between the governments of Jahangir and James in order to elevate his status at the expense of the other European diplomats and officials at court. As Subrahmanyam and Banerjee demonstrate, Roe creates religious and political distinctions between the English and the Indians in order to establish his authority with the governors of the EIC and justify the delays in fulfilling his mission in India.

I. Religion and the Marketplace

Roe's Embassy represents one of many Anglo-Muslim alliances that were brokered under Elizabeth I. Nabil Matar writes that Elizabeth was the first European ruler to sign trade agreements with the "infidel" rulers of Turkey and Morocco, and that she did so in order to counter the threat that the Spanish, the Portuguese, and the Dutch posed to England's commercial prospects in the Mediterranean and Indian Ocean.[10] By 1600, the year the EIC was formally established as a joint-stock company, this strategy had facilitated diplomatic and commercial exchanges between England and three major Islamic empires: the Ottomans in Turkey, the Safavids in Iran, and the Mughals in India. While early modern merchants carried religious and theatrical stereotypes about the violent and bloodthirsty Turk, their anti-Christian leader, "Mahomet," and their religious text, the Alcoran, on their travels to the region, these images existed alongside recognition of the commercial prospects that trade in the Mediterranean offered.[11] These images were less prominent in the EIC's engagement in India where the Muslim ruling class practiced a syncretic version of Islam and advocated religious tolerance for the primarily Hindu population they governed.[12] Terry's and Roe's reports on the Mughal court were nonetheless shaped by their belief in the distinction between Christian and non-Christian princes and subjects.

Like the English alliances with Turkey and Morocco, Roe's Embassy to India was designed to repair past hostilities over trade, allay religious differences, and heighten economic ties between the nations.[13] His primary objective was to win the Mughals' favor so that they would grant the EIC a *farman,* or signed imperial decree, that would allow it to expand its factories in the country.[14] The EIC had already secured an unsigned *farman* in 1612 that promised them "diverse Rytes, Libertyes, and Privileges for their peacable trade and commerce with his People," a pledge that James I commanded Roe to expand on with a signed treaty that would enable the "Maintaynance and Continuance of the Amity and Course of Marchandiz betweene Us."[15] The treaty that Roe signed with the Mughals achieved some of these goals. It allowed the EIC's agents to transport goods without harassment; pay customs duties only at the ports where they landed; lease warehouses in which to store their goods; and defend themselves from attack.[16] At the same time, the treaty prevented the EIC from building fortifications and permitted only a limited number of agents to carry arms in Mughal territory. While Roe did not succeed in gaining a blanket *farman* for trade in India, he did increase the EIC's commercial prospects and bring them closer to attaining parity with the Portuguese Estado and the Dutch VOC.[17]

These corporations were part of an emerging system of global exchange that connected goods in Asia, Africa, and the Mediterranean with consumers in Europe. The Portuguese Estado had a hundred-year lead in this regard; its ships had landed on the south-west coast of India in 1499, and its agents had established an administrative state governed by a Viceroy and protected by a powerful navy by the sixteenth century.[18] The Portuguese also had close diplomatic and commercial ties with the Mughals by the time the English began setting up their first factories in India. If the Portuguese threatened English expansion on the west coast of India, the Dutch hindered their growth to the east. Created two years after the EIC, the Dutch VOC had a monopoly over the spice trade in the Moluccas, Indonesia, and Sri Lanka.[19] The Portuguese and the Dutch organizations had another advantage over the EIC: they were organized on a military footing with fortifications and factories that protected their goods when they moved into new territories.[20] The presence of these fortifications meant that the EIC, which was a commercial enterprise without a military component, lacked the means to challenge its European rivals in its first two decades of its existence. However, as Emily Erikson notes, the absence of a cumbersome bureaucracy and military allowed the EIC to build a more dynamic commercial network in the long run.[21] These distinctions allowed the EIC's agents to form autonomous social networks, shape trade policy, and adapt to local markets at a faster pace than the Estado and VOC.[22]

At the time of Roe's arrival, the EIC had established only one factory in Surat on the west coast, though it would go on to establish large settlements in Madras in 1639 and Bombay in 1661.[23] The factory served as a base for three different forms of trade in which the EIC was engaged: bilateral trade that involved exporting Asian commodities, primarily spices, indigo, and calico, to England; re-export trade that involved selling these commodities in Europe; and "country trade" that involved selling Indian goods to ports in Asia.[24] Their primary goal in the first two decades was to expand their existing factories—warehouses and trading posts where they stored goods for export—in the country. Since England's main commodity, woolen cloth, had few buyers in the Asian markets, the EIC relied on the profits generated by its role in the "country trade" in Asia and reexport trade with Europe to secure the bullion they would need to purchase goods in the Indies.[25] The EIC was wildly successful in the first two decades of its operation, returning a profit of 155 percent on voyages between 1601 and 1610 and 87 percent on those between 1613 and 1623, respectively.[26] While religion did not appear to play a major role in England's trade with Asia, the distinction between Christianity and Islam was nonetheless a recurring issue in attacks and defenses of the EIC.

In particular, the EIC's practice of exporting bullion to purchase Asian goods ignited heated criticism of its activities by mercantilist writers like Gerard

Malynes, who argued that its agents hurt English manufacturers by underselling native commodities abroad and flooding the domestic market with cheap foreign goods.[27] These attacks were especially vociferous during a period of economic depression in the 1620s and were both economic and religious in orientation. According to Gitanjali Shahani, the arguments against the EIC took on a xenophobic note that "variously presaged local unemployment, bemoaned the loss of precious English bullion, and cautioned against the infiltration of heathen goods into the Christian world."[28] The EIC was accused of endangering the health of the nation by bringing dangerous foreign goods into its environs and by carrying precious silver out of it. As Andrea Finkelstein writes, "The general perception was that the East India Company exported bullion, draining Christendom in general and England in particular of that 'sinews of war' and 'vitall spirit' of trade that was silver coin."[29] The EIC was a convenient scapegoat for England's financial woes since its representatives could be credibly accused of being unpatriotic and anti-Christian by placing private profit above the well-being of the nation. The EIC's critics appeared vindicated when a ban on the import of cotton textiles from India was instituted in 1721. While the ban might have preserved the figurative health of the nation by expelling "heathen" goods, it occurred nearly a century after its first voyage at a time when its settlements in India were well established.

The EIC's chief defenders, Edward Misselden and Thomas Mun, countered the claims that it was unpatriotic and unchristian by emphasizing its service to the nation and its religious mission. They promoted the EIC's nationalist *bona fides* by arguing that the EIC preserved the nation's store of bullion by sending only the Spanish silver it derived from its reexport trade with Europe to the Indies.[30] In *A Discourse of Trade from England unto the East Indies* (1621), Mun writes, "For if the rule be true, that when the value of our commodities exported doth overbalance the worth of all those forraigne wares which are imported and consumed in this kingdome, then the remainder of our stocke which is sent forth, must of necessity returne to us in Treasure."[31] Mun defends the EIC by claiming that it brings more bullion to England through its trade with Europe than it expends on purchasing goods abroad. Mun and Misselden also seek to silence their detractors by positing that the nation's prosperity should be measured by its balance of trade—the total cost of its exports weighed against its imports—rather than by debating the amount of bullion required to buy goods from other nations.[32] In addition, they counter Malynes' argument that the outflow of bullion was unpatriotic by outlining the ways in which the EIC's activities enriched the nation. Misselden lists these benefits in *The Circle of Commerce* (1624), stating, "It promiseth Renowne to the King, Revenue to the Crowne, treasure to the Kingdome, a purchase for the land, a prize for the sea, Ships for Navigation, Navigation for ships, Mariners for both: entertainment of the rich, employment for the poor, advantage for the adventurers, and increase of trade to all the Subjects."[33] Misselden asserts that the EIC enhanced the economy by employing agents and factors, sailors, and shipbuilders.[34] Both men responded to the criticism that the EIC depleted the nation's reserves by asserting that the wealth from their commercial ventures flowed to the king and his subjects as well as to individual shareholders.

Finally, Mun and Misselden refuted the charge that the EIC enabled "heathen" goods to infiltrate English shores by arguing that its mission facilitated the triumph of Christianity over Islam. As Joost Hengstmengel explains, early modern mercantilists believed in the doctrine of universal economy which held that "God himself had designed the world for an international exchange of goods."[35] This theological explanation underlines Misselden's and Mun's claims that the EIC's agents were fulfilling their Christian duty by facilitating global trade. In *A Discourse of Trade*, Mun adds to this image by presenting the EIC's activities as part of a providential plan to end the Ottoman Empire's monopoly over trade with Asia:

> But by the Providence of almightie God, the "discoverie" of that Navigation to the East Indies …hath not onely much decayed the great commerce, between the Indians and the Turkes in the Red Sea; and in the Persian Gulfe (to their infinite hurt and the great increase of Christian trade) but it hath also brought a further happinesse unto Christendome, in generall, and to the Realme of England in particular, for the venting of more English commodities; and for exporting of a lesse quantitie of silver out of Europe, unto the Infidels, by many thousand poundes yeerly, then hath beene accustomed in former time.[36]

Mun justifies the EIC's activities to its detractors by situating it in the context of a holy war between Christianity and Islam. It is in this context that he presents the discovery of a sea passage to Asia as the manifestation of a providential system that favors Christian merchants over Muslim ones. He asserts that the EIC's agents not only enrich the nation by trading along the new route, but also thwart the Turks, "the common enemie of Christendom," in doing so.[37] The defenders of the EIC presented its efforts as part of a providential plan that promoted Christianity, served the king, and enriched the nation. As Mun's views on battling the Turk demonstrate, the EIC's representatives could simultaneously declare vehement opposition to Islam and advocate for close commercial ties with the Ottomans, Safavids, and Mughals. Terry's and Roe's accounts express similar contradictions as they both condemn the despotism and corruption of the Mughals and call for trade concessions from them.

II. Edward Terry and divinely sanctioned commerce

Edward Terry makes a similar case for the EIC's service to the nation in *The Merchant and Mariner's Oration* (1649), a sermon that he delivered at St. Andrew's Undershaft, its parish Church, on September 6, 1649.[38] Like Mun and Misselden, Terry subscribes to the theory of a cosmopolitan universal economy in which nations engage in trade with their neighbors because "The state of the World cannot stand without buying and selling, traffique and transportation."[39] Terry counters the xenophobic attacks against the EIC's domestic trade by advocating for the movement of foreign goods to England:

> You by your Adventures can bring India, and Turky, and Egypt, nay Europe, Asia, Affrica, America, I meane all parts and places the world over, that know Commerce, in their rich and usefull Commodities home unto us. *Certainely, as your calling is honourable, so 'tis very profitable and usefull to all Kingdomes and commonwealths; a calling very lawfull while lawfully used* [italics mine].[40]

Terry presents the EIC's agents as conduits who carry tributes from other nations to enrich England, which he places at the center of a hierarchical system of exchange. He also invokes the Calvinist belief that individuals have a spiritual and a secular duty to God when he suggests that the EIC's pursuit of profit is divinely sanctioned.[41] The EIC's representatives thus display their faith and enrich the nation when they labor diligently in their chosen profession. Terry's sermon was delivered three decades after his return from India, but it demonstrates the popularity of Mun and Misselden's defense of global commerce among those connected to the EIC.

Terry adopts a similar stance in *A Voyage to East-India* (1655), where he revises and expands the notes from his travels that were first published in Samuel Purchas's *Hakluytus Posthumus or Purchas his Pilgrimes* (1625).[42] In *A Voyage*, Terry adds to the portrait of the EIC's merchants and mariners from his sermon by situating them within a humanist discourse of virtue. According to Philip Stern, advocates for the EIC adopted "a vocabulary of activity, vitality, industriousness, consular government, balance, and public good" associated with Protestant humanism in order to counter accusations that their enterprise was driven by a desire for profit.[43] Terry used the language of virtue to draw religious and moral distinctions between the English, and the Dutch, their chief rivals in the spice trade. He laments that the EIC currently holds the smallest share of the Asian market, with "free Trade for no kind of Spice, but for that, which is one of the lowest prized, namely Pepper, which they fetch from Bantim" and holds the duplicitous behavior of the Dutch responsible for its condition.[44] Terry concludes that, unlike the English whose honest behavior entitles them to greater rewards, the Dutch are unworthy of the monopolies they enjoy because they are "engrossing Hucksters" that "make very bold with God in cases that seem to give advantage unto their high *Thoughts and Commodities: for what evill cannot Ambition and Covetousnesse do*, when are backt with arbitrary and unlimited power here below."[45] Terry valorizes the EIC's commercial activities on the grounds that its agents are more faithful and honest than the Dutch. Marjorie Rubright writes that the English stationed in Indonesia made similar distinctions between their ventures, which they described as "lawful and innocent of corruption," and those of the Dutch, which they portrayed as "degenerate and strange."[46] The EIC's agents hoped that the contrast between English honesty and Dutch greed would increase their share of the spice trade by presenting them as better trading partners to the local inhabitants. Terry notes, moreover, that the English treat the Dutch as "Neighbours and Brethren" in those countries where they have monopolies, whereas the Dutch fail to return the favor "in other places, where they had the like advantage of us, they dealt with us neither like Christian, nor Men."[47] Terry attributes the Dutch's commercial success to their lack of faith and unethical business practices.

Terry finds the "heathen" inhabitants of India even less worthy of the commercial advantages they enjoy. He describes them as cowardly, indolent and idle and implies that their commercial success stems from lack of competition.[48] He elides the contribution of human labor in his description of a country that is enriched by the effortless flow of silver to its shores: "And this is the way to make any Nation of the World rich to bring and leave Silver in it and to take away Commodities. And as all Rivers run into the Sea so many Silver Streams run into this Monarchy, and there Stay."[49] He writes that cotton cloth, the chief commodity exported by the Mughals, is so highly prized that merchants "from grand Cairo in Egypt, as from many other parts of the Turks Dominions to trafique; hither they come from Prester Johns Countrey which lyes on the other side of the Arabian Gulfe" travel to the Red Sea port of Moha to purchase it.[50] Terry's description of the flow of silver into India resembles his image of the EIC's ships bringing goods to England in the *Merchant and Mariner's Oration*. The similarities between these narratives speak to his desire to replicate, even replace, the system of trade that enriches the Indians with one that benefits the English.

In *Voyage*, Terry suggests that the English should enjoy the same commercial advantages as the Indians not only because they are superior soldiers and mariners, but also because their Christian faith energizes their economic activity. In contrast, Terry writes that, Indian commerce is dependent on weak ships, unprepared soldiers, and poorly planned trade routes, which hinder its ability to compete in global markets. He describes Indian ships as "very ill built, like an overgrown Liter, broad and short, but made exceeding big, on purpose to waft passengers forward and backward" and suggests that, although they have "good Ordnance, but those Navigators know not well how to use them for their defence."[51] Terry tempers his admiration of Mughal wealth by noting that their reliance on unwieldy ships and untrained sailors makes them vulnerable to attack. In addition, he claims that these ships are poorly constructed because their primary task is religious, not commercial. He observes that the ships fulfill their commercial goals by unloading goods in the Red Sea port of Moha, but also notes that their chief purpose is to transport Muslim pilgrims "who goe on purpose to visit Mahomets sepulcher at Medina near Mecca."[52] Terry traces the fleet's voyage from the west coast of India to Mocha in Yemen and Mecca and Medina in Saudi Arabia in order to demonstrate that its religious mission is treated as more important than its economic one. Terry's views on Muslims' annual pilgrimage to holy sites in the Middle East are similar to his critique of their call to prayer, during which "They likewise rehearse the names of God and Mahomet certayne times every day upon beads, like the misse-led Papist, who seems to regard the number rather than the weight of prayers."[53] Terry aligns Muslims with Catholics in order to highlight their investment in a false faith that is dependent on empty rituals and abject signs of devotion. The Muslims' devotion to religious rituals seems to confirm Terry's assessment that their faith impedes their ability to compete in international markets. He suggests that the combination of faith and industriousness displayed by the EIC's agents is more likely to succeed in the global marketplace than the dated and unwieldy religious and economic framework on which Mughal commerce depends.

Terry creates a system of distinctions to separate the EIC's commercial prospects from that of the Dutch and the Indians in *Voyage to East-India.* He condemns the Dutch for failing to align their religious ideals with their financial honesty like the English. In a similar manner, Terry posits that Protestant virtue inspires the EIC's economic endeavors whereas the practice of Islam detracts from the commercial activity of the Indians. In *A Voyage*, Terry presents English Christianity as a positive force that is tied to virtue and that entitles its adherents to a greater share of the global marketplace.

III. Thomas Roe and the Christian art of the deal

Roe's views on the marketplace are filtered through a more material lens than Terry's as he sets out to obtain a *farman* that will allow the English to expand their factories in India. Roe also particularizes the differences between the English and the Indians, where Terry treats them as abstract and collective. This strategy allows Roe to emphasize his efforts on behalf of the EIC by portraying himself as an advocate for free and ethical trade, while condemning the Indians he negotiates with as corrupt and tyrannical. Like Terry, Roe distinguishes between his identity as a Christian subject and that of the Mughal emperor whom he treats as a dangerous Muslim "other." I read these distinctions as performative strategies that serve a dual purpose for Roe: they help him call for greater concessions from the Mughals and build his reputation as a credible broker with the EIC's directors in London. Roe also magnifies the obstacles he faces and his success in overcoming them in order to parley his modest achievements in India into a diplomatic career in Europe.

Roe arrived in India with a set of disadvantages that had the potential to derail his mission. He did not speak Persian, the language of the Mughal court; he had no prior diplomatic experience in Asia; and his agreement with the EIC stipulated that he had no authority over their agents. Roe addresses these deficits by relying on a combination of complaint, threat, and compromise to achieve his goals. He draws on the first of these strategies—complaint—to build his credit with the EIC's directors so that they favor his advice on trade over that of their factors or agents in India, who wished to imitate the Portuguese and build fortifications in Gujarat. Roe sought to counter the factors' demands, which he found the Mughals unwilling to grant, and replace them with his own views on trade. In a letter to the EIC's directors, Roe laments, "your jealousy to give me any authority of your business or favors hath disabled me to look into many things that should have redounded to your profitt."[54] Roe claims that the factors' desire for fortifications would divert funds from the pursuit of trade and compel the EIC to invest in a form of militarization that had been harmful to the Portuguese and the Dutch. Roe illustrates the benefits of peaceful commerce by stating:

> A war and trafique are incompatible. By my consent, you shall no way engage your selves but at sea, where you are like to gayne as often as to loose. It is the beggaring of the Portugall, notwithstanding his many rich residences and teritoryes, that hee keeps souldiers that spends it; yet his garrisons are meane. He never Profited by the Indyes since hee defended them. Observe this well. It hath beene also the error of the Dutch who seeke Plantation here by the sword....lett this bee received as a rule that if you will Profitt, seeke it at Sea, and in quiet trade; for without controversy it is an error to affect Garrisons and Land wars in India.[55]

Roe suggests that the Portuguese and the Dutch had exhausted their resources by building fortifications in Asia. These structures forced them to defend their territory at the expense of expanding their trade in the region. As M. G. Aune notes, the English recognized that they would be unable to achieve military parity with the Mughals or build the heavily armed fleets favored by their European rivals: "Rather, they saw a trading relationship with India as a means to increase economic power, stabilize their own economy and protect themselves from foreign threats, all goals that could be met without the colonial investment made by the Portuguese or the Spanish."[56] Roe uses these observations on trade to present himself as better advocate for the EIC's concerns than its agents because his approach distinguishes the EIC's practices from those of their European rivals. The agreement that Roe ultimately obtained was in keeping with his advice to the directors since it expanded the EIC's commercial infrastructure in India without giving the factors the fortifications they desired.

Roe adopts a similar strategy with the Indian customs officers he meets upon landing, with the caveat that he uses his cultural, not commercial, *bona fides*, to oppose their demands. The officers ask to search his goods when he arrives on shore; Roe responds with a formal complaint about their violation of diplomatic protocol, asserting:

> That I was the Ambassador of a Mightie and free prince: that I would never dishonor my Master so much whose Person I bare, as to subject myself to so much slavery: I would engage my Honor (which I esteemed as my life) that no follower of mine had the worth of a Pice of trade or Marchandice: and that in Europe and most Parts of Asia all Ambassadors and their trains were so far priviledged as not to be subject to Common and barbarous usage... for that I could not answer it with my head to loose the right and freedom due to the Ambassador of a Christian king.[57]

Roe uses a series of moral distinctions to align himself with Christianity, freedom, and honesty while presenting the Indian officials as barbaric, enslaved, and corrupt. He suggests, moreover, that his allegiance to a Christian king places him above the representatives of other nations and even gives the right to travel unmolested in non-Christian lands. When the officials insist that it was "the Custome of this Cuntrie" to search all visitors, Roe responds that he expects them to "entertain and honor me, not to enslave and entangle me with barbarous Customes."[58] Roe uses the word "barbarous" to create racial distinctions between the English and the Indians as well as to align the Indians with religious and political subjection from which he believes he is exempt.[59] Roe combines these complaints about his mistreatment with threats of violence against the officials. He accuses them of "base treachery" when they try to search his goods and states that he "laid my hand on my sword" and "called for a case of Pistolls," insisting that he "was free landed and I would die so…if any of them durst touch any belonging to me."[60] Roe draws on his ability to inflict violence on the officials when his authority as a Christian subject and his position as a diplomat fail to convince them. The threat of violence works, and the officials agree to forego the search and allow him to travel from the shore to his residence unharmed. The incident demonstrates how Roe uses the rhetoric of virtue to paint his opponents as corrupt and despotic and redraw the boundaries of their disagreement to favor his position.

Roe uses similar tactics, with less agreeable results, in his negotiation for the *farman* with Prince Khurram, the heir to the throne and governor of Gujarat, the state where the EIC's factories were located.[61] The manner in which Roe frames the encounter between them suggests that his rhetoric is both a sign of religious and cultural animus and a strategic maneuver to win better terms for the EIC. Roe presents Khurram as an implacable foe from the outset, writing of their first meeting: "I was informed he was enemy to all Christians and therefore feared some affront. He answered I should be welcome and receive the same Content I had from his father. Hee is lord of Suratt, our chef residence, and his favor important for us."[62] Roe overlooks Khurram's civil response by casting it as a disguise for anti-Christian prejudice that will derail the agreement between them. Roe shares similar concerns with his readers a year later when he expresses his fears about Khurram's succession to the throne: "wee shalbe the loosers, for hee is most earnest in his superstition, a hater of all Christians, Proud, Subtill, false, and barbarously Tyranous."[63] Roe seeks to delegitimize Khurram's views on trade before they begin negotiations by casting him as an eastern despot whose objections to a treaty stem from his misguided religious beliefs. Focusing on Khurram's hostility to the English allows Roe to depict the EIC's demands as reasonable, even virtuous, in comparison and present the treaty he signs as a major achievement.

The orientalist stereotypes that Roe invokes mask the compromises he makes to reach an agreement that will suit both parties. The distinction that Roe seeks to draw between Christian honesty and Mughal duplicity falters when Roe reveals his desire to take Khurram "in his own Nettes" by flattering him into forming an alliance with the English. Khurram reacts to Roe's advances "with scorne that his father nor hee needed nor our assistance: he ment not war with the Portugall for our sakes, neyther would ever deliver any fort to us to receive his owne at our Curtesye: if wee cam as Merchantes wee were welcome: wee had Suratt for our Port...or any other Citty was free for us to abyde, buy, and sell: in what could wee in reason demand more?"[64]

The Prince demonstrates that he is more attentive to the threat of European geopolitical rivalries than Roe gives him credit for. He makes note of the danger that naval battles between the English and the Portuguese would pose to Indian merchants and seems eager to maintain cordial relations with both nations in order to prevent such an occurrence. Roe presents his negotiations with Khurram as a Herculean struggle against a tyrannical opponent, but a closer inspection of his journal illustrates the Mughals' desire to limit English ambitions in the region. The agreement they sign is a result of careful compromise that Roe downplays in his letters to the EIC. Doing so allows him to magnify his skill at delicate trade negotiations and burnish his credentials as diplomat to his superiors in London.

Like Terry, Roe weds commercial and religious imperatives in his description of the Embassy. In a letter to the EIC, Roe lists the obstacles that Khurram poses to his Embassy—withholding money that was owed to them and appropriating gifts they wished to bestow on the Emperor—only in order to assert that he remedied these lapses by previous factors when he arrived at court. He notes: "I have this yeare passd many difficultyes by the Perversenes of Sultan Coronne, Lord of Suratt; but by Gods direction I have overcome them."[65] Roe takes a providential view of his mission by suggesting that God helps direct his activities on behalf of the EIC. Two years later, Roe takes a similar position on the divine hand in the marketplace, advising the EIC's directors, "You will find it is not many factories here that gettes you a penny. I will forecast your ease, and by godes grace, settle not only your priviledges but your Profittes."[66] Roe reiterates his previous advice on prioritizing trade over militarism, but also adds a religious element to it by presenting his efforts to increase their wealth as part of a divine plan.

The *farman* that Roe signed was the result of sustained negotiations and, while it increased the EIC's mandate to trade in India, its terms were less favorable to the English than its directors and factors desired.[67] In the three years leading to these negotiations, Roe built his social and economic credit with the EIC's directors by contrasting his religious and moral mandate on matters of trade with the advice of their factors and the corrupt practices of the Indians. Roe used these distinctions to both magnify his achievements in a system that he claimed was stacked against him and as the pathway to a diplomatic career in Europe. Roe rehearsed his credentials as a public servant in a letter to the EIC's directors that he wrote before he left India: "I desier every way to lett you know I ayme at Creditt, not at money."[68] Roe is careful to distinguish between the financial and social connotations of credit as he outlines ambitions for the future. Roe's efforts with the EIC's directors paid off as he was appointed to several diplomatic posts on leaving India.[69] He parleyed his success in securing an agreement with the Mughals into a joint appointment as ambassador and commercial agent for the Levant Company in Constantinople from 1621 to 1629; helped negotiate a truce between Sweden and Poland in 1629; and served as the chief negotiator for talks between France, Sweden, Denmark, the Netherlands, and England in 1638.[70] Roe was never enthusiastic about undertaking an Embassy to the Mughal court, nor was he at ease with the linguistic, religious, and cultural differences he encountered in India. Nonetheless, his ability to negotiate a *farman* and his advocacy for free trade shaped his career as a diplomat and had a material impact on the first two decades of EIC policy in India.

Roe's *Embassy* and Terry's *Voyage* are among the earliest English narratives about Mughal India. Their description of the emperor, Jahangir, his courtiers, and merchants are informed by popular stereotypes of the Islamic "other" that were in circulation in the early modern period. Roe and Terry draw on these tropes to create a system of religious, economic, and social distinctions between the EIC's representatives, on the one hand, and the Dutch and the Indians, their chief rivals in the local marketplace, on the other. Their accounts use the rhetoric of virtue to present the English as honest and industrious in matters of trade while treating their co-religionists, the Dutch, as duplicitous. This framework is especially acute in their portrayal of the Mughal ruler and his heir as Eastern despots and their assessment of the merchants and officers whom they govern as abject and corrupt. The moral landscape that Roe and Terry inhabit is inextricable from their religious affiliation since both men attribute the success of the EIC's mission to the Protestant faith of its employees.

The combination of religious and economic thinking on display in their writing is in keeping with the views of the EIC's earliest defenders, Edward Misselden and Thomas Mun, who suggested that its profits would benefit Christian nations by breaking the Turks' hold on global commerce and benefit Christian nations. Terry makes a similar case in the *Voyage* when he notes that their Christian faith spurs the industriousness of the EIC's agents whereas Islamic rituals and prayers hinder the trading patterns of Indian merchants. In the same vein, he suggests that local merchants did not deserve the profits they enjoyed because they were unable to harness the full potential of the nation's resources or defend their goods from external attacks. Like Terry, Roe maintained that there was a divine hand helping him navigate the obstacles that the EIC's factors and Mughal aristocrats posed to his Embassy. He addressed these obstacles by framing his negotiations for a treaty as a series of religious, political, and economic battles which he won because of God's grace and his honest and incorruptible nature. Thomas Roe and Edward Terry were early proponents of a discursive system which held that the English had a right to shape the Indian marketplace and the Mughals had a duty to facilitate their work. Their accounts rehearsed a series of religious and moral distinctions between the two nations that were firmly established by the generations that followed.

Notes

1 Sir Thomas Roe, *The Embassy of Sir Thomas Roe to the Court of the Great Mogul, 1615–1619, as Narrated in His Journal and Correspondence*, ed. William Foster (London: Bedford Press, 1926), 550. All quotes by Roe are from Foster's 1926 edition.

2 Edward Terry, *A Voyage to East-India* (London: T.W. for J. Martin and J. Allstrye, 1655).

3 Jyotsna G. Singh notes the presence of "incipient colonial ideology" that presented Christian beliefs as superior to non-Christian ones in her seminal work on early English writing on India, *Colonial Narratives/Cultural Dialogues: "Discoveries" of India in the Language of Colonialism* (New York: Routledge, 1996), 22; Gerald MacLean coins the term "imperial envy" to describe early English descriptions of the Ottoman Empire, a classification that is equally applicable to English descriptions of the Mughals, *Looking East: English Writing and the Ottoman Empire before 1800* (New York: Palgrave Macmillan, 2007), 20–21.

4 Richmond Barbour, "Sir Thomas Roe and the Embassy to India, 1615–1619," in *Before Orientalism: London's Theatre of the East, 1576–1626*, Cambridge Studies in Renaissance Literature and Culture, series no. 45 (New York: Cambridge University Press, 2003), 147; Kate Teltscher, *India Inscribed: European and British Writing on India, 1600–1800* (New York: Oxford University Press, 1995), 22. I agree with Barbour's and Teltscher arguments that Roe's orientalism functions as a compensatory gesture, but also expand on their claims by focusing on the economic implications of his writing.

5 Jyotsna G. Singh, "History or Colonial Ethnography? The Ideological Formation of Edward Terry's *A Voyage to East India* (1655 & 1665) and *The Merchants and Mariners Preservation and Thanksgiving* (1649)," in *Travel Knowledge: European "Discoveries" in the Early Modern Period*, eds. Ivo Kamps and Jyotsna G. Singh (New York: Palgrave, 2001), 200–01.

6 Ania Loomba, "Of Gifts, Ambassadors, and Copy-cats: Diplomacy, Exchange and Difference in Early Modern India," in *Emissaries in Early Modern Literature and Culture: Mediation, Transmission, Traffic, 1550–1700*, eds. Brinda Charry and Gitanjali Shahani (Burlington, VT: Ashgate, 2009), 43. On similar arguments regarding Roe's engagement with the Mughal court, see Nandini Das, "'Apes of Imitation': Imitation and Identity in Sir Thomas Roe's Embassy to India," in *A Companion to the Global Renaissance: English Literature and Culture in the Era of Expansion*, ed. Jyotsna G. Singh (Malden, MA: Wiley Blackwell, 2007), 125, and Pramod K. Nayar, "Object Protocols: The 'Materials' of Early English Encounters with India," in *The English Renaissance, Orientalism, and the Idea of Asia*, eds. Debra Johanyak and Walter S. H. Lim (New York: Palgrave Macmillan, 2010), 195.

7 Daniel Vitkus refers to this process as "discursive imperialism" in his study of the early modern Mediterranean, *Turning Turk: English Theater and the Multicultural Mediterranean, 1570–1630*, Early Modern Cultural Studies (New York: Palgrave Macmillan, 2003), 21.

8 Sanjay Subrahmanyam, "Frank Submissions: The Company and the Mughals Between Sir Thomas Roe and Sir William Norris," in *The Worlds of the East India Company*, eds. H.V. Bowen, Margarette Lincoln, and Nigel Rigby (Rochester, NY: The Boydell Press, 2002), 77. For a similar argument on orientalism as a strategy that dehumanizes the Indians, see Pramod K. Nayar, *English Writing and India, 1600–1920: Colonizing Aesthetics* (New York: Routledge, 2008), 41.

9 Rita Banerjee, "Thomas Roe and the Two Courts of Emperor Jahangir and King James," *Etudes Anglaises: Revue du Monde Anglophone* 70, no. 2 (2017): 149. Rahul Sapra makes a similar argument about the difference between Roe's representation of the Mughals in his journal and his letters to the EIC, *The Limits of Orientalism: Seventeenth-Century Representations of India* (Newark, DE: University of Delaware Press, 2011), 63.

10 Nabil Matar, "Turks and Moors in England," in *Turks, Moors, and Englishmen in the Age of Discovery* (New York: Columbia University Press, 1999), 19–20.

11 Gerald MacLean and Nabil Matar, *Britain and the Islamic World, 1558–1713* (New York: Oxford University Press, 2011), 26–28.

12 MacLean and Matar, *Britain and the Islamic World*, 9, 40.

13 The EIC's ships had been refused entry to the port of Surat and one of its captains, Sir Henry Middleton, had retaliated against Indian ships in the Red Sea in 1609–10, actions that did not endear the English to the Mughals and demonstrated the need to establish diplomatic ties with Jahangir, K. N. Chaudhuri, *The English East India Company: The Study of an Early Joint-Stock Company 1600–1640* (London: F. Cass, 1965), 42–43.
14 On the difference between the English interpretation of a *farman* as a contract and the Mughal understanding of the term as a material embodiment of the ruler, see Bernard S. Cohn, "The Command of Language and the Language of Command," in *Subaltern Studies: Writings on South Asian History and Society*, vol. IV, ed. Ranajit Guha (London: Oxford University Press, 1985), 280. On the *farman* as a sign of agency by Asian rulers, see Peter Good, "The East India Company's Farman," in Medieval and Early Modern Orients, 3 August 2020. https://memorients.com/articles/the-east-india-companys-farman
15 Roe, *Embassy*, 549–50.
16 Roe, *Embassy*, 506–8.On the limitations of the *farman*, see Barbour, *Before Orientalism*, 185, and Guido Van Meersbergen, "Dutch and English Approaches to Cross-Cultural Trade in Mughal India and the Problem of Trust, 1600–1630," in *Beyond Empires: Global, Self-Organizing, Cross-Imperial Networks, 1500–1800*, eds., Cátia A. P. Antunes and Amelia Polónia, vol. 21, *European Expansion and Indigenous Response* (Leiden, The Netherlands: Brill, 2016), 81–82.
17 Roe was the only English man to serve as ambassador to India in the seventeenth century. The next ambassador to serve in the Mughal court, Sir William Norris, arrived in India in 1699 when the company's presence was well established, Subrahmanyam, "Frank Submissions," 84–85.
18 Charles H. Parker, *Global Interactions in the Early Modern Age, 1400–1800*, Cambridge Essential Histories (New York: Cambridge University Press, 2010), 22.
19 Parker, *Global Interactions*, 23.
20 Emily Erikson, *Between Monopoly and Free Trade: The English East India Company, 1600–1757*, Princeton Analytical Sociology Series (Princeton, NJ: Princeton University Press, 2014), 12.
21 On the continuities between the first English joint-stock corporation, the Merchant Adventurers Company, and later joint-stock ventures like the Levant Company and EIC, see Robert Brenner, "The Social Basis of English Commercial Expansion, 1550–1650," in *Merchant Networks in the Early Modern World*, ed. Sanjay Subrahmanyam, (Brookfield, VT: Variorum, 1996), 376–77.
22 Erikson, *Between Monopoly and Free Trade*, 15.
23 On the EIC's early settlements in India, see Philip J. Stern, *The Company State: Corporate Sovereignty and the Early Modern Foundations of the British Empire in India* (Oxford: Oxford University Press, 2011), 19–22.
24 Chaudhuri, *The English East India Company*, 16–18.
25 Chaudhuri, *The English East India Company*, 9–10.
26 Andrea Finkelstein, *Harmony and the Balance: An Intellectual History of Seventeenth-Century English Economic Thought* (Ann Arbor, MI: University of Michigan, 2000), 63.
27 Gerard Malynes, *The Center of the Circle of Commerce* (London: VVilliam Iones, 1623), G3f–G5f.
28 Gitanjali Shahani, "'A Foreigner by Birth': The Life of Indian Cloth in the Early Modern Marketplace," in *Global Traffic: Discourses and Practices of Trade in English Literature and Culture from 1550 to 1700*, eds. Barbara Sebek and Stephen Deng, Early Modern Cultural Studies, 1500–1700 (New York: Palgrave Macmillan, 2008), 180.
29 Finkelstein, *Harmony and the Balance*, 69.
30 On Mun's views regarding free trade, see Jonathan Gil Harris, *Sick Economies: Drama, Mercantilism, and Disease in Shakespeare's England* (Philadelphia: University of Pennsylvania Press, 2004), 6–9.
31 Thomas Mun, *A Discourse of Trade, from England unto the East-Indies* (London: Nicholas Okes, 1621).
32 Finkelstein, 89, and Harris, 168–71.

33 Edward Misselden, *The Circle of Commerce* (London: Iohn Dawson, 1623), sigs. Ggv–Gg2r. For Misselden's views on the balance of trade, see sigs. Ddv–Dd2r.
34 The EIC's governors similarly claim that the EIC's activities enhance the strength, wealth, safety, treasure, and honor of the nation in East India Company, *The Petition and Remonstrance of the Governor and Company of Merchants of London, Trading to the East Indies* (London, 1628).
35 Joost Hengstmengel, *Divine Providence in Early Modern Economic Thought*, Routledge Studies in the History of Economics (New York: Routledge, 2019), 89.
36 Thomas Mun, *A Discourse of Trade*, sig. Cv. The mercantilist writer, Edward Misselden, makes a similar argument on the balance of trade in *The Circle of Commerce*, sigs. Ddv-DD2r.
37 On the theory of providential economy promoted by Mun, see Harris, *Sick Economies*, 7.
38 An unauthorized edition of Terry's notes on the voyage was acquired by Thomas Purchas and included in his travel narrative, *Hakluyts Posthumus, or Purchas His Pilgrimes* (London: William Stamsby, 1625). Terry published an expanded account of his travels in *A Voyage to East-India* (1655), which ends with a lengthy sermon comparing the religious customs of the two countries. For a discussion of the *Voyage*'s publication history, see "Edward Terry," in *Early Travels in India, 1583–1619*, ed. William Foster (London: Oxford University Press, 1921), 325 and 362.
39 Edward Terry, *The Merchants and Mariners Preservation and Thanksgiving* (London, 1649), 15.
40 Terry, *The Merchants and Mariners*, 14.
41 On the connection between spiritual and secular labor, see R. H. Tawney, *Religion and the Rise of Capitalism* (New York: Verso, 2015), 363–64.
42 Foster, *Early Travels in India*, 289–90.
43 Philip Stern, "Corporate Virtue: The Languages of Empire in Early Modern British Asia," *Renaissance Studies* 26, no. 4 (2012): 518.
44 Terry, *Voyage to East-India*, 112.
45 Terry, *Voyage to East-India*, 112.
46 Marjorie Rubright, *Doppelgänger Dilemmas: Anglo-Dutch Relations in Early Modern English Literature and Culture* (Philadelphia: University of Pennsylvania Press, 2014), 210.
47 Terry, *Voyage to East-India*, 111 and 113.
48 Terry, *Voyage to East-India*, 163 and 312–13.
49 Terry, *Voyage to East-India*, 118–19.
50 Terry, *Voyage to East-India*, 137.
51 Terry, *Voyage to East-India*, 137–8.
52 Terry, *Voyage to East-India*, 137–8.
53 Terry, *Voyage to East-India*, 317. It is worth noting that Terry's comments on Indian religion are riddled with contradictions. He comments favorably on the Mughals' tolerance for multiple religions and praises the Muslims for their devotion, while also condemning them for practicing polygamy. He likewise praises Hindus or Gentiles for their industriousness but condemns their idolatrous sects and belief in reincarnation, 307–08 and 320–25.
54 Roe, *Embassy*, 87.
55 Roe, *Embassy*, 97–98. On similar objections, see 286 and 468.
56 M. G. Aune, "Elephants, Englishmen and India: Early Modern Travel Writing and the Pre-Colonial Moment," *Early Modern Literary Studies* 11, no. 1 (May 2005), accessed March 19, 2021, https://extra.shu.ac.uk/emls/11-1/auneelep.htm.
57 Roe, *Embassy*, 47–48. For similar responses, see Roe, *Embassy*, 81–82 and 99–100.
58 Roe, *Embassy*, 48.
59 On the significance of the word "barbarous" as a marker of racial difference, see Martin Orkin and Alexa Alice Joubin, *Race* (New York: Routledge, 2019), 10–12.
60 Roe, *Embassy*, 50.

61 On stereotypes of Indian deceit in EIC and VOC writing, see Meersbergen, "Dutch and English Approaches," 71. Amrita Sen discusses the persistence of tropes of Indian corruption in descriptions of local agents who were valued by the EIC in "Searching for the Indian in the English East India Company Archives: The Case of Jadow the Broker and Early Seventeenth-Century Anglo-Mughal Trade," *Journal for Early Modern Cultural Studies* 17, no. 3 (2017): 50.
62 Roe, *Embassy*, 109.
63 Roe, *Embassy*, 283.
64 Roe, *Embassy*, 287–88. Roe makes another attempt to manipulate Khurram by offering to sell him a unicorn's horn, an offer Khurram rejects, 291.
65 Roe, *Embassy*, 346.
66 Roe, *Embassy*, 468.
67 On the factors' complaints about the *farman*'s limitations, see Meersbergen, 82.
68 Roe, *Embassy*, 478.
69 Roe, *Embassy*, lvi–lvii. Roe's preference for diplomatic posts in Europe, see Subrahmanyam, "Frank Submissions," 7.
70 Michiel Janszoon van Miereveldt, "Roe, Sir Thomas (1581–1644)," in *Oxford Dictionary of National Biography* (September 23 2004), accessed March 19, 2021, https://doi.org/10.1093/ref:odnb/23943.

Bibliography

Aune, M. G. "Elephants, Englishmen and India: Early Modern Travel Writing and the Pre-Colonial Moment." *Early Modern Literary Studies*, 11.1 (2005). https://extra.shu.ac.uk/emls/11-1/auneelep.htm

Banerjee, Rita. "Thomas Roe and the Two Courts of Emperor Jahangir and King James." *Etudes Anglaises: Revue du Monde Anglophone*, 70.2 (2017): 147–66.

Barbour, Richmond. "Sir Thomas Roe and the Embassy to India, 1615–1619." In *Before Orientalism: London's Theatre of the East, 1576–1626*, 146–93. Cambridge Studies in Renaissance Literature and Culture, series no. 45. New York: Cambridge University Press, 2003.

Brenner, Robert. "The Social Basis of English Commercial Expansion, 1550–1650." In *Merchant Networks in the Early Modern World*, ed. Sanjay Subrahmanyam, 361–84. Brookfield: Variorum, 1996.

Chaudhuri, K. N. *The English East India Company: The Study of an Early Joint-Stock Company 1600–1640*. London: F. Cass, 1965.

Cohn, Bernard S. "The Command of Language and the Language of Command." In *Subaltern Studies: Writings on South Asian History and Society*, Vol. IV, ed. Ranajit Guha, 276–329. New York: Oxford University Press, 1985.

Das, Nandini. "'Apes of Imitation': Imitation and Identity in Sir Thomas Roe's Embassy to India." In *A Companion to the Global Renaissance: English Literature and Culture in the Era of Expansion*, ed. Jyotsna G. Singh, 114–28. Malden: Wiley Blackwell, 2007.

East India Company. *The Petition and Remonstrance of the Governor and Company of Merchants of London, Trading to the East Indies*. London: Nicholas Bovrne, 1628.

Erikson, Emily. *Between Monopoly and Free Trade: The English East India Company, 1600-1757*. Princeton Analytical Sociology Series. Princeton: Princeton University Press, 2014.

Finkelstein, Andrea. *Harmony and the Balance: An Intellectual History of Seventeenth-Century English Economic Thought*. Ann Arbor: University of Michigan, 2000.

Foster, William, ed. "Edward Terry." In *Early Travels in India, 1583–1619*, 288–332. London: Oxford University Press, 1921.

Harris, Jonathan Gil. *Sick Economies: Drama, Mercantilism, and Disease in Shakespeare's England.* Philadelphia: University of Pennsylvania Press, 2004.

Hengstmengel, Joost. *Divine Providence in Early Modern Economic Thought.* Routledge Studies in the History of Economics. New York: Routledge, 2019.

Loomba, Ania. "Of Gifts, Ambassadors, and Copy-cats: Diplomacy, Exchange and Difference in Early Modern India." In *Emissaries in Early Modern Literature and Culture: Mediation, Transmission, Traffic, 1550–1700,* eds. Brinda Charry and Gitanjali Shahani, 41–77. Burlington: Ashgate, 2009.

MacLean, Gerald. *Looking East: English Writing and the Ottoman Empire Before 1800.* New York: Palgrave Macmillan, 2007.

MacLean, Gerald, and Nabil Matar. *Britain and the Islamic World, 1558–1713.* New York: Oxford University Press, 2011.

Malynes, Gerard. *The Center of the Circle of Commerce.* London: VVilliam Iones, 1623.

Matar, Nabil. "Turks and Moors in England." In *Turks, Moors, and Englishmen in the Age of Discovery*, 19–42. New York: Columbia University Press, 1999.

Misselden, Edward. *The Circle of Commerce.* London: Iohn Dawson, 1623.

Mun, Thomas. *A Discourse of Trade, from England unto the East-Indies.* London: Nicholas Okes, 1621.

Nayar, Pramod K. *English Writing and India, 1600–1920: Colonizing Aesthetics.* New York: Routledge, 2008.

Nayar, Pramod K. "Object Protocols: The 'Materials' of Early English Encounters with India." In *The English Renaissance, Orientalism, and the Idea of Asia*, eds. Debra Johanyak and Walter S. H. Lim, 185–202 New York: Palgrave Macmillan, 2010.

Orkin, Martin, and AlexaAlice Joubin. *Race.* The New Critical Idiom. New York: Routledge, 2019.

Parker, Charles H. *Global Interactions in the Early Modern Age, 1400–1800.* Cambridge Essential Histories. New York: Cambridge, 2010.

Purchas, Thomas. *Hakluyts Posthumus, or Purchas His Pilgrimes.* London: William Stamsby, 1625.

Roe, T. *The Embassy of Sir Thomas Roe to the Court of the Great Mogul, 1615-19, as Narrated in His Journal and Correspondence*, ed. William Foster. London: Bedford Press, 1926.

Rubright, Marjorie. *Doppelgänger Dilemmas: Anglo-Dutch Relations in Early Modern English Literature and Culture.* Philadelphia: University of Pennsylvania Press, 2014.

Sapra, Rahul. *The Limits of Orientalism: Seventeenth-Century Representations of India.* Newark: Delaware University Press, 2011.

Sen, Amrita. "Searching for the Indian in the English East India Company Archives: The Case of Jadow the Broker and Early Seventeenth-Century Anglo-Mughal Trade." *Journal for Early Modern Cultural Studies*, 17.3 (2017): 37–58.

Shahani, Gitanjali. "'A Foreigner by Birth': The Life of Indian Cloth in the Early Modern Marketplace." In *Global Traffic: Discourses and Practices of Trade in English Literature and Culture from 1550 to 1700*, eds. Barbara Sebek and Stephen Deng, 179–98. Early Modern Cultural Studies, 1500–1700. New York: Palgrave MacMillan, 2008.

Singh, Jyotsna G. *Colonial Narratives/Cultural Dialogues: "Discoveries" of India in the Language of Colonialism.* New York: Routledge, 1996.

Singh, Jyotsna G. "History or Colonial Ethnography? The Ideological Formation of Edward Terry's *A Voyage to East India* (1655 & 1665) and *The Merchants and Mariners Preservation and Thanksgiving* (1649)." In *Travel Knowledge: European "Discoveries" in the Early Modern Period*, eds. Ivo Kamps and Jyotsna G. Singh, 197–207. New York: Palgrave, 2001.

Stern, Philip. "Corporate Virtue: The Languages of Empire in Early Modern British Asia." *Renaissance Studies*, 26.4 (2012): 510–30.

Stern, Philip J. *The Company State: Corporate Sovereignty and the Early Modern Foundations of the British Empire in India*. Oxford: Oxford University Press, 2011.

Subrahmanyam, Sanjay. "Frank Submissions: The Company and the Mughals Between Sir Thomas Roe and Sir William Norris." In *The Worlds of the East India Company*, eds. H.V. Bowen, Margarette Lincoln, and Nigel Rigby, 69–97. Rochester: The Boydell Press, 2002.

Tawney, R. H. *Religion and the Rise of Capitalism*. New York: Verso, 2015.

Teltscher, Kate. *India Inscribed: European and British Writing on India, 1600–1800*. New York: Oxford University Press, 1995.

Terry, Edward. *The Merchants and Mariners Preservation and Thanksgiving*. London: John Downame, 1649.

Terry, Edward. *A Voyage to East-India*. London: T. W., 1655.

van Meersbergen, Guido. "Dutch and English Approaches to Cross-Cultural Trade in Mughal India and the Problem of Trust, 1600–1630." In *Beyond Empires: Global, Self-Organizing, Cross-Imperial Networks, 1500–1800*, eds. Cátia A. P. Antunes and Amelia Polónia, 69–87. Vol. 21 *of European Expansion and Indigenous Response*. Leiden: Brill, 2016.

van Miereveldt, Michiel Janszoon. "Roe, Sir Thomas (1581-1644)." In *Oxford Dictionary of National Biography*. 2004. DOI: 10.1093/ref:odnb/23943.

Vitkus, Daniel. *Turning Turk: English Theater and the Multicultural Mediterranean, 1570–1630. Early Modern Cultural Studies*. New York: Palgrave Macmillan, 2003.

6

MOVING IMAGES

Marketing the sacred in viceregal rural Peru

Sara González Castrejón

Introduction

Recently the parish priest of San Miguel Arcángel de Cayma in Arequipa (Peru) reversed the position of the two sculptures—Saint Dominic and Saint Francis—that adorn the main altarpiece together with Our Lady of Candlemas and patron Saint Michael. Saint Francis ended up on the left-hand side and Saint Dominic on the right-hand side. Aesthetically speaking, the effect is pleasing, as both effigies, with their prominent religious emblems (cross and skull/cross and church model), are looking away from each other, which makes them more visible and dynamic; but from the historical point of view, this would be an iconographic aberration. Or not? Under some sort of longstanding tacit agreement, Saint Dominic would sit on the left and Saint Francis on the right. Who decided on that? It is difficult to know, but position and color conventions prevail in Catholic religious iconography to denote social and political hierarchy and religious status… until they do not. This essay will investigate rearrangements and substitutions of sacred images in colonial churches of rural Peru and their making, remaking, change, exchange, placement, and displacement, which will give an insight into the dynamic realities of marginalized indigenous communities which aspired to be heard, seen, and acknowledged as politically mature and (synonymously) as generators, not only recipients, of evangelization. We will use some case studies, such as the above mentioned Our Lady of Candlemas of Cayma, who was subject to a fashionable body update in 1826 and underwent several display changes in the church's main altarpiece as the new Peruvian Republic was blackmailing older priests as potential royalists. We will also look at Our Lady of Copacabana in Santiago de Andajes, Santo Tomás de Cochamarca (Oyón Province), and San Juan Bautista de Tulpay (Huaura Province), a devotion exploited by native leaders for personal promotion in a hostile colonial environment which excluded

DOI: 10.4324/9781003082842-7

them from "far-reaching" decisions and the 1821 refurbishment of San Pedro de Naván (also in Oyón), a temple which was re-decorated to accommodate republican symbology when the village's prominent place as a traditional indigenous Eucharistic sanctuary was uncertain under the new political regime. These cases seem miscellaneous, but they have in common the fact that cult objects are at the forefront of ideological disputes and at the core of promising political careers. Such objects can be traded off or invested in, for the purposes of individual and community advancement.

This will allow us to explore the role their materiality and "character" plays in the construction of Christian local identities. By "character" we refer to the fact that each one of these representations is ascribed a personality, with the ensuing whims, predilections, desires, and even rages and vengeance, which manifest approval or disapproval of the cause to which they are attached. Catholic religious images, despite their magical aura, are, and always have been, far from untouchable, at least in the physical sense. In the case of Peru, since the arrival of Christianity in the sixteenth century and up to today, they can be lent, borrowed, gifted, ostracized, body-modified, promoted, neglected, and displaced. The faithful may become attached to them only temporarily due to momentum arising from an event, big or small: beatification, canonization, or canonical coronation (with the inevitable public joyful demonstrations, the account of which would be often printed and distributed), or a local word-of-the-mouth miracle. They may also be obliterated if a more fashionable devotion is taken on by the faithful. Let us go to our case studies.

Our Lady of Candlemas of Cayma (Arequipa): the reinvention of an old Marian sanctuary

Our Lady of Candlemas of Cayma ("Candelaria" or "Purificación" in Spanish) is an image with an interesting life. Legend has it that the actual sculpture was a present from Emperor Charles I of Spain (V of Germany, 1500–1558) to the Provinces of Peru, taken to Arequipa by Dominican friars who oversaw the evangelization of the area. Early modern historian Juan Domingo de Zamácola y Jáuregui, who was curate of Cayma between 1778 and 1823, wrote that the first shrine dedicated to Her was built on a place called Lari Lari, which later became the church's cemetery.[1] The current temple is now a famous pilgrimage destination, and the statue itself is one of the oldest Marian effigies in Peru (Figure 6.1). It is medium-sized, with delicate factions. It carries a metal candle and a basket with two pigeons in its right hand and holds an effigy of Baby Jesus ("Niño Jesús") with its left arm. The reference to the candle, the basket with pigeons, and Niño Jesús alludes to the presentation of Jesus at the Temple and Mary's subsequent purification after giving birth, which was a Jewish custom. This was a favorite devotion of the Dominican friars worldwide, but particularly in the Americas. Part of its appeal was the fact that it conveniently denoted

FIGURE 6.1 Our Lady of Candlemas of Cayma (Arequipa).

Source: Photograph by Sara González Castrejón with permission of local parish priests

Mary's purity while avoiding the thorny issue of Her Immaculate Conception: that is, the fact that She had been born free from original sin, then still a pious opinion (which the Order of Saint Dominic did not support), as it only became a dogma under the Pontificate of Pius IX.

The Order of Preachers (O.P.) was the first Christian congregation to arrive and try to evangelize what is today Peru. Dominicans were the custodians of the sanctuary of Our Lady of Candlemas in the isle of Tenerife (Canary Islands,

Spain), which was a mandatory stop on the long and perilous journey to the Americas. Therefore, the cult was widespread among seafarers, who also contributed to its dissemination across the globe. Its popularity in Peruvian lands let it take root in rural areas such as Cayma, where local indigenous authorities wasted no time in adopting it as a guarantor of their Catholic maturity and protector of their political legitimacy.

We mentioned above the Arequipa spot known as Lari Lari. According to local tradition, the Cayma statue of the Virgin Mary was being transported to Cuzco when it suddenly became heavy and the carriers heard the words *ccaiman, ccaiman*, which in the local language meant something like "not beyond this point." That meant Our Lady decided to stay there, with the *caymeños*. The fact is that Cayma was a Dominican *doctrina* (curacy) subordinate to the Convent of San Pedro de La Chimba, so it is very possible that the Candlemas statue was brought there by the friars themselves; however, the local aristocracy, among them the prominent Alpaca family, who were the *curacas* or rulers, were keen on the tradition of the prodigious arrival. This, together with the many miracles ascribed to the image, boosted devotion among *indios* and eventually among all *arequipeños*.

But independent of the image's origins, the *curacas* and other prominent *caymeños* orchestrated a permanent "marketing campaign" to promote the local Candlemas cult. As mentioned earlier, according to tradition, the Cayma Marian image's first destination was Cuzco, the Inca imperial city, which had a thriving Diocese that overshadowed the Church of Arequipa. Insisting on the idea that the Virgin Mary preferred rural Cayma over flashy urban Cuzco meant that She legitimated local indigenous religiosity, especially when in 1576 the Church of Arequipa was trying to become a Diocese independent from Lima, a project that apparently met with opposition from the Archbishop of Cuzco, Don Sebastián de Lartaún.[2] One of the canvases on the lower choir at Saint Michael the Archangel's depicts precisely the *ccaiman* episode (Figure 6.2): Our Lady's effigy is proudly displayed inside Her open transport case before Her astounded *indio* carriers pronouncing the word *CAIMAN*. On the bottom left there is an inscription that states: "Estos milagros [pintó] el M[aest]ro D[o]n Jacinto Carbajal. Por mandado de Juan Domingo de Zamacola y Jauregui Cura de Caima. Año de 1780" (Those miracles [painted] Master Don Jacinto Carbajal. By request of Juan Domingo de Zamácola y Jáuregui, parish priest of Cayma. Year 1780). There is also a caption that reads: "Es tradicion asentada, ser la S[eño]ra de Caima, una de las preciosas Joyas con q[ue] el Emperador Carlos V enrriqueciò este Ymperio. Y que al pasar por este Sitio, habló por dos ocasiones a los Yndios que la conducian: Caiman, Caiman I no la pudieron mover mas" (It is an accepted tradition that Our Lady of Cayma is one of the precious jewels with which Emperor Charles V adorned this Empire, and that when she was crossing this spot, she spoke on two occasions to the Indians who carried Her: Caiman, Caiman, and they could not move her any further). The scene is set in a paradise-like environment found in many colonial Andean paintings with Marian content: fertile fields with flowers, exuberant trees, exotic birds, a cascade, and the river Chili in the background. We can see what

FIGURE 6.2 Jacinto Carbajal, *Virgen of Cayma Worshipped by Natives*, 1780. Church of San Miguel Arcángel de Cayma (Arequipa).

Source: Photograph by Sara González Castrejón with permission of local parish priests

would have been the first chapel of the Virgin Mary of Candlemas in Lari Lari: a thatched house with a cross on top of the roof. The garden theme is traditionally associated not only with Eden (cf. Gen 2:9; 2:15; Ez 31:8) or Heaven (Lc 23:42–43; 2 Cor 12:3–4; Ap 2:7, Ap 22:14, 15) but, typologically, with Mary's purity and Her Immaculate Conception. According to the magistery of the Catholic Church, because of Her Immaculate Conception, Mary is the new Paradise of God, the new Creation, and because of her glorious Assumption, She represents the new eschatological Paradise already anticipated in Her. In the Biblical-Patristic tradition, flowery Eden represents the closed orchard, "enclosed garden, sealed fountain" (Cant 4, 12b) where the betrothal of God with mankind takes place.[3] This epiphany strongly suggests that *caymeño* Amerindians are welcome into such betrothal.

Let us remark, too, that the carriers feature colorful Pre-Hispanic-like outfits and some of them wear "exotic" feather headdresses whose colors match those of the birds and flowers in the garden, generating an even more solid identification between the indigenous people of Cayma and Mary's symbolic Eden. The small cascade on the left-hand side, which runs close to one of the worshipping carriers, could allude to Cayma as a new pristine garden where man is loyal to God, unlike our forefathers Adam and Eve. We must also look at how the river Chili is represented: as a sort of canopy that shelters both Our Lady of Candlemas and her new but unconditional *indio* followers. At this point, we must remember that patristic literature adds the canal or waterway to the Marian metaphors already discussed. For example, Saint Bernard, in his *First Christmas Sermon*, explains that since the ultimate source of Christ's fountain of life spouts from the Father, Mary was chosen as a channel between the Father and the Son. In our opinion, the painting represents, in local terms, what would have been the first *caymeño* conversion in history, which is attributed to divine wish. Although this canvas was painted in 1780 on Father Zamácola's orders, it was a copy of an older, damaged one, perhaps commissioned by locals, so its iconographical program could have helped both *caymeños* and their parish priest to publicize Saint Michael the Archangel as a Christian "hot spot" in Arequipa. Originally a "commodity," albeit a very precious one, the effigy of Our Lady inadvertently started a lucrative pilgrimage business in Cayma, supported by local Catholic hierarchies who wished to break away with the Archdiocese of Lima.

Missing and migrating saints, also in Cayma (Arequipa)

As hinted above and as we will see below, Father Zamácola was obsessed with the cult of Our Lady of Candlemas of Cayma. He was determined to revive his church as a popular Marian pilgrimage center. For that, he counted on the support of the local elites and that of his close friend and mentor, Arequipa Bishop Manuel Abad Yllana, O. Praem. (1771–1780), who was a zealous devotee of the Virgin Mary. According to record, Monsignor Abad Yllana always carried a rosary in his hand, which he did not put away even while eating or sleeping. He composed a Marian *Novena* which is still prayed in Cayma.[4] The illustrious prelate died in 1780, but his always faithful pupil Zamácola kept having copies made, and he also ordered a total of eight thousand prints featuring Our Lady sitting in her chapel for public distribution.[5]

As mentioned above, San Miguel Arcángel de Cayma was a Dominican doctrine until 1778, when it was placed under ordinary jurisdiction by King Charles III of Spain. Don Juan Domingo was in fact its first secular curate upon the demise of Fray Luis Hurtado de Mendoza, O.P. Don Juan Domingo immediately undertook an ambitious refurbishment program, as the temple and its surroundings were in disrepair.[6] As renovations went on, the iconographic setting changed radically. Our Lady of Candlemas and Saint Michael the Archangel retained their prominent location within the main altarpiece. In fact, they became even more visible due to repairs and embellishments done to the structure. However, other saintly figures were not so lucky and ended up forgotten, ostracized, traded, or perhaps destroyed by neglect and/or the forces of nature.

When Father Zamácola took up his post as Cayma's parish priest on the fourteenth of October 1778, a certified inventory of the church's contents was taken. The main altarpiece featured a gilded wooden three-level structure with eight niches: the upper level hosted an image of Saint Catherine Virgin and Martyr (that means, Catherine of Alexandria) flanked by the Virgin Mary and Saint Joseph; the middle part housed an effigy of the Patron Saint Michael (in the center) with Saint Hyacinth of Poland and Saint Rose of Lima. At the bottom could be seen a second Saint Joseph and a statue of Saint Vincent Ferrer: between them stood Our Lady's recess, made from plain wood.[7] Hyacinth of Poland and Vincent Ferrer are Dominican saints; the former was canonized in 1594 and the latter in 1455. Rose of Lima, for her part, was a member of the Third Order of Saint Dominic and Catherine of Alexandria although a figure of late antiquity, she had a prominent place in the Order of Preachers' hagiography in connection with Saint Catherine of Siena.

The 1784 earthquake ruined the church and all furnishings had to be temporarily taken down. In 1788 a chapel for Our Lady of Candlemas was built, embedded in the front wall: it was octagonal, polychromed, and adorned with stained glass and curtains. Subsequently, the main altarpiece was rearranged around it and in 1797 Saint Joaquim and Saint Anne, two custom-made figures by sculptor Diego Cacerez, replaced Saint Hyacinth of Poland and Saint Rose of Lima on the middle level. Medieval saints Isidore the Laborer and Maria Torribia (Santa María de la Cabeza in Spanish), also created by Cacerez, arrived in 1800 and took the spot of the second Saint Joseph and Saint Vincent Ferrer on the bottom level. The Virgin Mary and Saint Joseph remained on the top part of the altarpiece, but their positions were reversed: Mary was displayed on the right-hand side and Joseph on the left-hand side, perhaps to keep some sort of visual harmony, female figures on the left and male figures on the right. Archangel Saint Michael proudly stood between them, his niche on top of the Virgin of Candlemas's chapel. As for Saint Catherine of Alexandria, she simply vanished, just like Saint Hyacinth of Poland or Saint Rose of Lima, who do not feature again in the *Libro de Ynbentarios y Aumentos* or any later inventories. Saint Vincent Ferrer, for his part, ended up in a not-quite-so-visible location, the side chapel of the Souls in Purgatory.

It would seem as if the transferal of San Miguel Arcángel de Cayma to Diocesan authority signaled the obliteration of all Dominican devotions. The available documents do not explain if the missing saints were destroyed in the 1784 earthquake of if they were given or traded away, but I cannot stop thinking that Father Zamácola considered them redundant and obsolete, as the Order of Preachers had no more to do with Cayma. Zamácola was a Peninsular (from the Bizkaia area) and a royalist, as demonstrated in his writings. Isidore the Laborer is the patron saint of Madrid, and Maria Torribia was reportedly his wife; he was canonized in 1619, and she was beatified in 1697 at the behest of the Spanish monarchy (she is not officially a saint yet, although she is popularly nicknamed "Santa"). They are protectors of husbandry, farming, and rural communities, and they also stand for the vocational meaning of marriage. Their presence in Cayma would have been pertinent at the time when the whole area was mostly agricultural. Patronage over saintly wedlock could have also been relevant because of the "bad habits" that Don Juan Domingo observed in his parishioners. As we can see, the time leading up to 1800 radically changed San Miguel de Cayma's iconographic program and general feel. Father Zamácola's and Monsignor Abad Yllana's efforts to promote the Marian sanctuary swapped the original ascetic, monastic-like ambiance for a more joyful atmosphere in which the Sacrament of Matrimony and the Virgin's divine filiation were celebrated. Mary of Candlemas stood solemn in her fashionable new chapel as the Mother of God, proudly displaying Niño Jesús to the people, celebrating Her own purity. Her position at the center of the altarpiece, below Saint Michael, referred to the connection between Michael's Biblical meaning, "Who like God?" (*Quis sicut Deus?*), and the Catholic motto "Who like Mary, Mother of God, conceived without original sin?"

This altarpiece was sadly demolished in 1851; mason Manuel Gómez completed the current one in 1854.[8] A photograph, apparently from 1893, shows Gómez's creation with Saint Michael in the main niche (lower body), Our Lady in the upper recess and Saint Joaquim and Saint Anne on the side pedestals.[9] The iconographic program insists on the sacred genealogy of the Virgin Mary and Her rank, above the Lieutenant of God. Saint Anne is still at Cayma, while Saint Joachim is not. Why some religious images stay while others go is unclear, especially in a seismic place like Arequipa, where temples get devastated time after time, but as we see, private initiative must not be underestimated. A curate's personal agenda could obliterate centuries-old devotions, promote "modern" cults, and revitalize classic ones. His parishioners would support his cause if they were moved by belief and the acquisition of status.

1780, two years into Father Zamácola's tenure, was an interesting time for church transformations at San Miguel Arcángel de Cayma. A brand-new image of Saint John of Nepomuk was brought in. Nepomuk was canonized in 1729, so he was a relatively new, trendy saint. According to legend, he was martyred and thrown into the river Vlatva in Prague by King Wenceslas IV of Luxemburg when he refused to break Queen Anne of Bohemia's confession secret. He quickly became a protector against flooding and drowning; he is in fact the patron saint of seafarers. Although his effigy was originally placed on the upper niche of Saint Anthony of Padua's altarpiece, Don Juan Domingo eventually sent it to the chapel of *Acequia Alta* together with a statue of Saint John the Baptist, another figure obviously related to water, in that case not with the water that destroys, but with the one that leads to the New Life. The two saints together form an attractive iconographic program: a pair of "aquatic" *Santos Juanes*, very pertinent in a location whose name in English means "High Irrigation Ditch." Apart from that, Saint John of Nepomuk is exemplary of what a good priest should be: someone who is faithful to the ministry until his death. Saint John the Baptist, for his part, becomes de facto an advocate for priesthood by baptizing Jesus. Therefore, the image replacement at the Cayma temples delivered a more coherent theological message to parishioners, as Nepomuk's deeds bear little relation with those ascribed to Saint Anthony but share a connection with the Baptist's, which spin around water and sacrality.

The following years also brought numerous changes. A statue of Saint John the Evangelist was added in 1790 to be part of the Calvary scene. Those of Saint Peter and Saint Augustin arrived in 1797 and a flamboyant effigy of Saint Anthony of Padua joined the team in 1806, when its original counterpart, small, and obviously not up to Father Zamácola's high aesthetic standards, was sent off to the newly inaugurated Church of San Fernando de Socabaya, a settlement built by Zamácola himself in 1794–1795 on orders of Bishop Pedro José Chávez de la Rosa (1786–1805). Other sculptures were given new prominent roles in individual reredos and a few "survivor outsiders" were adopted. A canvas of the Immaculate Conception was given to San Miguel Arcángel de Cayma by Archdeacon Francisco Xavier de Echeberría just after the 1784 earthquake, as its original location, San Juan's Church, was destroyed. An "ugly" (*de mal gusto*) Saint Michael figure which came in its own little display case, donated by a wealthy native man from the prairie named Don Bernardo del Pino, was promptly replaced with a better one salvaged from a cathedral refurbishment. One of the two "Saint Josephs" found by Don Juan Domingo in the main altarpiece in 1778 (we suspect the one at the bottom, as the other one was paired with an image of the Virgin Mary) was given his own place within a private chapel on a recycled display structure made with the discarded original niche of Our Lady of Candlemas. In the same year, 1806, the figure of Christ of the Descent had its body modified, almost totally rebuilt, because according to Father Zamácola, "the old one had no control of sculpture" (*...el viejo no tenía regla alguna de escultura*), and two decades later, in 1826 and under the tenancy of Zamácola's successor Don Mariano Martínez, the most poignant physical transformation of a religious image took place at Cayma: the removal of Our Lady of Candlemas's plasterboard outfit, which was attached to Her block-type body, and the reshaping of Her figure to suit the fashion of the times.[10] The result is a glamorous sculpture with an hour-glass silhouette which would rather correspond to Enlightenment European-imported styles than to viceregal iconographic tendencies. All in all, Fathers Zamácola and Martínez, in communion with the local elites, turned a neglected, rancid, and unrelatable building into one of the most modish temples and Marian sanctuaries in the whole of Arequipa. By acquiring, trading, rehousing, and "updating" saints' effigies, they achieved a modern, engaging church environment.

The insurrections against monarchic power that took place in the South of Peru in the period 1780–1814 profoundly depressed Zamácola, who registers in his parish accounts book (*Libro de cargo y data*) that in 1814, because of the political situation, he was too dispirited to accomplish anything. Don Juan Domingo was obviously referring to the insurrection of the Angulo brothers and Brigadier Mateo Pumacahua, who briefly occupied Arequipa that very year. Peninsular priests in Peru had a tough time in the period leading to emancipation and beyond, as their loyalty to the patriotic cause was questioned and they had to have their posts revalidated before the *Junta Eclesiástica de Purificación*, the Purification Church Tribunal, which would judge their adherence to the new regime. It is tempting to regard Our Lady of Candlemas's body change as a wink to and a sign of the new times. We can see how over 70 years, up-to-date devotions and their "looks" played an essential part in making a religious institution marketable and successful. The Alpaca family's, Abad Yllana's, Zamácola's and Martínez's efforts paid off, and on the eleventh of May 1947 the good old *Candelaria* statue was officially canonized by Lima's Archbishop Juan Gualberto Guevara in the presence of the President of the Republic and cheering multitudes. San Miguel Arcángel de Cayma became a national monument and it is now one of the most visited places in Arequipa.

Our Lady of Copacabana in Santiago De Andajes, Santo Tomás De Cochamarca (Oyón Province) and San Juan Bautista De Tulpay (Huaura Province), Lima region: the appeal of a fashionable urban devotion

Our Lady of Copacabana is a Candlemas advocation associated with a Marian shrine in Bolivia which hosts a sixteenth-century statue reportedly made by Francisco Tito Yupanqui, an Inca royal descendant. The place became a pilgrimage spot and replicas of the effigy were exported throughout the Peruvian Viceroyalty. In Lima, the Church of Copacabana became the most prestigious *indio* religious foundation: it started its days in the marginal district of San Lázaro, where a small chapel was erected in 1589. In 1590, when the Jesuits forcefully moved the San Lázaro natives to *Cercado* (Lima's *reducción* or Indian village), the image of Our Lady was installed in a makeshift chapel. One year later the building was vandalized, and Turibius of Mogrovejo, second Archbishop of Lima (1579–1606), organized a redress procession. As preparations were underway, the statue miraculously sweated in front of many witnesses and the illustrious prelate "adopted" it: he took it to the cathedral and founded a confraternity in its name. In 1606 the *mayordomos* (confraternity stewards) saw the opportunity to move Our Lady back to San Lázaro, where a new Copacabana temple was being built, although the solemn relocation did not take place till the twenty-eighth of December, 1633 on the anniversary of the miraculous sweat. At that point, and in order to avoid being dispossessed of the image again, the brethren approached King Charles II of Spain, who granted them patronage over the confraternity by royal charter of the twenty-eighth of January 1678.[11] This was a milestone in the struggle for Andean self-determination, which was actively led by members of the native elites: by calling themselves founders, benefactors, and patrons, they took every opportunity to contest European prejudices about "Indians" being neophytes and uncivilized.

An earthquake in 1687 destroyed the Church of Copacabana, though the image was undamaged. The temple was rebuilt with a *beaterio* (or informal convent) for the recollection and instruction of Andean noble maidens. That gave even more social prominence to Lima's ethnic aristocrats, as they could rival the religious sponsorship of wealthy Spaniards and creoles and demonstrate their status as generators, and not only recipients, of evangelization. The confraternity was re-founded on the fifteenth of March 1706, and in July 1708 its executive committee got permission from Lima's Archbishopric to appoint and dismiss the *beaterio*'s mother superior. It could almost be said that the Copacabana elite emulated the King of Spain's *Patronato Real*, the royal patronage that controlled major appointments of religious officials and the management of church revenues under terms set up in concordance with the Holy See.

This devotion was popular in the Andes north of Lima.[12] Archival records place it in villages of Huaura Province (San Pedro de Tongos, San Juan Bautista de Tulpay, Santiago de Maray, San Agustín de Puñún, San Agustín de Canín, San Juan Bautista de Moyobamba, San Miguel de Parquín, San Bartolomé de Picoy) and Oyón Province (Santo Tomás de Cochamarca, Santiago de Andajes, San Pedro de Naván, San Pablo de Acaín and San Pedro de Palpas). It could have been imported by *doctrineros* (catechists), but I suspect it was Archbishop Turibius of Mogrovejo who disseminated it, as he visited the area for the second time in 1605, after the image had acquired notoriety. In any case, local agency cannot be discarded, as *curacas* constantly travelled to Lima, where they had family and business contacts as well as religious and social engagements. Our Lady of Copacabana "walked" the other way around, from the Peruvian capital back to the mountains, and established solid bonds and social networks among the sierra inhabitants.

> It is indeed the case that the Church of Tulpay was founded to host a custom-made Copacabana statue:[13]Alonso Tarapaco and Pedro Vilcas, both natives and community leaders in the village of Tulpay in Santiago de Maray's Doctrine, Checras Province, say in our and our people's name that we own the said (Tulpay) settlement which is one league away Tongos, where we attend Mass and receive the Christian doctrine with a great effort from our part, as there is no temple in the said village of Tulpay, and the older men and women cannot attend (the services in Tongos) because

> of the big distance, their multiple impairments, and also because they have their houses and orchards in the abovementioned village of Tulpay, as it shows on the certification by Father Pedro Ruiz de Garfias, the local parish priest, attached to this petition. For these reasons, and given the fact that we own a sculpture of Our Lady of Copacabana for which we have no dedicated shrine:
>
> We ask and call upon your mercy to grant us a licence to erect a chapel in the said village of Tulpay where Mass and the (Copacabana) feast can be observed and people can pray to the sacred image on Christian teaching days, and we implore justice.

The said license arrived on the seventeenth of May 1651. The Tulpay settlement was originally consecrated to Saint John the Baptist, a traditional cult favored by the Dominican Order which also gave name to its Peruvian Province. It is interesting to see how a "fashionable," relatively recent devotion, was what moved the *curacas* to erect a brand-new temple, as if the *tulpayano* noblemen wished to mirror their peers in the prestigious Copacabana Lima confraternity. The fact that nowadays there is also a colonial effigy of the Virgin Mary of Cocharcas in the Church of Tulpay is compelling, too, as this is another Candlemas devotion associated with *indio* Christian initiative: tradition has it that a young Cocharcas man, Sebastián Quimichi, who was a descendant of *curaca* Chuquisullca, was accidentally injured and disabled during celebrations in honor of Apostle Peter, the local patron saint. Devastated and embarrassed, he emigrated to Cusco, where he first heard of the Copacabana shrine and Our Lady's healing powers. Hoping She would help his physical condition, Quimichi set off on a pilgrimage. One day, after a revealing dream, he woke up in full health, so once at the sanctuary, he decided to acquire a copy of the image to promote the devotion back in Cocharcas. With that in mind, he toured La Paz and Potosí taking donations, and eventually was able to buy a replica made by Francisco Tito Yupanqui. Now, here the story gets even more interesting, as the Prior of the Copacabana shrine confiscated the statue, accusing Quimichi of usurping religious authority. To get it back, Don Sebastián went all the way to Chuquisaca (nowadays Sucre in Bolivia) to present his case before the Bishop and the Real Audiencia (Royal High Court). He eventually succeeded and continued his journey home through Cusco, where Archbishop Antonio de la Raya had become suspicious of the *indio*'s true intentions before giving green light to his religious enterprise. Eventually the image of Cocharcas reached its destination and a famous shrine was founded. As stated above, Spaniards often dubbed Peruvian natives as defective Christians, prone to idol worshipping and in need of constant tutoring: Tulpay speaks volumes about indigenous Catholic pride, even in rural contexts. Old, Spanish-imposed saints such as John the Baptist or Peter, were unceremoniously traded for trendier Peruvian-born, indigenous-linked figures such as Our Lady of Copacabana or of Cocharcas.

The Copacabana devotion left nobody indifferent in the Lima Andes. It was synonymous with status and sometimes "practiced" in extreme ways. In 1646, the *indios* of the Andax *repartimiento* took Don Francisco de Cordova Guaras, their *curaca* and governor, to court under the accusation of "aggression and taunts", which included the fact that

> he violently extracted from the church of Cochamarca a large altarpiece of Our Lady of Copacabana, which belonged there, and forced some Indians to carry it on their shoulders to the village of Churín, where he resides, and the said altarpiece is in his home, as it has been proven, and although he admits to this, he denies that the altarpiece belongs to the church and [claims] it is his property, and [he also denies] that the Indians carried it on their shoulders, a statement which is improbable, because if the altarpiece really belonged to the governor, what was it doing in the church, and if he says he put [it there (torn)], why did he take it out in the first place, with which he appears convicted [...torn].[14]

And not satisfied with one single affront to "spiritual matters" (*las cossas espirituales*), Guaras had orchestrated another spoliation in the temple of Santiago de Andajes, where

> ... he bullied an Indian woman who was in charge of that church's warehouse or sacristy where accessories, chasubles and ornaments are kept, and out of ten *varas* of blue *damasco* or *lama* [cloth] that Father Fray Lucas de Mendoza had donated to make a mantle for Our Lady of Copacabana, he cut more than four '*varas*' and gave a paper or receipt for it to the confraternity's administrator saying that he would pay for it in two weeks, and this crime, contemplated the right way, is most serious.[15]

These documents tell us that Guaras somehow believed he owned the local Copacabana cult and therefore could trade with it for personal recognition. We are in no place to doubt his spiritual sincerity, but it is apparent that a devotion originally linked (at least in popular memory) to the Inca imperial family, which was also protected and promoted by Monsignor Mogrovejo, the saintly Archbishop of Lima, was a bonus when it came to competing for social acknowledgement with *encomenderos* and *doctrineros.* Old founding saints such as John the Baptist (Tulpay), Thomas (Cochamarca) and James (Andajes) did not possess as much charisma or appeal to stir up domestic religiosity as the flashy, urban newcomer, Our Lady of Copacabana.

San Pedro De Naván (Oyón Province), Lima region

Not many people will have heard of San Pedro de Naván, a remote village in the Lima Andes. Its church, dedicated to Saint Peter the Apostle, would be barely memorable from the outside if it were not because for painted façade, fruit of a restoration that took place in the early 2000s by the NGO Patrimonio Perú.[16] However, the interior surprises the visitor with pleasant remains of colonial murals in the form of an illusory dossel that covers the nave walls, a simulated, heavily decorated plinth, and fake textile and marble ornaments. The altarpieces, although agreeable to the eye, are very much like those in other temples of the surrounding area: standardized plaster neoclassical structures that seem to have been cast in the same workshop. However, the presbytery's vault holds a surprise: an 1821 untouched mural unlike anything one finds in Lima's rural churches (see Figure 6.3). It sharply contrasts with the traditional religious imagery painted inside other temples, based mainly on the Holy Trinity and Virgin Mary. It is linked to Our Lady, though: a big caption, held by angels, wrapped around in a red and white ribbon, containing the words:

> Magnificat anima mea Dominum: Et exultavit Spiritus meus in Deo Salvatore meo, quia respexit humillitatem ancilla suae: ecce enim ex hoc beatam me dicent omnes generationes, quia fecit mihi magna qui.
>
> My soul proclaims the greatness of the Lord, my spirit rejoices in God my Savior, for He has looked with favor on His humble servant. From this day all generations will call me blessed, the Almighty has done great things to me...

FIGURE 6.3 San Pedro de Naván (Oyón).

Source: Photograph by Sara González Castrejón with permission of local parish priests

This is the start of the *Magnificat*, the Song/Canticle of Mary, which can be found in Luke 1, 46–55. It is spoken by Mary upon the occasion of her Visitation to her cousin Elizabeth. In the narrative, after Mary greets Elizabeth, who is pregnant with John the Baptist, the latter moves within Elizabeth's womb. Elizabeth praises Mary for her faith and Mary responds with what is now known as the *Magnificat*. In Catholic theology, this prayer alludes to the fact that Mary is a compendium of the church, the New Eve: in her body the Old Testament and the New Testament meet, as the Only Begotten *Logos* encounters primeval Adam. Everything became new when the Word was incarnated to recover estranged mankind for God. Thus, *Magnificat* is a prophetic chant: Mary, in her pilgrimage throughout the mountains of Judaea, is the archetype and symbol of the future church that is still locked in her womb. At the same time, it is a joyful song: the vault murals show angels with musical instruments (bugle, bassoon, oboes, bass, *tromba marina*), accompanied by King David, who is composing the Book of Psalms and has the harp ready behind his throne. Red and white became the colors of the Peruvian flag at the time of emancipation from Spain, which was declared precisely in 1821: this could be one of the first artistic examples of the then emergent Peruvian Republic—full of optimism.

Also, if we pay attention, we will notice that the angels are all dressed in red and King David in red and white. We know that the Independentist Army passed by Naván on the eleventh of February that year and that commissioners Nicolás Chavarrea and José Cuaria Saavedra recruited eight young men. We must mention at this point that the village of Naván prided itself on the devotion to the Holy Sacrament: it was permanently displayed in the temple of San Pedro, even if it was just an annex of the local parish church, Santiago de Andajes. In 1789 the residents of Caujul, who run the vice-parish Church of San Juan Bautista, complained to the Archdiocese of Lima, and tried to dispossess Naván of the "Sacrament privilege," so mayor Josef Narciso and other prominent Naván neighbors wrote to Archbishop Juan Domingo González de la Reguera asking for permission to exhibit the Holy Wafer and hold the relevant ceremonies. They were endorsed by Doctor Bartolomé González de Orduña, the Vicar of the Ecclesiastical Province of Cajatambo. On the eleventh of March 1791 Monsignor González de la Reguera forbade the cult, remarking that San Pedro de Naván was not a parish or a vice-parish church and that there was no apparent license or even evidence that there were sufficient funds or people to support it. The congregation did not give up and appealed to the Third Chapter of Lima's Archbishopric's Synodal Constitutions, which stated that every spacious and comfortable church in the Peruvian territory should have a monstrance and an altar stone. After long-lasting negotiations, a license finally arrived on the eleventh of August 1810.[17]

It is not clear if the arrival of the Independentist Army had anything to do with the above mentioned mural or if its imagery was influenced at all by a patriotic "feel," but if it is the case, then a full religious building was marketed to suit changing political needs and perhaps also to avoid dispossession of the Holy Sacrament (Naván's main asset), or even retaliation against local clergy suspected of royalism.

Final reflections

Going back to San Miguel Arcángel de Cayma, the parish priest has just found a long-lost Saint Augustine sculpture which, according to early modern inventories, dates from 1797.[18] It was in the church warehouse and had lost its attributes (bishop's rod and model church, or book with burning heart). The Augustinian devotion was popular during the first evangelization of Peru, when the O.S.A. took care of catechizing rural populations and it is still found across the Peruvian geography. However, despite the Bishop of Hippo being a Founding Father of the church, his Cayma effigy was at some point ostracized, locked away, and forgotten about until January 2021. It is currently being restored to make it ready for display.

A bit different is Saint Anne's case: the fact that she belongs in a family, be it with Saint Joseph or with Mary and Baby Jesus (although she often parades with Saint James the Apostle in Catholic processions) makes her "widowed" in Cayma, and therefore more difficult to exhibit in context. Being only visible within the church's private premises, for now she is not spiritually marketable; her journey took her from replacing Saint Rose of Lima in the middle body of the main altarpiece at a time when religious Orders were being scrutinized by the Spanish Monarchy, to shining with Saint Joseph next to patrons Saint Michael the Archangel and Our Lady of Candlemas in a dazzling neo-classical setting, to being secluded in the little fortress which is the temple of Cayma.

Regarding the cult of Our Lady of Copacabana in the Lima Andes, what once was a bold, ubiquitous devotion that stood for *indio* piety is now basically forgotten and the Copacabana images decrepit. Confraternities, masses, and processions are long gone, and the same happened with rivalries and altercations surrounding patronage. Even in San Juan Bautista de Tulpay, founded on this Marian advocation, Saint John the Baptist—local cattle protector—and the Exaltation of the Holy Cross managed to obliterate Our Lady. Perhaps the "Copacabana" construct progressively lost its momentum as rural natives became more confident and defiant over their Christian prowess. In such contexts, newer, more fashionable devotions -especially Peruvian ones, such as the already mentioned Saint Rose of Lima, canonized in 1671—may have been a bonus for social recognition.

As for Santiago de Naván, it seems to be the irruption of General José de San Martín's army that triggered the display of novel, republican-related iconography on the presbytery's vault, just above the Holy Wafer in its monstrance, the privilege that so many decades had taken to secure. In this sense, it is possible that the local clergy sought a compromise between Navan's traditions, rooted in colonial values, and a new "enlightened" form of Catholicism which might pose a threat to anything looking "royalist." Naván's Church became a "product" which could satisfy everybody.

We are sometimes tempted to compare the complex religious panorama in Viceregal Peru with the stock market, although the "metaphor" may not be elegant. Marian and saints' devotions go up or down in value according to changing individual or communal needs or circumstances. The Virgin Mary and other holy figures were acknowledged, valued, protected, and loved, but at the same time they could be tokens for self-propaganda. What is certain is that this racking of holy images allowed sacred places to constantly reinvent themselves.

Notes

1 See, for example, AAA (Archivo Arzobispal de Arequipa), 3.1.3: Sección: Vicarías; Serie: Arequipa; Subserie: Cayma; Tipo de documento: Libro inventario: *Ynventario de la Yglesia Parroquial de San Miguel de Cayma fecho con toda prolijidad en el año de 1820 Siendo cura propio el Bachiller Don Juan Domingo de Zamácola y Jáuregui*, in Lenin Jesús Huayhua Alarcón, "La iglesia de Cayma en 1820", *Revista Archivo Arzobispal de Arequipa* 7, 2010: 217–30.

2 Antonio de Egaña, S.J., *Historia de la Iglesia en la América Española (Hemisferio Sur)* (Madrid: Biblioteca de Autores Católicos, 1966) 318.

3 See Jesús Casás Otero, *Tota Pulchra: María, esplendor de la belleza divina* (Salamanca: Secretariado Trinitario, 2015) 86–94.

4 "As the Most Illustrious Master Abad Yllana -my lord-, having arrived at this sanctuary where he spent more than one month giving Confirmations and renewing with his learned, elegant, and loving exhortations the already forgotten devotion of this Sanctuary, he undertook the task of writing a *Novena* of Our Lady of Cayma and he did, and on his orders, I gave it to the printing press. We have handed in one hundred copies to those who requested them, all for free, as I was instructed by Our Most Illustrious lord of glorious memory" ("Como el Yll[ustrísi]mo Señor Abad Yllana (mi señor) haviendo venido a este santuario en donde se mantuvo mas de un mes haciendo confirmaciones y renovando con sus doctas, elegantes, y amorosas exortaciones la devocion yà olvidada de este Santuario, puso en obra el escribir una Novena de Nuestra Señora de Cayma y en efecto la concluio, y por su orden la di a la [imp]renta, cien exemplares se han ido repartiendo a los q[u]e las han pido [*sic*] sin llevar por ellas precio alguno por havermelo asi mandado N[uest]ro Señor Yll[ustrísi]mo de gloriosa memoria."). See Juan Domingo Zamácola Jáuregui, *Libro de Ynbentarios y aumentos de la Yglesia Parroquial de San Miguel de Cayma, desde que tomò posesion de la dicha parroquia el Bachiller Don Juan Domingo de Zamacola y Jauregui que fue el dia 14 de Octubre de 1778*, unpublished manuscript, Archivo Parroquial de Cayma, ff. 15r–15v. Father Zamácola also wrote a biography of Monsignor Manuel Abad Yllana; see, among others, Rubén Vargas Ugarte, *Biblioteca peruana: Impresos peruanos (1763–1805)* (Lima: Taller Periodístico de la Empresa Tipográfica la Prensa, 1935), 358 and Antonio Unzueta, *Juan Domingo de Zamácola y Jáuregui y su obra en el Perú, s. XVIII* (Vitoria-Gasteiz: Servicio Central de Publicaciones del Gobierno Vasco, 1992).

5 Zamácola, *Libro de Ynbentarios*, f. 27r.

6 Zamácola, *Libro de Ynbentarios*, f. 12r onwards. The following pages of this section are based on the *Libro de Ynbentarios*.

7 Zamácola, *Libro de Ynbentarios*, f. 3v.

8 Ricardo Mariátegui Oliva, *El Santuario de Caima* (Lima: Empr. Graf. Stylo, 1952) in Ramón Gutiérrez, "La iglesia de Cayma. Una obra excepcional de la arquitectura Arequipeña" in *Revista del Archivo Arzobispal de Arequipa* 4 (1997) 52.

9 See Yarabaya, "Cayma," *Foto Vintage Arequipa* (blog), November 14, 2010, http://fotovintagearequipa.blogspot.com/2010/11/cayma.html.

10 Zamácola, *Libro de Ynventarios*, f. 31r.

11 For more information, see Fray Domingo Angulo, *Notas y monografías para la historia del barrio de San Lázaro de la ciudad de Lima: Origen y principios del barrio de San Lázaro* (Lima: E. R. Villarán, 1917).

12 See Sara González Castrejón, *Templos virreinales de la sierra de Oyón y Huaura: Estudio artístico e iconográfico* (Lima: USMP y Archivo del Obispado de Huacho, 2019).

13 AAL (Archivo Arzobispal de Lima), Capítulos, Santiago de Maray, VIII, 22, 8-6-1678, ff. 58r-59r: "Alonso Taparaco y Pedro Vilcas naturales y Prinçipales de el Pu[ebl]o de tulpai en la doctrina de Santiago de Maray en la Provincia de los checras en nuestro nombre y el del comun deçimos, que nosotros tenemos el asiento de el dicho Pu[ebl]o una legua del de Tongos donde con mucha incommodidad nuestra vamos a misa y a doctrina por no tener capilla en el dicho pu[ebl]o de Tulpai, y los viexos, y viexas, por su distançia no pueden yr tan lexos asi por su impedimento como Por tener sus cassas y chacras, en el dicho Pu[ebl]o de Tulpai como consta de la çertificasion que con ella presentamos de el Licençiado Pedro Ruiz de garfias cura de la dicha doctrina por lo qual y por aver echo una imagen de bulto de nuestra señora de copacavana y no tener donde collocarla: A V[uestra] m[erced] Pedimos y suplicamos se sirva de darnos liçencia para que podamos hazer una capilla en el dicho Pu[ebl]o de Tulpay donde se pueda deçir misa y celebrar la fiesta de la dicha ymagen y acudir a Reçar los dias de doctrina y pedimos justicia."

14 [...] con mano poderosa sacó de la yglecia de Cochamarca un retablo grande de nuestra S[eñor]a de Copacavana que estava en ella y le hiso llevar en ombros de los yndios al pueblo de Churín donde está su cassa y le tiene en ella como está provado y aunq[ue] confiessa este hecho niega fuesse de la ygleçia este retablo y q[ue] era proprio suio y también el que los yndios le llevasen en hombros con que del mismo descargo se conose lo inverisimil [sic] de él porque si era del d[ic]ho govern[ad]or el r[etabl]o como estava en la ygleçia y si diçe le avia pues [... roto] de que le saco con que se halla convencido [... roto]. Archivo General de Indias (AGI), Lima, 320, pages unnumbered.

15 "[...] hiso a una yndia a cuio cargo estava la despensa o sacristía en que se guardavan los aderesos casullas y ornam[ent]os de aquella ygleçia y de dies baras de damasco o lama asul que avía dado para un manto de mi Señora de Copa Cavana el P[adr]e Frai Lucas de Mendoça del Orden de las mercedes corto mas de quatro y dio un papel o rresibo de ello al maiordomo de la Cofradia diciendole que dentro de dos semanas lo pagaria y este delito considerado de la suerte que se debe es gravissimo." Archivo General de Indias (AGI), Lima, 320, pages unnumbered.

16 Patricia Navarro Grau, Patrimonio Perú: personal communication.

17 See Archivo Arzobispal de Lima (AAL), Papeles importantes, 23, 31, and 1790.

18 Zamácola, *Libro de Ynbentarios*, f. 27r.

Bibliography

Manuscript Sources

Archivo Arzobispal de Lima. Capítulos, Santiago de Maray, VIII.22 (1678).

Archivo Arzobispal de Lima. Papeles importantes, 23.31 (1790).

Archivo General de Indias. Lima, 320.

Archivo Parroquial de Cayma, Juan Domingo Zamácola Jáuregui. *Libro de Ynbentarios y aumentos de la Yglesia Parroquial de San Miguel de Cayma, desde que tomò posesion de la dicha parroquia el Bachiller Don Juan Domingo de Zamacola y Jauregui que fue el dia 14 de Octubre de 1778.*

Printed Sources

Alarcón, L. J. H. "La iglesia de Cayma en 1820." *Revista del Archivo Arzobispal de Arequipa*, 7 (2010): 217–30.

Angulo, Fray Domingo. *Notas y monografías para la historia del barrio de San Lázaro de la ciudad de Lima: Origen y principios del barrio de San Lázaro*. Lima: E. R. Villarán, 1917.

Calancha, Antonio. *Coronica del Orden de San Agustin en el Peru, con sucesos egenplares vistos en esta monarquia*. Barcelona: Pedro Lacavalleria, 1639.

Casás Otero, Jesús. *Tota pulchra: María, esplendor de la belleza divina*. Salamanca: Secretariado Trinitario, 2015.

Egaña, Antonio de. *Historia de la iglesia en la América Española (Hemisferio Sur)*. Madrid: Biblioteca de Autores Católicos, 1966.

González Castrejón, Sara. *Templos virreinales de la sierra de Oyón y Huaura: Estudio artístico e iconográfico*. Lima: USMP and Archivo del Obispado de Huacho, 2019.

Gutiérrez, Ramón. "La iglesia de Cayma: Una obra excepcional de la arquitectura Arequipeña." *Revista del Archivo Arzobispal de Arequipa*, 4 (1997): 41–62.

Oliva, Ricardo Mariátegui. *El Santuario de Caima*. Lima: Empr. Graf. Stylo, 1952.

Unzueta, Antonio. *Juan Domingo de Zamácola y Jáuregui y su obra en el Perú, s. XVIII.* Vitoria-Gasteiz: Servicio Central de Publicaciones del Gobierno Vasco, 1992.

Vargas Ugarte, Rubén. *Biblioteca peruana: Impresos peruanos (1763-1805)*. Lima: Taller Periodístico de la Empresa Tipográfica la Prensa, 1935.

Electronic Sources

Yarabaya. "Cayma." *Foto Vintage Arequipa* (blog). November 14, 2010. http://fotovintagearequipa.blogspot.com/2010/11/cayma.html

7

SANCTITY, ANTI-JUDAISM, AND THE EARLY MARKET ECONOMY

Anne L. Williams

No other figurehead embodies the intersection of sanctity with the emerging European market economy quite like Joseph of Nazareth, a saint promoted particularly by fourteenth- and fifteenth-century mendicant preachers. Franciscan and Dominican altarpieces reveal a concerted effort to establish the foster-father of Jesus as a model of ideal nuclear paternity in the nascent market economies of *trecento* central Italy; this is frequently accomplished by presenting him as the Holy Family's treasurer in depictions of the Adoration of the Magi. Yet while Joseph plays a significant role in mendicant sermons as the fiscally responsible, ideal urban *paterfamilias*, his artistic depictions sometimes simultaneously complicate "official" theological doctrine by including a satirical undercurrent. While promoting the importance of safeguarding family wealth—espoused for example, by the Franciscan preacher Bernardino da Siena (1380–1444)—these works can simultaneously subvert these same ideals by portraying the elderly saint as an avaricious miser, fastidiously packing away the Magi's treasures into the family's chest or greedily ogling the precious gifts. By referencing popular Christian iconography associated with personifications of Avarice and Jewishness, the saint's depiction ties him to the Old Law, while revealing anxieties regarding the necessity of personal profit in the shadow of an earlier medieval worldview of attention to goods as the source of corruption. Yet in this case, satire binds lay and clerical concerns. Because Joseph was often a figure of identification for priests as the leaders of their congregations, and because, according to theologians including the Franciscan Peter John Olivi (1248–98), Joseph's status as the head of his family rendered him analogous to the pope, his depictions may have also carried an undercurrent of pre-Reformation subversion rooted in clerical satires of the Church's greed. Weaving together subversion and veneration, such images complicate prior conceptions of St. Joseph's pre-Reformation representation and function, which either interpret satire as

DOI: 10.4324/9781003082842-8

antithetical to the saint's veneration, or which negate satire's role entirely in arguing for the development of the saint's cult by the late fourteenth century.[1] Analyzing art, sermon material, and clerical satire, this chapter proposes that in certain Dominican and Franciscan altarpieces, veneration and caricature combined not only to promote the saint as a role model for urban fathers, but also to negotiate anxieties regarding the new necessity of personal profit in the emerging market economies of fourteenth-century central Italy.

Mockery and veneration: the Old Law, feudal morality, and the new economy

Bartolo di Fredi's Sienese *Adoration of the Magi* of c. 1385–88 (Pinacoteca Nazionale di Siena; Figure 7.1) presents a saintly role model whose appearance confounds a single interpretation, probably intentionally so. Joseph is dignified by his gilded halo, his scale, and his position as protector of his family from the fray. Yet with furrowed brow he turns away from the surging crowd of onlookers, clutching the Magus's precious golden gift as far away from them as possible, while casting a wary eye toward the unruly horses and servant of the holy kings. Somewhat redolent of worldly greed, yet reverently haloed, Bartolo presents a saintly model that defies a single interpretation or single moral message. The altarpiece was probably commissioned for the Sienese Church of San Domenico, specifically for its Altar of the Three Kings. An excess of Dominican saints in the *predella* bolsters the argument for a Dominican context, as does the fact that Bartolo and his son served as "official painters" of the Dominicans of Montalcino, for whom Bartolo executed an Adoration of the Shepherds (1374; Metropolitan Museum of Art, New York) with another prominent Joseph.[2]

Relatively little is known about the cult of Joseph in *trecento* central Italy. However, the Servite Fra Nicolo Pieri da Siena (Fra Niccolò di Pietro Barlettaio, d. 1349) preached sermons in the saint's honor early in that century. As the Ordo Servorum Mariae (Protectors of Mary), the Servites had adopted a feast of Saint Joseph in 1324, with the Franciscans to follow in 1399. Joseph's prominence in the frescoes of Siena Cathedral's "cripta"—indeed, the reverence that the painters accorded to the saint in that cycle—suggests that the saint had risen to importance as early as 1270 in that city, when the crypt was constructed, probably as a kind of lower chapel.[3] The mendicant role in promoting Joseph's cult is evident through the establishment of the saint's feast in the Roman calendar in 1479 by the former Minister General of the Franciscan Order, Pope Sixtus IV (1414–84), amplified by the saint's extensive promotion by Franciscan Observants.[4] But Joseph was espoused much earlier by Bernard of Clairvaux (1090–1153), whose writings on the saint were elaborated in the thirteenth and fourteenth centuries by the Dominicans Thomas Aquinas (1225–74) and Albertus Magnus (d. 1280), and the Franciscans Peter John Olivi, Ubertino da Casale (1259–1329), and Bartholomew of Pisa (1338–1401). Humor and satire also played an inextricable part of Joseph's rise in popularity in many locales, a tradition that is often

FIGURE 7.1 Bartolo di Fredi, *Adoration of the Magi*, panel from an altarpiece, 1385–1388. Tempera on panel, 195 × 163 cm. Pinacoteca Nazionale, Siena.

Source: Photo courtesy of the Ministry of Cultural Heritage and Tourism, Museale della Toscana, Pinacoteca Nazionale di Siena

sanitized in art historical scholarship that (rightly) argues for an earlier, fourteenth- and fifteenth-century rise in cult status.[5] However, for many worshippers, mild mockery and veneration were not at all antithetical. Clear evidence of Joseph's frequent caricatures in art lies in the writing of Jean Gerson, the theologian and Chancellor of the University of Paris, who bemoaned their prevalence and insisted in his *Josephina* (1414–18) on the saint's youth, vigor, and beauty.[6] According to Gerson, "He wasn't at all old, ugly, ineffectual, feeble, and so to speak, incapable of work."[7] But Joseph is consistently called *senex* (old man) in late medieval writings on the saint, a "problem" that persisted in art into the late fifteenth century, when the Franciscan preacher Bernardino Tommitano da Feltre (1439–94) complained that painters represented him as a *vechiarello,* an impotent "little old man."[8]

The satirical possibilities of the saint as keeper of the family's worldly goods were not overlooked by artists, even as the saint remained simultaneously an object of veneration. Signifiers of "otherness" infiltrated Joseph's sacred iconography both north and south of the Alps, particularly in works depicting the saint as family "treasurer," packing away the Magi's treasures into the family's chest (Figure 7.2), scrutinizing the gold coins in his hands (Figure 7.3), or ogling the precious gifts with a hint of worldly desire, all while the other protagonists admire the Christ child. Images like the Adoration scene from the Blankenberch Retable of c. 1430/40 (Figure 7.4), like the treasure chest imagery, characterize the saint as keeper of the treasure and perplexed head of the household. In such works, Joseph is frequently the smallest adult present and barred from the rest of the Adoration figures by some sort of barrier. He receives the Magus's precious gift, holds the treasure, or sometimes glances toward it with a look of desire or incredulity. Close attention to Giotto's *Adoration of the Magi* in the Metropolitan Museum of Art (c. 1320; Figure 7.5), a panel originally part of a series of seven probably produced for a Franciscan altarpiece, reveals that Joseph's line of sight extends not toward the Christ child, nor to Melchior, from whom he just received the precious gift of myrrh, but to the gold still held by Caspar. The recumbent Virgin Mary seems to cast an incredulous glance toward her husband, whose attention, stance, and wispy beard are mirrored by a four-legged, horned companion below—evoking his Jewishnesss and also his biblical nature as *cornuto.*[9] The panel's original intended location is debated, although it was undoubtedly a Franciscan church, supported by the presence of two friars in the background. The panels may have constituted part of an altarpiece for the Bardi Chapel of Santa Croce in Florence, but other proposed locations include the Church of San Francesco in Sansepolcro and the Church of San Francesco in Rimini, where Giotto also painted a crucifix.[10] Giotto indeed is well known for his wit in the Paduan Scrovegni Chapel (painted c. 1303–05), made manifest there particularly in his depictions of the elderly Joseph (although Joseph is not depicted as family treasurer in that fresco cycle, possibly because of its patron's associations with usury).[11]

In accordance with the ninth-century theologians Christian of Stavelot and Paschasius Radbertus, the Magi's offering of gold to the infant Jesus in scenes of the Adoration of the Magi could be interpreted as a reminder of the child's royal lineage. As the keeper of this gold in many Adoration scenes, Joseph is therefore the guardian of the Davidic line (and ultimately Jesus), and the devoted helpmate of Mary.[12] According to Bernard of Clairvaux, God gave Joseph to Mary to be her protector and "the nourisher of His human body," a role evoked in later preaching as well, as in the early fourteenth-century sermons of the Servite Fra Nicolo.[13] Nicolo's two preserved sermons on Joseph document the

FIGURE 7.2 Pupil of Meister Francke, Adoration of the Magi, *Preetz Altarpiece*, c. 1435, Preetz Abbey, Schleswig-Holstein. Inv. CC-BY-SA, Nationalmuseet, Copenhagen.

Source: Photo courtesy of the Nationalmuseet, Copenhagen

importance of the saint for the Servites of Siena and of Montesenario in Florence; they emphasize the saint's nobility as a descendent of the House of David and his worthiness to be considered "like a father" to Christ. In his first sermon, Nicolo describes how Joseph guards and defends the "treasure" (*thesaurum*) entrusted

FIGURE 7.3 Gherardo Starnina, *Adoration of the Magi*, from Florence, first quarter of the 15th century. Tempera on wood, 30.5 × 57.5 cm. Inv. 149, Escallier Bequest, 1857, Musée de la Chartreuse, Douai.

Source: Bridgeman Images

to him by God in the form of His earthly family. In his second sermon, Nicolo again describes three "treasures" that Joseph receives through his marriage to the Virgin: faith, the mother of the Son of God herself, and the Son who entrusted Joseph to command and nourish him.[14] The treasures for Fra Nicolo are the holy persons, not earthly goods, an irony probably not lost on Bartolo's Sienese Dominican patrons—and emphasized further by the frequent link between Joseph's nobility and poverty. Quoting the thirteenth-century Dominican friar and bishop Albertus Magnus in his *Summa Moralis* (printed 1477), the Dominican Archbishop of Florence Antoninus (1389–1459) emphasized Joseph's poverty as a component of his nobility as a descendent of David, asserting that upon receiving the Magi's precious gifts, Joseph gave them all away to the poor—possibly a reaction to the saint's earlier satirical depictions.[15]

But in emphasizing the saint's role as financial manager of his family's wealth, popular preachers like the Franciscan Bernardino of Siena (1380–1444), who was directly inspired by early *trecento* Sienese sermons on Joseph like those of Fra Nicolo, reveal a saint less emblematic of idealized poverty.[16] The emergence of the money economy beginning in twelfth-century Europe engendered a transformation in ideals of masculinity and parenting, particularly concerning the relationship of the head of the family to money.[17] The prevalence of the nuclear family in newly urbanized cities—indeed, its importance for the financial stability of the economy—became linked to individual responsibility, particularly for the *paterfamilias* as loyal provider and treasurer. The circulation of economic and theological ideas via sermons, humanist writers, and merchants resulted in a new ideal of masculinity rooted in monetary exchange; art and literature both constructed and reflected not only these new ideals, but also the anxieties generated by man's shifting relationship to money, rooted in the contradiction between the pervasive importance of acquiring wealth and continuing Christian

FIGURE 7.4 Circle of the Master of the Fröndenberger Marienretabels (after Conrad von Soest), *Blankenberch Retabel*, right wing, inside: Adoration of the Magi (detail), c. 1430/40. Oil on wood, 154.5 × 396.0 cm (overall). Inv. 6 WKV, LWL-Museum für Kunst und Kultur, Münster (Westfälisches Landesmuseum)/loan from the Westfälischer Kunstverein.

Source: Photo courtesy of the LWL-Museum für Kunst und Kultur, Münster

ideals of charity and poverty.[18] R. H. Tawney emphasizes the critical role of fifteenth-century preachers like Bernardino da Siena and Antoninus of Florence in adapting the earlier thought of Thomas Aquinas to the rapidly evolving requirements of a burgeoning capitalist system.[19] The mendicant preachers were

FIGURE 7.5 Giotto di Bondone, *Adoration of the Magi*, c. 1320. 45.1 × 43.8 cm. John Stewart Kennedy Fund, 1911, Accession Number 11.126.1, Metropolitan Museum of Art, New York.

Source: Photo © The Metropolitan Museum of Art, New York

integral as early as the thirteenth century in supporting the new social classes of the *popolo grasso* (merchant-bankers) and *popolo* (artisan-craftsmen) through ideological principles that brought their behavior into line with mercantile capitalism in Italy and Europe as a whole.[20]

Mendicant concepts of charity and properly "poor" uses of money, such as providing goods to one's community that were otherwise unattainable, allowed for a positive view of profit.[21] But money used improperly, particularly through usury or hoarding, was deeply condemned, with those who stored money away considered animalistic brutes.[22] Those who saw or owned images that depicted Joseph as preoccupied with material goods were familiar with an extensive visual history that strongly associated worldly wealth with moral depravity and attention to goods as a source of corruption.[23] The only other character so closely tied with many of Joseph's depictions as "treasurer" is Avarice, a personification closely linked with the infamous Judas Iscariot and medieval Christian conceptions of the "miserly Jew," a caricature often shown holding a moneybag or in proximity to chests of coins.[24] In Giotto's monochromatic frescoes of the seven vices in the Cappella Scrovegni of Padua, Envy and Avarice combine as the antithesis of Charity; *Karitas* (Figure 7.6) stands atop a pile of disused moneybags, unequivocally signifying her contempt for worldly goods. *Invidia* (Figure 7.7), by contrast, clutches her moneybag, while flames consume her, a uniquely indirect representation of Avarice that is dynamically fulfilled by the prominence of Judas, with his own 30 pieces of silver, in the chapel's cycle.[25] Mendicant popular preaching in the fourteenth and fifteenth centuries repeatedly emphasized the Jews as corrupt and Jews are characterized in Franciscan writings on economics

FIGURE 7.6 Giotto di Bondone, *Charity,* 1303–05, south wall, Scrovegni Chapel, Padua.

Source: Photo: Wikimedia Commons

FIGURE 7.7 Giotto di Bondone, *Envy,* 1303–05, north wall, Scrovegni Chapel, Padua.

Source: Photo: Wikimedia Commons

between 1260 and 1380 as enemies of poverty and dangerous usurers; preachers like Bernardino da Siena emphasized the socio-economic "dangers" of Jewish usury in exploiting the poor and the commune.[26]

In no example of late medieval Christian art does the holding of treasure or the packing away of goods convey unequivocally positive connotations. On the entrance portals of Gothic cathedrals, Avarice is shown rather ubiquitously packing her treasure away, as at Chartres and Amiens (Figure 7.8).[27] It is not surprising that Erwin Panofsky describes the Joseph of another Dominican Adoration scene, part of an altarpiece painted by the friar Meister Francke in 1424 (Figure 7.9), as "an amiable caricature of the Philistine's thrift and caution [...he] confiscates the precious gifts for which, he thinks, the Infant Jesus would have little use and which would be safer in the family's traveling chest."[28] Ruth Mellinkoff adds, "The deprecation is, I suggest, intensified because of Joseph's placement on the stool, in a dorsal position—scarcely an image to

FIGURE 7.8 Personification of the Vice of Avarice, Cathedral of Notre Dame, Amiens, west façade, central portal, 1220–1236.

Source: Photo © Stuart Whatling

be venerated."[29] Although the dorsal position in art does not always equate with derision, Joseph's small size and marginalization with respect to other depicted figures (see Figure 7.4) often do. Medieval Christian images of wealth and preoccupation with worldly goods were intrinsically tied to contemporary anti-Judaism, and especially to perceived evils associated with greed and lending money at interest. As early as the twelfth century, Joseph was clearly emphasized as Jewish in art, often through his headwear.[30] This was tied to his "unenlightened" state, as one who, at Christ's birth, does not immediately recognize the child as Savior. But with the rise of his cult in the thirteenth and fourteenth centuries, Joseph was simultaneously venerated as the first convert to the new religion during the Nativity. The saint's Jewishness was important as a typological statement of his ties to the Old Law, biblically fulfilled by the birth of Jesus, and the arrival of the New Law.[31] Satires of the saint's Jewishness in art underscored this typological relationship.

The negative connotations of Joseph's fascination with the Magi's gifts become clearer when compared with one of the most popular devotional treatises of the fourteenth century; according to the *Meditationes Vitae Christi* (Meditations on the Life of Christ, compiled c. 1300 or 1346–64 by a Franciscan), upon receiving

FIGURE 7.9 Master Francke, Adoration of the Magi, *St. Thomas* (*Englandfahrer*) *Altarpiece*, 1424. Tempera on oak, 91.8 × 84.3 cm. Inv. HK-493, Hamburger Kunsthalle, Hamburg.

Source: Photo: Wikimedia Commons

the Magi's precious gifts, the Virgin Mary immediately gave them all away to the poor.[32] Donations to charity were of particular concern to mendicant preachers including Bernardino da Siena and the Dominican Giovanni Dominici (1356–1419), who, unlike Bernardino, urged his followers against seeking material possessions.[33] For Dominicans like Giordano da Pisa (1260–1311), who preached in Florence between 1303 and 1307, the virtue of charity (*carità*) was the "supreme, all-encompassing virtue" for its ability to bring personal salvation to the giver.[34] But Joseph's fascination with the Magi's gold in works like those of Bartolo, Giotto, or Gherardo Starnina (Figure 7.3) are more redolent of greed than of charity. If such images were not intended to poke fun at Joseph's preoccupation with worldly wealth, then the saint's attentions would probably be directed elsewhere. The *Meditationes* is explicit:

> Did the poverty-stricken Lady keep it for herself, her old husband, and the little Child, that they might have the means to live, to spend or to save or to buy houses, fields, vineyards? God forbid that those devoted to poverty should concern themselves with these things. Since the Lady deeply longed for poverty and understood the desire of the Child, who taught her inwardly as well as by showing His desire in signs, perhaps by turning His face away from the gold in disdain, she distributed everything to the poor within a few days.[35]

Joseph's clutching of the Magus's precious gift on Bartolo's Dominican altarpiece and his eyeing of the gold on Giotto's Franciscan panel contrasts overtly with the beloved popular treatise and with mendicant aspirations to poverty and giving. It contrasts even more explicitly with the Dominican Antoninus's later assertion of Joseph's active role in his family's noble impoverishment in the *Summa Moralis*.[36] Despite his ambivalence toward the new moralities of the money economy, Giordano da Pisa characterizes excess worldly goods and profit unequivocally: modest aspirations are acceptable and worldly goods could be used in the pursuit of salvation, but a man who wishes to enrich himself works against this goal in pitting himself against other men:

> And thus riches are a great burden—too great—and are impossible to come by legitimately.... He who would gather treasure in this world must lose the treasure of heaven.... One cannot have both... for wherever you have, or wish to have, your treasure, there is your heart. So if your treasure is to be in heaven, your heart must be there; if it is to be here, then your heart is to be here too. And, thus, this vice is the very most dangerous, for it removes and severs your heart from God...whoever gathers his treasure on earth must despair of God, for he does not entrust himself to Him, nor to His power, wisdom, bounty, and richness. But whoever entrusts himself to God is well aided, and whoever trusts Him thoroughly will never be abandoned.[37]

As a model for earthly fathers, Joseph's subversive fascination with the infant's gift in fourteenth-century art complicates a clear-cut understanding. While upholding new ideals of fiscal responsibility preached in Siena and Florence and tied to the rise of the urban family, the "treasurer" Joseph seems to simultaneously subvert these ideals for their slippage into avarice.[38] The saint's depictions highlight a critical contradiction between the importance of acquiring wealth, emphasized by early fifteenth-century mendicant preachers like Bernardino da Siena, and continuing ideals of charity and poverty developed in earlier feudal societies—ideals advanced by the *trecento Meditationes*. Depictions of saints as clearly virtuous models and patrons, particularly the Virgin Mary, to whom the city of Siena was dedicated in 1260, played an important part in the consolidation of *trecento* Sienese identity.[39] But Giotto's and Bartolo's panels encourage us to consider fourteenth-century religious art as capable of much more than a presentation of a single set of morals. Rather, such images advance seemingly paradoxical themes—fiscal responsibility and the dangers attendant upon this—encouraging their viewers to meditate upon a rapidly changing, nuanced spectrum of moralities. Veneration and subversion, via the celebration of paternal responsibility and the satire of avaricious behavior, were perhaps not so antithetical; *trecento* satire could differ from its conventional definitions as a phenomenon intended to elicit a singular response, a "firm commitment to positive values contrary to the negative values it mocks."[40] The "miserly" Joseph played upon the saint's biblical lack of enlightenment regarding the most valuable thing present—his foster son—who he initially does not recognize as Savior. But the saint's imperfections ultimately called attention to his critical theological role as *paterfamilias,* and to his function as a relatable figure of identification for actual fathers, lay and clerical.

The Monti di Giuseppe, anti-Jewish preaching, and clerical satire

Probably influenced in part by these earlier representations of the saint as filial treasurer and miser, the sermons of Bernardino da Siena's followers demonstrate intriguing connections between Joseph, monetary concerns, and the fifteenth-century establishment of the first Christian-run credit unions intended to replace Jewish money-lending.[41] These sermons may represent an active recuperation of the saint to align with these new institutions and their concomitant values. The Franciscan Bernardino da Feltre fulfilled his predecessor's ideological mission by establishing about 30 Monti di Pietà throughout Italy; these were run essentially as civic pawnshops offering low-interest loans, supported by an accumulation of capital, or "monte."[42] Bernardino da Feltre's preaching against usury was linked to his preaching on Joseph; Monti di Pietà were also called Monti di Giuseppe.[43] In one of his sermons, he describes a miracle in 1490 in which a devotee had been robbed of a large sum. After praying before a statue of Joseph for future protection, his money was restored the very next night.[44] According to the Milanese Dominican reformer Isodoro Isolani (1475–c. 1528), who produced his *Summa de donis Sancti Joseph* in Pavia between 1514 and 1521, "The people who call on St. Joseph shall be repaid by him with interest from heaven while he himself in the majesty of his glory partakes of no mortal interest."[45]

Bernardino da Siena's early promotion (around 1425–27) of the idea behind the Monti di Pietà and the prevalence of anti-Jewish preaching in fourteenth- and fifteenth-century Tuscany revolved around a perceived need to target Jewish "avarice" and wealth acquired through the "unnatural" reproduction of funds through interest.[46] But Bernardino's fight, and that of his like-minded Franciscan and Dominican predecessors, was also anti-papal. In fourteenth-century Italy, the pope actively censured mendicant preaching against the Jews; the papacy recognized the necessity of Jewish lending for providing immediate liquidity, even after the establishment of the first Monti di Pietà by the Franciscans, and therefore not only allowed, but also promoted Jewish money-lending at a controlled interest rate. Despite mendicant-led efforts to dissuade Jewish moneylending and to outlaw it officially upon the establishment of the first Monti di Pietà, the papacy continuously intervened to counteract them. Ariel Toaff suggests that the papacy was one of the "'silent partners' in the Jewish banks, at least from the middle of the thirteenth century."[47]

But during the Western Schism (1378–1417), with its resultant decline in papal authority, mendicant preaching against the Jews could be undertaken with less fear of the consequences.[48] In light of lessened papal oversight against anti-Jewish fervor during the Schism, Bartolo's caricature of Joseph as the avariciousness embodiment of the Old Law may have extended, in the minds of some contemporaries, to a satire of avaricious ecclesiastical elites. Priests readily identified with Joseph as the leaders of their congregations, and according to Bernard of Clairvaux, Jean Gerson, Peter John Olivi, Fra Niccolo, Bernardino da Siena, Antoninus, and Isidoro Isolani, Joseph's status as the head of his family and spouse of Mary (who was theologically equated with *Ecclesia*) rendered him analogous to the head of the Church, the pope himself.[49] According to Peter John Olivi, "Joseph represents God the Father and Christ because he is the spouse of the Church; he is also the type of the bishops, spouses of the Church... And in the evangelical Word through the spirit of Christ, Joseph is also the image of the Roman pontiffs, installed as guardians of the Church."[50] A major focus of popular preaching was the overt greed of clergy-members, and the love of money was seen increasingly as characteristic of the papacy.[51] For Bartolo's Dominican and lay audiences, the avaricious saint could easily partake of this broader concern with greed: Jewish, Christian, and even papal. In addition to fervently disavowing Jewish money-lending, the Dominicans were less eager than the Franciscans to support Christian banking initiatives, including both the later fifteenth-century Monti di Pietà and the much earlier notion of public debt, a system established in 1345 via forced loans (*prestanze*) upon a commune's urban population.[52]

Clerical satires of papal and clerical avarice were not at all unusual in the fourteenth century.[53] So-called money-*centos,* satirical collections of Latin verses, satirize the curia's conduct by mimicking biblical passages and document growing worries among reform-minded clergy about the papacy's increasing reliance upon fundraising. The Money-Gospel was the most popular genre of *cento,* extant in 16 copies across western Europe ranging in date from the thirteenth century to the fifteenth. The extant copies' references to canonical texts confirm a learned clerical context, and references are sometimes made to particular orders including the Franciscans.[54] Most versions include the story of a poor cleric who is turned away from the curia's door because of his poverty, while a wealthy and simoniacal bishop gains immediate entrance by lavishly bestowing gifts. Clerical greed is reiterated through the manuscripts' use of wordplay; in the fifteenth-century Venice Money-Gospel, *carpinales* (graspers) replaces *cardinales* (cardinals). The performative, oral nature of these parodic *centos* bespeaks public deliverance, while other, less sophisticated satires on money were apparently so common that some have suggested their execution was a frequent exercise for schoolboys.[55] Michael Camille and Paul Binski document the prevalence of illuminated clerical satire on the margins of legal and liturgical manuscripts dating as early as the late twelfth century; this extensive tradition of visual satire on the margins of manuscripts and in the sculpted marginalia of cloisters and churches suggests that ecclesiastical propriety would not preclude satire's presence on an altarpiece.[56]

Conclusion

Fifteenth- and sixteenth-century associations in preaching between St. Joseph and money in Italy document an affiliation between the two that existed much earlier, evidenced in the works of Bartolo and Giotto. Joseph's appearance in fourteenth- and fifteenth-century art as a father preoccupied with worldly goods appears to have promoted his role as a proponent of the new ideals of masculinity in a mercantile economy, even if he sometimes directly mirrored the behavior of Avarice or the "avaricious Jew." At the heart of money-*centos*, sermons, and paintings like Bartolo's lay a confrontation that pitched the faith-based morals of an older system rooted in personal and associative relationships against a cash economy based on impersonal relationships and contracts. Extant sermons reveal that the popular preachers worked to facilitate the practical and salvatory successes of their audiences—the *popolo* and *popolo grasso*—in the new economy, frequently at the expense of Jewish communities. But painters like Bartolo and Giotto also reveal a negotiation of unquestionably prevalent feelings of anxiety in an economy where old morals and new necessities often conflicted—one where, for Christians, and for their foremost paternal role model, Jewishness and worldly wealth were simultaneously caricatured and critical precursors to salvation and survival. Sermons, *centos*, and religious art provided a means by which such anxieties were made manifest, negotiated, and ameliorated.[57] The Dominicans of Siena, for example, attracted audiences of merchants and bankers singularly focused on securing their economic positions; one can imagine Bartolo's grasping saint as a model and cautionary figure in its original Dominican context.[58] More than a mere presentation of a set of morals, or a straightforward rejection of sinful acts, Joseph's imagery was probably highly engaging, even meditative, inviting the audience to reexamine the nuances of morality, and how to best approach a wide spectrum of life's challenges. This diverges from concrete definitions of satire as intended to elicit a singular, directed response, for negativity, positivity, and culpability overlap across a thin line, and saints, laity, and clergy alike are implicated in issues of morality in the early market economy.

Notes

1 Erwin Panofsky was the first to introduce this idea: Erwin Panofsky, *Early Netherlandish Painting: Its Origins and Character* (Cambridge: Harvard University Press, 1953), 1: 164. See also Ruth Mellinkoff, *Outcasts: Signs of Others in Northern European Art of the Late Middle Ages* (Berkeley: University of California Press, 1994), 1: 82, 226; Louise O.Vasvari "Joseph on the Margin: The Mérode Tryptic and Medieval Spectacle," *Mediaevalia* 18 (1995): 168; Louis Réau, "Joseph," in *Iconographie des saints*, vol. 3, pt. 2 of *Iconographie de l'art chrétien* (Paris: Presses Universitaires de France, 1958), 752–5; Johan Huizinga, *The Autumn of the Middle Ages,* trans. Rodney J. Payton and Ulrich Mammitzsch (1919; repr., Chicago: University of Chicago Press, 1996), 177, 194–6; Teresa Rodrigues, ed., *Butler's Lives of the Saints: New Full Edition*, vol. 3. (Collegeville, MN: The Liturgical Press, 1993), 185–86; Margory Bolgar Foster, "The Iconography of St. Joseph in Netherlandish Art, 1400–1550" (PhD diss., University of Kansas, 1978), 249. By contrast, in much of the prior work on the saint's depictions in art, Joseph is cleansed of his humor, or the humor is simply unseen, while other arguments more consciously negate its presence with appeals to (convincing) arguments rooted in earlier medieval theological discourse. But a work's theological significance does not preclude the presence and function of humor. Sheila Schwartz, "St. Joseph in Meister Bertram's Petri-Altar," *Gesta* 24, no. 2 (1985): 147–56; Carolyn C. Wilson, *St. Joseph in Italian Renaissance Society and Art: New Directions and Interpretations* (Philadelphia: Saint Joseph's University Press, 2001), 95.

2 Wolfgang Loseries, "Altarpieces of the Adoration of the Magi and the Shepherds by Bartolo di Fredi: New Documentation and New Evidence," in *Bartolo di Fredi, The Adoration of the Magi: A Masterpiece Reconstructed* (Charlottesville, V.A.: University of Virginia Art Museum, 2012), 41–63; Francesca Fiorani, "Bartolo di Fredi's View of Siena as the New Jerusalem," in *Bartolo di Fredi, The Adoration of the Magi: A Masterpiece Reconstructed* (Charlottesville, V.A.: University of Virginia Art Museum, 2012), 32–5; Gaudenz Freuler, *Bartolo di Fredi Cini: Ein Beitrag zur sienesischen Malerei des 14. Jahrhunderts* (Disentis: Desertina, 1994), 284–96, and 476–8. See also Judith B. Steinhoff, *Sienese Painting After the Black Death: Artistic Pluralism, Politics, and the New Art Market* (Cambridge: Cambridge University Press, 2007), 62–63; Gaudenz Freuler, "Andrea di Bartolo, Fra Tommaso d'Antonio Caffarini, and Sienese Dominicans in Venice," *Art Bulletin* 69, no. 4 (1987): 578.

3 Evidence of Servite devotion to Joseph in Bologna and Todi also exists as early as 1301 and 1317, respectively; Joseph was chosen as protector of their general chapter at Orvieto in 1324. Further propelling overall devotion to St. Joseph, a Latin translation of the Hebrew *History of Joseph the Carpenter* appeared in Italy in the early fourteenth century. Angelo Battiston, "Deux sermons du fr. Nicolo Pieri de Sienne sur saint Joseph," *Cahiers de Joséphologie* 7, no. 1 (1959): 79–102; Angelo Battiston, "Le Patronage de Saint Joseph en Italie," *Actes du Congrès d'études tenu à l'Oratoire Saint-Joseph, Montréal, 1er 9 août 1955* (Montreal: Fides, 1956): 30–60; Wilson, *St. Joseph,* 6–7; Herbert L. Kessler, "Joseph in Siena," in *Joseph of Nazareth through the Centuries*, ed. Joseph F. Chorpenning (Philadelphia: Saint Joseph's University Press, 2011), 66–73.

4 Unofficial Franciscan devotion to St. Joseph probably dates to the early thirteenth century. Blaine Burkey, "The Feast of St. Joseph: A Franciscan Bequest," *Cahiers de Joséphologie* 19 (1971): 647–80. See also Francis Lad Filas, *Joseph: The Man Closest to Jesus* (Boston: St. Paul Editions, 1962), 538.

5 See, for example, Wilson, *St. Joseph,* 5–8; Carolyn C. Wilson, "Some Further Evidence of St. Joseph's Cult in Renaissance Italy and Related St. Joseph Altarpieces," in *Die Bedeutung des hl. Josef der Heilsgeschichte. Akten des IX. Internationalen Symposions über den hl. Josef,* ed. Johannes Hattler and Germán Rovira (Kisslegg: Fe-Medienverlag, 2006), 2: 904; Schwartz, "St. Joseph in Meister Bertram's Petri-Altar," 147–56.

6 Jean Gerson, *Considérations sur Saint Joseph*, III, 842–68; Jean Gerson, *Josephina*, IV, 753; Jean Gerson, *Sermo de natalitate beatae Mariae Virginis*, III, 1351, in *Opera omnia,* ed. Louis Ellies du Pin, 2nd ed., vols. 1–5 (1706; repr., Hildesheim: Olms, 1987).

7 Jean Gerson, *Oeuvres completes,* ed. Palémon Glorieux (Paris: Desclée, 1962), 7: 75: "ne fust point viel, lait, défecteux et febble et comme impotent au labeur." Quoted in David Herlihy, *Medieval Households* (Cambridge, MA: Harvard University Press, 1985), 128.

8 Bernardino da Feltre, *Sermoni del beato Bernardino Tomitano da Feltre,* ed. P. Carlo Varische da Milano, vols. 1–3 (Milan: Cassa di Risparmio delle Provincie Lombarde e Banca Monte, 1964), 1: 395. "Sed non conoscitur quia pingitur cossi un vechiarello, par cossi un tal christianello." Herlihy, *Medieval Households,* 127, notes 85 and 86.

9 In medieval Christian caricatures of Jewishness, like that of Judas on the Arena Chapel's east chancel arch, the pointed beard is evocative of the goat's beard, considered the favorite animal of Satan and Jews, and an animal associated with lechery. Jonathan B. Riess, "Luca Signorelli's *Rule of Antichrist* and the Christian Encounter with the Infidel," in *Reframing the Renaissance: Visual Culture in Europe and Latin America 1450–1650* (New Haven: Yale University Press, 1995), 286; Joshua Trachtenberg, *The Devil and the Jews: The Medieval Conception of the Jew and its Relation to Modern Antisemitism* (New Haven: Yale University Press, 1943), 46.

10 Keith Christiansen, "Fourteenth-Century Italian Altarpieces," *Metropolitan Museum of Art Bulletin* 40 (1982): 50–56; Martin Davies, *The Earlier Italian Schools* (London: National Gallery, 1951), 180–1, 304; Dillian Gordon, "A Dossal by Giotto and his Workshop: Some Problems of Attribution, Provenance and Patronage," *Burlington Magazine* 131 (1989): 524–31; Carl Brandon Strehlke and Machtelt Brüggen Israëls, *The Bernard and Mary Berenson Collection of European Paintings at I Tatti* (Florence: i Tatti, 2015), 320, and 322–9.

11 Andrew Ladis, "The Legend of Giotto's Wit and the Arena Chapel," *Art Bulletin* 68, no. 4 (1986): 581–96.

12 Gérard Mercier, "Saint Joseph dans les commentaires bibliques et les homéliares du IXe siècle," *Cahiers de Joséphologie* 19 (1971): 232–53; Schwartz, "St. Joseph in Meister Bertram's Petri-Altar," 147–56.

13 *Hom.* II:16; translated in Sheila Schwartz, "The Iconography of the Rest on the Flight into Egypt" (PhD diss., New York University, Institute of Fine Arts, 1975), 62.

14 Battiston, "Deux sermons du fr. Nicolo Pieri de Sienne sur saint Joseph," 91–7.

15 Antoninus of Florence, *Summa Moralis,* pt. 4, coll. 955 D.E., 956 A.D., cited in Timothy M. Sparks, "St. Antoninus of Florence on St. Joseph," *Cahiers de Joséphologie* 19 (1971): 451–52, note 60; Wilson, *St. Joseph,* 37; Keith Christiansen, Laurence B. Kanter, and Carl Brandon Strehlke, *Painting in Renaissance Siena: 1420–1500* (New York: Metropolitan Museum of Art, 1988), 209.

16 Bernardino laid out this position in a Christmas Eve sermon in Siena. He also preached his sermon on St. Joseph in Padua and Bologna. Bernardino da Siena, *Le prediche volgari sul Campo di Siena 1427,* ed. Carlo Delcorno. (Milan: Rusconi, 1989); Bernardino da Siena, *Le prediche volgari: Quaresimale Fiorentino del 1424,* ed. Ciro Cannarozzi, 2 vols. (Pistoia: Alberto Pacinotti, 1934); Bernardino da Siena, *Opera Omnia* (Florence: Collegio San Bonaventura, 1950–65), 7: 16–30. See also 4: 491, 546; 6: 89, 134, 140, and 328. For the Sienese sermon, see Battiston, "Le Patronage de Saint Joseph en Italie," 51. Battiston cites St. Bernardine, Codex Chig. c. IV. 163, f. 21 c.-24 c., Bibl. Laurenz., Florence. Like Bernardino, the Franciscan Fra Roberto Caracciolo da Lecce (c. 1425–95) also preached a Christmas Eve sermon on Saint Joseph in Padua. See also David Herlihy, "The Making of the Medieval Family: Symmetry, Structure, Sentiment." *Journal of Family History,* VIII (1983): 116–30.

17 Juliann Vitullo and Diane Wolfthal, "Trading Values: Negotiating Masculinity in Late Medieval and Early Modern Europe," in *Money, Morality, and Culture in Late Medieval and Early Modern Europe,* ed. Juliann Vitullo and Diane Wolfthal (Burlington, V.T.: Ashgate, 2010), 155–96.

18 For analyses of the monetary economy's effects on Christian ethics and morality, see especially Jacques Le Goff, *Your Money or Your Life: Economy and Religion in the Middle Ages,* trans. Patricia Ranum (New York: Zone Books, 1988) and Joel Kaye, *Economy and Nature in the Fourteenth Century: Money, Market Exchange, and the Emergence of Scientific Thought* (Cambridge: Cambridge University Press, 1998); Lester K. Little, *Religious Pov-*

erty and the Profit Economy in Medieval Europe (Ithaca: Cornell University Press, 1983), 3–41. See also Vitullo and Wolfthal, "Trading Values: Negotiating Masculinity in Late Medieval and Early Modern Europe," 155–96. For Tuscany particularly, see David Herlihy and Christiane Klapisch-Zuber, *Tuscans and Their Families: A Study of the Florentine Catasto of 1427* (New Haven:Yale University Press, 1985).

19 R. H. Tawney, *Religion and the Rise of Capitalism* (Harmondsworth: Penguin, 1964), 44–46.

20 Daniel R. Lesnick, *Preaching in Medieval Florence:The Social World of Franciscan and Dominican Spirituality* (Athens, G.A.: University of Georgia Press, 1989): 1 and 96–114.

21 Giacomo Todeschini, "Franciscan Economics and Jews in the Middle Ages: From a Theological to an Economic Lexicon," in *Friars and Jews in the Middle Ages and Renaissance*, ed. Steven J. McMichael and Susan E. Myers (London: Brill, 2004), 109–10.

22 Linda Hults, *The Print in the Western World* (Madison,W.I.: University of Wisconsin Press, 1996), 113–14; Vitullo and Wolfthal, "Trading Values: Negotiating Masculinity in Late Medieval and Early Modern Europe," 167–71; Odd Inge Langholm, *Wealth and Money in the Aristotelian Tradition: A Study in Scholastic Economic Sources* (Bergen: Universitetsforlangen, 1983).

23 For literary and visual depictions of avarice, see Richard Newhauser, *The Early History of Greed: The Sin of Avarice in Early Medieval Thought and Literature* (Cambridge: Cambridge University Press, 2000). See also Richard Newhauser, ed., *The Seven Deadly Sins: From Communities to Individuals* (Leiden: Brill, 2007); Richard G. Newhauser and Susan J. Ridyard, ed., *Sin in Medieval and Early Modern Culture* (York: York Medieval Press, 2012); Juliann Vitullo and Diana Wolfthal, ed., *Money, Morality, and Culture in Late Medieval and Early Modern Europe* (Burlington, V.T.: Ashgate, 2010).

24 See Roberto Rusconi, "Anti-Jewish Preaching in the Fifteenth Century and Images of Preachers in Italian Renaissance Art," in *Friars and Jews in the Middle Ages and Renaissance*, ed. Steven J. McMichael and Susan E. Myers (London: Brill, 2004), 233–34, plates 10–11; Birgit Wiedl, "Laughing at the Beast: The *Judensau:* Anti-Jewish Propaganda and Humor from the Middle Ages to the Early Modern Period," in *Laughter in the Middle Ages and Early Modern Times: Epistemology of a Fundamental Human Behavior, its Meaning, and Consequences*, ed. Albrecht Classen (Berlin: De Gruyter, 2010), 325. For further Christian representations of Jews and Judaism, see Dana E. Katz, *The Jew in the Art of the Italian Renaissance* (Philadelphia: University of Pennsylvania Press, 2008); Debra Higgs Strickland, *Saracens, Demons, and Jews: Making Monsters in Medieval Art* (Princeton: Princeton University Press, 2003); Sara Lipton, *Images of Intolerance: The Representation of Jews and Judaism in the Bible Moralisée* (Berkeley: University of California Press, 1999); Mellinkoff, *Outcasts*; Heinz Schreckenberg, *The Jews in Christian Art: An Illustrated History* (New York: Continuum, 1996).

25 Anne Derbes and Mark Sandona, *The Usurer's Heart: Giotto, Enrico Scrovegni, and the Arena Chapel in Padua* (University Park, P.A.: Pennsylvania State Press, 2008), 14–48.

26 In early Franciscan writings, Judas is characterized as *avaris* and cast as the antithesis of Christ's perfect poverty. Todeschini, "Franciscan Economics and Jews in the Middle Ages," 102–3, note 12; Jeremy Cohen, *The Friars and the Jews: The Evolution of Medieval Anti-Judaism* (Ithaca: Cornell University Press, 1982), 238–41; Jeremy Cohen, *Christ Killers: The Jews and the Passion from the Bible to the Big Screen* (Oxford: Oxford University Press, 2007).

27 The implications of the treasure chest continued to resonate in later print culture, as in Hans Holbein's *The Rich Man* from his *Dance of Death*. David Kunzle, *The Early Comic Strip: Narrative Strips and Picture Stories in the European Broadsheet from c. 1450–1825* (Berkeley: University of California Press, 1973).

28 Panofsky, *Early Netherlandish Painting,* 1: 70. The so-called Saint Thomas Altarpiece was executed by the Dominican friar and painter Meister Francke for St. Thomas's Chapel in the Dominican church of St. John, Hamburg. Helmut R. Lippien, "Meister Francke," in *Goldgrund und Himmelslicht: Die Kunst des Mittelalters in Hamburg*, ed. Uwe M. Schneede (Hamburg: Dölling und Galitz, 1999), 140–53.

29 Mellinkoff, *Outcasts*, 1: 227.
30 Mellinkoff, *Outcasts*, 1: 62.
31 This dual significance continued to be celebrated in the seventeenth century as well; see Shelley Perlove and Larry Silver, *Rembrandt's Faith: Church and Temple in the Dutch Golden Age* (University Park: The Pennsylvania State University Press, 2009), 173–78.
32 Isa Ragusa and Rosalie B. Green, ed. and trans., *Meditations on the Life of Christ: An Illustrated Manuscript of the Fourteenth Century* (Princeton: Princeton University Press, 1961), 51–52. The manuscript was likely compiled in Tuscany by a Franciscan friar for a nun of the Poor Clares. Typically attributed to the anonymous "Pseudo-Bonaventure," the text has been ascribed specifically to Giovanni de Caulibus de Sancto Gemeniano. Recent work dates it between 1346 and 1364. See Sarah McNamer, "Further Evidence for the Date of the Pseudo-Bonaventuran Meditationes vitae Christi," *Franciscan Studies* 50 (1990): 235–61; Sarah McNamer, "The Origins of the *Meditationes vitae Christi*," *Speculum* 8 (2009): 905–55; Sarah McNamer, *Affective Meditation and the Invention of Medieval Compassion* (Philadelphia: University of Pennsylvania Press, 2010).
33 Giovanni Dominici, *Regola del governo di cura familiare*, ed. Piero Bargellini (Florence: Fiorentina, 1927), 88–90, 133; Dominici, MS Ricc. 1301, Predica 13, lines 294–98, cited in Nirit Ben-Aryeh Debby, *Renaissance Florence in the Rhetoric of Two Popular Preachers: Giovanni Dominici (1356–1419) and Bernardino da Siena (1380–1444)* (Turnhout: Brepols, 2001), 165.
34 Lesnick, *Preaching in Medieval Florence,* 131.
35 Ragusa and Green, *Meditations on the Life of Christ,* 51–52.
36 Dominici, *Regola*, 126; Debby, *Renaissance Florence in the Rhetoric of Two Popular Preachers*, 163.
37 Giordano da Pisa, *Prediche del B. Fra. Giordano da Rivalto, recitate in Firenze dal MCCCII al MCCCVI,* ed. Domenico Moreni (Florence: Magheri, 1831), 1: 6; translated in Lesnick, *Preaching in Medieval Florence,* 123. Preached in February 1305 or 1306.
38 Frederick Goldin, *German and Italian Lyrics of the Middle Ages: An Anthology and a History* (Garden City, N.Y.: Anchor Press, 1973), 107; Laura Kendrick, "Medieval Satire," in *A Companion to Satire: Ancient and Modern*, ed. Ruben Quintero (Oxford: Blackwell Publishing, 2007), 62.
39 Diana Norman, *Siena and the Virgin: Art and Politics in the Late Medieval City State* (New Haven: Yale University Press, 1999); Diana Webb, *Patrons and Defenders: The Saints in the Italian City-States* (London: Bloomsbury, 1996), 249–75; Henk van Os, *Sienese Altarpieces, 1215–1460: Form, Content, Function,* vols. 1–2 (Groningen: Bouma's Boekhuis, 1984); Judith Steinhoff, "Urban Images and Civic Identity in Medieval Sienese Painting," in *Art as Politics in Late Medieval and Renaissance Siena,* ed. Timothy Smith and Judith Steinhoff (Burlington, V.T.: Ashgate, 2012), 15–38; Steinhoff, *Sienese Painting After the Black Death*; Gerald Parsons, *Siena, Civil Religion and The Sienese* (Aldershot: Ashgate, 2003), xiv–xvii; Hayden B. J. Maginnis, *The World of the Early Sienese Painter* (University Park: The Pennsylvania State University Press, 2001), 29–32.
40 Edwin M. Duval, "Rabelais and French Renaissance Satire," in *A Companion to Satire: Ancient and Modern,* ed. Ruben Quintero (Oxford: Blackwell Publishing, 2007), 72.
41 Brian Pullan, *Rich and Poor in Renaissance Venice* (Cambridge, M.A.: Harvard University Press, 1971), 443–75; Debby, *Renaissance Florence in the Rhetoric of Two Popular Preachers*, 195. For Bernardino da Siena's preaching against the Jews (and others), see Franco Mormando, *The Preacher's Demons: Bernardino of Siena and the Social Underworld of Early Renaissance Italy* (Chicago: University of Chicago Press, 1999).
42 Carol Bresnahan Menning, "The Monte's 'Monte': The Early Supporters of Florence's Monte di Pietà," *Sixteenth Century Journal* 23, no. 4 (1992): 661.
43 Battiston, "Le Patronage de Saint Joseph en Italie," 51; Wilson, *St. Joseph,* 7, note 30.
44 Bernardino da Feltre, *Sermoni,* 1: 402; Herlihy, *Medieval Households,* 128–29; Schwartz, "The Iconography of the Rest on the Flight into Egypt," 131; Wilson, *St. Joseph,* 14, note 87.
45 *Summa,* Part 3, ch. 8; English translation quoted in Filas, *Joseph,* 506–7.

46 See especially: Steven J. McMichael and Susan E. Myers, ed., *Friars and Jews in the Middle Ages and Renaissance* (Leiden: Brill, 2004); Bernardino da Siena, *Le prediche volgari sul Campo di Siena 1427*, 2: 1033.
47 Ariel Toaff, "Jews, Franciscans, and the First *Monti di Pietà* in Italy (1462–1500)," in *Friars and Jews in the Middle Ages and Renaissance*, ed. Steven J. McMichael and Susan E. Myers (London: Brill, 2004), 247; Kenneth Stow, "The Good of the Church, the Good of the State: The Popes and Jewish Money," in *Christianity and Judaism*, ed. Diana Wood (Oxford: Blackwell, 1992), 241; Nirit Ben-Aryeh Debby, "Jews and Judaism in the Rhetoric of Popular Preachers: The Florentine Sermons of Giovanni Dominici (1356–1419) and Bernardino da Siena (1380–1444)," *Jewish History* 14, no. 2 (2000): 186.
48 Nirit Ben-Aryeh Debby notes that Dominici's preaching is vigorously anti-Jewish in a manner that would have probably provoked papal censure in a time of greater papal authority. Debby, "Jews and Judaism in the Rhetoric of Popular Preachers," 175–80; Kenneth R. Stow, "Papal and Royal Attitudes toward Jewish Lending in the Thirteenth Century," *AJS Review* 6 (1981): 161.
49 Schwartz, "St. Joseph in Meister Bertram's Petri-Altar," 147–56; Brian Patrick McGuire, "Becoming a Father and a Husband: St. Joseph in Bernard of Clairvaux and Jean Gerson," in *St. Joseph of Nazareth Through the Centuries,* ed. Joseph F. Chorpenning (Philadelphia: Saint Joseph's University Press, 2011), 49–61; Sparks, "St. Antoninus of Florence on St. Joseph," 429–55.
50 Schwartz, "The Iconography of the Rest on the Flight into Egypt," 152.
51 Martha Bayless, *Parody in the Middle Ages: The Latin Tradition* (Ann Arbor: The University of Michigan Press, 1996), 135. Poggio Bracciolini's *De avaritia* documents Bernardino da Siena's moving of his audience to laughter when discussing usurers. Poggio Bracciolini, "On Avarice," in *The Earthly Republic: Italian Humanists on Government and Society*, ed. Benjamin Kohl and Ronald G. Witt (Philadelphia: University of Pennsylvania Press, 1989), 247; Poggio Bracciolini, *De avaritia (Dialogus contra avaritiam),* ed. Giuseppe Germano (Livorno, Belforte: 1994).
52 Debby, *Renaissance Florence in the Rhetoric of Popular Preachers,* 171.
53 Greedy clerics were frequently described as predatory beasts, like the wolf, or mocked for their gluttony and guzzling of wine. See Kendrick, "Medieval Satire," 55–58; John A. Yunck, *The Lineage of Lady Meed: The Development of Mediaeval Venality Satire* (Notre Dame: University of Notre Dame Press, 1963), 112–14.
54 Contained within the same manuscript as the fifteenth-century Venice Money-Gospel is a satirical "letter" addressed to Franciscans: *Fratres, gaudete in domino semper…quia in stadio currents bravium accepistis et quod erat alienum pecuniae largitione arripuistis…* ("Brothers, rejoice in the Lord always….for you who run in the race receive the prize, and you seize what belongs to another by lavishing money…"). Quoted in Francesco Novati, "La parodia sacra nelle letterature moderne," in *Studi critici e letterari* (Turin: E. Loescher, 1889), 308; quoted and translated in Bayless, *Parody in the Middle Ages,* 156.
55 Yunck, *Lady Meed*, 183–84; Bayless, *Parody in the Middle Ages,* 135–42, 154, and 176. See also John A. Yunck, "Economic Conservatism, Papal Finance, and the Medieval Satires on Rome," *Mediaeval Studies* 23 (1961): 334–51; Rodney M. Thomson, "The Origins of Latin Satire in Twelfth Century Europe," *Mitellateinisches Jahrbuch* 13 (1978): 73–83.
56 Here I disagree with the assertion that "such textual affronts to decorum—which of course presuppose a grip on the whole concept of decorum in the first place—are unknown in the central images of Christianity." Paul Binski, *Gothic Wonder: Art, Artifice, and the Decorated Style, 1290–1350* (New Haven: Yale University Press, 2014), 292; Michael Camille, *Image on the Edge: The Margins of Medieval Art* (Cambridge: Harvard University Press, 1992), 10; Lilian M. C. Randall, *Images in the Margins of Gothic Manuscripts* (Berkeley: University of California Press, 1966).
57 Humor and satire commonly appeared in the fourteenth- and fifteenth-century sermons of the Servites, Dominicans, and Franciscans. Although the truly humorous elements of fourteenth-century sermons were never written down (lest the laity take such sensational forms of preaching into their own hands), Bernardino da Siena's preserved

sermons of the early fifteenth-century document this tradition to particular theatrical effect. Lina Bolzoni, *The Web of Images: Vernacular Preaching from its Origins to St. Bernardino da Siena* (Burlington, V.T.: Ashgate, 2004), 124–25; Lesnick, *Preaching in Medieval Florence,* 93–171.

58 Nirit Ben-Aryeh Debby discusses the complexities of Dominican perceptions of the Jews in Florence, for example, in the frescoes of Santa Maria Novella. Nirit Ben-Aryeh Debby, "Art and Sermons: Dominicans and the Jews in Florence's Santa Maria Novella," *Church History and Religious Culture* 92, no. 2/3 (2012): 171–200.

Bibliography

Battiston, Angelo. "Deux sermons du fr. Nicolo Pieri de Sienne sur saint Joseph." *Cahiers de Joséphologie*, 7.1 (1959): 79–102.

"Le Patronage de Saint Joseph en Italie." In *Actes du Congrès d'études tenu à l'Oratoire Saint-Joseph, Montréal, 1er 9 août 1955*, 30–60. Montreal: Fides, 1956.

Bayless, Martha. *Parody in the Middle Ages: The Latin Tradition*. Ann Arbor: The University of Michigan Press, 1996.

Bernardino da Feltre. *Sermoni del beato Bernardino Tomitano da Feltre*, ed. P. Carlo Varische de Milano. 3 vols. Milan: Cassa di Risparmio delle Provincie Lombarde e Banca Monte, 1964.

Bernardino da Siena. *Le prediche volgari: Quaresimale Fiorentino del 1424*, 2 vols., ed. Ciro Cannarozzi. Pistoia: Alberto Pacinotti, 1934.

——. *Le prediche volgari sul Campo di Siena 1427*, ed. Carlo Delcorno. Milan: Rusconi, 1989.

——. *Opera omnia*, 9 vols. Florence: Collegio San Bonaventura, 1950–65.

Binski, Paul. *Gothic Wonder: Art, Artifice, and the Decorated Style, 1290–1350*. New Haven: Yale University Press, 2014.

Bolzoni, Lina. *The Web of Images: Vernacular Preaching from Its Origins to St. Bernardino da Siena*. Burlington: Ashgate, 2004.

Bracciolini, Poggio. *De avaritia (Dialogus contra avaritiam)*, ed. Giuseppe Germano. Livorno, Belforte: 1994.

——. "On Avarice." In *The Earthly Republic: Italian Humanists on Government and Society*, eds. Benjamin Kohl and Ronald G. Witt, 241–92. Philadelphia: University of Pennsylvania Press, 1989.

Burkey, Blaine. "The Feast of St. Joseph: A Franciscan Bequest." *Cahiers de Joséphologie*, 19 (1971): 647–80.

Camille, Michael. *Image on the Edge: The Margins of Medieval Art*. Cambridge: Harvard University Press, 1992.

Chorpenning, Joseph F., ed. *St. Joseph of Nazareth through the Centuries*. Philadelphia: Saint Joseph's University Press, 2011.

Christiansen, Keith. "Fourteenth-Century Italian Altarpieces." *Metropolitan Museum of Art Bulletin*, 40 (1982): 50–6.

Christiansen, Keith, Laurence B. Kanter, and Carl Brandon Strehlke. *Painting in Renaissance Siena: 1420–1500*. New York: Metropolitan Museum of Art, 1988.

Cohen, Jeremy. *Christ Killers: The Jews and the Passion from the Bible to the Big Screen*. Oxford: Oxford University Press, 2007.

——. *The Friars and the Jews: The Evolution of Medieval Anti-Judaism*. Ithaca: Cornell University Press, 1982.

Davies, Martin. *The Earlier Italian Schools*. London: National Gallery, 1951.

Debby, Nirit Ben-Aryeh. "Art and Sermons: Dominicans and the Jews in Florence's Santa Maria Novella." *Church History and Religious Culture*, 92.2/3 (2012): 171–200.

——. "Jews and Judaism in the Rhetoric of Popular Preachers: The Florentine Sermons of Giovanni Dominici (1356–1419) and Bernardino da Siena (1380–1444)." *Jewish History*, 14.2 (2000): 175–200.
——. *Renaissance Florence in the Rhetoric of Two Popular Preachers: Giovanni Dominici (1356–1419) and Bernardino da Siena (1380–1444)*. Turnhout: Brepols, 2001.
Derbes, Anne and Mark Sandona. *The Usurer's Heart: Giotto, Enrico Scrovegni, and the Arena Chapel in Padua*. University Park: The Pennsylvania State University Press, 2008.
Dominici, Giovanni. *Regola del governo di cura familiare*, ed. Piero Bargellini. Florence: Fiorentina, 1927.
Duval, Edwin M. "Rabelais and French Renaissance Satire." In *A Companion to Satire: Ancient and Modern*, ed. Ruben Quintero, 70–85. Oxford: Blackwell Publishing, 2007.
Filas, Francis Lad. *Joseph: The Man Closest to Jesus*. Boston: St. Paul Editions, 1962.
Fiorani, Francesca. "Bartolo di Fredi's View of Siena as the New Jerusalem." In *Bartolo di Fredi, the Adoration of the Magi: A Masterpiece Reconstructed*, 32–5. Charlottesville, VA: University of Virginia Art Museum, 2012.
Foster, Marjory Bolgar. "The Iconography of St. Joseph in Netherlandish Art, 1400–1550." PhD diss., University of Kansas, 1978.
Freuler, Gaudenz. "Andrea di Bartolo, Fra Tommaso d'Antonio Caffarini, and Sienese Dominicans in Venice." *Art Bulletin*, 69.4 (1987): 570–86.
——. *Bartolo di Fredi Cini: Ein Beitrag zur sienesischen Malerei des 14. Jahrhunderts*. Disentis: Desertina, 1994.
Gerson, Jean. *Oeuvres complètes*, 10 vols., ed. Palémon Glorieux. Paris: Desclée, 1960–73.
——. *Opera omnia*. 2nd ed., 5 vols., ed. Louis Ellies du Pin. 1706. Reprint, Hildesheim: Olms, 1987.
Giordano da Pisa. *Prediche del B. Fra. Giordano da Rivalto, recitate in Firenze dal MCCCII al MCCCVI*, 2 vols., ed. Domenico Moreni. Florence: Magheri, 1831.
Goldin, Frederick. *German and Italian Lyrics of the Middle Ages: An Anthology and a History*. Garden City: Anchor Press, 1973.
Gordon, Dillian. "A Dossal by Giotto and his Workshop: Some Problems of Attribution, Provenance and Patronage." *Burlington Magazine*, 131 (1989): 524–31.
Herlihy, David. *Medieval Households*. Cambridge: Harvard University Press, 1985.
——. "The Making of the Medieval Family: Symmetry, Structure, Sentiment." *Journal of Family History*, VIII (1983): 116–30.
Herlihy, David and Christiane Klapisch-Zuber. *Tuscans and Their Families: A Study of the Florentine Catasto of 1427*. New Haven: Yale University Press, 1985.
Huizinga, Johan. *The Autumn of the Middle Ages*, Trans. Rodney J. Payton and Ulrich Mammitzsch. 1919. Reprint, Chicago: University of Chicago Press, 1997.
Hults, Linda C. *The Print in the Western World: An Introductory History*. Madison: University of Wisconsin Press, 1996.
Katz, Dana E. *The Jew in the Art of the Italian Renaissance*. Philadelphia: University of Pennsylvania Press, 2008.
Kaye, Joel. *Economy and Nature in the Fourteenth Century: Money, Market Exchange, and the Emergence of Scientific Thought*. Cambridge: Cambridge University Press, 1998.
Kendrick, Laura. "Medieval Satire." In *A Companion to Satire: Ancient and Modern*, ed. Ruben Quintero, 52–69. Oxford: Blackwell Publishing, 2007.
Kessler, Herbert L. "Joseph in Siena." In *Joseph of Nazareth Through the Centuries*, ed. Joseph F. Chorpenning, 63–76. Philadelphia: Saint Joseph's University Press, 2011.
Kunzle, David. *The Early Comic Strip: Narrative Strips and Picture Stories in the European Broadsheet from c. 1450 to 1825*. Berkeley: University of California Press, 1973.
Ladis, Andrew. "The Legend of Giotto's Wit and the Arena Chapel." *Art Bulletin*, 68.4 (1986): 581–96.

Langholm, Odd Inge. *Wealth and Money in the Aristotelian Tradition: A Study in Scholastic Economic Sources*. Bergen: Universitetsforlangen, 1983.

Le Goff, Jacques. *Your Money or Your Life: Economy and Religion in the Middle Ages*, Trans. Patricia Ranum. New York: Zone Books, 1988.

Lesnick, Daniel R. *Preaching in Medieval Florence: The Social World of Franciscan and Dominican Spirituality*. Athens: University of Georgia Press, 1989.

Lippien, Helmut R. "Meister Francke." In *Goldgrund und Himmelslicht: Die Kunst des Mittelalters in Hamburg*, ed. Uwe M. Schneede, 140–53. Hamburg: Dölling und Galitz, 1999.

Lipton, Sara. *Images of Intolerance: The Representation of Jews and Judaism in the Bible Moralisée*. Berkeley: University of California Press, 1999.

Loseries, Wolfgang. "Altarpieces of the Adoration of the Magi and the Shepherds by Bartolo di Fredi: New Documentation and New Evidence." In *Bartolo di Fredi, the Adoration of the Magi: A Masterpiece Reconstructed*, 41–63. Charlottesville, VA: University of Virginia Art Museum, 2012.

Maginnis, Hayden B.J. *The World of the Early Sienese Painter*. University Park: The Pennsylvania State University Press, 2001.

McGuire, Brian Patrick. "Becoming a Father and a Husband: St. Joseph in Bernard of Clairvaux and Jean Gerson." In *Joseph of Nazareth through the Centuries*, ed. Joseph F. Chorpenning, 49–61. Philadelphia: Saint Joseph's University Press, 2011.

McMichael, Steven J. and Susan E. Myers, eds. *Friars and Jews in the Middle Ages and Renaissance*. London: Brill, 2004.

McNamer, Sarah. *Affective Meditation and the Invention of Medieval Compassion*. Philadelphia: University of Pennsylvania Press, 2010.

——. "Further Evidence for the Date of the Pseudo-Bonaventuran Meditationes vitae Christi." *Franciscan Studies*, 50 (1990): 235–61.

——. "The Origins of the *Meditationes vitae Christi*." *Speculum*, 8 (2009): 905–55.

Mellinkoff, Ruth. *Outcasts: Signs of Others in Northern European Art of the Late Middle Ages*, 2 vols. Berkeley: University of California Press, 1994.

Menning, Carol Bresnahan. "The Monte's 'Monte': The Early Supporters of Florence's Monte di Pietà." *Sixteenth Century Journal*, 23.4 (1992): 661–76.

Mercier, Gérard. "Saint Joseph dans les commentaires bibliques et les homéliares du IXe siècle." *Cahiers de Joséphologie*, 19 (1971): 232–53.

Mormando, Franco. *The Preacher's Demons: Bernardino of Siena and the Social Underworld of Early Renaissance Italy*. Chicago: University of Chicago Press, 1999.

Newhauser, Richard. *The Early History of Greed: The Sin of Avarice in Early Medieval Thought and Literature*. Cambridge: Cambridge University Press, 2000.

Newhauser, Richard, ed. *The Seven Deadly Sins: From Communities to Individuals*. Leiden: Brill, 2007.

Newhauser, Richard G. and Susan J. Ridyard, eds. *Sin in Medieval and Early Modern Culture*. York: York Medieval Press, 2012.

Norman, Diana. *Siena and the Virgin: Art and Politics in the Late Medieval City State*. New Haven: Yale University Press, 1999.

Novati, Francesco. "La parodia sacra nelle letterature moderne." In *Studi critici e letterari*, 177–310. Turin: E. Loescher, 1889.

Panofsky, Erwin. *Early Netherlandish Painting: Its Origins and Character*, 2 vols. Cambridge: Harvard University Press, 1953.

Parsons, Gerald. *Siena, Civil Religion and the Sienese*. Aldershot: Ashgate, 2003.

Perlove, Shelley, and Larry Silver. *Rembrandt's Faith: Church and Temple in the Dutch Golden Age*. University Park: The Pennsylvania State University Press, 2009.

Pullan, Brian. *Rich and Poor in Renaissance Venice*. Cambridge: Harvard University Press, 1971.

Quintero, Ruben, ed. *A Companion to Satire: Ancient and Modern*. Oxford: Blackwell Publishing, 2007.

Ragusa, Isa and Rosalie B. Green, trans. and eds. *Meditations on the Life of Christ: An Illustrated Manuscript of the Fourteenth Century*. Princeton: Princeton University Press, 1961.

Randall, Lilian M. C. *Images in the Margins of Gothic Manuscripts*. Berkeley: University of California Press, 1966.

Réau, Louis. "Joseph." In *Iconographie des saints*, Vol. 3, pt. 2 of *Iconographie de l'art chrétien*. Paris: Presses Universitaires de France, 1958.

Riess, Jonathan B. "Luca Signorelli's *Rule of Antichrist* and the Christian Encounter with the Infidel." In *Reframing the Renaissance: Visual Culture in Europe and Latin America 1450-1650*, ed. Claire Farago, 283 -91. New Haven: Yale University Press, 1995.

Rodrigues, Teresa, ed. *Butler's Lives of the Saints: New Full Edition*, Vol. 3. Collegeville: The Liturgical Press, 1993.

Rusconi, Roberto. "Anti-Jewish Preaching in the Fifteenth Century and Images of Preachers in Italian Renaissance Art." In *Friars and Jews in the Middle Ages and Renaissance*, eds. Steven J. McMichael and Susan E. Myers, 225–37. London: Brill, 2004.

Schreckenberg, Heinz. *The Jews in Christian Art: An Illustrated History*. New York: Continuum, 1996.

Schwartz, Sheila. "St. Joseph in Meister Bertram's Petri-Altar." *Gesta*, 24.2 (1985): 147–56.

——. "The Iconography of the Rest on the Flight into Egypt." PhD diss., New York University, Institute of Fine Arts, 1975.

Sparks, Timothy M. "St. Antoninus of Florence on St. Joseph." *Cahiers de Joséphologie*, 19 (1971): 429–55.

Steinhoff, Judith B. "Urban Images and Civic Identity in Medieval Sienese Painting." In *Art as Politics in Late Medieval and Renaissance Siena*, eds. Timothy Smith and Judith Steinhoff, 15–38. Burlington: Ashgate, 2012.

——. *Sienese Painting After the Black Death: Artistic Pluralism, Politics, and the New Art Market*. Cambridge: Cambridge University Press, 2006.

Stow, Kenneth R. "Papal and Royal Attitudes toward Jewish Lending in the Thirteenth Century." *AJS Review*, 6 (1981): 161–84.

——. "The Good of the Church, the Good of the State: The Popes and Jewish Money." In *Christianity and Judaism*, ed. Diana Wood, 237–52. Oxford: Blackwell, 1992.

Strehlke, Carl Brandon and Machtelt Brüggen Israëls. *The Bernard and Mary Berenson Collection of European Paintings at I Tatti*. Florence: I Tatti, 2015.

Strickland, Debra Higgs. *Saracens, Demons, and Jews: Making Monsters in Medieval Art*. Princeton: Princeton University Press, 2003.

Tawney, R. H. *Religion and the Rise of Capitalism*. Harmondsworth: Penguin, 1964.

Thomson, Rodney M. "The Origins of Latin Satire in Twelfth Century Europe." *Mitellateinisches Jahrbuch*, 13 (1978): 73–83.

Toaff, Ariel. "Jews, Franciscans, and the First *Monti di Pietà* in Italy (1462–1500)." In *Friars and Jews in the Middle Ages and Renaissance*, eds. Steven J. McMichael and Susan E. Myers, 239–54. London: Brill, 2004.

Todeschini, Giacomo. "Franciscan Economics and Jews in the Middle Ages: From a Theological to an Economic Lexicon." In *Friars and Jews in the Middle Ages and Renaissance*, eds. Steven J. McMichael and Susan E. Myers, 99–117. London: Brill, 2004.

Trachtenberg, Joshua. *The Devil and the Jews: The Medieval Conception of the Jew and its Relation to Modern Antisemitism*. New Haven: Yale University Press, 1943.

van Os, Henk. *Sienese Altarpieces, 1215–1460: Form, Content, Function*, 2 vols. Groningen: Bouma's Boekhuis, 1984.

Vasvari, Louise O. "Joseph on the Margin: The Mérode Tryptic and Medieval Spectacle." *Mediaevalia*, 18 (1995): 164–89.

Vitullo, Juliann and Diane Wolfthal. "Trading Values: Negotiating Masculinity in Late Medieval and Early Modern Europe." In *Money, Morality, and Culture in Late Medieval and Early Modern Europe*, eds. Juliann Vitullo and Diane Wolfthal, 155–96. Burlington: Ashgate, 2010.

Vitullo, Juliann and Diane Wolfthal, eds. *Money, Morality, and Culture in Late Medieval and Early Modern Europe*. Burlington: Ashgate, 2010.

Webb, Diana. *Patrons and Defenders: The Saints in the Italian City-States*. London: Bloomsbury, 1996.

Wiedl, Birgit. "Laughing at the Beast: The *Judensau:* Anti-Jewish Propaganda and Humor from the Middle Ages to the Early Modern Period." In *Laughter in the Middle Ages and Early Modern Times: Epistemology of a Fundamental Human Behavior, its Meaning, and Consequences*, ed. Albrecht Classen, 325–64. Berlin: De Gruyter, 2010.

Wilson, Carolyn C. "Some Further Evidence of St. Joseph's Cult in Renaissance Italy and Related St. Joseph Altarpieces." In *Die Bedeutung des hl. Josef der Heilsgeschichte. Akten des IX. Internationalen Symposions über den hl. Josef*, Vol. 2, eds. Johannes Hattler and Germán Rovira, 903–33. Kisslegg: Fe-Medienverlag, 2006.

——. *St. Joseph in Italian Renaissance Society and Art: New Directions and Interpretations*. Philadelphia: Saint Joseph's University Press, 2001.

Yunck, John A. "Economic Conservatism, Papal Finance, and the Medieval Satires on Rome." *Mediaeval Studies*, 23 (1961): 334–51.

——. *The Lineage of Lady Meed: The Development of Mediaeval Venality Satire*. Notre Dame: University of Notre Dame Press, 1963.

8

TIMEO HIBEROS ET CRUCES FERENTES

Jesuit missiology as Iberian colonialism in early modern Abyssinia

Luis Salés

On February 22, 1637, the coccydynious Latin Catholic[1] patriarch Afonso Mendez, briefly imposed on Ethiopia, wrote from Goa to the Sacred Congregation for the Propagation of the Faith bemoaning relatively recent events in Abyssinia and calling for decisive intervention:

> An extremely violent tempest of persecution has expelled me, together with many others of the Jesuit Society who are cultivators of the Ethiopian vineyard, from the boundaries of that land, and has tossed us—following the seizure of all our property… to India. Here, I am wholly occupied in procuring a fleet with which the island of Məṣəwwa', now a Turkish tributary, might be captured. For this is the mouth through which all merchandise passes into and out of Ethiopia, and through this alone is it possible to secure entry and departure for missionary preachers, a residence for the Roman patriarch and the bishops until the storm abates, and an asylum and a refuge for the Catholics who have been driven out and brought to ruin. I earnestly beg Your Eminences, therefore, to persuade our Most Holy Lord by your authority and prayers to write to His Catholic Majesty with the gravity of language that the urgency of this matter demands. For indeed, the entire restoration of Ethiopia turns on this hope.[2]

Several points about this excerpt are significant for the purposes of this study. First, it is clear that by the mid-1630s Mendes sees no substantive difference between Iberian[3] religious and economic ascendency in the region: military intervention secures both in the Horn of Africa. Second, he seems to imply that the "reduction" of Ethiopians to what the Ethiopians themselves tellingly called "that profane faith of the *'afrənj*" (ሃይማኖተ፡ አፍርንጅ: ርኩስተ፡ እንተ)[4]—a term largely designating western Europeans, often with some distaste—could be effected by

DOI: 10.4324/9781003082842-9

the force of arms. And third, Mendes is convinced that a forceful occupation of Ethiopia can be designated "restoration," as if that land had ever belonged to Latin Catholics. And yet, the message that the Habesha (as Abyssinians commonly called themselves) sent to Mendes and his colonizing compadres was unmistakable: they had overstayed their welcome. By the early 1630s, the shrewd Abyssinians harbored little doubt that the Iberians' motives were to annihilate their culture and religion and quite likely, to occupy and exploit their territories.[5] Habesha sources voicing these concerns were not unsubstantiated paranoia, as the Iberians themselves made no mystery of these ambitions and rightly earned censure, even by fellow Europeans, for taking the first steps in that direction.[6] Indeed, it bears mentioning that some scholarship on this episode (see below) may risk occluding the distinct economic leverage the Iberians sought to obtain in the region when the sole criterion for evaluation of Habesha-Iberian dynamics is that of interreligious or intercultural encounter: to pretend, even tacitly, that the Iberians were utterly disinterested in the exploitable natural and human capital of the region is disingenuous and an exercise in dishonest source selection. The Habesha did well to distrust and expel the *'afrənj*, and that decision uniquely altered the course of their history relative to all other African peoples.

Iberian interventionism in Abyssinia had begun some 80 years earlier. In the mid-sixteenth century, the predominantly Christian Abyssinian empire nearly collapsed after a string of military defeats at the hands of imam Aḥmad b. Ibrāhīm al-Ġazi (or "Grañ"), leader of the Adal sultanate (then encompassing parts of what today are Somalia, Eritrea, Djibouti, Sudan, and Ethiopia). Ləbnä Dəngəl, and later his successor Gälawdewos, led the defense of Ethiopia while emissaries to European-occupied India succeeded in securing the military assistance of some 400 Portuguese soldiers captained by Cristóvão da Gama. The conflict ended in a few years with a bittersweet Christian victory: Ləbnä Dəngəl, Grañ, and da Gama were dead and their armies suffered heavy casualties. Most of the Portuguese survivors remained in Abyssinia, where they were joined in 1557 by a group of Iberian Jesuits headed by Andrés de Oviedo.[7] While these priests were ostensibly there to care for their fellow Catholics' spiritual well-being, ample evidence to be considered here indicates that their simultaneous proselytization of the Ethiopians was deliberately premeditated and was from the beginning complicit in a larger religious-political complex of ecclesiological and economic expansionism. Predictably, these missionary efforts were at first met with a mixture of amusement and dignified disinterest. After all, there was a newborn Latin Catholic order attempting to convert the Abyssinians (whose established religion had been Christianity for incomparably longer than any nation in Western Europe) to a branch of Christianity that nearly all Christian traditions for most of Christian history considered schismatic at best; these unsolicited Jesuit endeavors failed. However, Jesuit fortunes reversed with a new wave of Iberian arrivals in 1603. While both waves aimed to convert Abyssinia to Latin Catholicism, they differed methodologically about how to implement a colonial campaign of cultural and religious extermination that increasingly acquired dimensions of political, military, and economic domination as Iberian access to power in the region grew.[8] But the success of these newcomers, too, was short-lived. In the early 1630s, the *nəgusä nägäst* (king of kings) Susənyos walked back his conversion to the *'afrənj* religion and his successor Fasilädäs permanently disinvited them. Ethiopia was never colonized.

In light of these considerations, it is surprising that scholarship on this episode has shown little interest in designating this Iberian intervention as colonial. The tacit consensus (tacit, as few have entertained the question as such) is that the Jesuits may have been culturally and religiously insensitive, but colonizers they were not.[9] Granted, if colonialism is regarded solely as the economic exploitation of a people that materially benefit the homeland of the colonizers, the case for Iberian colonialism in Ethiopia is merely an example of European failure to impose a regime of resource extraction. But extensive developments in postcolonial theory have pointed beyond this simplistic view of colonialism by drawing special attention to ideologies of cultural and religious domination through discursive constructions of otherness that often accompany or precede runaway economic exploitation;[10] I would maintain that was precisely the case in Iberia's attempted colonization of Ethiopia. That the Iberians disastrously failed hardly absolves them from deploying colonial-ideological indoctrination, engaging in widescale political manipulation, occupying and fortifying strategic landmarks,[11] and machinating schemes of economic profiteering, all of which resulted in thousands of native deaths and decades of civil strife.

Wendy Belcher has recently bucked the scholarly trend of disregarding the colonial dimensions of Iberian intervention in Abyssinia while arguing for Habesha noblewomen's pivotal role in defeating the Jesuits. She notes: "Oddly, few scholars have commented on this annihilation of a European proto-colonial effort, its absolute failure. And colonial effort it was."[12] I find Belcher's final interjection especially significant because it intimates that scholarship has not recognized this effort as colonial—an intimation readily confirmed from surveying scholarship on the episode. Specifically, I demonstrate here that the Jesuits deliberately and premeditatedly sought to exterminate Ethiopian Orthodox Täwaḥədo Christianity as a lived religious and cultural identity as part of a larger geopolitical campaign of economic and military domination of the strategic region. Because the evidence for this thesis is overwhelming, the approach of this study is a close reading of key passages in the writings of the Jesuit architects of this endeavor, Ignacio de Loyola and Pedro Páez. While this chapter focuses on Jesuit texts, I nonetheless give Abyssinians the final word on the matter and anticipate a future and lengthier Habeshacentric investigation of this pivotal moment in Abyssinian history.

Ignacio de Loyola

Ignacio de Loyola defined the primary features of Iberian colonial ideology for the "reduction" of Abyssinia to Latin Christianity, which effectively functioned as a guidebook for several generations of Jesuits given his significance for the order.[13] But for all its ecclesiastical appearance, de Loyola's ideology was also implicated in larger structures of empire-building and economic interventionism that were inextricable from his epistemological horizons. On this point, Giuseppe Marcocci has convincingly shown that "Rome was… the real source of legitimacy of the Portuguese Empire. Papal bulls had allowed the crown to make war and conquer in a very wide geographical area in exchange for an unprecedented effort of evangelization. The universal conversion, with all its millenarian implications, had become a political issue."[14] De Loyola's efforts were situated in this interplay of religious, political, and economic domination of eschatological proportions that dominated Iberian thought between the mid-sixteenth and late-seventeenth centuries. In this interim, several Iberian factions had formed that differed about their understanding of empire. While some wanted looser mercantile alliances, de Loyola's ideology was compatible with those who "insisted on military conquest and political subjection of new territories, stressing the importance of the providential apostolic mission of the Portuguese in the history of [hu]mankind."[15] This apostolic mission extended to non-Latin Christians and non-Christians alike; the only difference in dominating them was methodological.[16]

Thus, as early as February 20, 1555, de Loyola wrote a letter to his Jesuit compadre Juan Núñez, one of a dozen Jesuits initially responsible for the "reduction of Ethiopia." The letter's title all but spells out its sinister intentions: *Recuerdos que podrán ayudar para la redución de los reynos del preste Juan á la unión de la Yglesia y religión Cathólica, embiados al P. Juan Núñez* ("*Reminders that might help in the reduction of the kingdoms of Prester John to union with the Catholic Church and religion, sent to Fr. Juan Núñez*"). And yet, for a letter of an ostensibly religious character, de Loyola tellingly begins by emphasizing the importance of the Lusitanian crown for subjecting the Abyssinian monarch to the Latin Pope. The preface reads as a subtle reminder to the Habesha ruler of the force of European arms, so recently instrumental in defeating the Adal sultanate, with the implication that Núñez should not hesitate to invoke European might should subtler diplomacy fail. To broker Iberian demands, de Loyola suggests establishing an ambassador from Portugal, who can "go to visit Prester[17] and to offer him the patriarch and assistant bishops and the other priests… so that it is no longer needful to take patriarchs from the lands of the Moors or from schismatic Christians [i.e., Copts]. And if this gesture is done with the uttermost solemnity on behalf of His Highness, the [Latin] patriarch will appear to possess all the more authority for the divine service."[18] The upshot of this letter is that Ethiopian ecclesiastical demographics would be permanently occupied by Latin operatives; Ethiopian autocephaly was nowhere in view.

By extension, the measures de Loyola pushes would sever Ethiopia's ties with Alexandria and place all of Abyssinia under the political-religious-economic jurisdictional complex of the Latin Pope and the Iberian crowns. This strategy would entail a multi-tier triumph, as the *nəgusä nägäst* would answer to a European patriarch, but as understood by the theopolitical framework of Latin

Catholicism (tellingly, the Ethiopian *abunä*, Sə'mon, was tortured, murdered, and beheaded in 1617).[19] Consistent with de Loyola's global ambitions, this strategy would prime Ethiopian lands for European occupation and (almost certainly) economic exploitation under the façade of pontifical authority. The reason for promoting this approach is obvious, as Mendes intimated in his letter cited earlier: Abyssinia was located in a key strategic position that would establish Iberian control of the Red Sea, thereby mediating the Indian Ocean and the Mediterranean basin through an unbroken mercantile route that would circumvent Ottoman taxes on eastern imports.[20] While Mendes came close to realizing this vision, de Loyola first proposed the concomitance of Latin Papal authority over Abyssinia and economic, military, and political hegemony in the region.[21] For de Loyola and his followers, Ethiopian religion and culture was not only an acceptable casualty in furthering Iberian millennialism; its eradication was inherently good while benefitting European crowns and miters.[22]

There is no ambiguity about de Loyola's intentions, as after this politicized preface he outlines a playbook for the cultural and religious eradication of Ethiopian Orthodoxy that defined Jesuit measures progressively and successfully implemented between 1603 and 1632. The Jesuit masks this agenda of cultural and religious extermination with the euphemism "reduction" (*reducción* or *redução*), which has not garnered attention as a colonial term in this context designating the deliberate and sustained effort to annihilate ancient religious customs and cultural practices by supplanting them with Latin religion and culture. For example, Andreu Martínez D'Aloys explains that for de Loyola the term "reduction" refers to "a process in which a reality in potency becomes an act, wherein disorder and confusion are addressed towards unity and order."[23] Certainly, that is its sense in a recycled Thomistic Aristotelianism, but absent from this intellectualized explanation are the real, tangible implications behind the term, that is, the premeditated erasure of Habesha religious and cultural identities.[24] This sense of "reduction" is readily apparent throughout de Loyola's letter, as he emphasizes that "there is no hope of being saved outside of the Roman Catholic Church; and that what she determines concerning faith and mores must be believed to be saved."[25] Accordingly, de Loyola enumerates an extensive list of Abyssinian "errors" that his envoys must purge, such as intense fasting, certain baptismal practices, abstinence from pork, circumcision, and Sabbath observance.[26] Conversely, de Loyola proposes the imposition of distinctly Latin practices and beliefs, such as confession, final rites, and original sin. Throughout his directives, de Loyola inserts suggestions for effectively manipulating the natives to comply with these impositions.[27]

The beating heart of the document, however, is the indoctrination of the Abyssinian youth. De Loyola orders the Jesuits to "make many schools for reading and writing... and colleges for instructing the youth... in the Latin language and in Christian customs and doctrine."[28] Manifestly, de Loyola presupposes the non-existence of Abyssinian pedagogy and their consequent failure in training the youth in "Christian customs and doctrine." The preposterousness of his assumptions aside, the Jesuit's plan entails the systematic elimination of native Ethiopian forms of knowledge production by targeting the youth; once more, in his colonial imaginary, Ethiopian Orthodoxy and Ge'ez are acceptable and necessary casualties for universalizing a megalomaniac, Europeanized Christianity. Ironically, the Jesuits' assumption of Ethiopian intellectual inferiority was frequently weaponized against them—especially by women.[29] My point here is that de Loyola's objective was a colonial strategy of domination and extermination of native forms of knowledge that would have the longest-lasting consequences if they had prevailed because of the effects of indoctrinating the youth. I would therefore underscore that the success of de Loyola's agenda would have meant the eradication of one of the oldest and most authentic apostolic Christian traditions and the permanent loss of one of a few native African Christianities. This is no small matter and has yet to receive censure commensurate with the degree of its ethical severity.

Despite the extensive recommendations about subtlety and psychological manipulation he offered Núñez, de Loyola failed to take his own advice when addressing an epistle to the Abyssinian emperor Gälawdewos, dated February 16, 1555. His attitude exudes cultural and religious superiority, squarely operating in what the postcolonial historian Santiago Castro-Gómez calls "the hubris of point zero," that is, the widespread European ideology that their contingent epistemological positionality was identical to objective representational truth.[30] Accordingly, de Loyola presents a series of doctored datapoints by which he expects the Abyssinian emperor to accept the Latin Pope as the supreme religious head of his nation. For example, he claims that at the Chalcedonian council (451) "all exclaimed with a single voice and called Pope Leo the most holy, apostolic, and universal"[31] and adds that a similar outcome was decided in the ecumenical council of Constantinople (presumably Constantinople II, 553) and the synod of Florence (1439).

While it is true that some of these councils were attended by "Greeks [i.e., Romans], Armenians, and Jacobites [i.e., West Syrians]," it is simply not true that a universally accepted decision was reached. De Loyola may be reminded that the Tome of Leo wreaked irreversible havoc on the Chalcedonian council and that by Aksumite, Coptic, West Syrian, and Armenian accounts (that is, by the account of a considerable number of delegate factions) the Latins broke with the ecumenical tradition of Ephesus (431) by embracing Leo's Nestorian Christology. So it is fundamentally dishonest to state that the conciliar delegations affirmed anything "with a single voice." Needless to add, the factions that rejected Chalcedon also rejected every subsequent "ecumenical" council (Constantinople II, III, and Nicaea II) and did not deem their determinations dogmatically binding. Likewise, the Romans, Armenians, and west Syrians promptly rejected what they regarded as the unacceptably coercive and theologically flawed determinations of the sham Latin synod of Ferrara-Florence, which was just a ruse to secure military aid against the Ottomans that never, in fact, materialized on the scale promised or needed to make a substantive difference. In reality, de Loyola was absurdly overplaying the ecclesiological significance of the Latin Church for other Christians: when he penned this letter, Latin Catholics had been excommunicated by virtually every catholic, apostolic Christian tradition and were beleaguered further by the irreversible rise of Protestantism. Perhaps embedded in this domineering posturing was the attempt to compensate for Latin Christianity's ecclesiological insignificance for other apostolic Christians by executing a campaign of global expansionism forcefully to impose political catholicity where religious catholicity had failed.

This suggestion is hardly an uncharitable exaggeration. Consider, for example, de Loyola's imperiously hollow words when he directly informs—on whose authority?—the *nəgusä nägäst* Gälawdewos that "we decree and order that the Holy Apostolic See and the Roman Pontiff have primacy over the entire orb of the earth,"[32] meaning, of course, over Abyssinia as well. Clearly, de Loyola believes that Rome's ecclesiastical jurisdiction can be asserted, as though by fiat, to legitimate the Jesuits' spiritual and cultural occupation of Ethiopia. De Loyola's rationale is as insulting as it is unsolicited, as he further tells the emperor that the Alexandrian patriarchate, from which Ethiopia derived its apostolic status, beloved patriarchs, and theologoumena for twelve centuries, was a "severed, putrid member of the Church's mystical body" that "has neither movement nor virtue" as it was "schismatic and segregated from the Holy Apostolic See and from the head of the whole Church."[33] Accordingly, de Loyola proposes to dispatch a dozen Jesuits to Abyssinia, and a patriarch to follow, to eradicate Ethiopian Orthodoxy—albeit not stated in those terms. In sum, Ignacio de Loyola defined Iberian colonial ideology as the "reduction" of Abyssinia to Latin Catholicism. Central to this ideology was his belief that Latin Christianity was the true faith, that all other Christians had to submit to the Latin Pontiff, and that the bishop of Rome's jurisdiction was universal, thereby warranting his ecclesiastical operatives' spiritual and cultural occupation of the Christian other's existential landscapes worldwide. These ecclesiastical maneuvers were interwoven with imperial expansionism: where Iberian missionaries went, colonialism soon followed.

Such communications with Abyssinia predictably did not succeed in accomplishing their aims. In his *Confession of Faith*, Gälawdewos reassures his people as much as he rebukes the foreigners that Ethiopia is not subject to European jurisdiction. The emperor subtly invokes his regnal name, አጽናፍ ሰገድ ('Aṣnaf Sägäd, "The Uttermost Borders Bow [To Him]"), as a warning to the *'afrənj* that they were dealing with a monarch in his own right and would do well not to test his abundant generosity. Gälawdewos does not equivocate on the contested points: his and his nation's religious credentials are not in question, seeing as "my faith" (ሃይማኖትየ) is "the faith of my fathers, the Israelite kings [ነገሥት፡ እስራኤላዊያን], and the faith of my flock [መርዔትየ] who are in the boundaries of my empire."[34] Here the emperor's deliberate allusion to his Solomonid lineage (though doubtless legendary) is meant to trump Latin apostolic roots by over a millennium. He affirms the three ecumenical councils (conspicuously not the fourth) and offers a slight paraphrase of the Nicene-Constantinopolitan Creed (predictably, sans *filioque*).[35] Gälawdewos concludes by addressing his people's observance of Sabbath, circumcision, and abstinence from certain meats: Sabbath is observed in his nation because apostolic tradition celebrates Eucharist on Sabbath, as the ዲድስቅልያ (*Didəsqəlya*, part of the Ethiopic canon) affirms; circumcision is a cultural practice of Ethiopia, such as face tattooing in Nubia or ear-piercing in India, and that will not change on account of misplaced *'afrənj* pietistic posturing;[36] finally, the *'afrənj* err in Christian charity when censoring Abyssinians' abstinence from pork, for Paul tells the Romans, "Let the one who eats not abhor the one who does not eat, for God accepts all" (Rom 14:3).[37] Here Gälawdewos criticizes *'afrənj* intolerance by alluding with disdain, in subtle parallel, to a story about the Roman emperor Konstantinos I, who forced Jews to eat pork. Gälawdewos disapproves of such forceful actions, and instead reasonably proposes that if some people like fish, they should eat fish, and if chicken, chicken. Regardless, he concludes that there is no canon (ቀኖና) in the New Testament regarding meat because "to the pure, everything is pure" (ኵሉ፡ ንጹሕ: ለንጹሓን, Tit 1:15).[38] Gälawdewos cleverly implies his people's purity and leaves the question hanging: can the same be said of the *'afrənj*?

Pedro Páez

The Jesuits dispatched to Ethiopia during Gälawdewos's rule failed to make any headway after decades of efforts. However, Pedro Páez's arrival with a company of Jesuits in 1603 dramatically changed the course of events. Although Páez was largely forgotten by his contemporaries in the aftermath of the expulsion of the Iberians from Abyssinia in the 1630s, his significance for this reversal features prominently in modern scholarship.[39] Páez's meeker and subtler style is often (at times quasi-hagiographically)[40] contrasted with Mendes's insensitive authoritarianism.[41] Yet, while I grant Páez's and Mendes's methodological differences, the distinction strikes me as ethically immaterial as their objective was the extermination of an entire Christian tradition and culture. It is frankly disconcerting that much of scholarship cares more about nuancing their colonizing idiosyncrasies than it does about censoring their shared goal of religious and cultural annihilation. This misguided approach has yielded bewildering statements, such as that "The work [i.e., *História da Etiopía*] of Páez becomes… a safeguard for the survival of Ethiopian culture."[42] How it is possible to make this assertion about a man whose success would have meant the irretrievable loss of the culture he is here credited with safeguarding is unclear. Perhaps some of the positive scholarly assessment of Páez's work hinges on assuming the discursive transparency of his *História da Etiopía* (henceforth *HdE*).[43] But in my reading, large portions of this work amount to a colonizing ethnography replete with deliberate misrepresentations, literary misdirection, cultural stereotyping, and unrelenting condescension. Simply put, Páez misses no opportunity for establishing Iberian cultural, spiritual, and moral superiority to legitimate the eradication of

Ethiopian Orthodoxy. Attention to these details highlights the more malevolent features of Páez's work.

Páez's *História da Etiopía* responds to the Dominican Luis de Urreta's *Historia de la Sagrada Orden de Predicadores, en los remotos Reynos de la Etiopia* (Valencia, 1611). While de Urreta's book is at best a dishonest work of fantasy masqueraded as history and the unenviable gold standard in colonial exoticism and excess, Páez's self-assured insistence on truth-telling is also misleading for its calculated veneer of verisimilitude. So, while Páez has been rightly praised for producing extensive sections of largely credible content, it bears mentioning that the most accurate portions of his work are concerned with economic, geographic, and political data that a hypothetical invader would doubtless find of inestimable value—one must wonder, for example, whether Páez's sustained ponderances about the potential to cultivate the Ethiopian highlands with Iberian crops is simply academic theorizing.[44] The events that unfolded during Páez's time and immediately after—including especially the establishment of Jesuit strongholds in some of the most affluent and strategically valuable regions of the Ethiopian highlands—suggest that these surprisingly detailed and precise catalogs of the natural wealth of the land, the fertility of the soil, and the kinds of crops already growing there were most likely an early-stage blueprint for the exploitability of the land. But when it comes to Páez's representation of the natives, his tenor changes; his assessment of the locals sharply contrasts with his positive appraisal of the fructiferous geological conditions: what Ethiopia has in natural resources, it lacks in intellectual or cultural mettle—that is his implied estimation of the state of affairs. Simply put, Páez's representation of the Abyssinian land and religion is meant simultaneously to motivate Iberian economic profiteering while legitimating such an intervention by appealing to Habesha religious and cultural inferiority.[45] Of course, nothing about this approach was new to the Iberian colonizers, who in the same century had already deployed nearly identical strategies of infiltration and domination across massive swaths of land in America, Asia, and increasingly in Africa, with one eye on Catholicization and the other on tightening their grip on local resource supplies in the interest of economic hegemony over the global marketplace. So while the Iberians failed in the end, every indication suggests that they were intent on following similar patterns to colonize Abyssinia and would likely have succeeded had the Ethiopians not expelled them from their lands.

As de Loyola, Páez also underscores the inferiority of Abyssinian education to justify supplanting it with Jesuit pedagogy and Latin Catholic content. For example, in *HdE* 1.1.22 Páez refutes de Urreta's reports that the Habesha have seminaries and universities comparable to the Europeans' by describing their educational practices with unconcealed disdain. He explains that most youths are taught to read and often to write by non-cloistered monks and fails to conceal his injured misogynistic sensitivities when he reports that Habesha girls "learn not just to read but also to understand Saint Paul and the Gospel."[46] Páez seems to expect the reader to join him in shared outrage at this scandalous practice—clear proof (to like-minded misogynists) that Ethiopians have truly lost their way.

Predictably, Páez is unimpressed by the Abyssinian educational system[47] and launches into a protracted character assassination of these teacher-monks to sanction Jesuit indoctrination of Habesha boys (girls were already dangerously over-educated in his mind and indeed proved to be a persistent thorn in his side). He writes: "The truth is that if they [the monks] were to teach reasonably, they would bear much fruit, but they do not so much aspire (*pretendem*) to the good of the souls, as to honor and wealth... And when telling some of them aside (*em particular*) why they do not declare the truth of the faith... they answer that they do not dare, as they would lose their sustenance and they would harm them."[48] It is of course extremely convenient for the Jesuit that these monks would confess in private (thus overlaying their words with a façade of credibility) that they do not teach the truth because they are driven by greed—as if anyone would confess such a thing. But in this way, Páez can contrast the mendacious, greedy, and fearful monastics with Jesuits, who courageously teach the truth for free. To this point, Páez further relays the words of the son-in-law of the emperor Athanatewos, also spoken in private and thus seemingly most trustworthy: "Father, we do not have teachers. These, our monks, are like Pharisees, seeking nothing but honor and wealth, nor do they know anything. And if they do understand something, they dare not say."[49] Once again, the Jesuit reserves his harshest words for the mouth of a native to increase their weightiness, while simultaneously portraying Jesuit presence in Abyssinia as messianic and locally desired—all of these distinctive features of Iberian imperial millennialism. Páez thus engages in commonplace discursive strategies of colonial misrepresentation aimed here at justifying the imposition of Jesuit pedagogy and Iberian culture on the natives as part of a larger campaign of global economic, military, political, and religious hegemony. Predictably, Páez fails to mention in this allegedly altruistic moment that the Jesuits themselves, their vows of poverty notwithstanding, had accumulated considerable economic wealth during their time in Abyssinia, especially in the form of extensive land grants, which were the primordial means of capital generation in late medieval Abyssinia, and that they had taken further steps to increase land yields and protect their investitures through the development of defensive structures in strategic positions, as in the case of the 'Adwa plateau. Indeed, if the Jesuits' motives were purely religious and fully divorced from capital considerations, the confiscation of what property, precisely, was Mendes bemoaning in his letter, cited earlier? The simplest answer here is likely the most accurate and sincere: Mendes was not solely anguished by having lost hierarchical authority over Abyssinia, but also by the irretrievable loss of the significant material wealth that accompanied his and his compadres' elevated ecclesiastical status in the land.[50]

Páez next takes aim at the state of theological education of Ethiopians in particular, inserting that "they are most weak and replete with errors."[51] Once again, Páez will reserve his harshest words for a native, this time the emperor. In this scene, the Jesuit introduces a conveniently nameless monk who used to teach theology and Scripture to Susənyos before criticizing his understanding of difficult Scriptural passages. For instance, Páez reports that the monk interpreted the "sons of God" in Genesis 6 as referring to angels and maintains instead, with derision, that it refers to the sons of Seth. Needless to add, Páez shows his ignorance of the larger Biblical canon and commentary literature; this monk would ostensibly have interpreted Genesis 6 in light of Enoch's Book of the Watchers (1–10), which speaks of 200 angels who wreaked havoc on the earth. Páez enumerates further hermeneutical "errors" of this monk and occupies Susənyos' mouth to report that at these interpretations: "The emperor laughed a lot and said, 'Here your reverence will see of what type our teachers are; and indeed, this one was one of the most famed we have.'"[52] As before, the Jesuit's objective is to delegitimate the native Ethiopian theological authorities, especially by castigating them through the words of the Abyssinians themselves—and who could dispute the emperor's assessment concerning "one of the most famed we have"? This strategy remains constant across the breadth of the two tomes but is especially significant here as it sets up a full-tilt assault on Ethiopian Orthodoxy in the following book.

Book two contains some valuable information, such as detailed descriptions of the Abyssinian liturgy and the rites of ordination, but on the whole the book is a catalog of what Páez deems serious ritual and theological Abyssinian errors despite his acknowledgment of their ancient apostolic status (1.2.1). The irony, of course, is that Páez seems oblivious that where he finds fault with Ethiopian Orthodoxy, he is in fact finding fault with apostolic traditions and practices that predate the institutionalization of his own church's considerably later innovations. In sketch form, these include: the *filioque* controversy (1.2.2); Chalcedonian vs. non-Chalcedonian Christology (1.2.3–5); psychogenesis, psychology, psycho-somatic relations, and universal resurrection (1.2.6); observance of "Jewish" customs (1.2.8); baptismal practices (1.2.9); the absence of confirmation, extreme unction, and penance in Abyssinian liturgical life (1.2.10); differing marriage practices (1.2.14); and the absence of purgatory in Abyssinian eschatology (1.2.16). Again, Páez's success in imposing his agenda here would have meant the eradication of distinctive, ancient, apostolic Christian customs and beliefs, and their replacement with dubious dogmas denounced by most apostolic Christian traditions.

As before, Páez puts his own words in native mouths, but also gives a weak and uncompelling voice to his Abyssinian detractors to amplify his fabricated theological triumphs over throngs of native scholars. There is much reminiscent here of the *majlis* (مجلس) dialogic practiced in the early medieval Middle East and Iberia, including the unsurprising victory of the narrator's religion and the ensuing conversion of his religious other in the face of such compelling evidence.[53] But even the most tendentious Christian *majlis*, especially under the 'Abbasids, had the self-respect of at least putting real and often valid points in the mouths of the theological opponent to edify readers; Páez does not, which signals his marked departure from the mutual respect that existed in such discussions. Instead, Páez embraces a distinctly colonial approach that infantilizes his opponents, casts them as incapable of intellectual thought, and accuses them of deceit when all else fails.[54]

Páez first uses these representational structures in *HdE* 1.2.2, where he allegedly debates with a large group of Abyssinian monks about the *filioque*. The theological content Páez reproduces is nothing new for those who have traced the development of this controversy, but simply amounts to a reiteration of well-known points that were first criticized by the patriarch of Constantinople, Photios, about seven centuries prior. But in the Iberian's rendition of these debates, apparently no Ethiopian could offer a rejoinder to his arguments. Of course, I am skeptical of Páez's report, but that is immaterial; what is significant here is his colonizing representation of the events. For example, he claims that "Celá Christós" (the brother of the emperor),

> Being at first… so contrary to our holy faith that—as he himself tells me many times now—our beliefs seemed worse than those of the Moors, but after he understood them, he received them with so much affection and believes them with such firmness, that he put himself in danger of death to defend them, and now that he already confesses and takes communion with us, he says publicly that the faith of the Roman Church is the true one and that no one can be saved outside of it. And to those who contradict him on this subject, regardless of how greatly lettered they may be, he convinces them with his reasonings, like children.[55]

It is true that *ras* Śəʾəlä Krəstos was among the early Abyssinian noblemen who converted to Catholicism, and one must perhaps allow for his own theological forays to debate with his countryfolk. But regardless of these discussions' actual dynamics, Páez not only puts a Latin confession in a native's mouth—a portion of which is virtually identical to that previously cited in de Loyola's letter to Gälawdewos, but also deploys the enduringly colonial trope of paternalism to justify Iberian authority over greatly lettered Ethiopians as though they were children. The content matters less here than its representation: Páez deploys a common colonial formula for dominating religious others that belies the episode's discursive transparency.

A similar structure plays out when Páez debates the *filioque* with the "best" scholars of Ethiopia. He informs them that this dogma "is declared by sixteen general councils and determined as an article of faith, it is clearly deduced from the holy gospel and from S. Paul, who says that the Holy Spirit is the Spirit of the Father and of the Son, which is why all the holy doctors and even the books of Ethiopia teach it thus."[56] Páez senses the urge to affirm this point because he maintains that the Ethiopians, like the "Greeks" (i.e., Romans), deny that the Holy Spirit proceeds from the Son and only proceeds from the Father. As is well known, the *filioque* was a unilateral Latin addition to the Nicene-Constantinopolitan creed some two centuries after it had been adopted in Constantinople I (381) and was thus predictably not to be found in any other apostolic Christian tradition:

the *filioque* was inconsistent with Nicene-Constantinopolitan trinitarianism. Gregorios of Nazianzos, the patriarch of Constantinople for most of the council, had established that predicates attributed to a single person (ὑπόστασις) refer to hypostatic particularities (ἰδιότητα), while those predicated of more than one person belong to a substance (οὐσία) and apply to all three.[57] In the ninth century, Photios of Constantinople's *Mystagogy of the Holy Spirit* systematically outlines the heretical affirmations that result from taking the *filioque* seriously. Most significantly, the *filioque* shatters the substantive union of the Trinitarian persons by making a predicate (to give procession) apply to two persons (Father and Son) alone.[58]

Similar arguments against the *filioque* had been available for centuries. But instead of reporting what would have doubtless been a fascinating exchange of ideas, Páez resorts to a condescending strategy of proof-texting from Abyssinian scripture. When he allegedly identifies places in the Apostolic Constitution that seem to support the *filioque*, the native scholars' response in his reconstruction of the event is not to offer a hermeneutically savvy riposte, but secretly to erase it from their texts. And when Páez points out that the words have been erased, the same scholars somehow manage to copy the entire Apostolic Constitutions (approximately 100 pages long) without the *filioque*-supporting phrases (in the course of a single debate!) to show that it is not part of the original.[59] The episode of course borders on self-aggrandizing absurdity and insults the intellectual capabilities of the Abyssinians as though they were devious children who must resort to cheap tricks to win an argument—the irony of such a representation must have been lost on Páez. As before, the content itself is unreliable, but the style is significant: it signals that Páez follows established conventions of Western European colonial discourse to affirm his cultural and religious superiority and thereby to sanction the eradication of Ethiopian otherness through "reduction" to Latin Christianity.

However, Abyssinian sources tell a different story about *'afrənj* persuasiveness. One of the most important sources in this regard is the *Gädlä Wälättä Ṗeṭros* (*Life of Wälättä Ṗeṭros*, abbreviated hereafter as *GWP*), which has the distinct advantage of being relatively close to the events, while also enjoying some hindsight to weigh their significance. Although predictably favorable to the Ethiopian Orthodox faction, the general picture in the *GWP* can be corroborated by Abyssinian and Iberian sources and the interactions between Wälättä Ṗeṭros and the Jesuits are unremarkably casual when contrasted with Páez's bloated self-representation.[60] The *GWP* generally (but unceremoniously) documents that despite significant energy expenditure the Jesuits routinely failed to convert Habesha women, who often humiliated them or otherwise ignored their incessant efforts. This is a far cry from the heroic self-portrait Páez conjures up of his insurmountable genius; that is because his objective was not to retell events as they happened (his protestations to the contrary notwithstanding) but to represent Christian alterity as desperately thirsting for the waters of Latin Catholic truth and culture to justify Iberian colonialism in Abyssinia.

The *GWP* does not give that impression. Consider, for example, the uncontrived simplicity with which the text reports Wälättä Ṗeṭros's exchanges with three Jesuits that were sent to "deceive" her into abandoning "the true religion of Dioskoros [ሃይማኖተ፡ ዲዮስቆሮስ፡ ርትዕት] and to adopt the profane religion of Leo [ሃይማኖተ፡ ልዮን፡ ርኩስት]."[61] We are simply told: "And she argued with them, and she defeated them, and she humiliated them [ወተዋቀሠት፡ ምስሌሆሙ፡ ወሞዓቶሙ፡ ወአስተኃፈረቶሙ]," and somewhat later that "she laughed and heaped scorn on them [ትስሕቅ፡ ወትሣለቅ፡ ላዕሌሆሙ]" for calling themselves "teachers," when only Christ should be called a teacher (Mt 23:8).[62] The Gəʿəz account here intimates, as Páez's clearly displays, the Jesuits' deliberate efforts to cast themselves as the pedagogues of an otherwise intellectually and dogmatically hopeless people. But for all the cleverness that Páez reports on his own behalf, these Jesuits failed to persuade Wälättä Ṗeṭros—one must wonder how truly disruptive she must have been to have received such attention when, by Páez's account, a single Jesuit sufficed to defeat all the learned men of Ethiopia. If the *GWP* can be trusted, Wälättä Ṗeṭros must have been a troublemaker of an unusual sort, as the emperor dispatched her to Mendes as a final resort. Mendes reportedly spent every Saturday morning for months attempting to persuade Wälättä Ṗeṭ ros, but, as his colonial mission, failed.[63] If there is some truth to these reports, the unilateral Jesuit handle on the intellectual landscape of Ethiopia was not as firm as Páez made it appear. Wälättä Ṗeṭros lived to see and celebrate the permanent expulsion of the Iberians from Abyssinia, a land that never was, and never would be, theirs.

Conclusion

A clear picture begins to emerge from this investigation. The Jesuits in Abyssinia were not innocent bystanders solely concerned with the spiritual health of their fellow Iberians. Rather, they were active agents in a premeditated, decades-long campaign to subdue Ethiopia to the dual power complex of Latin Catholicism and the Iberian crowns through the determined eradication of Ethiopian religion and culture. Simply put, Jesuit missiology was instrumentally the overture to the would-be Iberian colonization of Abyssinia. In effect, the late writings of this episode (ca. 1622–1632, as well as texts written in the aftermath of the expulsion of the Iberians) indicate that under Afonso Mendes the missionary project was metamorphosizing into a new form of power dynamics, cultural suppression, and early-stage economic profiteering that was, simultaneously, one of the major reasons the endeavor collapsed. By the late 1620s and early 1630s, Habesha and European sources point to Iberian economic interest in the region, not solely for securing the Red Sea trade route, but for exploiting the fructiferous land itself. And judging from the Iberian track record from the preceding century that was not an unfounded fear. Some of the evidence considered here suggests that prominent Ethiopians had accurately predicted the direction in which Abyssinia was headed under the influence of the Jesuits, particularly by making inroads for the extraction of resources and exploitation of the land. That much is readily apparent from even the most cursory survey of the territories that had been granted to the Iberians between 1603 and 1630, whose common characteristics are relative fertility, proximity to trade routes, and the subsequent development of defensive edifices under the guise of feeling insecure—a fear that was probably well-founded, but, for that, clear evidence that their economic ascendency in Abyssinia was alarming to the populace.

All the same, the patriarchal impostor's uncompromising superiority complex vastly overestimated the purchase his cultural and religious capital had on the natives and, ironically, his distortedly condescending regard for the Habesha led him to underestimate their organizational capabilities and political astuteness. Jesuit failure in Ethiopia partially pivoted on self-delusion brought on by a colonial ideology of their own invention. But above all, the Iberian phantasy of colonizing Ethiopia failed because it persisted in the recalcitrant, Unchristian assumption of the other's inferiority. That is, in time the Iberians tacitly answered Gälawdewos's hanging question in the *Confession of Faith* and they were found wanting.

Notes

1 I do not use "Roman Catholic" as a designation for Christians whose ecclesiastical head was the bishop of Rome because this terminology, though almost universally used and accepted, is complicit in the colonial discursive erasure of Roman religion and culture (that is, the religion and culture of the Roman Empire) that were set in irreversible decline after 1453 (arguably in 1204, but certainly not earlier). The Romans were both Roman and Catholic; they were not subject to the bishop of Rome, nor did they regularly commune with Western Europeans. Here, "Romans" means the peoples of the Roman Empire; "Latin Catholics" refers to Christians ecclesiastically under the jurisdiction of the bishop of the city of Rome. Finally, I differentiate the Coptic and Latin popes by variant references to their episcopal sees, namely, Alexandria and Rome. On the general problems in relation to the Latin tradition of Western Europe and the Romans, see Anthony Kaldellis, *Romanland: Ethnicity and Empire in Byzantium* (Cambridge, MA: Belknap Press, 2019) and *The Byzantine Republic: People and Power in New Rome* (Cambridge, MA: Harvard University Press, 2015); George Demacopoulos, *Colonizing Christianity: Greek and Latin Religious Identity in the Era of the Fourth Crusade* (New York: Fordham University Press, 2019).

2 Patriarch Mendes, "Patriarch Mendes to the Sacred Congregation for the Propagation of the Faith, Goa, 22 February 1637," in *The Jesuits in Ethiopia (1609–1641): Latin Letters in Translation*. Ed. Wendy Laura Belcher, trans. Jessica Wright, Leon Grek, and Leonardo Cohen, trans. (Wiesbaden: Harrassowitz Verlag, 2017), 168.

3 By "Iberian" I primarily mean the subjects of the various crowns of the Iberian Peninsula, and though I acknowledge their cultural and linguistic differences, these were quite porous—e.g., Ignacio de Loyola and Pedro Páez, the two central figures in this study, were both Castilian but operated extensively at the behest of the Portuguese (indeed, Páez' wrote his largest work in Portuguese)—as were their political alliances; effectively, for most of the period covered here, there was little appreciable political difference between the Spanish and Lusitanian monarchical spheres of influence. See Marina Alfonso Mola and Carlos Martínez Shaw, "Pedro Páez y la misión jesuítica en Etiopía en el contexto de la unión de las Coronas de España y Portugal," *Historia Moderna* 17 (2004): 59–75, especially n. 1.

4 E.g., in Gälawdewos, *Vitae Sanctorum Indigenarum: I: Acta S. Walatta Petros*, ed. Carlo Conti Rossini, CSCO 68 (Rome, Paris, Leipzig: Karolus de Luigi, 1912), 25 (henceforth *GWP*).

5 See Wendy Laura Belcher, "Sisters Debating the Jesuits: The Role of African Women in Defeating Portuguese Proto-Colonialism in Seventeenth-Century Abyssinia," *Northeast African Studies* 13, no.1 (2013): 121–66, here especially 125–7 and nn. 37–42.

6 Three figures are especially notable in this regard: Fray Manuel de Asunción, Michael Geddes, and James Bruce. For further commentary, see Leonardo Cohen, *The Missionary Strategies of the Jesuits in Ethiopia (1555–1632)* (Wiesbaden: Harrassowitz Verlag. 2009) and "'Imprudentia Maxima': fray Manuel de Asunción y su crítica de la actuación de los Jesuitas en Etiopía," *Lusitania Sacra* 32 (2015): 81–104, as well as his references (n. 1) to Hervé Pennec, *Des jésuites au royaume du Prêtre Jean* (Paris: Centre Culturel Calouste Gulbenkian, 2003) and "La mission Jesuite en Ethiopie au temps de Pedro Páez (1583–1622) et ses rapports avec le pouvoir ethiopien," *Rassegna di Studi Etiopici*. 36, 37, 38 (1992–1994), 77–115, 135–65, and 139–81. Michael Geddes, *The Church History of Ethiopia* (Albany, NY: The Ages Digital Library, 1997), 4–5 (see further, Cohen, "Imprudentia Maxima," 82. James Bruce, *Travels to Discover the Source of the Nile in the Years 1768, 1769, 1770, 1771, 1772, and 1773*, vol. 3 (Edinburgh: J. Ballantyne, A. Constable, and Co, 1804–1805), 403 (see further, Cohen, "Imprudentia Maxima," 83).

7 See further Samantha Kelly, "Introduction," in *A Companion to Medieval Ethiopia and Eritrea*, ed. Samantha Kelly (Leiden: Brill, 2020), 1–4, and Amélie Chekroun and Bertrand Hirsch, "The Sultanates of Medieval Ethiopia" and "The Muslim-Christian Wars and the Oromo Expansion: Transformations at the End of the Middle Ages (ca. 1500–1560)," in *Companion to Medieval Ethiopia and Eritrea*, 86–112 and 454–76.

8 See Andreu Martínez d'Alòs-Moner, *Envoys of a Human God: The Jesuit Mission to Christian Ethiopia (1557–1632)* (Leiden: Brill, 2015), 145–6, 160–80, and 202 and Víctor M. Fernández, "Enlivening the Dying Ruins: History and Archaeology of the Jesuit Missions in Ethiopia, 1557–1632," in *Culture and History Digital Journal* 2, no. 2 (2013): 1–32.

9 E.g., Martínez d'Alòs-Moner, *Envoys*, 182–5 (the author even suggests the Jesuits had a positive influence on Ethiopian social fabric and political structures—but compare with 195), 199–214, and 239–40; Elena Serrano Bertos, "Episodio exótico de la misión jesuita en Etiopía: Pedro Páez en Etiopía," *Mutatis Mutandis* 8, no. 1 (2015): 67–82, and Marta Torres Santo Domingo, "La aventura de los misioneros en Etiopía: recorrido bibliográfico desde la Biblioteca Histórica," in *Pecia Complutense* 7, no. 13 (2010): 53–63; somewhat by contrast, Leonardo Cohen draws attention to the more negative sides of the intervention without outright examining it as colonial in *Missionary Strategies*, xviii, while Merid Wolde Aregay rightly highlights—in contrast with most scholars (see below)—the sinister profile of Pedro Páez; see Merid Wolde Aregay, "El conocimiento de Pedro Páez de la teología de la Iglesia Ortodoxa etíope," in *Conmemoracion del IV centenario de la llegada del sacerdote español Pedro Páez a Etiopía*, eds. Merid Wolde Aregay and Enrique Gismero (Madrid: AEdCI, 2007), 76–9.

10 Especially in relation to postcolonial theory and eastern Christianity, see most recently Demacopoulos, *Colonizing Christianity*, 1–9; M. N. Todorova, *Imagining the Balkans* (Oxford and New York: Oxford University Press, 2009) and "The Balkans: From Discovery to Invention," *Slavic Review* 53, no. 2 (1994): 453–82; M. Bakic-Hayden, "Nesting Orientalisms: The Case of Former Yugoslavia," *Slavic Review* 54, no. 4 (1995): 917–31 and "Orientalist Variations on the Theme 'Balkans': Symbolic Geography in Recent Yugoslav Cultural Politics," *Slavic Review* 51, no. 1 (1992): 1–15; J. Prawer, *The Crusaders' Kingdom: European Colonialism in the Middle Ages* (New York: Prager, 1972); C. Johnson, "He Has Made the Dry Bones Live: Orientalism's Attempted Resuscitation of Eastern Christianity," *Journal of the American Academy of Religion* 82, no. 3 (2014): 811–40; S. Henderson, "The Elephant in the Room: Orientalism and Russian Studies," *Slovo* 19, no. 2 (2007): 125–35; and Kaldellis, *Romanland*, 1–38.

11 See further, Martínez d'Alòs-Moner, *Envoys*, 189–90.

12 Belcher, "Sisters," 125.
13 Generally, see Markus Friedrich, "Ignatius's Governing and Administering the Society of Jesus," in *A Companion to Ignatius of Loyola: Life, Writings, Influence*, ed. Robert Maryks (Leiden: Brill, 2014), 123–40; John M. McManamon, *The Texts and Contexts of Ignatius Loyola's "Autobiography"* (New York: Fordham University Press, 2013), 115–34. More specifically, see Chekroun and Hirsch, "Muslim-Christian Wars," 454 and 467.
14 Giuseppe Marcocci, "Prism of Empire: The Shifting Image of Ethiopia in Renaissance Portugal (1500–1750)," in *Portuguese Humanism and the Republic of Letters*, eds. M. Berbara and K. A. E. Enenkel (Boston: Brill, 2012), 451.
15 Marcocci, "Prism," 454.
16 See Martínez d'Alòs-Moner, *Envoys*, 139, 144, 146 and Cohen, *Missionary Strategies*, 53.
17 Prester John was a common European designation for a quasi-legendary Christian king somewhere in Africa that eventually was applied to the Abyssinian emperor.
18 Ignacio de Loyola, *Monumenta Ignatiana* (henceforth *MI*) 8 (Madrid: Imprenta de Gabriel López del Horno 1909), 681.
19 Compare with *GWP*, 17 and Gälawdewos, *The Life and Struggles of Our Mother Walatta Petros*, ed. and trans. by Wendy Laura Belcher and Michael Klein (Princeton: Princeton University Press, 2015), 106, n. 4.
20 On this, see further Anaïs Wion, "Medieval Ethiopian Economies: Subsistence, Global Trade and the Administration of Wealth," in *Companion to Medieval Ethiopia and Eritrea*, ed. Samantha Kelly, 452–4.
21 Compare with Mendes's speech at the "conversion ceremony" of Susənyos in 1626 as recounted by Manuel de Almeida; on this, see Leonardo Cohen, "The Catholic Kingdom of Ethiopia: Father Manuel de Almeida's Account of the Imperial Conversion Ceremony," in *Lusitania Sacra* 29 (2014): 143–79.
22 Cohen, "Imprudentia Maxima," 89 and Martínez d'Alòs-Moner, *Envoys*, 139–41, but compare with Serrano Bertos, "Episodio exótico," 69.
23 Martínez d'Alòs-Moner, *Envoys*, 144.
24 Indeed, Martínez d'Alòs-Moner even pushes back against the colonial dimensions of the Iberian mission. See especially *Envoys*, 182, and n. 200.
25 Loyola, *MI* 8, 682.
26 Loyola, *MI* 8, 683–6.
27 E.g., Loyola, *MI* 8, 687: "Although there is a view to reducing them to uniformity with the Catholic Church, go easy and without doing violence to their sentiments (*ánimos*), as they are habituated to a different way of life."
28 Loyola, *MI* 8, 685.
29 See especially Belcher, "Sisters."
30 Santiago Castro-Gómez, *La hybris del punto cero: ciencia, raza e ilustración en la Nueva Granada (1750–1816)*. (Bogotá: Editorial Pontificia Universidad Javeriana, 2005).
31 In J. Deramey, "Une lettre de Saint Ignace de Loyola a Claudius, Roi d'Éthiopie ou d'Abyssinie," in *Revue de l'histoire des religions* 27 (1893): 50.
32 Deramey, "Une lettre," 50.
33 Deramey, "Une lettre," 48.
34 Edward Ullendorff, "The *Confessio Fidei* of King Claudius of Ethiopia," in *Journal of Semitic Studies* 32, no. 1 (1987): 166.
35 Ullendorff, "*Confessio Fidei*," 166–7.
36 Ullendorff, "*Confessio Fidei*," 168.
37 Ullendorff, "*Confessio Fidei*," 169.
38 Ullendorff, "*Confessio Fidei*," 169.
39 See Chekroun and Hirsch, "Muslim-Christian Wars," 468; Serrano Bertos, "Episodio exótico," 68–71; Alfonso Mola and Martínez Shaw, "Pedro Páez," 67–9; Martínez d'Alòs-Moner, *Envoys*, 159–60.
40 See especially Alfonso Mola and Martínez Shaw, "Pedro Páez," 75, where he is put on a pedestal with saints such as Matteo Ricci and Francisco Xavier.

41 See Cohen, "Imprudentia Maxima," 84 and Belcher, "Sisters," 122–4.
42 Elena Serrano Bertos, "Episodio exótico," 77.
43 Especially Martínez d'Alòs-Moner, *Envoys*, 159–60 and Alfonso Mola and Martínez Shaw, "Pedro Páez," 71, who expressly articulate as much.
44 Compare with Serrano Bertos, "Episodio exótico," 74.
45 Agreeing on this point with Martínez d'Alòs-Moner, *Envoys*, 161.
46 Pedro Páez, *História da Etiopía*, eds. Isabel Boavida, Hervé Pennec, and Manuel João Ramos (Lisbon: Assírio & Alvim, 2008), 211.
47 Ironic, given lackluster literacy levels in Castile. See, e.g., Serafín Tapia, "Nivel de alfabetización en una ciudad castellana del siglo XVI: Sectores sociales y grupos étnicos en Ávila," in *Studia Historica: Historia Moderna* 6 (1988): 481–502.
48 Páez, *História*, 211.
49 Páez, *História*, 211.
50 On the significant wealth of these lands see Cohen, "Imprudentia Maxima," 90.
51 Páez, *História*, 213.
52 Páez, *História*, 214.
53 There are numerous such encounters, perhaps one of the earliest recorded in Arabic being مجادلة الراهب إبراهيم الطبراني (*The Disputation of the Monk Abraham the Tiberian*), though many more were penned after, perhaps the most famous being the multi-recension *Dispute of the Monk George with Muslim Scholars*, which is reported to have happened under Saladin. In Syriac, the literature also was well established, particularly since the legendary Patriarch Timothy I was supposed to have had a several-day dispute with none other than al-Mahdi himself. For a recent republication of the edition, see Alphonse Mingana, *The Apology of Timothy the Patriarch before the Caliph Mahdi* (Piscataway, NJ: Gorgias Press, 2009); Sidney Griffith, "The Monk in the Emir's *Majlis*: Reflections on a Popular Genre of Christian Literary Apologetics in Arabic in the Early Islamic Period," in *The Majlis: Interreligious Encounters in Medieval Islam*, eds. Hava Lazarus-Yafeh, et al. (Wiesbaden: Otto Harrassowitz, 1999), 22–37 and "Disputing with Islam in Syriac: The Case of the Monk of Bet Hale and a Muslim Emir," *Hugoye: Journal of Syriac Studies* 3, no. 1 (2000); Giacinto Bulus Marcuzzo, *Le dialogue d'Abraham de Tibériade avec 'Abd al-Rahman al-Hashimi à Jérusalem vers 820.* (Rome: G. B. Marcuzzo, 1986); Georges Vajda, "Un traité polémique christiano-arabe contre les juifs attribué à 'Abraham de Tibériade,'" *Bulletin: Institute de recherche et d'histoire des textes* 15 (1967–1968): 137–50, etc.
54 See, by comparison, John Murphy, "Legitimation and Paternalism: The Colonial State in Kenya," *African Studies Review* 29, no. 3 (1986): 55–65; see also Bernal Díaz del Castillo, *Historia verdadera de la conquista de la Nueva España*, ed. Guillermo Serés (Madrid: UNED, 2016), 189–93.
55 Páez, *História*, 293.
56 Páez, *História*, 295.
57 Gregorios of Nazianzos, *Oration* 31.9, 28, 29, 31, in *Grégoire de Nazianze. Discours 27–31*, eds. and trans. Paul Gallay and Maurice Jourjon. Sources Chrétiennes 250 (Paris: Éditions du Cerf, 1978).
58 For an excellent survey, see Tia Kolbaba, *Inventing Latin Heretics: Byzantines and the Filioque in the Ninth Century* (Kalamazoo, MI: Medieval Institute Publication, 2008).
59 Páez, *História*, 296–9.
60 See further, Belcher, "Sisters," 144–48; P. Gundani, "Christian Historiography and the African Woman: A Critical Examination of the Place of Felicity, Walatta Pietros and Kimpa Vita in African Christian Historiography," *Studia Historiae Ecclesiasticae* 30, no. 1 (2005): 75–89; Sevir Chernetsov, "A Transgressor of the Norms of Female Behaviour in the Seventeenth-Century Ethiopia: The Heroine of The Life of Our Mother Walatta Petros," *Khristianski Vostok* 10 (2005): 48–64; and Maria Rosaria Papi, "Una santa abissina anticattolica: Walatta-Petros," *Rassegna di Studi Etiopici* 3, no. 1 (1943): 87–93.
61 *GWP* 45.
62 *GWP* 46.
63 *GWP* 46–7.

Bibliography

Alfonso Mola, Marina, and Carlos Martínez Shaw. "Pedro Páez y la misión jesuítica en Etiopía en el contexto de la unión de las Coronas de España y Portugal." *Historia Moderna*, 17 (2004): 59–75.

Aregay, Merid Wolde. "El conocimiento de Pedro Páez de la teología de la Iglesia Ortodoxa Etíope." In *Conmemoracion del IV centenario de la llegada del sacerdote español Pedro Páez a Etiopía*, eds. Merid Wolde Aregay and Enrique Gismero, 69–91. Madrid: AEdCI, 2007.

Bakic-Hayden, M. "Orientalist Variations on the Theme 'Balkans': Symbolic Geography in Recent Yugoslav Cultural Politics." *Slavic Review*, 51.1 (1992): 1–15.

Bakic-Hayden, M. "Nesting Orientalisms: The Case of Former Yugoslavia." *Slavic Review*, 54.4 (1995): 917–31.

Belcher, Wendy Laura. "Sisters Debating the Jesuits: The Role of African Women in Defeating Portuguese Proto-Colonialism in Seventeenth-Century Abyssinia." *Northeast African Studies*, 13.1 (2013): 121–66.

Bruce, James. *Travels to Discover the Source of the Nile in the Years 1768, 1769, 1770, 1771, 1772, and 1773*, Vol. 3. Edinburgh: J. Ballantyne, A. Constable, and Co., 1804–1805.

Bulus Marcuzzo, Giacinto. *Le dialogue d'Abraham de Tibériade avec 'Abd al-Rahman al-Hashimi à Jérusalem vers 820*. Rome: G. B. Marcuzzo, 1986.

Castro-Gómez, Santiago. *La hybris del punto cero: ciencia, raza e ilustración en la Nueva Granada (1750–1816)*. Bogotá: Editorial Pontificia Universidad Javeriana, 2005.

Chekroun, Amélie, and Bertrand Hirsch. "The Muslim-Christian Wars and the Oromo Expansion: Transformations at the End of the Middle Ages (ca. 1500–1560)." In *Companion to Medieval Ethiopia and Eritrea*, ed. Samantha Kelly, 454–76. Leiden: Brill, 2020.

Chekroun, Amélie, and Bertrand Hirsch. "The Sultanates of Medieval Ethiopia." In *Companion to Medieval Ethiopia and Eritrea*, ed. Samantha Kelly, 86–112. Leiden: Brill, 2020.

Chernetsov, Sevir. "A Transgressor of the Norms of Female Behaviour in the Seventeenth-Century Ethiopia: The Heroine of The Life of Our Mother Walatta Petros." *Khristianski Vostok*, 10 (2005): 48–64.

Cohen, Leonardo. *The Missionary Strategies of the Jesuits in Ethiopia (1555–1632)*. Wiesbaden: Harrassowitz Verlag, 2009.

Cohen, Leonardo. "The Catholic Kingdom of Ethiopia: Father Manuel de Almeida's Account of the Imperial Conversion Ceremony." *Lusitania Sacra*, 29 (2014): 143–79.

Cohen, Leonardo. "'Imprudentia Maxima': fray Manuel de Asunción y su crítica de la actuación de los Jesuitas en Etiopía." *Lusitania Sacra*, 32 (2015): 81–104.

de Loyola, I. *Monumenta Ignatiana* 8. Madrid: Imprenta de Gabriel López del Horno, 1909.

Demacopoulos, George. *Colonizing Christianity: Greek and Latin Religious Identity in the Era of the Fourth Crusade*. New York: Fordham University Press, 2019.

Deramey, J. "Une lettre de Saint Ignace de Loyola a Claudius, Roi d'Éthiopie ou d'Abyssinie." *Revue de l'histoire des religions*, 27 (1893): 37–75.

Díaz del Castillo, Bernal. *Historia verdadera de la conquista de la Nueva España*, ed. Guillermo Serés. Madrid: UNED, 2016.

Fernández, Víctor M. "Enlivening the Dying Ruins: History and Archaeology of the Jesuit Missions in Ethiopia, 1557–1632." *Culture and History Digital Journal*, 2.2 (2013): 1–32.

Friedrich, Markus. "Ignatius's Governing and Administering the Society of Jesus." In *A Companion to Ignatius of Loyola: Life, Writings, Influence*, ed. Robert Maryks, 123–40. Leiden: Brill, 2014.

Gälawdewos. *Vitae Sanctorum Indigenarum: I: Acta S. Walatta Petros*, ed. Carlo Conti Rossini, Vol. 68 of Corpus Scriptorum Christianorum Orientalium. Rome: Karolus de Luigi, 1912.

Gälawdewos. *The Life and Struggles of Our Mother Walatta Petros*, eds. and trans. Wendy Laura Belcher and Michael Klein. Princeton: Princeton University Press, 2015.

Geddes, Michael. *The Church History of Ethiopia*. Albany: The Ages Digital Library, 1997.

Gregorios of Nazianzos. "Oration 31.9." In *Grégoire de Nazianze. Discours 27–31*, eds. and trans. Paul Gallay and Maurice Jourjon. Sources Chrétiennes 250. Paris: Éditions du Cerf, 1978.

Griffith, Sidney. "The Monk in the Emir's *Majlis*: Reflections on a Popular Genre of Christian Literary Apologetics in Arabic in the Early Islamic Period." In *The Majlis: Interreligious Encounters in Medieval Islam*, eds. Hava Lazarus-Yafeh, Mark R. Cohen, Sasson Somekh, and Sidney H. Griffith, 22–37. Wiesbaden: Otto Harrassowitz, 1999.

Griffith, Sidney. "Disputing with Islam in Syriac: The Case of the Monk of Bet Hale and a Muslim Emir." *Hugoye: Journal of Syriac Studies*, 3.1 (2000): 29–54.

Gundani, P. "Christian Historiography and the African Woman: A Critical Examination of the Place of Felicity, Walatta Pietros and Kimpa Vita in African Christian Historiography." *Studia Historiae Ecclesiasticae*, 30.1 (2005): 75–89.

Henderson, S. "The Elephant in the Room: Orientalism and Russian Studies." *Slovo*, 19.2 (2007): 125–35.

Hirsch, Bertrand. "The Muslim-Christian Wars and the Oromo Expansion: Transformations at the End of the Middle Ages (ca. 1500–1560)." In *Companion to Medieval Ethiopia and Eritrea*, ed. Samantha Kelly, 454–76. Leiden: Brill, 2020.

Johnson, C. "He Has Made the Dry Bones Live: Orientalism's Attempted Resuscitation of Eastern Christianity." *Journal of the American Academy of Religion*, 82.3 (2014): 811–40.

Kaldellis, Anthony. *The Byzantine Republic: People and Power in New Rome*. Cambridge: Harvard University Press, 2015.

Kaldellis, Anthony. *Romanland: Ethnicity and Empire in Byzantium*. Cambridge: Belknap Press, 2019.

Kelly, Samantha. "Introduction." In *A Companion to Medieval Ethiopia and Eritrea*, ed. Samantha Kelly, 1–30. Leiden: Brill, 2020.

Kolbaba, Tia. *Inventing Latin Heretics: Byzantines and the Filioque in the Ninth Century*. Kalamazoo: Medieval Institute Publication, 2008.

Marcocci, Giuseppe. "Prism of Empire: The Shifting Image of Ethiopia in Renaissance Portugal (1500–1750)." In *Portuguese Humanism and the Republic of Letters*, eds. M. Berbara and K. A. E. Enenkel, 447–65. Boston: Brill, 2012.

Martínez d'Alòs-Moner, Andreu. *Envoys of a Human God: The Jesuit Mission to Christian Ethiopia (1557–1632)*. Leiden: Brill, 2015.

McManamon, John M. *The Texts and Contexts of Ignatius Loyola's "Autobiography"*. New York: Fordham University Press, 2013.

Mendes, Patriarch. "Patriarch Mendes to the Sacred Congregation for the Propagation of the Faith, Goa, 22 February 1637." In *The Jesuits in Ethiopia (1609–1641): Latin Letters in Translation*, ed. Wendy Laura Belcher, Trans. Jessica Wright, Leon Grek, and Leonardo Cohen, 168–9. Wiesbaden: Harrassowitz Verlag, 2017.

Mingana, Alphonse. *The Apology of Timothy the Patriarch before the Caliph Mahdi*. Piscataway: Gorgias Press, 2009.

Murphy, John. "Legitimation and Paternalism: The Colonial State in Kenya." *African Studies Review*, 29.3 (1986): 55–65.

Páez, Pedro. *História da Etiopía*, eds. Isabel Boavida, Hervé Pennec, and Manuel João Ramos. Lisbon: Assírio & Alvim, 2008.

Papi, Maria Rosaria. "Una santa abissina anticattolica: Walatta-Petros." *Rassegna di Studi Etiopici*, 3.1 (1943): 87–93.

Prawer, J. *The Crusaders' Kingdom: European Colonialism in the Middle Ages*. New York: Prager, 1972.

Santo Domingo, Marta Torres. "La aventura de los misioneros en Etiopía: recorrido bibliográfico desde la Biblioteca Histórica." *Pecia Complutense*, 7.13 (2010): 53–63.

Serrano Bertos, Elena. "Episodio exótico de la misión jesuita en Etiopía: Pedro Páez en Etiopía." *Mutatis Mutandis*, 8.1 (2015): 67–82.

Tapia, Serafín. "Nivel de alfabetización en una ciudad castellana del siglo XVI: Sectores sociales y grupos étnicos en Ávila." *Studia Historica: Historia Moderna*, 6 (1988): 481–502.

Todorova, M. N. "The Balkans: From Discovery to Invention." *Slavic Review*, 53.2 (1994): 453–82.

Todorova, M. N. *Imagining the Balkans*. Oxford: Oxford University Press, 2009.

Ullendorff, Edward. "The *Confessio Fidei* of King Claudius of Ethiopia." *Journal of Semitic Studies*, 32.1 (1987): 159–76.

Vajda, Georges. "Un traité polémique christiano-arabe contre les juifs attribué à 'Abraham de Tibériade'." *Bulletin: Institute de recherche et d'histoire des textes*, 15 (1967–1968): 137–50.

Wion, Anaïs. "Medieval Ethiopian Economies: Subsistence, Global Trade and the Administration of Wealth." In *A Companion to Medieval Ethiopia and Eritrea*, ed. Samantha Kelly, 395–424. Leiden: Brill, 2020.

9

RACIALIZED SACRED SPACES

Commodifications of race in Þingeyrar, Iceland (c.1470–1700)

Lorenz A. Hindrichsen

Introduction

Historians have long recognized the significance of racialized objects in late medieval and early modern culture, and the extent to which their production, dissemination, and showcasing shaped emerging racial codes at the time. In her groundbreaking study *Things of Darkness: The Economies of Race and Gender in Early Modern England* (1995), Kim F. Hall demonstrated how the making and exchange of bejeweled sixteenth-century cameos featuring royals and aristocrats alongside anonymized black figures served to articulate racial hierarchies and normalize a commodification of color that went hand in hand with the promotion of colonial settlements and the commodification of human labor.[1] Later studies like Peter Erickson's reading of black servants in early modern portraits established the pan-European dimension of this reification of racial hierarchies, while also highlighting the presence of subversive, dissonant texts that empower disenfranchised voices and question the racial oppression normalized in much early modern artistic representation.[2]

How and to what extent religious artifacts echoed, amplified, or undercut this secular dialectic of exclusion and inclusion is still imperfectly understood. Studies on medieval and early modern religious art have fruitfully explored race through the lens of influential narratives (e.g. the Adoration of the Magi), important Biblical figures (e.g. the Queen of Sheba), racialized apocryphal characters (e.g. Judith's ethnicized maidservant), or devotional practices (e.g. the veneration of Black Madonnas), illustrating how artistic representation was often shaped by, and reinforced colonial discourse.[3] In many cases, though, establishing direct ties between racialized artifacts and colonial contexts is fraught with complications, as evidence is scant or inconclusive. The gradual fading away of Black Saint Maurice in Germany in the 1530s, for example, has been read as a response to

DOI: 10.4324/9781003082842-10

the incipient transatlantic slave trade, whose economic and cultural repercussions reached far into Europe's *hinterland* and supposedly eroded the demand for black saints.[4] In terms of artistic production, though, the Reformation seems to have been even more influential, as it not only curbed the demand for *devotionalia* venerating saints at large but also stalled manufacturing at Magdeburg and Halle—which had a monopoly on the commodification of Black Maurice—after these cities turned Protestant.[5]

While many aspects relating to the representation and commodification of figures like Saint Maurice remain unresolved, a growing number of studies on religion and race in the early modern period recognize that religious texts, artifacts, rituals, and devotional practices played a key role in shaping narratives on color throughout the European continent.[6] The scope of religious artifacts that were deliberately ethnicized is extensive. Racialized altarpieces, pulpits, statues, baptismal fonts, prayer books, church bells, chalices, or candlesticks can be found virtually anywhere in Europe, from Palermo to Iceland's north coast, from Lisbon to the Baltic, from cosmopolitan Antwerp to remote Swiss mountain villages.[7] A major factor fueling this wide distribution of racialized artworks was trade: medieval and early modern religious artifacts were sold internationally, while fixed installations such as stained-glass windows and murals were often created by itinerant craftsmen. Many religious representations of Blackness thus permeated national, linguistic, cultural, and even denominational boundaries, contributing to a buoyant, heterogeneous religious marketplace.[8]

The way these religious artworks portray color often echoes representational patterns familiar from secular art. In many visual renderings the Black Magus is reduced to the status of a colonial subject: physically marginalized (trailing the other Magi), exoticized (through Oriental dress), sexualized, infantilized, and heavily commodified (bestowing lavish gifts while "gift[ing] himself" in the process).[9] It is reasonable to assume that the many images of a disenfranchised Black Magus played a role in normalizing Northern Europe's participation in the Black Atlantic economy, especially since many of these visual interpretations were produced and sold in the Netherlands at a time when the nation was on the verge of becoming Europe's foremost hub for art, investments, and international trade, including the slave trade.[10] At the same time, one can also find visual texts that challenge the code of an effete, reluctant, disingenuous Black Magus. Some dissenting artists elevate him compositionally (privileging him above other Magi), dignify him physically (removing stigmatizing attributes), ennoble him emotionally (lending him an air of authenticity and trust), or strengthen him narratively (by making him gaze directly at the viewer), thereby making a powerful socio-political statement.[11]

Arguably the most influential locus where this dialectic between inclusive and exclusive visions unfolded in a communal setting was the parish church. Medieval and early modern congregations played a key role in integrating people of color into a given community. Recent studies on ecclesiastical records in England show a substantial number of Black congregants throughout the sixteenth and seventeenth centuries,[12] and case studies on some of these suggest that, it was through Church membership that non-white individuals acquired the right to carry out a trade, marry, buy property, or issue a will.[13] Conversely, exclusionary practices by seventeenth-century Caribbean Churches serving a white Protestant Plantocracy functioned as a social barrier preventing non-Whites from being recognized as true Christians and, in consequence, from ever achieving the status of freemen.[14]

While a church interior need not offer clues to a community's racial politics, nor a racialized artifact shape a congregation's views on color, there is reason to believe that the showcasing of racialized artifacts often constituted a conscious racializing of sacred space, similar to the gendering and social stratifying of space we find in many early modern churches.[15] There are documented cases from the seventeenth century in which the presence of inclusive artwork went hand in hand with—and perhaps facilitated—inclusion, notably the baptism of non-White congregants. The St. Johannis Church in Schweinfurt, Bavaria, for example, records the baptisms of several Jewish, Turkish, and Black congregants from the early fifteenth to the late seventeenth centuries, many of which were performed underneath a massive mural celebrating the baptism of the Ethiopian chamberlain from the Acts.[16] Also, it seems that the increasing customization of artwork throughout the early modern period, whereby artists would work from a given template and tailor it to a particular place or audience, allowed for modifications that accommodated local views and values, including attitudes to race. Indeed, one can find many variants of near-identical visual texts where artists faithfully copied the main narrative and stylistic elements yet tinkered with the ethnicity and skin color of selected figures, thereby strategically altering the racial politics in those texts.[17]

A deliberate racializing of sacred spaces by early modern communities would have been complicated, though, by the presence of older artwork already installed by previous generations. Many parishes collected artwork over a long period of time that turned their churches into *Wunderkammer*-like museal spaces in the process. Consecrated objects such as altarpieces were viewed as valuable and sacred, and were unlikely to be removed for the sake of racial politics.[18] As a result, many early modern congregations encountered not only contemporary but also older racialized artifacts that promoted distinctly different understandings of ethnicity and race. That these older artifacts were not just retained for material or symbolic value but fully engaged with, is confirmed by their very prominent showcasing within many churches; medieval Black Madonnas, or shrines with the Black Magus were often given pride of place, underscoring their significance for early modern communities.[19] The eclectic, heterogeneous mix of racialized artifacts hailing from different places and time periods thus offered multiple visions of exclusion or inclusion which would have informed a congregation's thinking on color.

A perfect test case for close-reading the dynamics and complexities of racialized sacred spaces can be found at Þingeyrar in Northern Iceland, a place whose remoteness seems particularly suited to demonstrating the full scope of medieval and early modern distribution networks. The following analysis will close-read two artifacts found at the local parish church: an English medieval altarpiece and a late seventeenth-century Danish baptismal font. This discussion will explore the racializing of Þingeyrar Church through these artifacts by considering their

a. spatiality, both geographical (the dissemination of an artifact) and compositional (how interior space is deployed to present objects),
b. materiality (the materials and surfaces used to create visual narratives on color),
c. iconography (the use of prominent signifiers that build visual narratives, such as exotic headdress or oriental clothing),
d. representation of emotions (specifically the articulation of power relationships through ritualized body language),

and

e. relevant socio-economic and political contexts (notably Iceland's status as a colony and the so-called "Turkish raids" of 1627).

As the following discussion hopes to show, studying visual representations of color in a parish church can provide valuable insight into the racializing of sacred spaces through such objects while offering valuable clues to the distribution networks sustaining the trade in racialized religious art. Close-reading the two artifacts from Þingeyrar Church also reveals a distinct shift in production from a late medieval mass manufacturing of largely uniform artifacts to early modern customization of religious art that considers cultural norms, especially attitudes to race. Historicizing the emerging of such customization seems useful for arriving at a closer understanding of the interplay between evolving early modern concepts of race and the commodifying of alterity through religious artifacts.

Spatiality

Þingeyrar Church on Iceland's north-east coast, at the site of Iceland's oldest monastery (inaugurated 1133, dissolved 1551), houses two artifacts that are very helpful for exploring medieval and early modern economies of race: an alabaster altarpiece from Nottingham (c. 1470), whose far left relief shows four Black flagellators tormenting Christ (Figure 9.1); and a richly adorned Danish baptismal font (1697), whose illustrations include a representation of the baptism of the Ethiopian chamberlain by Deacon Phillip from the Acts (8:27–39) (Figure 9.2).[20] The baptism of the Ethiopian is highly important both for exegesis and discussions of race, as it marks the first baptism of a Gentile, and the most favorable representation of a sub-Saharan African (Greek αἰθίοψ, *Vulgate* aethiop, *King James Bible* Ethiopian) in the New Testament.[21] The myth of Black flagellators

FIGURE 9.1 Left panel of the altarpiece at Þingeyrar Church, produced in Nottingham (c. 1470).

Source: Photograph by Katharina Kley

tormenting Christ is not rooted in the Scriptures and is purely apocryphal, yet features prominently in medieval and early modern art.[22] The rather unexpected convergence of these narratives at Þingeyrar points towards very extensive distribution networks for racialized religious art in the medieval and early modern period. Alabaster altarpieces similar to the one at Þingeyrar can be found in France, Italy, Croatia, and on the Iberian Peninsula, and attest to the commercial success of the English alabaster industry (centered around Nottingham) in the

FIGURE 9.2 Illustration from the baptismal font at Þingeyrar Church, donated by Laurits Gottrup in 1697.

Source: Photograph by Katharina Kley

fifteenth century.[23] The template used for the Ethiopian on the baptismal font at Þingeyrar was also used for a range of artworks across Europe, including paintings, murals, book illustrations, stained-glass windows, and fonts in England, France, Switzerland, Germany, and Poland.[24]

The Nottingham alabaster altarpiece (c. 1470) reached Þingeyrar during the so-called "English Age" (c. 1415–75), when England controlled most of Iceland's foreign trade, even though it nominally belonged to the Danish crown. With England's alabaster industry still in full swing (the industry collapsed in the early sixteenth century and was dealt a death blow by the iconoclasm of the Reformation), the altarpiece managed to reach Iceland just as the "English Age" was coming to a close, giving rise to a "German Age" for the next five decades.[25] That the Þingeyrar altarpiece was not just a fluke, but part of a larger consignment of English alabasters, emerges from the presence of two very similar altarpieces on Iceland's north coast, at Hólar Cathedral (*Hóladómkirkju*, 30 miles east) and Möðruvellir Church (*Möðruvallakirkja*, 60 miles east).[26] The three alabasters were all made in Nottingham in the 1470s and are uniform in composition and style, though the scenes they portray vary. All three altarpieces contain a similar relief showing the Resurrection; the Hólar altarpiece also includes the flagellation of Christ from Þingeyrar in a largely identical version.[27]

The baptismal font of 1697 reached Iceland under very different circumstances. Denmark had declared a trade monopoly on Iceland in 1602, and controlled the island politically, ecclesiastically, and economically. The Danish governor of the northern province, Laurits Gottrup, donated the font as a gift for the new church he had built two years previously, along with a pulpit (dated 1696, Figure 9.3), presumably to strengthen the relationship between Denmark and its northernmost colony, which was struggling considerably at the time.[28] While there is no evidence to confirm that Gottrup personally handpicked the baptism of the Ethiopian to be one of the eight narratives displayed on the font, there is reason to believe that its selection was not accidental. As the local authority overseeing secular and spiritual matters in the northern province, Gottrup would have seen many analogies between his role and his concerns on the one hand and the biblical episode on the other. The baptism of the Ethiopian chamberlain ultimately deals with issues of leadership, enfranchisement, cultural difference, and inclusion—topics Gottrup would have cared about in his role as colonial administrator.

That race constituted a key concern when the font was installed emerges clearly from its strategic positioning within the apse. The font is placed at a short distance from the altarpiece, and level with the pulpit. It is turned so that the baptism of the Ethiopian directly faces the left panel of the altarpiece where the Blackfaced tormentors flagellate Christ (Figure 9.3). Octagonal in shape with a different biblical

FIGURE 9.3 Interior view of the apse at Þingeyrar Church.

Source: Photograph by Katharina Kley

scene adorning each side, the font could have legitimately been turned any other way; the juxtaposition of these two narratives—the only ones at Þingeyrar that discuss color—thus hardly seems an accident. By having the Black flagellators directly face the Deacon Phillip baptizing the Ethiopian, and vice versa, the apse becomes a dialectic space where diametrically opposed narratives intersect: a story of otherness and difference meets a story of sameness and inclusion. The tension between these two narratives is further enhanced by some of the characters breaking through the fourth wall as if to interact with the figures across the apse. Two of the four flagellators seem to grin and jeer at Phillip while whipping Christ; the Evangelist calmly returns their gaze while ceremoniously baptizing the Ethiopian with his right.

How this dialectic of exclusion and inclusion would have been received by early modern audiences is hard to tell. Would the font's inclusive vision have superseded the apocryphal, xenophobic narrative of the altarpiece? Or would the altarpiece on account of its age be seen as invalidating the font's narrative? Last, might audiences have attempted to synthesize the two narratives, seeing them as canceling each other out, or as suggesting that color could render individuals "almost the same, but not quite"?[29]

No matter how audiences would have responded, it is clear that the Þingeyrar apse was designed as a discursive space that encouraged reflection and debate on color, and on the spiritual, religious, social, and economic implications of including or excluding ethnically different individuals from the congregations. This debate, I argue, is sustained through the pairing of significant artistic choices: the objects' materiality, their iconography, the representation of emotion, and references to significant contexts.

Materiality

The form, function, and materiality of the altarpiece and the font are a central part of this conversation. The altarpiece asks a congregation to bear witness to the passion of Christ. Designed as a rectangular relief, it resembles a stage where the passion is performed for the congregation in the pews. Its tripartite story arc—flagellation, crucifixion, resurrection—offers a dramatic backdrop to the priest officiating at the altar, complementing the liturgy with a poignant rendering of Christ's suffering and redemption. The parallel arrangement of the altarpiece and pews invites a solemn witnessing from a static point of view, with the three-dimensionality of the figures adding tension and suspense, thus partly offsetting the physical distance between audience and artifact.

Conversely, the font invites congregants to enter the apse and be close at hand when the sacrament is being administered. This participatory function is supported by the font's octagonal design (mimicking the pulpit's hexagonal shape), which inevitably hides most of the painted panels from view unless congregants circle the font and approach it from different sides. The font's free accessibility (situated between the first and second pew, Figure 9.3) allows for an intimacy that the altarpiece—only seen from distance, and placed behind altar rails—clearly lacks. The different degree to which congregants may interact with these artifacts have a direct bearing on how their representations of Blackness are received, as audiences can establish a close rapport with the baptized Ethiopian, yet experience the Black tormentors as remote figures only seen from a distance.

The artifacts' liturgical function is also highly relevant. Representing Blackfaced enemies of Christ on an altarpiece authenticates them and conceals their apocryphal origin. The succinct caption underneath the Black flagellators ("flagellat[us] est [Jesus Christus]"—"Christ is being flagellated"), which is echoed verbatim on the virtually identical relief at Hólar Cathedral,[30] adds to that effect by firmly anchoring the scene in the Gospel, thus asking congregants to accept the panel's interpretation as a literalization of the Holy Writ. Mounted as a fixture that is visible throughout the year (having lost its wings, which would have covered the flagellation for some part of the liturgical cycle),[31] the relief may be said to further, or at least normalize, color prejudice, especially since there is little in the artifact that would seem suspect, or unreliable to an early modern audience. The availability of similar altarpieces displaying Blackfaced flagellators, both locally (at Hólar) and abroad, would have strengthened such a view.[32]

In contrast, finding the baptism of the Ethiopian on a baptismal font is quite extraordinary by European, and especially Scandinavian, standards. Most Scandinavian fonts originate from the eleventh to the thirteenth century and feature simple carvings of biblical emblems, often in combination with heathen symbols.[33] When biblical scenes are chosen, they are usually popular ones like the Fall of Eden, Noah's Ark, or the baptism of Christ. The baptism of the Ethiopian chamberlain does not seem to appear on other Scandinavian fonts and features on very few European ones.[34] By visualizing two baptisms (Christ's and the Ethiopian's), the Þingeyrar font promotes the power of its own sacrament. Pairing the baptism of Christ with the baptism of the Ethiopian also celebrates inclusivity and asserts that neither physical nor cultural difference should bar anyone from receiving the said sacrament.

The materialities of font and altarpiece likewise impact how the two narratives are received. The altarpiece's widely available, soft white alabaster rock, which sparked a mass manufacturing boom in the fifteenth century,[35] is perfect for carving and coloring sculptures; it is also economical as craftsmen can forgo white paint by leaving surfaces untouched. The Þingeyrar altarpiece makes extensive use of such bare rock to represent white clothing (Christ's as well as the flagellators') and white skin (Christ's). The shared white dress code aligns Christ and flagellators socially, signaling courtly status; Blackfacing the flagellators revokes that equity, marking them as malevolent and profane. To what extent Christ's whiteness was meant to connote ethnic, proto-racial Whiteness is unclear, especially since Western concepts of Whiteness were still evolving at the time.[36] Even if no ethnic reference was intended, the decision to represent Christ's physicality through white pure rock (as opposed to white paint) seems significant, as it would have facilitated associations of color with impurity. Using white alabaster as a base material can thus be seen as strengthening a binary that would eventually be used to justify disenfranchisement on the basis of assumed moral depravity.[37]

The extensive use of gilded paint on the intricate frames surrounding the altarpiece's scenes elevates the alabaster (prestigious in the fourteenth century, but much less so in the 1470s)[38] to a more refined commodity, thereby evaluating its narratives as exclusive and authoritative. A similar illusion of grandeur is evoked on the baptismal font. Made out of plain wood yet painted in a veined pattern mimicking red marble, the font's base and octagonal encasing form an elaborate ploy that feigns status and prestige. The font's baroque touches are echoed on the accompanying octagonal canopy which praises its "noble and wise" patron Laurits Gottrup in gilded capitals; a similar inscription adorns the matching pulpit completed one year previously (Figure 9.3).[39]

This discourse of alleged wealth and generous patronage feeds directly into the story of the Ethiopian's baptism. The rich use of colors—Nordic baptismal fonts are usually monochrome— dignifies the narrative and highlights selected details from Matthäus Merian's etched template (Figure 9.4). Deacon Phillip,

FIGURE 9.4 The baptism of the Ethiopian chamberlain from *Icones Biblicae* by Matthäus Merian (1625)

Source: Merian, Matthaeus. "Icones Biblicae: Praecipuas Sacrae Scripturae Historias Eleganter & Graphice Repraesentantes = Biblische Figuren Darinnen Die Fürnembsten Historien in Heiliger Göttlicher Schrifft Begriffen [...]." Strassburg: Lazari Zetzners Erben, [1625]–1630. Zentralbibliothek Zürich, Rv 76, https://doi.org/10.3931/e-rara-24422/, Public Domain Mark

an ageing figure on the etching, appears youthful (sporting flowing chestnut hair), vigorous (wearing a vibrant red cape), and seemingly close to the viewer (being painted in distinctly lighter tones than his surroundings). The Ethiopian's skin color, which closely matches Deacon Phillip's in the etching (Figure 9.4), is likewise accentuated and effectively offset by his white toga, thereby identifying race as a central theme in the narrative.[40] The use of color also allows for a bucolic pink Nordic sky that frames this encounter between gracious Deacon Phillip (a double for Laurits Gottrup?) and the Ethiopian as a serene transformative moment facilitated by the Deacon's benevolent patronage.

Form, function, and materiality of font and altarpiece thus play a key role in articulating the racial codes they promote. Placed at a distance behind altar rails, the Blackfaced flagellators are othered spatially as well as materially, through the impurity that defines them. In contrast, the Ethiopian's proximity and his accessibility humanize him. Strong parallels between narrative (the Ethiopian's baptism) and form (the baptismal font) invites the congregation to realize this narrative in their midst and make their community inclusive. Conversely, using spatial distance to alienate the emotionally distanced flagellators achieves the opposite effect, and normalizes an othering of color characteristically found in English alabasters.

Iconography

Medieval and early modern representations of ethnic and cultural differences rely heavily on props and dress to connote otherness. Artists frequently opt for generic attributes like turbans that lack a precise geographical or cultural referent. The Þingeyrar altarpiece echoes such practice by equipping the flagellators with curiously feathered headpieces to mark them as savage and non-Western. The blurring of ethnic geographies (an African, Asian, or American headdress?) is reminiscent of illustrated travel accounts from the late fifteenth century, where identical ethnic props reappear in scenes supposedly taking place on different continents.[41] Feathers and Blackface aside, the Þingeyrar flagellators appear curiously European, both in physiognomy and dress, which suggests a distinct lack of familiarity with actual non-Europeans. Such generic Blackness may have been deliberate to some extent: a marketing ploy allowing pan-European viewers to project the Blackfaced flagellators onto a specific, localized Other.[42] The ethnically indistinct alterity of the flagellators also mirrors a fifteenth-century manufacturing process whereby artisans would carve alabasters independent of any specifications from customers and opt for generic designs that would speak to a broad pan-European market.[43]

In contrast, the highly customized baptismal font reveals subtle changes to its iconography, as reflected in a repositioning of the most important ethnic prop, the turban placed at Deacon's Phillip's feet, which encodes the cultural and religious roots the Ethiopian severs by receiving the sacrament. In process of adapting Merian's etched template to the font's wooden encasing, the artist has shifted the turban slightly upwards and to the right, moving it from below Phillip's feet (Figure 9.4) to below his left hand (Figure 9.2). As a result, the turban no longer appears like an object Phillip towers above or dominates, but one he points at and acknowledges as if to stress the double transformation taking place here: by becoming Christian, the Ethiopian also sheds his cultural Otherness. That the (unbaptized) servant steering the Ethiopian's chariot still wears his turban confirms the point.[44] By echoing the turban's whiteness several times in the picture, the painting adds multiple ties linking the Ethiopian's roots to his new-found spiritual purity (shown in his white dress), his purification (reflected in the water mirroring sunlight), and the spiritual source of this light (the Scriptures on his chariot). A pattern of reds (in the turbans, Phillip's cape, and the servant's dress) further binds the characters together and unifies the scene.

In both texts, the presence and absence of weapons are also crucial for characterization. The flagellators wield massive whips whose thick strands cling to Christ's limbs like snakes, possibly as a reference to the Fall, which Christ redeems through his suffering. (The column to which Christ is tied uncannily resembles the Forbidden Tree in medieval iconography.) The firmness with which the flagellators brandish their whips, sometimes even using two hands, shows their determination to defile Christ.

On the baptismal font, it is the conspicuous absence of weapons that is striking. Most early modern interpretations of the scene accompany the turban with a discarded scimitar to highlight the Ethiopian's peaceful intent and his unconditional acceptance of Christianity. Some versions further expand on the scimitar by transferring the scene onto a battlefield: Abraham Bloemaert's massive oil painting (1620), originally intended for an altarpiece, shows the Ethiopian's baptism stall an Ottoman army advancing under a dark, overcast sky.[45] Crucially, the Þingeyrar font not only removes the scimitar tucked underneath the turban on Merian's template (Figure 9.4); it also replaces it with the caption "ACTORUM VIII," referencing the Biblical source of the episode, the eighth book of the Acts of the Apostles. This unusual substitution—captions like these are common, but removing key props are not—makes for a powerful statement, and suggests that in this biblical episode, and perhaps in the Þingeyrar community at large, the word is indeed mightier than the sword.

The power of the word is further celebrated through the brightly illuminated Scriptures on the Ethiopian's chariot, serving as an extension of his Self. Foregrounding the book acts as a reminder of the Ethiopian's learning, as his desire to be baptized arises from his curiosity about a cryptic passage in the Prophet Isaiah. Many other early modern representations, such as Abraham Bloemaert's oil painting mentioned above, remove the book from the scene altogether, thus erasing a central aspect of the Ethiopian's character, casting him as a blind follower of Deacon Phillip.[46] By accentuating the Ethiopian's literacy and learning, and by replacing the scimitar (or Oriental belligerence) with the Scriptures, the image minimizes the cultural gap between Phillip and the Ethiopian, thus honoring, dignifying, and celebrating his presence.

The Black flagellators on the altarpiece distinctly lack any signifiers that might encode piety or learning. Their white stockings and white dress superficially align them with Christ, as does their similarity in height. The savagery of their actions, though, echoed in their feathered headgear, undercuts this superficial likeness, and stresses the wide gulf separating them from the Christ and the baptized Ethiopian across the apse.

Emotions

Recent histories of emotions have studied how pre-bureaucratic societies relied on dramatic, ritualized displays of emotion to consolidate existing power structures. Loyalty and fealty, cornerstones of feudal hierarchies, were rarely confirmed in writing, but more frequently enacted as social texts performed on public occasions. Subservience, dissent, forgiveness, and gratitude were expressed using a vocabulary of ritualized displays which made emotions visible, recognizable, and recordable.[47] Such performative displays of emotion were also central to cross-cultural encounters, where language barriers, cultural differences, volatile trade relationships, and loose governing structures made communities privilege social texts over written texts. Colonial encounters, in particular, relied on performative acts (such as ritualized ceremonies and interactions) to build stable power structures between trading partners, allies, colonizers, and colonized.[48]

The artifacts at Þingeyrar tap into familiar repertoires of performed emotion to define relationships, and to relate to the viewers. The Blackfaced flagellators offer a prime example of performed emotion as most of their poses seem staged and self-aware rather than impulsive. The two flagellators on the left, who wield their whips fervently, seem strangely unconcerned with where their blows are landing as they primarily seek eye-contact with the viewer—arms suspended in mid-air—as if to ensure their tormenting of Christ will be registered. The two flagellators on the right look on in apathy while lazily pulling Christ's hair and holding the rope tying him to the pole, as if waiting for the next cue. Their facial expressions are rigid and mask-like, with a glassy stare and furrowed brow. The orchestrated feel of the entire group, which differs significantly from more life-like renderings in contemporary paintings, also arises from the curious legwork of the flagellator at the bottom left and of Christ, whose right legs move in parallel motion. This synchronicity, coupled with the strangely identical white dress worn by Christ and the flagellators, offers a clue as to what these figures were most likely based on: a group of Morris dancers. With their short coats, stockings, and pointed shoes, the flagellators on the Þingeyrar panel uncannily resemble the Morris dancers from the Lancaster Castle Panel (c. 1500) and from Continental sources.[49]

The purpose of the "Morris dance" at Þingeyrar—to continue the analogy—seems less to inflict pain than to rule and own Christ, and force him into submission. Contemporary representations of Christ tied to the pole show him in a wide range of poses: confrontational, defiant, oblivious, unresponsive, silently enduring, bent and broken, pitying his tormentors, twisting in pain, or hiding behind the pole in shame.[50] The body language of Christ and his tormentors is usually complementary: a stoic Christ will fuel his tormentors' fury, while a charging Christ will make his flagellators retreat, and so on.[51] Nottingham alabaster pieces break with that tradition by showing Christ and flagellators mirror each other's movements and advance in parallel, as if conscious of their performance.[52] The crowding of Christ by two flagellators rising above him intensifies the scene and re-emphasizes the dominant theme of Christ being overpowered by stereotypical villains and driven into their demoniacal dance. The combination of static and dynamic elements—Christ and the flagellators on the left constantly moving forward, and the passive tormentors on the right completing the loop—sustain that energy, and lends the panel unity. That the Nottingham artists should base their representation of ethnic otherness on Blackfaced Morris dancers is not devoid of irony, and shows how constructions of ethnicity in the late medieval and incipient early modern period heavily depended on recycling of stereotypes whereby Westernized ritualistic figures often fed back into the perception and construction of Otherness.[53]

The performative elements on the baptismal font draw from a different tradition, one of the ritualized ceremonies. Deacon Phillip, earnestly facing the viewer as if to ascertain the witnessing of this momentous occasion, seems to stop midway through the ceremony in a freeze frame. His torso no longer faces the Ethiopian (like in Merian's etching, Figure 9.4), but the viewer, who becomes his primary interlocutor while the Ethiopian turns into a mute presence that is attended to, but not conversed with. Significantly, Phillip's gestures are directed at the viewer, not at the Ethiopian; the raised admonishing index finger we see in other versions has become an open palm gesturing at the turban, as if to attest to the miraculous transformation taking place. Phillip is also moved closer to the observer as objects originally placed in front of Phillip on Merian's etching are moved to the back or erased altogether (Figure 9.4). The framing has been adjusted so that Phillip and the Ethiopian appear larger and take up more space, while the surroundings are shrunk to a minimum, which again strengthens Phillip's protagonism.

The Ethiopian's pose, clasping his hand in intense prayer, complements Phillip's dignified pose perfectly. For a modern reader distinct echoes of the eighteenth-century Abolitionist emblem "Am I Not a Man and a Brother"[54] seem inevitable. Significantly, though, the Ethiopian bows his head not upwards toward Phillip, but slightly downwards, thus signaling spiritual awareness and piety rather than supplication to the Evangelist. His torso has also been slightly turned so that he no longer faces Phillip on his right (as in Merian's print), but looks more toward the viewer; this allows the audience to study his pose and facial expression more closely, thus establishing a stronger emotional connection between congregants and the praying Ethiopian.

Probably the most obvious visual referents for both Phillip and the Ethiopian, though, would be the congregation themselves, comprised of the priest performing a baptism and the praying parishioners. Deacon Phillip's unusual frontal view, his upright stance, and his direct eye contact privilege the viewer over the Ethiopian, thus making a personalized ritual a public one. The Ethiopian's intense prayer, from a lowered position (as he stands knee-deep in water), makes him assume the pose of congregants praying in the pews. The image invites parishioners to imitate and pray with the Ethiopian, thus including him in their midst. It is this performative element uniting congregants and the Ethiopian which renders the painting truly inclusive.

The distinctly Scandinavian setting further reinforces that connection between local parishioners and the font. The artist replaced the lush vegetation and steep Alpine cliffs in Merian's print with a characteristically Nordic vision of a calm lake, a dark-green forest, and a gentle snow-clad mountain against a pink sky. Such local touches might have prompted Þingeyrar parishioners to contemplate connections between themselves and the Ethiopian. Iceland was often celebrated as the northernmost outpost of Christianity and Western culture, as well as the last bastion separating Europe from the pagan natives of Greenland. Scandinavian countries frequently celebrated Iceland for its contributions to a common Nordic culture, particularly its famous sagas. Then again, Icelanders were also frequently patronized as boorish and uncivilized: prompting several early modern Icelandic authors to counter such stereotypes in descriptions of their country.[55]

Such stigmatizing might have facilitated an identification with the marked outsider baptized by the Deacon. The Ethiopian appears nobler and prouder than in most other variants, including Merian's etching. The upper body is almost upright, unlike the bent shapes found in many other versions, and the typical fawning characteristics are clearly missing.[56] The unambiguous ethnicizing of the Ethiopian—unlike the whitewashing in many other contemporary versions[57]—also ennobles his origin and color; the Ethiopian at Þingeyrar, it seems, ranks among most dignified representations of a Black biblical figure in the early modern period.

Then again, as the carefully programed acting by Phillip and the Ethiopian reveal, what is being enacted here is the spectacle of a dignified and mutually respectful baptism which minimizes, but fails to erase, the difference in status. As a colonial allegory dramatizing intercultural encounters, the Þingeyrar font represents color as a natural attribute that should not bar an individual from joining the congregation. At the same time, membership does not mean equity, the painting suggests.

Contexts

Produced two centuries apart, the artworks preserved at Þingeyrar articulate widely divergent visions of color, mainly because they emerge from—and cater to—very different markets. The altarpiece from the 1470s resembles in many ways a pre-colonial text, which imagines rather than response to cross-cultural encounters. It is ritualistic demonizing of color echoes the pan-European tradition of the Morris dance, in which Blackfaced dancers assume vaguely Orientalized identities for entertainment. The very wide market distribution of similar Nottingham altarpieces—reaching the Mediterranean, the French Atlantic coast, the North Atlantic, and Central Europe—underscores a popularity which may have been strengthened by, yet cannot be solely attributed to, visions of Otherness on flagellation panels; after all, not every Nottingham altarpiece included such a scene,[58] nor is it likely that the systematic racializing of selected figures (which distinguishes English alabasters from alabasters produced in the Netherlands and elsewhere) took precedence over economically more significant factors like production cost, distribution networks, or market access.[59]

The flagellators we find on different fifteenth century altarpieces vary in terms of ethnic attributes: some are turbaned, some have thick curly hair, some are feathered, some have non-Western features. What unites them is the binary opposition they help to establish between an idealized white-clad, white-complexioned courtly community on the one hand, and the grotesque mocking of such a community through generic Blackness on the other. The marketing appeal of such cultural politics seems obvious, particularly toward the end of the fifteenth century, when the advance of the Ottoman Empire, the successful Reconquista in Spain, the gradual circumnavigation of Africa, and imminent exploratory voyages toward East and West challenged the ways Europeans constructed their identities. The altarpiece thus commodifies the cultural appropriation of ethnicity under the mantle of religiosity, and sanctifies the use of cultural stereotypes for the purpose of commercial gain.

The Þingeyrar baptismal font of 1697 caters to a very different audience, drawing from very different traditions. As a Danish export, it most likely references the Danish colonial experience and can be seen as a commentary on the expanding Danish overseas trade, which increased exponentially in the late seventeenth century. Given Denmark's intensifying involvement in the slave trade at the time, the font might have been intended as a wider political statement, arguing for the enfranchising of enslaved Africans shipped across the Atlantic.[60] The disinterest of Northern European Protestant nations in baptizing and franchising their enslaved laborers suggests as much.[61]

Then again, given Iceland's status as a Danish colony, governor Laurits Gottrup's gift to Iceland might be seen as a shrewd political coup, and an attempt to curry favor with the local population. Iceland underwent considerable economic hardship in the sixteenth and seventeenth centuries, largely resulting from unfavorable conditions for fishing, and from the near-isolation due to the trade monopoly imposed by Denmark in 1602.[62] Governor Laurits Gottrup seems to have fought hard to alleviate Icelandic hardship during his tenure, several sources suggest, as he expressly sailed to Denmark to petition the Danish crown for more favorable economic conditions for Icelanders shortly after donating the font.[63] By commissioning a font showing a gracious, authoritative Deacon Phillip blessing a devout and sincere Ethiopian, Gottrup might have tried to boost his image as a generous, kind administrator while idealizing Danish-Icelandic relations as peaceful and mutually respectful. (The extensive inscriptions in the church lauding Laurits's generosity—as the donor of the font, and benefactor of the region—support such a reading.)

A third interpretation arises from a national trauma that shook Iceland in the early seventeenth century and scarred national consciousness for centuries to come: the notorious "Turkish raids" of 1627, whereby a small fleet of Algiers-based pirates, led by a Nordic renegade commander, sailed up to Iceland's south coast, ransacked several village and churches and returned to North Africa with 400 captives—a heavy blow for the Iceland's community and its fragile economy. Faced with a hefty ransom that Iceland could not pay by itself, the community struggled greatly to repatriate the captives; when the ransom finally reached North Africa almost ten years later in 1636, it only resulted in the freeing of 34 captives.[64] The "Turkish raid" (the ethnic label is a misnomer connoting Oriental Otherness) was still very fresh in the national consciousness by the late seventeenth century and shaped Icelandic views on foreign nations for many generations to come. Given the impossibility of protecting the vast Icelandic coastline against future intruders without considerable Danish financial support, which was not forthcoming at the time, many Icelanders sought refuge in spirituality (rather than xenophobia) to deal with the very real threat of renewed attacks.[65]

The pacifist strain of the baptismal font, expressed in the strategic removal of the scimitar at Deacon Phillip's feet, can be seen to articulate precisely such a response. The Ethiopian chamberlain, rather than arrive armed, is essentially a man of peace, asking for Deacon Phillip's blessing. As an idealized version of a Black visitor, he is stepping into an idealized Nordic landscape to accept his baptism with dignity and grace. His narrative would be uncannily echoed a century later in the extraordinary story of the Caribbean slave Hans Jonatan, who fled his Danish slave owner, and the Danish authorities in Copenhagen, and reached Iceland, where he settled, married, founded a family, and remained undetected for the rest of his life.[66]

Conclusion

The artifacts at Þingeyrar Church showcase well the complex and multifaceted nature of commodifying race in the medieval and early modern period. Part of this complexity stems from the transnational origin of many artifacts on race. Medieval and early modern Europe constituted a fairly porous marketplace where mass-manufactured artifacts and bespoke artworks were traded widely. Even remote and economically shielded areas like Iceland were influenced by other nations and their discourse on color, as exemplified by the Þingeyrar altarpiece and baptismal font, which echo artworks found all over Europe. Reading these artifacts as localized variants of shared pan-European texts is not only helpful for arriving at a deeper understanding of various economies of race; such an approach also aligns with the artistic process underlying these artifacts, whereby designs and templates crisscrossed national boundaries, resulting in pan-European distribution networks that increasingly offered tailor-made artifacts for localized markets.

A by-product of this cultural exchange is the presence of multiple, and often mutually conflicting, narratives co-existing side by side, as encapsulated in the curious dialectic space at Þingeyrar Church, which can be seen as representing a larger trend. Incidentally, in the same year that Matthäus Merian published his *Icones Biblicae* (1625), which served as a template for the Þingeyrar font, Paul Peter Rubens completed a painting that echoes the racialized tormentors shown on the Þingeyrar altarpiece.[67] The simultaneity of these pieces obviously challenges the idea of a monolithic pan-European view on color. How might one define the *zeitgeist* on the race for the year 1625, and on what basis? Which texts and narratives might one select for such a purpose? And what larger national, cultural, or geographical entities might a particular artwork actually represent? Answering these questions is particularly challenging for cosmopolitan artists like Merian and Rubens, who were influenced by various national and local traditions, and catered to an international clientele.[68]

A useful framework for a differentiated appreciation of racialized artifacts in a localized spiritual setting, I suggest, is the one modeled in the discussion above. Considering an artifact's distribution (local, national, or regional?), its spatial arrangement (approachable or distanced?), its form and function (statue, window, or font?), materiality (alabaster or canvas?), iconography (turban or feathers?), and relevant contexts (local, national, and regional) can lead to a closer understanding of the choices made by artists as they were reaching out across national, linguistic, cultural, and denominational lines. Knowing one's marketplace and understanding how the race was viewed by various communities increasingly became a key criterion of success for artists and craftsmen in the early modern period. The race for new markets and the marketing of race often went hand in hand.

Notes

1 Kim F. Hall, *Things of Darkness: Economies of Race and Gender in Early Modern England* (Ithaca, NY: Cornell University Press, 1995), 211–26.
2 Peter Erickson, "Invisibility Speaks: Servants and Portraits in Early Modern Visual Culture," *Journal for Early Modern Cultural Studies* 9, no. 1 (2009): 36–8, https://doi:10.1353/jem.0.0027.
3 Paul H. D. Kaplan, *The Rise of the Black Magus in Western Art* (Ann Arbor, MI: UMI Research Press, 1985); on the Queen of Sheba, see Kim F. Hall, "Object into Object? Some Thoughts on the Presence of Black Women in Early Modern Culture," in *Early Modern Visual Culture: Representation, Race, and Empire in Renaissance England, ed. Peter Erickson and Clark Hulse (Philadelphia: University of Pennsylvania Press,* 2000), 346–79; Judith's apocryphal Black maidservant is discussed in Paul H. D. Kaplan, "Isabella d'Este and Black African Women," in *Black Africans in Renaissance Europe*, ed. Thomas F. Earle

and K. J. P. Lowe (Cambridge: Cambridge University Press, 2005), 125–54; Monique Scheer, "From Majesty to Mystery: Change in the Meanings of Black Madonnas from the Sixteenth to Nineteenth Centuries," *The American Historical Review* 107, no. 5 (2002): 1412–40, https://doi.org/10.1086/ahr/107.5.1412.

4 Gude Suckale-Redlefsen and Robert Suckale, *Mauritius: Der Heilige Mohr/The Black Saint Maurice (German and English text)* (Houston: Menil Foundation, 1987), 122–3. The concept *hinterland* has been effectively leveraged in studies showing that remote, land-locked territories of Central Europe often had close economic ties to the transatlantic slave trade (Felix Brahm and Eve Rosenhaft, *Slavery Hinterland: Transatlantic Slavery and Continental Europe, 1680–1850* (Suffolk: Boydell Press, 2016).

5 Luther personally attacked the "idolatrous" veneration of Maurice at Halle in 1521, and many statues of Maurice were destroyed in the iconoclasm in Magdeburg in 1524 (Suckale-Redlefsen and Suckale, *Mauritius: Der Heilige Mohr, 108–11).*

6 Two recent studies that effectively demonstrate the impact of religious practice onto colonial contexts are Katharine Gerbner, *Christian Slavery: Conversion and Race in the Protestant Atlantic World* (Philadelphia: University of Pennsylvania Press, 2018) and Dennis Austin Britton, *Becoming Christian: Race, Reformation, and Early Modern English Romance* (New York: Fordham University Press, 2014).

7 See, for example, the statues dedicated to Benedict of Palermo in Southern Europe (Erin Kathleen Rowe, *Black Saints in Early Modern Global Catholicism* (Cambridge: Cambridge University Press, 2019), 1–11) or artifacts celebrating Saint Maurice in Tallinn and Riga (Anu Mänd, "Black Soldier—Patron Saint: St Maurice and the Livonian Merchants," *Ikonographisk Post: Nordisk Tidskrift för Ikonografi/Nordic Review of Iconography*, no. 1 (2014): 56–75.

8 See, for example, the stained windows at Balliol College Chapel, Oxford, by the Dutch artist Abraham van Linge, 1637, showing Deacon Phillip preaching to the Ethiopian chamberlain (Van Linge, Abraham, *St. Philip Preaching to the Eunoch [sic]* (Oxford: Balliol College Chapel, 1637),n. 6," Medieval Renaissance Gothic Stained Glass and Sculpture Photograph Archive, accessed September 17, 2020, https://www.therosewindow.com/pilot/Oxford-Balliol-col/n6-det1.htm). Or see the altarpiece from Jorg Leerer's workshop in Southern Germany (1508) featuring the Black Magus, which travelled 150 miles to the remote Swiss mountain village of Brigels ("Kapelle St. Martin, Brigels," Pleiv Breil/Brigels Catolica-Romana, accessed September 17, 2020, https://www.pleiv-breil.ch/sankt-martin/. Also note that many early modern artists like Albrecht Dürer catered to both Catholic and Protestant patrons (Anja Grebe, *Albrecht Dürer: Künstler, Werk und Zeit* (Darmstadt, Germany: WGB, 2006), 134).

9 David Bindman and Henry Louis Gates Jr., eds., *The Image of the Black in Western Art: From the "Age of Discovery" to the Age of Abolition: Artists of the Renaissance and Baroque*, Volume III, Part 1 (Cambridge: Harvard University Press, 2010), 60.

10 Perhaps the strongest articulation of such a view can be found in Yona Pinson, "Connotations of Sin and Heresy in the Figure of the Black King in Some Northern Renaissance Adorations." *Artibus et Historiae* 17, no. 34 (1996): 159–75.

11 Versions where the Black Magus appears as the first of the Magi are hard to come by. Examples include the frontispiece to the Jesuit missionary Alonso de Sandoval's *Tomo … De Instauranda Aethiopum Salute* (1647) (Alonso de Sandoval, *Tomo … De Instauranda Aethiopum Salute*, Vol. 1 (Madrid, Paredes: 1647), UB Heidelberg: Heidelberger Historische Beständ— Digital, accessed September 18, 2020, https://digi.ub.uni-heidelberg.de/diglit/sandoval1647bd1/0003) and the stained-glass coat of arms of the abbots at Wettingen, Switzerland (1623) (*Coat of Arms of the Abbots at Wettingen, Wikimedia Commons*, https://commons.wikimedia.org/wiki/File:Kloster_Wettingen_S%C3%BCd_11.jpg).

12 Imtiaz Habib, *Black Lives in the English Archives, 1500–1677: Imprints of the Invisible* (London: Routledge, 2017), 2–3.

13 Miranda Kaufmann, *Black Tudors: The Untold Story* (London: OneWorld, 2017), 109–10, 12–6, and 159–63.
14 Gerbner, *Christian Slavery*, 31–42.
15 Will Coster and Andrew Spicer, eds., *Sacred Space in Early Modern Europe* (Cambridge: Cambridge University Press, 2005), 9–10.
16 The chronicler of the Schweinfurt Church records, among other things, the baptism of a 15-year-old male from Barbados in 1660 ("'Schweinfurt St. Johanniskirche Geschichte,' Schweinfurtführer—Ein Führer Durch Schweinfurt und Seine Geschichte, accessed September 19, 2020, https://www.schweinfurtfuehrer.de/geschichte/geschichte-und-beschreibung-der-st-johannis-kirche-aus-beck-sche-chronik/).
17 Whitewashed versions of the baptism of the Ethiopian at Þingeyrar (Fig. 2, discussed below) include a stained-glass window from Berne, Switzerland (1634) ("Bildscheibe Samuel Gruner und Albrecht Manuel mit Philippus bei der Taufe des Kämmerers aus dem Mohrenland,"Vitrosearch, accessed September 19, 2020, https://vitrosearch.ch/en/objects/2471743), a version on the coffered ceiling at Hospitalkirche Hof, Germany (1699) (*The Christening of the Ethiopian Chamberlain*, Hospitalkirche Hof, accessed September 19, 2020, https://www.hospitalkirche-hof.de/index.php/bildtafel?imgid=30133), and a French illustrated Bible by Nicolas Fontaine from 1699 (Nicolas Fontaine, *L'Histoire du Vieux et du Nouveau Testament*, Google Books, https://books.google.co.ao/books?id=aPZgAAAAcAAJ&printsec=frontcover&hl=pt-PT&source=gbs_ge_summary_r&cad=0#v=twopage&q&f=false).
18 See, for example, the failed attempt by a zealous Lutheran priest to remove an "idolatrous" pre-Reformation altarpiece in Zwickau, Saxony, in 1560 against the will of a traditional-minded congregation and city council (Aleksandra Lipińska, "'Ein Tafell von Alabaster zu Antorff Bestellen': Southern Netherlandish Alabaster Sculpture in Central Europe," *Simiolus: Netherlands Quarterly for the History of Art* 32, no. 4 (2006): 231, https://www.jstor.org/stable/20355336).
19 See, for example, the prominent showcasing of the fifteenth-century Black Madonna at Einsiedeln Abbey, Switzerland (Scheer, "From Majesty to Mystery," 1414–5).
20 For a detailed introduction to Þingeyrar Church and its artifacts, see Margrét Hallgrímsdóttir, Þorsteinn Gunnarsson, Karl Sigurbjörnsson, and Kristín H. Sigurðardóttir, "Þingeyrakirkja." *Kirkjur Íslands* 8 (2006), 286–69 and 297–8.
21 "Strong's Greek: 128. Αἰθίοψ (Aithiops)—Ethiopian," Bible Hub: Search, Read, Study the Bible in Many Languages, accessed December 1, 2020, https://biblehub.com/greek/128.htm. The baptism of the Ethiopian was frequently used by missionaries, Blacks, and abolitionists as an argument for inclusive baptisms. See, for example, the case of Mathew from Barbados (1760) in Katherine Gerbner's *Christian Slavery* (Gerbner, *Christian Slavery*, 192).
22 A wide-ranging collection of Black and Orientalized flagellators can be found in Ruth Mellinkoff, *Outcasts: Signs of Otherness in Northern European Art of the Late Middle Ages*, 1994 ed. (Berkeley: University of California Press, 1993), Figs. I.12, I.29, I.39, I.40, VI.24, VI.25, VII.35, VII.37, VII.38.
23 Francis Cheetham, *English Medieval Alabasters: With a Catalogue of the Collection in the Victoria and Albert Museum* (Woodbridge, UK: Boydell & Brewer, 2005), 57–9.
24 The same template is used for an illustrated version of the *Book of Common Prayer* (1667) (*Philip and the Ethiopian Eunuch*, in *The Book of Common-Prayer* [...], "Philip and the Ethiopian Eunuch | Pitts Digital Image Archive | Emory University," Pitts Theology Library, last modified 1667, https://pitts.emory.edu/dia/image_details.cfm?ID=132938) and for a baptismal font at Lubin, Poland ("Baptismal font of the Protestant Church at Lubin, Poland," Lüben – Bilder, Geschichten, Dokumente, accessed September 19, 2020, https://www.lueben-damals.de/taufbecken.html). For examples from France, Switzerland, and Germany, see footnote 17.
25 A good overview of the political, economic, and ecclesiastical forces shaping Iceland throughout the early modern period is offered by Baldur Þórhallsson and Þorsteinn

Kristinsson, "Iceland's External Affairs from 1400 to the Reformation: Anglo-German Economic and Societal Shelter in a Danish Political Vacuum," *Icelandic Review of Politics & Administration* 9, no. 1 (2013): 113–37.

26 Harðardóttir, "Þingeyrakirkja," 286.

27 "Nottingham alabaster altarpiece at Hólar Cathedral," accessed December 1, 2020, https://www.mr.is/~gk/jfr/ordskyr/a/altarisbrik_hdk.htm. For the Mödruvalla altarpiece see "Altarisbrík [Mödruvalla altarpiece] Ekki úr Landi," Fréttir – Mbl.is, last modified May 20, 2009, https://www.mbl.is/greinasafn/grein/1283881/.

28 Harðardóttir, "Þingeyrakirkja," 266, 295–8.

29 Homi Bhabha, "Of Mimicry and Man: The Ambivalence of Colonial Discourse," October 28 (1984): 126.

30 "Nottingham alabaster altarpiece at Hólar Cathedral," https://www.mr.is/~gk/jfr/ordskyr/a/altarisbrik_hdk.htm.

31 Harðardóttir, "Þingeyrakirkja," 286. Note that the very similar alabaster altarpiece at Hólar Cathedral still has both its wings intact.

32 The wide distribution of Blackfaced figures on such altarpieces is confirmed by W. L. Hildburgh, the early twentieth-century authority on English alabaster, who states that "the representing as black the faces of executioners, torturers, and similar nefarious folk" is an "iconographical peculiarit[y]" characteristic of fifteenth-century English alabasters (W. L. Hildburgh, "Iconographical Peculiarities in English Medieval Alabaster Carvings," *Folklore* 44, no. 2 [1933]: 149).

33 John Carlsen, "De Små Veltalende Ting," *Siden Saxo* 2 (2018): 31.

34 Examples include two Restoration fonts by Grinling Gibbons in London, the first at St. Margaret's Lothbury ("St Margaret's Lothbury Tour Guide—St Margaret Lothbury & St Mary Woolnoth," St Margaret Lothbury & St Mary Woolnoth—Church of England Parish Churches at the Heart of the City of London, accessed September 19, 2020, https://stml.org.uk/tour/), and the second one at St. James Church, Piccadilly ("Baptismal Font showing the baptism of the Ethiopian chamberlain," St James's Church Piccadilly London, accessed September 19, 2020, https://www.sjp.org.uk/font.html). There is also evidence of a now lost font formerly in the Protestant Church at Lubin, Poland (see footnote 18).

35 Cheetham, *English Medieval Alabasters*, 11.

36 Kimberly Poitevin, "Inventing Whiteness: Cosmetics, Race, and Women in Early Modern England," *Journal for Early Modern Cultural Studies* 11, no. 1 (2011): 59–89.

37 See, for example, the instrumentalizing of Noah's curse on Ham in justifications of slavery (Stephen R. Haynes, *Noah's Curse: The Biblical Justification of American Slavery* (New York: Oxford University Press, 2002).

38 Kim Woods, "The Master of Rimini and the Tradition of Alabaster Carving in the Early Fifteenth-Century Netherlands," *Netherlands Yearbook for History of Art/Nederlands Kunsthistorisch Jaarboek* 62, no. 1 (2012): 60–1.

39 The font's inscription reads: "This font was donated by the noble and wise administrator for Northern and Western Iceland, Lauritz Christensen Gottrup, and his beloved Cathrina Peters to Þingeyrar Church for use and ornament" (translation mine), Harðardóttir, "Þingeyrakirkja," 297. The pulpit's inscription is very similar in tone.

40 Note how this distinguishes the Þingeyrar font from many whitewashed versions based on Merian's template (for examples, see footnote 17).

41 Stephanie Leitch, "Burgkmair's Peoples of Africa and India (1508) and the Origins of Ethnography in Print," 134.

42 Note that the near-identical altarpiece at Hólar Cathedral fashions the flagellators into Oriental rather than African stereotypes by lightening their complexions and painting massive black mustaches ("Nottingham Alabaster Altarpiece at Hólar Cathedral," https://www.mr.is/~gk/jfr/ordskyr/a/altarisbrik_hdk.htm).

43 Lynn F. Jacobs, "The Marketing and Standardization of South Netherlandish Carved Altarpieces: Limits on the Role of the Patron," *The Art Bulletin* 71, no. 2 (1989): 208–29.

44 The font here expresses what appears to be a distinct minority view in Northern Europe, especially among Protestants (Britton, *Becoming Christian*, 1–5 and 8–11).

45 Abraham Bloemaert, *The Baptism of the Eunuch*, 1620, Wikimedia Commons, https://commons.wikimedia.org/wiki/File:The_Baptism_of_the_Eunuch_by_Abraham_Bloemaert_Centraal_Museum_11225.jpg.

46 Bloemaert's removal of the book may be related to his Catholicism. (Xander Van Eck, "The Artist's Religion: Paintings Commissioned for Clandestine Catholic Churches in the Northern Netherlands, 1600-1800," *Simiolus: Netherlands Quarterly for the History of Art* 27, no. 1/2 (1999): 73). Note, however, that there are extant Catholic versions displaying the Ethiopian's book; see, for example, the illustrated French Bible by Nicolas Fontaine (1699, footnote 17), which is based on Merian and faithfully replicates the open Bible on the chariot.

47 For a useful introduction to reading emotions as performances, see Barbara H. Rosenwein and Riccardo Cristiani, *What is the History of Emotions?* (New York: John Wiley & Sons, 2017), 45–9.

48 A good overview of reading emotions in various colonial settings appears in Harald Fischer-Tiné, ed., *Anxieties, Fear and Panic in Colonial Settings: Empires on the Verge of a Nervous Breakdown* (New York: Springer, 2017).

49 Anne G. Gilchrist, "A Carved Morris-Dance Panel from Lancaster Castle," *Journal of the English Folk Dance and Song Society* 1, no. 2 (December 1933): 86. See also the status of Morris dancers at the Münchner Stadtmuseum (1480) (Erasmus Grasser, *The Morris Dancers*, 1480, https://www.muenchner-stadtmuseum.de/en/collections/applied-arts-collection/the-morris-dancers).

50 For a figure of Christ hiding behind the pole, see "*Death of Judas; Flagellation of Christ* from BL Arundel 157, f. 10," n.d. https://picryl.com/media/death-of-judas-flagellation-of-christ-from-bl-arundel-157-f-10-f79e62.

51 See, for example, the Yates Thompson MS from the British Library (France, fifteenth century) (Yates Thompson 3 f. 133v, *Flagellation of Christ*, n.d., British Library, accessed December 1, 2020, https://www.bl.uk/catalogues/illuminatedmanuscripts/ILLUMIN.ASP?Size=mid&IllID=5863).

52 The same synchronicity of movement can be observed on altarpieces at the British museum (*The Flagellation of Christ*, Museum number 1891,0521.1," n.d., https://www.britishmuseum.org/collection/object/H_1891-0521-1), and at the Chazen Museum of Art (*Flagellation of Christ*, n.d. Wikimedia Commons, https://commons.wikimedia.org/wiki/File:English_reliefs,_1_of_3,_Flagellation_of_Christ,_perhaps_Nottingham,_c._1440-1450,_alabaster_with_traces_of_polychromy_and_gilding,_lent_by_the_Metropolitan_Museum_of_Art_-_Chazen_Museum_of_Art_-_DSC02024.JPG).

53 For a general introduction to Morris dancing, see John Forrest, *The History of Morris Dancing, 1438–1750: Studies in Early English Drama* (Toronto: University of Toronto Press, 1999). Another religious representation of Blackness that is inspired by the Morris dance is the mural of St. Maurice at Roskilde, Denmark, which shows the Black saint stepping forward in a typical Morris-dance-like fashion (David Bindman and Henry Louis Gates Jr., eds., *The Image of the Black in Western Art: From the Early Christian Era to the "Age of Discovery": From the Demonic Threat to the Incarnation of Sainthood*, Volume II, Part 1 [Cambridge: Harvard University Press, 2010], 12).

54 Lindsey Barrett, "'Am I Not a Man and a Brother?': The Political Power of the Image," *The Black Atlantic*, last modified February 10, 2014, https://sites.duke.edu/blackatlantic/2014/02/10/am-i-not-a-man-and-a-brother-the-political-power-of-the-image/.

55 Kristín Loftsdóttir and Gísli Pálsson, "Black on White: Danish Colonialism, Iceland and the Caribbean," *Scandinavian Colonialism and the Rise of Modernity*, 2013, 39.

56 For examples of a fawning, servile Ethiopian, see the oil painting by Jan van der Elburcht, originally intended as an altarpiece (Jan Van der Elburcht, *Baptism of the Ethiopian Chamberlain*, n.d., Museum Boijmans Van Beuningen, Rotterdam, Wikimedia Commons,

https://commons.wikimedia.org/wiki/Category:Jan_van_der_Elburcht#/media/File:Jan_van_der_Elburcht_The_Baptism_of_the_Eunuch.jpg).

57 For examples see footnote 17.

58 Möðruvellir Church, situated 60 miles east of Þingeyrar, does not include the flagellation (see footnote 27).

59 For introductions to the fifteenth-century alabaster industry in the Netherlands, see Jacobs, "The Marketing and Standardization of South Netherlandish Carved Altarpieces," 208–14 and Woods, "The Master of Rimini," 61–77.

60 For a short introduction to the Danish slave trade, see Erik Gøbel, "Danish Shipping Along the Triangular Route, 1671–1802: Voyages and Conditions on Board," *Scandinavian Journal of History* 36, no. 2 (2011): 135–55.

61 Gerbner, *Christian Slavery*, 31–42.

62 Thráinn Eggertsson, "No Experiments, Monumental Disasters: Why It Took a Thousand Years to Develop a Specialized Fishing Industry in Iceland," *Journal of Economic Behavior & Organization* 30, no. 1 (1996): 1–23.

63 Jon Olassen, "Biographiske Efterretninger om Arne Magnusen," in *Nordisk Tidsskrift for Oldkyndighed*, Vol. 3 (Copenhagen: J. D. Quist, 1835), 75–6.

64 Þorsteinn Helgason, "Historical Narrative as Collective Therapy: The Case of the Turkish Raid in Iceland," *Scandinavian Journal of History* 22, no. 4 (1997): 277–8.

65 Helgason, "Historical Narrative as Collective Therapy," 275–89. Helgason notes that for most Icelandic writers "[t]he main lesson of the Raids was a religious one" (1997: 285). Bishops, in particular, called for contributions to the ransoms and prayers. No local leader seriously argued for military reinforcements to prevent a further attack, mainly due to the heavy taxation and limitations of the Icelandic economy (1997: 282).

66 Loftsdóttir and Pálsson, "Black on White," 47.

67 Peter Paul Rubens, *The Flagellation of Christ*, 1625, Church of St. Paul, Antwerp, Wikimedia Commons, https://commons.wikimedia.org/wiki/File:Flagellation-of-christ-_Rubens.jpg.

68 Rubens painted for and visited at the courts of Charles V of Spain, Charles I of England, and Marie de Medici, widow of Henry IV of France. (Mark Lamster, *Master of Shadows: The Secret Diplomatic Career of the Painter Peter Paul Rubens* (New York: Nan A Talese, 2009)). Merian worked for the famous engraver Theodor de Bry, who illustrated many of the most influential travel accounts of the period. He later married de Bry's daughter and took over the business after de Bry's death (Lucas H. von Wüthrich, *Matthaeus Merian d.Ä: Eine Biographie* (Hamburg: Hoffmann u Campe Verlag, 2007)).

Bibliography

"Altarisbrík [Mödruvalla altarpiece] Ekki úr Landi." Fréttir – Mbl.is. Accessed May 20, 2009, https://www.mbl.is/greinasafn/grein/1283881/.

"Baptismal font of the Protestant Church at Lubin, Poland." Lüben – Bilder, Geschichten, Dokumente. Accessed September 19, 2020. https://www.lueben-damals.de/taufbecken.html.

"Baptismal Font showing the baptism of the Ethiopian chamberlain." St James's Church, Piccadilly, London. Accessed September 19, 2020. https://www.sjp.org.uk/font.html.

Barrett, Lindsey. "'Am I Not a Man and a Brother?': The Political Power of the Image." *The Black Atlantic*, Accessed February 10, 2014. https://sites.duke.edu/blackatlantic/2014/02/10/am-i-not-a-man-and-a-brother-the-political-power-of-the-image/.

Bhabha, Homi. "Of Mimicry and Man: The Ambivalence of Colonial Discourse." *October*, 28 (1984), 125–33. doi:10.2307/778467.

"Bildscheibe Samuel Gruner und Albrecht Manuel mit Philippus bei der Taufe des Kämmerers aus dem Mohrenland." Vitrosearch. Accessed September 19, 2020. https://vitrosearch.ch/en/objects/2471743.

Bindman, David, and Henry Louis Gates Jr., eds. *The Image of the Black in Western Art: From the "Age of Discovery" to the Age of Abolition: Artists of the Renaissance and Baroque*, Vol. III, Part 1. Cambridge: Harvard University Press, 2010.

Bindman, David, and Henry Louis Gates Jr., eds. *The Image of the Black in Western Art: From the Early Christian Era to the "Age of Discovery": From the Demonic Threat to the Incarnation of Sainthood*, Vol. II, Part 1. Cambridge: Harvard University Press, 2010.

Bloemaert, Abraham. *The Baptism of the Ethiopian Eunuch*. 1620. *Wikimedia Commons*. https://commons.wikimedia.org/wiki/File:The_Baptism_of_the_Eunuch_by_Abraham_Bloemaert_Centraal_Museum_11225.jpg.

Brahm, Felix, and Eve Rosenhaft. *Slavery Hinterland: Transatlantic Slavery and Continental Europe, 1680–1850*. Suffolk: Boydell Press, 2016.

Britton, Dennis Austin. *Becoming Christian: Race, Reformation, and Early Modern English Romance*. New York: Fordham University Press, 2014.

Carlsen, John. "De Små Veltalende Ting." *Siden Saxo*, 2 (2018), 28–39.

Cheetham, Francis. *English Medieval Alabasters: With a Catalogue of the Collection in the Victoria and Albert Museum*. Woodbridge: Boydell & Brewer, 2005.

Coat of Arms of the Abbots at Wettingen. *Wikimedia Commons*. 1623. Cloister, south section, https://commons.wikimedia.org/wiki/File:Kloster_Wettingen_S%C3%BCd_11.jpg.

Coster, Will, and Andrew Spicer, eds. *Sacred Space in Early Modern Europe*. Cambridge: Cambridge University Press, 2005.

"*Death of Judas; Flagellation of Christ* from BL Arundel 157, f. 10." n.d. British Library. https://picryl.com/media/death-of-judas-flagellation-of-christ-from-bl-arundel-157-f-10-f79e62.

de Sandoval, Alonso. *Tomo … De Instauranda Aethiopum Salute*, Vol. 1. Madrid: Paredes, 1647. UB Heidelberg: Heidelberger Historische Bestände – Digital. Accessed September 18, 2020. https://digi.ub.uni-heidelberg.de/diglit/sandoval1647bd1/0003.

Eggertsson, Thráinn. "No Experiments, Monumental Disasters: Why It Took a Thousand Years to Develop a Specialized Fishing Industry in Iceland." *Journal of Economic Behavior & Organization*, 30.1 (1996): 1–23. doi:10.1016/s0167-2681(96)00839-6.

Erickson, Peter. "Invisibility Speaks: Servants and Portraits in Early Modern Visual Culture." *Journal for Early Modern Cultural Studies*, 9.1 (2009): 23–61. doi:10.1353/jem.0.0027.

Fischer-Tiné, Harald., ed. *Anxieties, Fear and Panic in Colonial Settings: Empires on the Verge of a Nervous Breakdown*. New York: Springer, 2017.

"*The Flagellation of Christ*, Museum number 1891,0521.1." n.d. The British Museum. Accessed December 1, 2020. https://www.britishmuseum.org/collection/object/H_1891-0521-1.

Flagellation of Christ. *Wikimedia Commons*. n.d. Chazen Museum of Art. Accessed December 1, 2020. https://commons.wikimedia.org/wiki/File:English_reliefs,_1_of_3,_Flagellation_of_Christ,_perhaps_Nottingham,_c._1440-1450,_alabaster_with_traces_of_polychromy_and_gilding,_lent_by_the_Metropolitan_Museum_of_Art_-_Chazen_Museum_of_Art_-_DSC02024.JPG.

Fontaine, Nicolas. *L'Histoire du Vieux et du Nouveau Testament*. Google Books. Last modified 1699. https://books.google.co.ao/books?id=aPZgAAAAcAAJ&printsec=frontcover&hl=pt-PT&source=gbs_ge_summary_r&cad=0#v=twopage&q&f=false.

Forrest, John. *The History of Morris Dancing, 1438–1750: Studies in Early English Drama*. Toronto: University of Toronto Press, 1999.

Gerbner, Katharine. *Christian Slavery: Conversion and Race in the Protestant Atlantic World*. Philadelphia: University of Pennsylvania Press, 2018.

Gilchrist, Anne G. "A Carved Morris-Dance Panel from Lancaster Castle." *Journal of the English Folk Dance and Song Society*, 1.2 (1933): 86–8.

Gøbel, Erik. "Danish Shipping Along the Triangular Route, 1671–1802: Voyages and Conditions on Board." *Scandinavian Journal of History*, 36.2 (2011): 135–55. doi:10.1080/03468755.2011.564065.

Grasser, Erasmus. *The Morris Dancers*. 1480. Münchner Stadtmuseum. https://www.muenchner-stadtmuseum.de/en/collections/applied-arts-collection/the-morris-dancers.

Grebe, Anja. *Albrecht Dürer: Künstler, Werk und Zeit*. Darmstadt: WGB, 2006.

Habib, Imtiaz. *Black Lives in the English Archives, 1500–1677: Imprints of the Invisible*. London: Routledge, 2017.

Hall, Kim F. *Things of Darkness: Economies of Race and Gender in Early Modern England*. Ithaca: Cornell University Press, 1995.

Hall, Kim F. "Object into Object? Some Thoughts on the Presence of Black Women in Early Modern Culture." In *Early Modern Visual Culture: Representation, Race, and Empire in Renaissance England*, eds. Peter Erickson and Clark Hulse, 346–79. Philadelphia: University of Pennsylvania Press, 2000.

Hallgrímsdóttir, Margrét, Þorsteinn Gunnarsson, Karl Sigurbjörnsson, and Kristín H. Sigurðardóttir. "Þingeyrakirkja." *Kirkjur Íslands*, 8 (2006): 261–314.

Haynes, Stephen R. *Noah's Curse: The Biblical Justification of American Slavery*. New York: Oxford University Press, 2002.

Helgason, Þorsteinn. "Historical Narrative as Collective Therapy: The Case of the Turkish Raid in Iceland." *Scandinavian Journal of History*, 22.4 (1997), 275–89. doi:10.1080/03468759708579357.

Hildburgh, W. L. "Iconographical Peculiarities in English Medieval Alabaster Carvings." *Folklore*, 44.2 (1933), 123–50. doi:10.1080/0015587x.1933.9718489.

Jacobs, Lynn F. "The Marketing and Standardization of South Netherlandish Carved Altarpieces: Limits on the Role of the Patron." *The Art Bulletin*, 71.2 (1989): 208–29. doi:10.2307/3051194.

"Kapelle St. Martin, Brigels." Pleiv Breil/Brigels Catolica-Romana. Accessed September 17, 2020. https://www.pleiv-breil.ch/sankt-martin/.

Kaplan, Paul H. D. *The Rise of the Black Magus in Western Art*. Ann Arbor: UMI Research Press, 1985.

Kaplan, Paul H. D. "Isabella d'Este and Black African Women." In *Black Africans in Renaissance Europe*, eds. Thomas F. Earle and K. J. P. Lowe, 125–54. Cambridge: Cambridge University Press, 2005.

Kaufmann, Miranda. *Black Tudors: The Untold Story*. London: OneWorld, 2017.

Lamster, Mark. *Master of Shadows: The Secret Diplomatic Career of the Painter Peter Paul Rubens*. New York: Nan A Talese, 2009.

Leitch, Stephaine. "Burgkmair's Peoples of Africa and India (1508) and the Origins of Ethnography in Print." *The Art Bulletin*, 91.2 (2009): 134–59. https://www.jstor.org/stable/40645477.

Lipin´ska, Aleksandra. "'Ein Tafell von Alabaster zu Antorff Bestellen': Southern Netherlandish Alabaster Sculpture in Central Europe." *Simiolus: Netherlands Quarterly for the History of Art*, 32.4 (2006): 231–58. https://www.jstor.org/stable/20355336.

Loftsdóttir, Kristín, and Gísli Pálsson. "Black on White: Danish Colonialism, Iceland and the Caribbean." In *Scandinavian Colonialism and the Rise of Modernity*, eds. M. Naum and J. Nordin, 37–52. New York: Springer, 2013. doi:10.1007/978-1-4614-6202-6_3.

Mänd, Anu. "Black Soldier – Patron Saint: St Maurice and the Livonian Merchants." *Ikonographisk Post: Nordisk Tidskrift för Ikonografi/Nordic Review of Iconography*, 1 (2014): 56–75.

Mellinkoff, Ruth. *Outcasts: Signs of Otherness in Northern European Art of the Late Middle Ages*, 1994 ed. Berkeley: University of California Press, 1993.

"Nottingham alabaster altarpiece at Hólar Cathedral." Accessed December 1, 2020. https://www.mr.is/~gk/jfr/ordskyr/a/altarisbrik_hdk.htm.

Olassen, Jon. "Biographiske Efterretninger om Arne Magnusen." In *Nordisk Tidsskrift for Oldkyndighed*, Vol. 3, 1–166. Copenhagen: J. D. Quist, 1835. https://books.google.dk/books?id=D7JQAAAAcAAJ&pg=PA76&dq=%22laurits+gottrup%22&hl=en&sa=X&ved=2ahUKEwi1yLGMpffrAhVx-yoKHaCsA_EQ6AEwAHoECAIQAg#v=onepage&q=%22laurits%20gottrup%22&f=false.

Philip and the Ethiopian Eunuch. In *The Book of Common-Prayer [.]*. "Philip and the Ethiopian Eunuch | Pitts Digital Image Archive | Emory University." Pitts Theology Library. Last modified 1667. https://pitts.emory.edu/dia/image_details.cfm?ID=132938.

Pinson, Yona. "Connotations of Sin and Heresy in the Figure of the Black King in Some Northern Renaissance Adorations." *Artibus et Historiae*, 17.34 (1996): 159–75. doi:10.2307/1483528.

Poitevin, Kimberly. "Inventing Whiteness: Cosmetics, Race, and Women in Early Modern England." *Journal for Early Modern Cultural Studies*, 11.1 (2011): 59–89. doi:10.1353/jem.2011.0009.

Rosenwein, Barbara H., and Riccardo Cristiani. *What is the History of Emotions?* New York: John Wiley & Sons, 2017.

Rowe, Erin Kathleen. *Black Saints in Early Modern Global Catholicism*. Cambridge: Cambridge University Press, 2019.

Rubens, Peter Paul. *The Flagellation of Christ*. 1625. Church of St. Paul, Antwerp. Wikimedia Commons. https://commons.wikimedia.org/wiki/File:Flagellation-of-christ-_Rubens.jpg.

Scheer, Monique. "From Majesty to Mystery: Change in the Meanings of Black Madonnas from the Sixteenth to Nineteenth Centuries." *The American Historical Review*, 107.5 (2002): 1412–40. https://doi.org/10.1086/ahr/107.5.1412.

"Schweinfurt St. Johanniskirche Geschichte." Schweinfurtführer – Ein Führer Durch Schweinfurt und Seine Geschichte. Accessed September 19, 2020. https://www.schweinfurtfuehrer.de/geschichte/geschichte-und-beschreibung-der-st-johannis-kirche-aus-beck-sche-chronik/.

"St Margaret's Lothbury Tour Guide – St Margaret Lothbury & St Mary Woolnoth." St Margaret Lothbury & St Mary Woolnoth – Church of England Parish Churches at the Heart of the City of London. Accessed September 19, 2020. https://stml.org.uk/tour/.

"Strong's Greek: 128. Aἰθίοψ (Aithiops) – Ethiopian." Bible Hub: Search, Read, Study the Bible in Many Languages. Accessed December 1, 2020. https://biblehub.com/greek/128.htm.

Suckale-Redlefsen, Gude, and Robert Suckale. *Mauritius: Der heilige Mohr/The Black Saint Maurice (German and English Text)*. Houston: Menil Foundation, 1987.

Þórhallsson, Baldur, and Þorsteinn Kristinsson. "Iceland's External Affairs from 1400 to the Reformation: Anglo-German Economic and Societal Shelter in a Danish Political Vacuum." *Icelandic Review of Politics & Administration*, 9.1 (2013): 113–37. doi:10.13177/irpa.a.2013.9.1.6.

The Christening of the Ethiopian Chamberlain. Hospitalkirche Hof. Accessed September 19, 2020. https://www.hospitalkirche-hof.de/index.php/bildtafel?imgid=30133.

Van der Elburcht, Jan. *Baptism of the Ethiopian Chamberlain*. n.d. Museum Boijmans Van Beuningen, Rotterdam. *Wikimedia Commons*. https://commons.wikimedia.org/wiki/Category:Jan_van_der_Elburcht#/media/File:Jan_van_der_Elburcht_The_Baptism_of_the_Eunuch.jpg.

Van Eck, Xander. "The Artist's Religion: Paintings Commissioned for Clandestine Catholic Churches in the Northern Netherlands, 1600–1800." *Simiolus: Netherlands Quarterly for the History of Art*, 27.1/2 (1999): 70–94. doi:10.2307/3780879.

Van Linge, Abraham. 1637. *St. Philip Preaching to the Eunoch*. Oxford: Balliol College Chapel – n.6. Medieval Renaissance Gothic Stained Glass and Sculpture Photograph Archive. Accessed September 17, 2020. https://www.therosewindow.com/pilot/Oxford-Balliol-col/n6-det1.htm.

Woods, Kim. "The Master of Rimini and the Tradition of Alabaster Carving in the Early Fifteenth-Century Netherlands." *Netherlands Yearbook for History of Art/Nederlands Kunsthistorisch Jaarboek*, 62.1 (2012): 56–83. doi:10.1163/22145966-06201004.

von Wüthrich, Lucas H. *Matthaeus Merian d.Ä: Eine Biographie*. Hamburg: Hoffmann u Campe Verlag, 2007.

Yates Thompson 3 f. 133v. *Flagellation of Christ*. n.d. British Library. Accessed December 1, 2020. https://www.bl.uk/catalogues/illuminatedmanuscripts/ILLUMIN.ASP?Size=mid&IllID=5863.

10

THE MIRACLE OF THE BLACK LEG

Medical knowledge, race + territorialization

Cecilio M. Cooper

This chapter focuses on a scene of amputation as a visceral instantiation of anti-black depredation. In it, saints expropriate an anonymous black figure's limb during miraculous healing. According to the Miracle of the Black Leg (MoBL), a Roman dreamt that Cosmas and Damian amputated an Ethiopian's healthy limb so that it could be transplanted onto his own ailing body. The MoBL merits this sustained attention because it evidences how Renaissance worldviews shape visual representations of humanity's differentiation from divinity and each other. Blackness operates cosmologically within the miracle as a sign of heathen physiognomic difference and disease. It illuminates how church authority, commerce, and medical knowledge converge as a backdrop for European conquest into Africa and the New World. The original version of the miracle did not hinge upon the racial differences between the amputee and the recipient. I argue that the racial metamorphosis of MoBL literary accounts and visual iconography were sparked by the onset of the trans-Atlantic slave trade. In other words, the once-white donor leg was blackened as part of a rhetorical move to justify territorializing parts of the globe as legitimately enslavable. This chapter uses the divine possession chronicled in the Miracle of the Black Leg's cross-racial transplant imagery to theorize human bodies as sexualized and racialized territories that index larger geographic territories. Moreover, it affords an opportunity to show how the racialized trade in chattel slaves throughout early modern marketplaces is among the dynamic contexts where libidinal economies and political economies converge. Quests to possess land, persons, or goods were as influenced by emergent psychic investments in white sovereign personhood as the ordering of territory in accordance with monotheist religious doctrine.

My study examines fifteenth- through seventeenth-century Italian and Spanish woodcut, sculpture, and paintings alongside hagiographies, surgical texts, and anatomy atlases. The artistic renderings are not treated as mimetic

DOI: 10.4324/9781003082842-11

illustrations of the literary depictions but as a heterogeneous collection of visual symbology that is intelligible when examined within colonial systems of meaning. Most exist as paintings, but woodcuts, sculptures, and drawings are also addressed as less frequent occurrences. The paintings and sculptures don't appear before the fifteenth century and taper off altogether after the seventeenth century. [1] The preponderance of visual portrayals does not merely seem a practical way to communicate *The Golden Legend* to illiterate masses but also speaks to visuality's role in articulating early modern racial distinctions, scales of value in globalizing marketplaces, and scientific knowledge.

Advancements in anatomical science were made possible by sexual experimentation on black bodies. In 1702 Alexis Littre recounted his clinical tests to determine the source of dark coloring in African skin in *Histoire de Academie Royale des Sciences*.[2] This was a replication of Marcello Malpighi's microscopic study of African skin, which resulted in the identification of the skin layer that holds pigmentation (now called the Malpighian layer). Littre tested Malpighi's findings by dissecting the penis of an enslaved person, and from Buffon's estimation concluded "that the end of the glans, which was not covered with the prepuce, was black, and that the part of it which was covered was perfectly white. This observation demonstrates that the air is necessary to produce the blackness of Negroes."[3] Though flesh could be excised from any other part of the patient, exposed tissue from genitals was more desirable because the skin samples seemed to provide more veridical evidence about black skin. This 1665 breakthrough is regarded as "undoubtedly the most important skin-related discovery of the early-modern era" because "he identified a third and separate layer of gelatinous 'African' skin located in between the outer 'scarf' skin and the inner 'true' skin."[4] The Italian microanantomist asserted that a gelatinous black substance gave African skin its swarthy hue. The benefits of this scientific research on genitals were not strictly applied to reproductive medicine, but the discoveries about the skin it enabled had far-reaching effects throughout disciplines concerned with the human body. This experiment is one of the countless instances where black skin has been medically scrutinized. The process of *epidermalization*, as described by Frantz Fanon, pathologizes dark skin and the subsurface flesh as bodily expressions of slave status and black inferiority.[5]

By this logic, the Ethiopian in the Miracle of the Black Leg seemed an appropriate source for the replacement flesh because he represented an otherwise extraneous and disposable population. British, Dutch, and French demands for black slaves intensified after Spanish, Italian, and Portuguese colonizers seized African territory. In 1441 Prince Henry the Navigator of Portugal commissioned captains Nuno Tristão and Antão Goncalves to lead an expedition to West Africa. When they enslaved a Mauritanian and brought him back to their benefactor, they helped inaugurate Europe's participation in the Atlantic slave trade and expand domestic slave markets in Benin and Congo to a cross-continental scale. Eager to gain a competitive edge in the contest for territorial acquisitions, Catholic monarchs Queen Isabella I of Castile and her spouse King Ferdinand of Aragon financed Christopher Columbus's explorations half a century later. The

Italian discovered exotic wildlife along with Taino and Arawak peoples indigenous to the Caribbean islands. These were places he and his Iberian counterparts had previously believed uninhabitable. In the 1494 Treaty of Tordesillas, Spain and Portugal negotiated which segments of Atlantic territory beyond Europe they would claim as within their purview. The Catholic Church initially decreed that the newfound islanders were legitimately enslavable because they lived in heathen lands that had not yet received the Word of God. After amending his pro-slavery views in 1515, Dominican friar Bartolomé de las Casas would challenge theologian Juan Ginés de Sepúlveda's assertion that Amerindians were sub-human natural slaves. Las Casas advocated missions to protect and civilize them while urging Spain to import Black Africans. These replacement captives seemed better suited for the harsh conditions of enslavement. Race, exemplified by blackness, eventually displaced kinship, and religion as slavery's organizing principle in the Atlantic World.[6]

I concur with Saidiya Hartman that "premature death persists as one of the definitive markers of Blackness," as does vulnerability to wanton violence for those who survive.[7] From J. Marion Sims's gynecological procedures on enslaved women to the Tuskegee syphilis study to medical schools grave robbing black corpses to the harvesting of Henrietta Lacks's genetic material, black people have been subjected to violent medical practices in the name of progress. Blackness more readily casts us as objects of medical manipulation than active subjects who are treated as interlocutors key to the generation of medical knowledge. My examination of the MoBL builds upon this robust body of evidence. It leads me to ponder what bioethical concerns arise when we try to account for medicine's indifference to antiblack violence in the MoBL all while embracing Cosmas and Damian's sacrifice and innovation? How does the MoBL invite us to think about race, scientific knowledge, capital, and conquest in the early modern Atlantic World?

The Miracle's Origins

"Where can we get flesh to fill in where we cut away the rotted leg?" queries the saint to his brother. After being martyred, Cosmas and Damian amputated the limb of an Ethiopian (in some versions, a Moor) and transplanted it onto a Roman church official to replace his cancerous limb. The swarthy foreigner had recently been buried in the cemetery of Saint Peter in Chains. The verger prayed to be healed, and the saints appeared to him in a dream. The surgery was performed while he slept, and he awoke pain-free and astonished that the healthy black leg had been seamlessly fused to him. In some versions, the leg was severed below the knee and, in others, the gangrenous tissue rose up through his hip joint. A Catalonian derivation states that the hole left after a chunk of flesh had been carved from the Roman's thigh was filled with tissue from the exhumed Moor/Ethiopian. The diseased flesh was then reattached to the disinterred corpse. For performing this groundbreaking surgery and many other healing miracles, the twin brothers were canonized as patron saints of physicians. Cosmas is derived from the Greek *kosmos*, which multiply signifies order, the material world, universe, ornamentation, and cleanliness. Damian or *Damianus* is a portmanteau from "*Domini manus*, the hand of the Lord."[8] The earliest iteration of their supernatural feat was documented in the medieval hagiography *The Golden Legend* (which is alternately entitled *The Lives of Saints*). While early modern portrayals of the twin saints' activities abound, this chapter is especially interested in the subset of available reproductions depicting Cosmas and Damian's Miracle of the Black Leg (aka "The Miracle of the Moor's (Black) Leg").

The duo was purportedly born around 250 A.D. in the Roman province Aegea, which is located in the south-central region of present-day Turkey. The municipality of Çukurova lies near both the Mediterranean coast and the Syrian border. Cosmas and Damian were medically trained in their homeland. Many cults dedicated to the twin saints are believed to have originated in the Northern part of Syria during their lifetimes. This is also the site of their oldest preserved icons. Their remains (chiefly their bones) were dispersed throughout Europe after they were martyred. These corporeal relics attracted the worship of more Christians, so the number of their cults grew and expanded west. Cultists made pilgrimages and engaged in a holy practice called incubation. This entails sleeping at the foot of the shrines with the hopes of having a curative dream like the one experienced by the MoBL's transplantee. The legend of the twin saints that circulates most widely today in Europe and North America is actually a synthesis of three pairs, each with distinct veneration days and birthplaces. The Eastern Orthodox Church venerates a pair of Arab brothers on October 17, the Orthodox Church's celebration of Mesopotamian twins occurs on November 1, and the Roman Catholic Church commemorates Italian siblings on September 26.[9] Over 60 posthumous miracles are attributed to Cosmas and Damian. With over 1,500 purported depictions of the MoBL, they are among the most iconographically represented physician-saints in Byzantine and post-Byzantine art.[10] Images of the MoBL don't appear in images commissioned by the Orthodox Church but do appear in Roman Catholic images after 1270. Various literary and visual depictions attest that Cosmas and Damian were subjected to tortures so great; they were eventually canonized as martyrs.

Roman Emperor Diocletian persecuted Cosmas and Damian for passing off acts of chicanery as healings by divine possession. He commanded them to renounce their Christian faith, pledge fealty to Olympian deities, and reveal to him the true secular secrets behind their abilities. They refused. The pair was bound with chains and thrown into the sea, yet still, they would not drown. After withstanding stretching on a rack, attempts were then made to crucify them. Angels deflected the stones and arrows launched at them so that they rebounded upon the shooters. Flames meant to consume them at the stake instead engulfed both punishers and onlookers. Burning at the stake was considered a particularly severe punishment because it caused the soul to be separated from the body. Cosmas and Damian survived the fire, though their other five brothers perished from beheadings. After surviving a litany of abuses, the twins were also finally murdered by decapitation. They were buried together and consecrated.[11]

A striking resonance seems to exist between the fragmenting violence that precipitated the twin saints' martyrdom and the means through which they posthumously performed the transplantation.

To neutralize Protestant charges that saints were demonic imposters, the Catholic council devised strict criteria for researching and validating miracles.[12] Stories of martyrdom were investigated from the Inquisition through to the council of Trent (1545–1563), after which Roman Catholic leadership standardized the processes for bestowing sainthood. The reforms made by this ecumenical council were motivated by the Protestant Reformation and also included increased regulation of sexuality in Latin America.[13] From then on, Cosmas and Damian were presented in imagery as vessels for divine healing through overt reference to Angels, Mary, Jesus, etc. Otherwise, they risked being misconstrued as charlatans or sorcerers. Kees Zimmerman attributes the eventual decline in depictions of the miracle to skepticism about the veracity of the miraculous events and a widespread crisis of faith.

Images of the legend have been recovered throughout Western Europe, but paintings by Spanish and Italian artists constitute the majority. Solo or smaller clusters of early modern imagery have also been found in Portugal, Greece, Germany, Switzerland, Brazil, Belgium, and the Netherlands. MoBL imagery can be placed in three groups: 1) those where the black replacement leg is shown on the white recipient with the amputated black body in the frame (as in fig. 10.1),[14] 2) the black replacement limb is shown but the black donor is absent (as in fig. 10.2),[15] and 3) representations of the miracle where the replacement leg is white. Additional categorical subdivisions are: 1A) where the sickly white leg has been reattached to the black body and 2A) where it lies detached and the black donor is absent. *Predella* paintings present episodes or scenes in the lives of these saints and are meant to be viewed sequentially.[16] In the San Marco predellas, Cosmas and Damian are likened to the disciples whom Christ entreats to heal the ailing while taking vows of poverty. The scholarship on the legend has generally been contextualized in religious studies of Cosmas and Damian as saints, art historical accounts of relics and iconography, and histories of medicine. The blackness of the leg is often remarked upon as a curiosity but has gone largely under-theorized. My study deploys analytical frames from black critical thought to challenge and complement existing work on MoBL (Figures 10.1 and 10.2).

The earliest visual depictions of the MoBL appear as two *predella* panels in Rinuccini Chapel in Florence, which follows the first literary depiction of the miraculous transplantation as a black leg in the thirteenth century. An antecedent to *Golden Legend* version dates back to the fifth century as the "Miracle of the Anagyri," which sets the miracle in a different location and describes the miracle occurring while the saints were still alive. *Anagyri* is a Greek word meaning men without silver. Tantamount to pennilessness, they were described as such because they piously refused payment for their divinely bestowed healing powers.[17]

The fifteenth-century artistic works that were produced in the fraught political context where Spain was struggling to expel invaders from North Africa

FIGURE 10.1 Fernando del Rincon, *Milagros de los santos médicos Cosme y Damián*, 1510, Oil on panel, 188 × 155 cm, P02549.

Source: Museo del Prado-Pinture. Madrid, Spain © Album/Alamy Stock Photo

and Asia fomented portrayals of the limb as coming from a swarthy Moor. This reflected Spanish desire to harm darker-skinned foreigners, imagined as a physiognomically and morally distinct population, for the benefit of the empire. Renderings created by Spanish artists are extraordinary because, unlike German and Italian creations in the MoBL tradition, they show the macabre presence of a mutilated living black donor.[18] The patient is often shown to be sleeping as described in the legend. Earlier accounts state that the rest of the Moor's corpse remained in the cemetery, but some artists include the black body next to the bed. This results in a powerful juxtaposition of color further distinguished by a

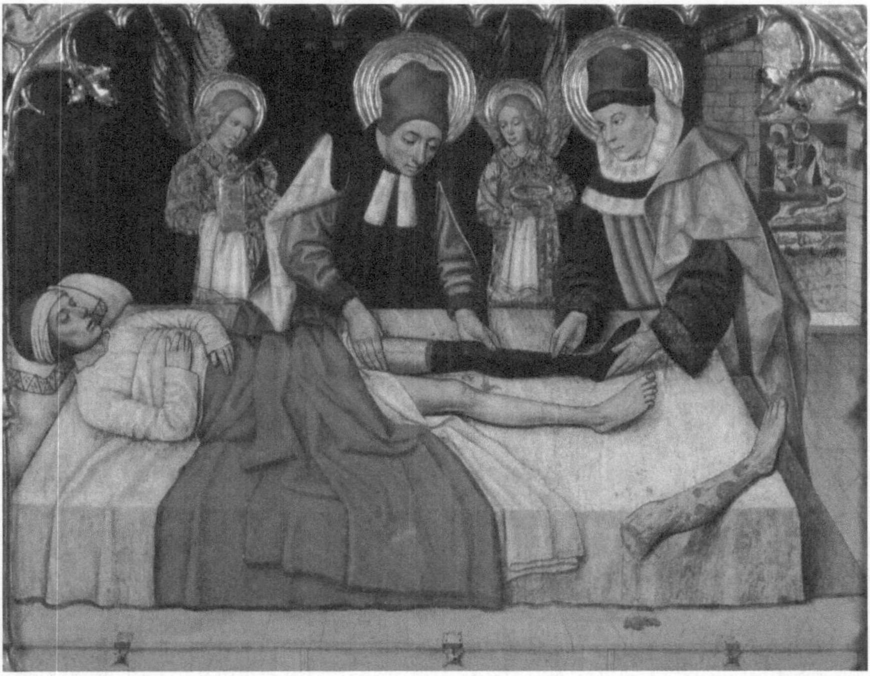

FIGURE 10.2 Jaime Huguet, Predella of the altarpiece of the saints Abdón and Senén, 1460. *Miracle of the gangrenous leg*, San Cosme and San Damián, Tempera painting of egg on board, 301 × 225 cm.

Source: Church of Santa María, Terrasa © Album/Alamy Stock Photo

difference in height. The spatial placement of the black body on the floor below the white person on the bed accentuates the racial hierarchies between the two.

Red and orange—signaling royalty—predominate several of the paintings. They are often included with other primary colors of yellow or blue throughout. In other instances, the warm hues are complemented by green accents. They are generally depicted as identical twins dressed in matching tunics and crowned in golden halos. The German Wurttgemburishces Landesmuseum paintings are exceptions in that the surgeons appear to be fraternal twins wearing dissimilar tunics and mantles. In some, they are clean shaven, while they appear bearded in other depictions. Depending on perspective, some show the twins adjacent to each other attending to the side of the body from which the leg is cut, and others have them flanking the bed-ridden invalid. Some images show an intimate scene only featuring the saints and their patients. Another subset includes mortals as witnesses and angels to provide divine guidance for the surgical procedure. The *mise-en-scene* (design, surroundings, etc.) of the images enrich the narrative of the depictions, including clothing, furnishings, and medical paraphernalia (mantles, mortars, scalpels, ointments, etc.).

Race, Language + Visuality

What does the imagery around the interracial amputation and transplantation depicted in the MoBL reveal about race, the transatlantic slave trade, science, and early modern visuality? Existing scholarship on the Miracle generally includes a clear aversion to framing the MoBL as indicative of antiblack racism. *Proto-racism,* racism's historical antecedent, is deemed a more appropriate descriptor. This includes Joseph Ziegler's and Peter Biller's assessments of proto-racial thought in medieval science through case studies on Jewish men and black women. Their work is featured in the edited volume *The Origins of Racism in the West,* which suggests that early Christian associations of evil with black skin and Graeco-Roman associations of black with the underworld buttress racial ideologies of Classical Antiquity and the Middle Ages. Instead, the transplantation imagery is described as occurring between persons of same or different ethnicities.[19] In his discussion of the MoBL as exemplifying the origins of antiblack racism in the New World, David Brion Davis finds the potential insight of Benjamin Isaac's use of *proto-racism* is undermined by his understanding of racism, which "focuses only on ideas and attitudes and excludes behavior, practices, and consequences."[20] Geraldine Heng's book *The Invention of Race in the European Middle Ages* challenges "canonical race theory" scholarship that argues race is strictly a modernist conception. Heng engages influential pre-modernist work concerned with ethnicity as an antecedent to Enlightenment racial logic.[21] Drawn largely from the perspectives of historians and anthropologists, *Black Africans in Renaissance Europe* addresses the influx of black Africans to Europe during the voyages of discovery.[22] The collection targets readers versed in African diasporic history and interrogates whether the terms race or racism are anachronisms for the study of blacks in the Renaissance. Kim F. Hall's *Things of Darkness* posits the centrality of black skin for social constructions of Renaissance beauty in literature. The emergent sense that sixteenth–seventeenth century Englishness heavily relied upon an imagined symmetry between a person's interiority and their physiognomy. Moreover, black skin has been deemed the obverse of white (feminine) virtue.[23] Lorraine Daston's and Katharine Parks' influential *Wonders and the Order of Nature, 1150–1750* is one of only a few historical analyzes of monstrosity and curiosity. It shows that "symmetric monstrosities" (like conjoined twins) were considered unseemly though not unnatural occurrences. These monstrous births were subject to dissection in order to clarify knowledge about normal versions of organisms.[24] These Renaissance-focused works illuminate the varying ways bodily differences circulated in Europe. Famed navigator Amerigo Vespucci wrote in his travel narrative about a voyage to the West Indies that he anticipated finding Amerindian cannibals that were exclusively female. Seven years after Columbus, the Italian feared that a savage would dismember and roast the flesh of European explorers after ripping away their penises with her teeth. In "Some Could Suckle over Their Shoulder," Jennifer Morgan argues that these anthropophagi were threats because of their perceived "female sexual insatiability."[25] Widely-circulated cartographic texts like Leo Africanus's *A Geographical*

Historie of Africa mapped black cannibalistic licentiousness from black bodies onto the intemperate locales through climatic theory. With these contributions in mind, I draw connections between the MoBL, biomedicine, and commodified blackness in the Atlantic world. This mythical event exemplifies how European somatic integrity is constituted through African corporeal loss.

Medievalists and Classicists may claim that their disregard for antiblackness is meant to defend against supposed anachronistic impositions of race onto pre-1500 phenomena. Complementary moves attempt to distinguish "pre-racial" conceptions of blackness (or neutral "non-racial" blackness) from the racial in order to identify an earlier idyllic time when blackness' negative connotations had no bearing on the concurrent bigotry directed toward black persons. I find these to be untenable distinctions that mystify the quaquaversal intensity with which antiblackness pervades Western modernities. The aforementioned positions safeguard antagonistically antiquated scholarship away from critiques about how racism not only shapes what are deemed appropriates objects of study but also whose vantages are relentlessly licensed to conduct such studies. My research shows that ethnicity functions as a sub-genre of Man[26] and secondary level of classification of race, so that it is *never* a non-racial marker of difference. Ethnicity is commonly invoked in scholarship as a way to disavow how antiblackness forms the bonds of non-black/non-slave cultural filiation. The MoBL scandalizes claims to pre-modernist pre-racial ethnicity because it unequivocally betrays how presumption of physiognomic, moral, and chromatic incongruity between Africans and Europeans drives its spectacular narrative arc.

The MoBL circulates in print via William Caxton's first translation of the *Golden Legend* from Voragine's original Latin into English. Wynken de Worde published the second edition of Caxton's translation in 1487 with an important modification from the 1483 first edition. This change circulates many subsequent versions: "Moryans" is used in place of "Ethyopyens." In her discussion of the MoBL, Sheetal Lodhia states "Moorishness increasingly comes to signify blackness, such that blackness stands for both racial and religious difference."[27] Moor here does render the Africanity of the Ethiopian figure inoperable but instead augments its meaning so that his Otherness—his blackness—is intensified. Rather than address the variety of designations for the donor as a problem of historical accuracy that needs to be verified, the slippages in categorization for both the saints and the dark-skinned non-Roman figure betray the convoluted and complicated way blackness serves as a roving target used to delineate liminal human status. While some argue that Moor chiefly connotes religious or ethnic Otherness, I believe the term also has racial inflections that are legible in the MoBL. Moor is derived from *maurus*, which is a Greek word for black. It becomes fused to blackness as the suffix of the term *blackamoor.* Scholars working with early modern texts may translate *Aethiops* and *Maurus* as either "nigger," "blackavised Moor," "Negro," "black Moor", or "blackamoor."[28] A.C. Saunders claims that "in the 5th century the word for slave was *mouro*, Moor."[29] Free Moors were *mouros forros,* and black slaves *mouros negros* or blackamoors. The

Muslim or pagan connotations of *moor* compelled the Portuguese to use *escravo* to specifically denote black slaves from 1459 onward.[30]

It's also important to note the ambiguity of geographic labels during this period. The territory that Europeans referred to as Ethiopia, as origin place for Ethiopians, is not synonymous with the contemporary East African nation-state. In his study on antiblack racism in Abrahamic faiths (i.e. Christianity, Judaism, and Islam), David Goldenberg finds that Ethiopia was associated with outermost geographical categorization and the limit of the inhabited world.[31] For the untraveled European, Ethiopian functioned as a generic term for black Africans. The scope of *Afriqa/Afriqi* could mean North Africa or sub-Saharan black Africa in rabbinic literature. African and Ethiopian became interchangeable with Moor because then it wasn't assumed that Arabia and Africa were distinct regions. Their residents were even thought to share ancient ancestry. Greeks and Romans alternately romanticized Ethiopia or Guinea or Nubia or Kush as places rich in gold and the homeland of the darkest-skinned peoples.[32] Ethiopians/Moors/Africans were used to signify anthropological racial, and geographical extremes.

The Miracle was resurrected during the Renaissance and circulated widely in religious and medical contexts. Remarkably, it is still rehearsed in contemporary scholarship on *phantom limb syndrome*. First recorded in the sixteenth century, the term *phantom limb* was coined to describe a neurological phenomenon that causes amputees to feel missing body parts because they project mental images of their physiques that extrapolate from the bounds of injured flesh. Some renditions of *The Golden Legend* state that the black leg was harvested from a disinterred corpse, while others affirm that the donor was alive when his leg was severed. How does phantom limb syndrome, as describing a present absence, help us imagine how black suffering was understood in early modernity through the dismemberment of the unnamed black figure in the MoBL? Alternately, how does the desecration of this black corpse further the accrual of medical knowledge while fueling the religious transcendence of white subjects? Many of the written accounts of the MoBL neglect to explicitly describe the replacement limb as African-derived. However, the racialized adaptation is disproportionately represented in the visual iconography of the *Golden Legend* created in the Roman Catholic tradition. It appears that Roman Catholics had a more intense need than their Orthodox counterparts for the race to not only be *read*, but also *seen*. To what can we attribute this asymmetry of interpretation? My research finds that the MoBL is an opportunity to gain a clearer understanding of how literary and visual culture shape early modern expressions of antiblackness.

My work is less concerned with the material circulation of the hagiographies, paintings, and sculptures as precious material objects than what they illuminate about how blackness becomes a "visually knowable"[33] "thing to see,"[34] and how it circulates for a range of fungible uses. Blackness is indexed both by spectacular physiognomic markers and less obvious indicators of sin and disease. Antiblackness enacts a forceful visual grammar in responses to the troubling disaggregation black opacity poses to the Western visual field. Here I mean the dual inflection of opacity as 1) obscuring meaning/confusing and 2) an impediment to translucence/making vision cloudy. Hypervisibility is associated with the disproportionate display of images that foreground black abjection. Hypervisibility is inextricable from invisibility because the latter is premised on the simultaneous occlusion or disappearing of black persons as seeing agents. An antiblack world endeavors to deny black people access to the "right to look."[35] To be excessively seen and almost endlessly available to surveillance means for black people that the antiblack world that watches you violently works to veil itself from your perception.

The "ocular desire" at play in mapping bodies and territory reflects the centrality of the colonial gaze in projects of empire.[36] Visuality has a temporalizing function that ahistorically valorizes presence. Seeing is believing. Blackness is most immediately experienced as a visual occurrence that is most readily described through the registers of color, light, and texture. It persists through excessive presence, which manifests as hypervisibility. To fully know and dominate blackness requires purveying it from all angles. Increased attention to the way blackness and antiblackness, tethered in a kind of attraction-repulsion *pas de deux*, impact the deeper registers of visual culture also has relevance for the natural sciences. Psychic expressions of antiblackness, as phobic forces, extend from physiognomic between Men and natives through humanist sciences. The hypervisibility of blackness and consequent criminalization of black persons is bound up with the paradox of *ocularcentrism*, the fetishistic investment in and hierarchization of the visual realm in ways that shore up the "primacy of the image."[37] Blackness' non-origins amidst the shadows of modernity enables its continued objectification even within projects that aim to redress histories of loss.

It seems that there is a contradictory process of identification (formation of ego libido) and disidentification at play in the Miracle images, which is not only reflected in their formal elements, but also in the stories they tell. The averted gaze of the black amputees highlights how they serve doubly as objects to the white actors painted in the frame and to the white spectators looking at the images on the walls of homes or churches. Viewers are invited to interpolate themselves into the scene by adopting/sharing the look of the white actor while also observing how the white actors look. Painting spectators are also then prodded to engage the images as sadistic voyeurs who take pleasure in the harm of another without being seen or harmed themselves. Unlike the stolen glances of a peeping tom, the voyeurism of the Miracle imagery is hallowed and licit. The visual grammar is part of a larger project through which European subjectivity becomes codified and disseminated by artists and scientists who train lay people and each other on how to properly look at Others and themselves. In this way, the paintings serve didactic functions beyond the simple transmission of saint hagiography.

The narcissistic potential of the white viewer to find himself mirrored in the eyes of the injured black amputee is foreclosed by the visual grammar of the Miracle paintings. The prone submissive comportment amplifies the gross vulnerability to violation that made the black person available to the enactment of this violent scene in the first place. When represented as dark faceless corpses, the bodies are shown to have utility despite their lack of individuation.[38] The facelessness of the corpse in the paintings echoes the namelessness of the black donor in the literary accounts of the Miracle.[39] Though circulating prior to the onslaught of racialized slavery, black bodies are represented as a fleshy amalgam comprised of interchangeable units. The authorship, sponsorship, and circulation of these Renaissance paintings rest on assurances that the intended audience for the paintings was white—whether servants, patricians, or royalty.

Conclusion

This chapter not only shows how the MoBL emerged from the confluence of religious beliefs with commercial demands but also the ways that early modern medical culture betrays inextricable tethers between embodiment, violence, and visuality. Moreover, the MoBL is a fascinating testament to church-sanctioned authority over the unsparing instrumentalization of flesh—both living and dead. MoBL imagery proliferated amidst a dynamic sphere of occultist influence undergirded by both the libidinal economies and political economies of antiblackness. Thoroughly enmeshed within burgeoning racial logic, we must keep in mind that "the affluent 'modern' makers of the unconventional *Miracle of the Black Leg* worked for the politically powerful and slave-owning ecclesiastical elite."[40] After examining accounts of the dissection and amputation performed by medicine's patrons saints, I'm left to conclude that the MoBL provides more compelling evidence corroborating that racial stratification is foundational to scientific-medical discourse, capitalism's onset, and Atlantic World visual culture. Clearly, the MoBL emblematizes how human bodies were simultaneously regarded as objects of scientific analysis, spiritual vessels, and units of economic exchange.

Notes

1 Kees Zimmerman, ed., *One Leg in the Grave Revisited: The Miracle of the Transplantation of the Black Leg by the Saints Cosmas and Damian*. Groningen: Barkhuis, 2013, 18.
2 Andrew Curran, *Anatomy of Blackness: Science and Slavery in an Age of Enlightenment*. John Hopkins UP, 2011, 122.
3 Georges-Louis Leclerc and Comte de Buffon, "The Geographic and Cultural Distribution of Mankind," *Race and the Enlightenment: A Reader.* Ed. Emmanuel Chukwudi Eze. Oxford: Blackwell, 1997, 23.
4 Leclerc and Buffon, 23.
5 Frantz Fanon, *Black Skins White Masks.* Trans. Charles Lam Markmann. Grove Press, 1967, 11.
6 Saidiya Hartman, *Lose Your Mother: A Journey Along the Atlantic Slave Route*. New York: Farrar, Straus and Giroux, 2007, 72–3.
7 Saidiya Hartman, "The Dead Book Revisited." *History of the Present* 6, no.2 (2016): 210.
8 Jacobus de Voragine, "*The Golden Legend:* Saints Cosmas and Damian." Translated by William Granger Ryan. In *One Leg in the Grave Revisited: The Miracle of the Transplantation of the Black Leg by the Saints Cosmas and Damian*. ed. Kees Zimmerman. Groningen: Barkhuis, 2013, 33.
9 The Roman date was originally September 27, but was moved a day earlier so not overshadowed by St. Vincent's celebration.

10 Dimitris Beldekos, et al. "The Medical Vestment and Surgical Instruments of Saint Cosmas and Damian on Sinai Icons From the Seventh to the Eighteenth Century," *Journal of Religion and Health* 54, no.6 (2015): 2020–32. https://link.springer.com/article/10.1007/s10943-014-9899-y

11 Douglas B. Price and Neil J. Twombly, *The Phantom Limb Phenomenon: A Medical, Folkloric & Historical Study: Texts & Translations of 10th to 20th century Accounts of the Miraculous Restoration of Lost Body Parts.* No. 10. Georgetown UP, 1978. + Kees Zimmerman, ed. *One Leg in the Grave Revisited: The Miracle of the Transplantation of the Black Leg by the Saints Cosmas & Damian.* Groningen: Barkhuis, 2013.

12 Lorraine Daston, "The Nature of Nature in Early Modern Europe," *Configurations* 6, no .2 (1998): 149–72. https://muse.jhu.edu/article/8141

13 Martha Few, "'That Monster of Nature': Gender, Sexuality, and the Medicalization of a 'Hermaphrodite' in Late Colonial Guatemala," *Ethnohistory* 54, no.1 (2007): 170. https://doi.org/10.1215/00141801-2006-042

14 See MoBL imagery from Rincon de Figueroa, di Pietro, Rinuccini, St. Michael's Church in Munich, di Lorenzo in Carmen Fracchia, *"Black but Human": Slavery and Visual Arts in Hapsburg Spain, 1480–1700.* New York: Oxford University Press, 2019.

15 See MoBL imagery from Stuttgart, Huguet, Sao Paolo fresco, Berruguete, Balbases, Fra Angelico, Pesselino, *Legenda Aurea* in Carmen Fracchia, *"Black but Human."*

16 J.L. de Jong, "Transplantation and Salvation," Edited by Kees Zimmerman, *One Leg in the Grave Revisited: The Miracle of the Transplantation of the Black Leg by the Saints Cosmas and Damian.* Groningen: Barkhuis, 2013, 41.

17 Consequently, some orthodox Greek versions refer to them as Saints *Anagyri* (or *Anagyroi*) or Saints Unmercenaries. Nebojša Jović and Marios Theologou, "The Miracle of the Black Leg: Eastern Neglect of Western Addition to the Hagiography of Saints Cosmas and Damian," *Acta Medico-Historica Adriatica* 13, no. 2 (2015): 330. https://hrcak.srce.hr/152049

18 See fifteenth-century Spanish paintings by unknown artist and Rubio Rincón de Figueroa as well as Isidro Villoldo's painted woodcarving in Carmen Fracchia, *"Black but Human."*

19 Peter Biller, "Proto-racial Thought in Medieval Science," *The Origins of Racism in the West*, Ed. Miriam Eliav-Feldon, et al. Cambridge: Cambridge University Press, 2009, 157–80; Joseph Ziegler, "Physiognomy, Science, and Proto-racism 1200–500," *The Origins of Racism in the West*, Ed. Miriam Eliav-Feldon, et al. Cambridge: Cambridge University Press, 2009, 181–99.

20 David Brion Davis, *Inhuman Bondage: The Rise and Fall of Slavery in the New World.* New York: Oxford University Press, 2006, 341.

21 Geraldine Heng, *The Invention of race in the European Middle Ages.* Cambridge: Cambridge University Press, 2018.

22 Thomas Foster Earle and Kate J.P. Lowe, eds., *Black Africans in Renaissance Europe.* Cambridge: Cambridge University Press, 2005.

23 Kim F. Hall, *Things of Darkness: Economies of Race and Gender in Early Modern England.* Ithaca: Cornell University Press, 1995.

24 Lorraine Daston and Katharine Park, *Wonders and the Order of Nature, 1150–750.* New York: Zone Books, 1998.

25 Jennifer L. Morgan, *Laboring Women: Reproduction and Gender in New World Slavery.* Philadelphia: University of Pennsylvania Press, 2011.

26 My position on this rests on Sylvia Wynter's interventions on overrepresentations of Man via engagement with Michel Foucault on the "invention of Man," Anibal Quijano on the "coloniality of power," and Walter Mignolo on "colonial difference." She insists that rather than a non-racial universal category, Man is actually an ethnoclass through which white European embodiment comes to erroneously typify the entire human category.

27 Footnote 45, page 37. Sheetal Lodhia, Dissertation. *Material Self-fashioning and the Renaissance Culture of Improvement.* ProQuest, 2008. "Moreover, that black flesh with a potentially black soul has the potential to taint the Sacristan," 24.

28 Dorothy Hoogland Verkerk, "Black Servant, Black Demon: Color Ideology in the Ashburnham Pentateuch," *Journal of Medieval and Early Modern Studies* 31, no.1 (2001): 72. http://muse.jhu.edu/article/16483.
29 Alastair Corston de Custance Maxwell Saunders, *A Social History of Black Slaves and Freedmen in Portugal, 1441–555*. Cambridge: Cambridge University Press, 1982, xiii.
30 Ibid.
31 David M. Goldenberg, *The Curse of Ham: Race and Slavery in Early Judaism, Christianity, and Islam*. Princeton: Princeton University Press, 2009, 23.
32 Valentin Y. Mudimbe. "*Romanus Pontifex* (1454) and the Expansion of Europe." In *Race, Discourse, and the Origin of the Americas: A New World View*, edited by Rex Nettleford and Vera Lawrence Hyatt. Washington, DC: Smithsonian Institution, 1995, 60.
33 Nicole R. Fleetwood, *Troubling Vision: Performance, Visuality, and Blackness.* Chicago: University of Chicago Press, 2011, 6.
34 Jasmine Nichole Cobb, *Picture Freedom: Remaking Black Visuality in the Early Nineteenth Century*. New York: New York University Press, 2015, 42.
35 Nicholas Mirzoeff, *The Right to Look: A Counterhistory of Visuality*. Durham: Duke University Press, 2011.
36 Martin Jay, "The Rise of Hermeneutics and the Crisis of Ocularcentrism," *Poetics Today* 9, no. 2 (1988): 311. https://doi.org/10.2307/1772691
37 Jay, "The Rise of Hermeneutics and the Crisis of Ocularcentrism," 323.
38 See MoBL images by Rincón de Figueroa, Rinuccini Chapel, and St. Michael's Church in Munich in Carmen Fracchia, *"Black but Human."*
39 Natasha D. Trethewey, *Thrall: Poems*. Boston: Houghton Mifflin Harcourt, 2012, 11.
40 Carmen Fracchia, *"Black but Human": Slavery and Visual Arts in Hapsburg Spain, 1480–700*. New York: Oxford University Press, 2019, 147.

Bibliography

Beldekos, Dimitris, et al. "The Medical Vestment and Surgical Instruments of Saint Cosmas and Damian on Sinai Icons From the Seventh to the Eighteenth Century." *Journal of Religion and Health*, 54.6 (2015): 2020–32. https://link.springer.com/article/10.1007/s10943-014-9899-y

Cobb, Jasmine Nichole. *Picture Freedom: Remaking Black Visuality in the Early Nineteenth Century*. New York: New York University Press, 2015.

Curran, Andrew. *Anatomy of Blackness: Science and Slavery in an Age of Enlightenment*. Baltimore: John Hopkins University Press, 2011.

Daston, Lorraine. "The Nature of Nature in Early Modern Europe." *Configurations*, 6.2 (1998): 149–72. https://muse.jhu.edu/article/8141

Daston, Lorraine and Katharine Park. *Wonders and the Order of Nature, 1150–1750*. New York: Zone Books, 1998.

Davis, David Brion. *Inhuman Bondage: The Rise and Fall of Slavery in the New World*. New York: Oxford University Press, 2006.

Earle, Thomas Foster and Kate J.P. Lowe, eds. *Black Africans in Renaissance Europe*. Cambridge: Cambridge University Press, 2005.

Eliav-Feldon, Miriam, Benjamin H. Isaac, and Joseph Ziegler, eds. *The Origins of Racism in the West*. Cambridge: Cambridge University Press, 2009.

Fanon, Frantz. *Black Skins White Masks*, Trans. Charles Lam Markmann. New York: Grove Press, 1967.

Few, Martha. ""That Monster of Nature": Gender, Sexuality, and the Medicalization of a "Hermaphrodite" in Late Colonial Guatemala." *Ethnohistory*, 54.1 (2007): 159–76.

Fleetwood, Nicole R. *Troubling Vision: Performance, Visuality, and Blackness*. Chicago: University of Chicago Press, 2011.

Fracchia, Carmen. *'Black but Human': Slavery and Visual Arts in Hapsburg Spain, 1480–1700.* New York: Oxford University Press, 2019.

Goldenberg, David M. *The Curse of Ham: Race and Slavery in Early Judaism, Christianity, and Islam.* Princeton: Princeton University Press, 2009.

Hall, Kim F. *Things of Darkness: Economies of Race and Gender in Early Modern England.* Ithaca: Cornell University Press, 1995.

Hartman, Saidiya. *Lose Your Mother: A Journey Along the Atlantic Slave Route.* New York: Farrar, Straus and Giroux, 2007.

Hartman, Saidiya. "The Dead Book Revisited." *History of the Present*, 6.2 (2016): 208–15. https://doi.org/10.5406/historypresent.6.2.0208

Heng, Geraldine. *The Invention of Race in the European Middle Ages.* Cambridge: Cambridge University Press, 2018.

Jay, Martin. "The Rise of Hermeneutics and the Crisis of Ocularcentrism." *Poetics Today*, 9.2 (1988): 307–26. https://doi.org/10.2307/1772691

Jović, Nebojša and Marios Theologou. "The Miracle of the Black Leg: Eastern Neglect of Western Addition to the Hagiography of Saints Cosmas and Damian." *Acta Medico-Historica Adriatica*, 13.2 (2015): 329–44. https://hrcak.srce.hr/152049

Leclerc, Georges-Louis, and Comte de Buffon. "The Geographic and Cultural Distribution of Mankind." In *Race and the Enlightenment: A Reader*, ed. Emmanuel Chukwudi Eze. Oxford: Blackwell, 1997:15-28.

Lodhia, Sheetal. *Material Self-fashioning and the Renaissance Culture of Improvement.* PhD diss., Queen's University, 2008.

Mirzoeff, Nicholas. *The Right to Look: A Counterhistory of Visuality.* Durham: Duke University Press, 2011.

Morgan, Jennifer L. *Laboring Women: Reproduction and Gender in New World Slavery.* Philadelphia: University of Pennsylvania Press, 2011.

Mudimbe, Valentin Y. "*Romanus Pontifex* (1454) and the Expansion of Europe." In *Race, Discourse, and the Origin of the Americas: A New World View*, eds. Rex Nettleford and Vera Lawrence Hyatt. Washington, DC: Smithsonian Institution, 1995.

Price, Douglas B., and Neil J. Twombly. *The Phantom Limb Phenomenon: A Medical, Folkloric & Historical Study: Texts & Translations of 10th to 20th century Accounts of the Miraculous Restoration of Lost Body Parts.* Washington, DC: Georgetown University Press, 1978.

Saunders, Alastair Corston de Custance Maxwell. *A Social History of Black Slaves and Freedmen in Portugal, 1441–1555.* Cambridge: Cambridge University Press, 1982.

Trethewey, Natasha D. *Thrall: Poems.* Boston: Houghton Mifflin Harcourt, 2012.

Verkerk, Dorothy Hoogland. "Black Servant, Black Demon: Color Ideology in the Ashburnham Pentateuch." *Journal of Medieval and Early Modern Studies*, 31.1 (2001): 57–77. http://muse.jhu.edu/article/16483

Wynter, Sylvia. "Unsettling the Coloniality of Being/Power/Truth/Freedom: Towards the Human, After Man, Its Overrepresentation—An Argument." *CR: The New Centennial Review*, 3.3 (2003): 257–337.

Zimmerman, Kees, ed. *One Leg in the Grave Revisited: The Miracle of the Transplantation of the Black Leg by the Saints Cosmas and Damian.* Groningen: Barkhuis, 2013.

EPILOGUE

Kristin M. S. Bezio

As is probably clear to the readers of this volume, it is now a fundamental and nearly-universally recognized truth that the medieval and early modern worlds were far more interconnected and global than most moderns—from the seventeenth century forward—have traditionally acknowledged. Thanks to trade routes, missions of religious conversion, and the expansion of global empires—the Ottoman, British, and Holy Roman among them—the medieval and early modern worlds must be recognized not as eras cut off from globalization, but as precursors to the twenty-first century's global and globalizing culture and economy.

Traditional historiography has situated a global economy—whether of markets or religions—as being a *modern* phenomenon. Classrooms have taught and articles and monographs asserted that "colonialism," per se, did not appear on the global map until much later, pointing to the seventeenth and even eighteenth centuries, the peak of the Triangle Trade, and the rapid expansion of the British and Spanish colonial empires in those centuries as the "origins" of empire. And yet to do so requires us to ignore the evidence of historic, religious, artistic, and literary cultures. Empires existed long before the fall of feudalism, with the Roman Empire that so dramatically shaped most of Europe serving as a prime example. Empires existed in the Middle East, in Africa, in Asia, and in the Americas, and yet our too-frequently Eurocentric view of civilization pointedly ignores or obscures such accomplishments of human politics and engineering. Instead, European history lays claim to the "origins" of colonialism and empire with the end of feudalism, seeking to center themselves within a rhetoric of expansion and innovation that seems to inexorably lead to the industrial revolution and European expansion to both the West and East.

Needless to say, such a narrative, as popular as it has historically been, particularly among scholars trained in Europe and the Americas, effectively silences and effaces the significant contributions of centuries of cultures and civilizations based in Asia, Africa, and among the indigenous peoples of the Americas and Australia. As such, it is incumbent upon us, as scholars of the medieval and early modern eras, to remove the often willfully-adopted blinders that were instilled in so many of us during our undergraduate and graduate careers. Historical scholarship defined by boundaries of both geography and chronology limits not only our understanding of historical reality, but forces us into intellectual and ideological silos that—as we have seen all too tragically in the global spread first of populism and anti-scientific rhetoric, and then, so shortly after, in the novel coronavirus pandemic that began in 2019—limit our ability to relate to one another as human beings. In the historical fields, we all too often forget the forward-reaching implications of our research in terms of what the medieval and early modern eras might show us about the trends, patterns, and belief systems that have shaped and continue to shape our globally interconnected world. In particular, much of the so-called global "West" (a misnomer perpetuated by colonial and imperial authorities which is useful only insofar as it is a recognizable designation) has perpetuated claims of intellectual, scientific, economic, and religious superiority over a very, very long historical trajectory.

As Kim F. Hall points out in her seminal *Things of Darkness*, the language of racialization formed a fundamental component of early understandings not only of cross-cultural interactions but of empire and the development of nationalist rhetoric across Europe.[1] These encounters immediately took on valences that were both mercantile and religious, with early explorers working for merchant companies and religious missions (and sometimes both). Across the rapidly-expanding medieval and early modern worlds, marketplaces became loci of exchange, not only of goods and coin but of ideas and (often religious) ideologies.

The examinations contained in this volume both recognize and interrogate the assumptions that were necessarily a part of such encounters in terms of one key component: the perennial claim made on the part of a nearly endless stream of religious figures of authority that there is a separation between the material and spiritual, and that the spiritual—so often associated with the white, European, and male—takes precedence in the eyes of God. Yet throughout these chapters, we see again and again, in many locations and across centuries, the critical intersection of religion and market, whether a geographical marketplace or a more abstract marketplace of ideas or doctrines.

What is perhaps most interesting about the volume's attention to the intersection of marketplace and religion is the focus on the lengths to which people went in order to apply religious judgment and justification to fiscal and trade marketplaces. In the *Essais* of Montaigne as in the market square of Groningen and the missions of colonial Peru, the philosophical and geographical intersection of economics and religion produced a cultural hybridity that sought to justify economic interests within a spiritual (or at least pseudo-spiritual) framework that valorized both the religious and the economic as the work of God and good Christians. It is particularly evident throughout the European-based chapters that markets and marketplaces are inextricably intertwined with religious doctrine and rhetoric, whether or not the proponents of such language were willing to admit the intersection.

It is equally clear, if we examine the chapters that venture elsewhere in the world—Africa, the Americas, and India, in particular—that this economic religiosity (or sacralized marketplace, if you will) forms a fundamental pillar of colonial expansion, regardless of whether that imperial impulse finds its origins in Spain, Portugal, Italy, England, or elsewhere, and irrespective of Catholic, Protestant, or Orthodox doctrinal assertions. It also becomes apparent that "race," although not so clearly defined as it would become in later periods, played a significant role in the commodification of religion and religious objects, as well as in the marketplace of religious conversion that accompanied geographical expansion. As Hall remarks, the goal of European encounters with other cultures may have been economic, but "trade, rather than fostering a mixing of cultures, will eradicate religious as well as cultural and gender differences under one patriarchal God."[2] Whether in the tangible material goods of an altarpiece in Iceland, the visual depiction of interracial limb transplantation in Italy, or in direct encounters between Spanish missionaries and Abyssinian Christians, even inclusion of racial "Others" seeks to reinforce European anxiety about religious and economic superiority.

With the beginning of the 2020s, a decade in which not only a global pandemic, but also an international movement to recognize the historical oppression of indigenous peoples and peoples of color—particularly in the United States with the Black Lives Matter movement and the removal of Confederate, slaveholder, and imperialist statues (such as Christopher Columbus) around the world—it is more important than ever for medieval and early modern scholarship to acknowledge the underpinnings of this oppression in our chosen eras and regions of study. In this post-2020 era, decolonization of history and texts has become not simply *en vogue*, but an ethically necessary step in the evolution of medieval and early modern studies. We can no longer consider our work within the ostensibly-safe boundaries of nations, religious schemas, or even historical epochs. Rather, it is our moral obligation, in such a post-colonial age, to recognize the complicity and participation of the medieval and early modern ages in the construction, dissemination, and perpetuation of rhetorics of empire and oppression. By thus acknowledging the problems in our histories, we might better position ourselves, our colleagues, and our students to begin the process of dismantling the very institutions that were so firmly planted in the medieval and early modern periods.

Notes

1 Kim F. Hall, *Things of Darkness: Economies of Race and Gender in Early Modern England* (Ithaca: Cornell University Press, 1995).
2 Hall, 57.

Bibliography

Hall, Kim F. *Things of Darkness: Economies of Race and Gender in Early Modern England*. Ithaca: Cornell University Press, 1995.

INDEX